ARTIFICIAL AND HUMAN THINKING

ARTIFICIAL AND HUMAN THINKING

Edited by

ALICK ELITHORN AND DAVID JONES

Elsevier Scientific Publishing Company
Amsterdam · London · New York 1973

ARTIFICIAL AND HUMAN THINKING

Proceedings of a Nato Symposium entitled
Human Thinking: Computer Techniques for its Evaluation

Edited by Alick Elithorn and David Jones

For the U.S.A. and Canada:

JOSSEY-BASS INC. PUBLISHERS
615 MONTGOMERY STREET
SAN FRANCISCO, CALIF. 94111

For all other areas:

ELSEVIER SCIENTIFIC PUBLISHING COMPANY
335 JAN VAN GALENSTRAAT
P.O. BOX 1270   AMSTERDAM, THE NETHERLANDS

Library of Congress Card Number 72-83203

ISBN 0-444-41023-6

Printed in The Netherlands

Contents

Preface   xi
   David Barton

Introduction 1

1. PROGRAMMING THOUGHT. 17

The Programming of Deduction and Induction
   Bernard Meltzer 19
Syntactic Models of Cognitive Behavior
   Ira Pohl 34
The Frame Problem and Related Problems in Artificial Intelligence
   Patrick J. Hayes 45
The Computer Simulation of Inductive Thinking
   N.E. Wetherick 60
Simplicity of Concepts, Training and the Real World
   Ranan B. Banerji 70

2. TECHNIQUES 81

Computer Based Psychological Testing
   David Jones and John Weinman 83
Individualizing Computer-Assisted Instruction
   J.A.M. Howe 94
The Use of an Interactive Computer Terminal to Simulate Decision Making
Situations
   J. Gedye 102

The Ombudsman: A Computer Model of Dialogue in Instruction and Conflict
Mediation
    Roulette W. Smith 114
A Psychophysical Experiment With a Dependent Experimental Rule
    Pierre Bovet 125
The Use of Multivariate Statistical and Distance Models in the Study of
Schematic Concept Formation
    Richard M. Fenker 132

3. GAMES PLAYING AND THE STUDY OF THINKING 143

Rules in Games
    Rivka R. Eifermann 147
Design Considerations in Relation to Computer Based Problems
    Alick Elithorn and Alex Telford 162
Computer Experiments on the Formation and Optimization of Heuristic Rules
    Nicholas V. Findler 177
Some Ideas for a Chess Compiler
    M.R.B. Clarke 189
The Organization of Search Procedures
    Alick Elithorn and Richard Cooper 199
Effects of Simulated Opponent in an Experimental Game
    Dirk Revenstorff, Norbert Mai, Roman Ferstl and Wolfgang Grude . . . 214

4. MODEL BUILDING AND PSYCHOLOGICAL THEORY 225

An Evaluation of Computer Simulated Models of Human Problem Solving
    M. Fuat Turgut 227
A Mathematical Model for Individual Differences in Problem Solving
    P.O. White 235
Strategies in Concept Identification
    Jean-Francois Richard and Dominique Lepine 241
Models for Some Elementary Problem Solving Processes
    Uwe Mortensen 252
Capacity and Limit of the Computer in the Study of Problem Solving. An
Example: Solving Arithmetical Problems
    Gerard Vergnaud 264
The Interpretation of Implication
    D.S. Bree , ... 273
Modelling the Mind's Eye
    George W. Baylor 283

viii

5. EXPERIMENTAL STUDIES OF HUMAN THINKING 299

The Development of Strategies of Solution in Problem Solving
    Gerd Lüer 301
Illegal Thinking
    Dietrich Dörner 310
An Experimental Comparison of Two Models of Analysing the Problem
Solving Performances of Groups and Individuals
    Hüsnü Arici 319
Problem Solving as Choice Behaviour: Cost-Payoff Arrangements and
Optimality of Performance
    Ali S. Gitmez 324
Language and Thinking Processes
    H.J.A. Rimoldi 331

6. OVERVIEW 341

Problems of Psychological and Artificial Intelligence
    Gerard de Zeeuw 343

Bibliography 353

Contributors 371

Author Index 375

Subject Index 379

Preface

As neither a psychologist nor a computer scientist it was with some misgivings that I agreed to introduce "Artificial and Human Thinking," which reports the NATO Symposium on Human Thinking held at St. Maximin in August 1971. The central importance of the theme to human understanding as a whole, and to scientific thought especially, mitigates the impertinence of a statistician commenting on the proceedings, without making him any better informed about some of the points at issue. The Symposium was aptly so called, for once, and did provide a genuine exchange of ideas. If there was more than one Alcibiades and less than one Socrates, such was doubtless a reflexion of the youth of the subject under debate. The high degree of interaction was partly due to the relatively small number of actively contributing participants. It was also due to the balance of their interests, and this must be largely attributed to Dr. Elithorn's organizing efforts, aided by serendipity.

The matter of the Symposium was essentially the impact of the computer on the psychologist's understanding of human rational processes, especially in respect of so-called Artificial (or Machine) Intelligence. The neurophysiological basis of human thinking, its pathology, the physical functioning and perceptual effects of our receptors were not explicitly under discussion. Nor were questions of its biological function and evolutionary development. The human concern was with ratiocination; induction and deduction, particularly in relation to problem solving and game playing, with some reference to social, developmental and comparative studies. Memory and internal representation of percepts and concepts, processes of concept formation and thinking strategies, were features of reasoning selected for particular consideration by contributors, as were the more "elementary" processes of induction and logic. There was a merciful absence of epistemological argument. On the contrary a refreshing amount of experimental studies were reported and referred to. It is a truism that such studies are necessarily concrete records of particular events whose general implications require a further inductive argument and which indeed will always admit alternative interpretations. But how infinitely they are to be preferred to introspection and speculation unvalidated by subsequent critical testing.

The advent of the computer has affected psychology at diverse levels of sophistication and in several modes. At its simplest it has facilitated computation to such a degree that erstwhile esoteric mysteries like Factor Analysis, Multidimensional Scaling or Maximum Likelihood estimation in complex stochastic learning models have become everyday tools. At an apparently similar level, extensive Monte Carlo simulation of stochastic models (in learning or problem solving for example) has become a straightforward matter. This enormous increase in facility has meant that much more realistic, or at least more elaborate, models may be erected, simulated and compared with experiment. For example, in the case of protocols of thinking strategies in problem solving contexts, it became clear from the discussion at the Symposium that the computer-experimentation relationship had led to considerable increase in precision of the experimental psychologists' own conceptual paraphernalia. At what may be a deeper level of interaction, the study of heuristics in game playing and other attempts to use the machine to imitate intelligent human behaviour in dynamic situations also serve to sharpen the psychologist's thinking about thinking and suggest hypotheses to be subjected to experimental test. The once fashionable "cybernetic" ideas of human thinking seem to have settled down into a status of a useful ideological background, too general or too superficial to provide testable hypotheses, and the crude equation of digital computer processes with human ones sometimes implicit in earlier enthusiasms has now been relegated to the realms of journalists' mythology. On the other hand the algebra of computer languages and its putative application to natural languages (and so to important aspects of human thinking) clearly remains a major source of aspiration, if less of inspiration. Godel's theorem and its ramifications of course tell us a great deal about the logical structure of mathematical processes. But these were essentially prior to the realization of computers in hardware terms. It is only now, when men try to use these mathematical processes in theorem proving, that there is a need to answer such humanly important questions as: what constitutes an interesting or useful theorem? what makes a theorem "deep"? what is an "insightful proof"? what is the role of analogy? what part is played by intermediate constructs, logically within the system but based on physical intuition − like continuity and orthogonality for example? Mathematicians will be compelled to think more scientifically about what they do and this will not only make it easier for them to talk with psychologists but also will tell us a great deal about the human thinking process. Undoubtedly the algorithmic principle is proving immensely fertile for the thinking of biologists in the context of the translation of genetic code into self-organising systems; both within the cell and in the differentiation and development of multicellular organisms. One may doubt whether it is as directly applicable to intellectual operations; but surely the enlargment of mathematicians' ambitions which it enables will lead to useful new tools for the psychologist. Clearly a pre-requisite for this is a much closer collaboration between psychologists and algebraists than exists at present and more willingness to learn each other's languages. It is the development of computer science which is mediating the beginnings of such collaboration and symposia such as this which will help initiate the dialogue. More elementary hindrances to useful discourse became clear at the Symposium; for example, the logician's abstractions are less easy to translate into elementary experiment than mathematicians would suppose. At a rather more sophisticated level, what is meant by a model of an intellectual process admits multiple ambiguity. A clearer distinction between the different levels of correspondence with, and descriptions of, mechanisms needs to be developed, and the role and purpose of such distinction requires investigation.

A symposium rarely covers all the ground that one would wish. At St. Maximin the psychologists as much as the computer scientists adopted a formal description of the human intellectual process. The roles of personality and emotions, of social and cultural conditioning and conventions, of rewards and motivation — the difference between individuals in these and other respects were touched on rather than discussed at length. At times, it seemed as if abstract, mechanical, uniform and homogeneous man was the subject; that the proper study of Mankind is Man — not Men. This oversimple approach may well be unavoidable at the beginning of a new field. Indeed, backhandedly the criticism may merely reflect the extent to which the symposium whets one's appetite for a more experimentally based approach to the understanding of human thinking in all its aspects.

David E. Barton
Institute of Computer Science and
Queen Mary College, University of London

Acknowledgements

On behalf of all the participants, the Editors would like to express their thanks to the N.A.T.O. Science Committee Advisory Group on Human Factors which made possible the Symposium and the publication of these Proceedings. The Editors also wish to thank firstly Mrs. Jane Burlinson and latterly Miss Deirdre Barker. Perhaps the vignettes of Alice between the two Queens symbolizes their untiring efforts in preparing the Symposium and producing the Proceedings.

In designing the jacket and including in the text vignettes by Sir John Tenniel from the original edition of Lewis Carroll's *Through the Looking Glass* the Editors attempt to present symbolically the interaction of logic and fantasy which characterizes creative human thinking. Hopefully, the vignettes of the White Knight and Alice, and the White Knight and the Old Man symbolize man-robot relations at their best.

Perhaps science sometimes takes itself too seriously, but when man programs a machine that can laugh at itself, will man then be laughing himself out of court?

Introduction

Fancy what a game of chess would be if all the chessmen had passions and intellects, more or less small and cunning; if you were not only uncertain about your adversary's men, but a little uncertain also about your own; if your Knight could shuffle himself on to a new square on the sly; if your Bishop, in disgust at your Castling, could wheedle your Pawns out of their places, and if your Pawns, hating you because they are Pawns, could make away from their appointed posts that you might get checkmate on a sudden. You might be the longest-headed of deductive reasoners, and yet you might be beaten by your own Pawns. You would be especially likely to be beaten, if you depended arrogantly on your mathematical imagination, and regarded your passionate pieces with contempt.

Yet this imaginary chess is easy compared with a game a man has to play against his fellow-men with other fellow-men for his instruments ...

George Eliot, 1866

Two things make a symposium successful: the level of the contributions, and the quality of the formal and informal discussion. In the first respect the standard of the contributions was as high or higher than in most symposia of this type; in the second respect the symposium was particularly fortunate. To capture, condense, and transmit the more valuable parts of such a discussion is indeed a difficult task. Less fortunate was the fact that technical and practical difficulties made it impossible to record the discussions verbatim though we are inclined to consider that such recordings raise almost as many problems as they solve. Indeed to transmit to those who were not there the full value of this most important aspect of the symposium is impossible. Consequently as editors we have decided in this respect to achieve what we can and not to be too concerned at our failure. In this introduction therefore we have tried to meet this challenge by summarising the contributions that the symposium has made to our own thinking and in doing so we acknowledge that of necessity we have plagiarised the ideas generated by the other participants. To attribute these meticulously to their origins would be impossible and in the current climate of beliefs about "think-tanks" and the origins of scientific thought it would be attempting a meaningless manoeuvre. Finally in introducing our introduction it is a pleasure to record that our task has been made immeasurably easier by the kindness and competence shown by Gerard de Zeeuw in preparing an overview which distills much of the consensus which was reached by a very mixed group of interdisciplinary workers.

The Problem of Definition

Strictly speaking human intelligence and human thinking were the subjects of the symposium. How, the participants were asking, can computer techniques contribute to research in this field?

In studying human thinking a recurring problem is that of definitions. Until quite recently thinking was regarded as a human prerogative and even now many people would regard human thinking as qualitatively, as well as quantitatively, different from that of animals. Whether the so-called lower animals use language or symbols to aid their thinking is essentially a semantic problem of definition. Any form of learning or memory involves some form of internal representation of past events. A set of internal representations is undoubtedly a set of symbols. The calculus of operations used to relate and manipulate symbols both to each other and to the external world is a system of thought. Language is a shared community of externalised symbols, and intelligence a comparative term that we use to describe our attempts to relate the thinking power of one organism to that of another. Using these terms in this way it is clear that intelligence and thinking are attributes of a very wide variety of biological organisms. *If* we define intelligence so that it is by definition adaptive i.e. is goal oriented, then again by definition it can *only* be a function of organisms which we thus define as biological.

These arguments may sound trivial, may be truisms, but if admitted they do have consequences that are not always accepted. If thinking and intelligence are not necessarily adaptive, but exist as functions in their own right, these functions clearly can be subsumed by mechanical devices.

Subtleties of definitions apart, at a common sense level the intelligence of a system defines the efficiency with which the system can process information. Since efficiency is often a value judgment the evaluation of the intelligence of a system can only be undertaken in terms of a cost analysis. Philosophically and for that matter in many practical situations the question "Is one system more intelligent than another?" is quite meaningless. Just as the question "Is rail transport a better system than road transport?" is meaningless unless the universe of service is defined, so questions of comparative intelligence can only be discussed in terms of a common problem domain. Provided this is not forgotten then the fundamental philosophical difficulties of defining intelligence are of little practical importance either to psychologists or to the students and midwives of artificial intelligence.

The Neurological Basis of Mind

To the regret of all who took part in the symposium, Professor Ennio de Renzi, who had served on the advisory committee, was prevented at the eleventh hour from presenting his paper reviewing the contributions which neurology and the relatively new discipline of neuropsychology have made to our understanding of the human intellect. In the absence of this paper it is appropriate to mention here one or two of the issues involved.

In their recent text on problem solving, Newell and Simon (1972) point out that the origins of their psychological approach are distinct from those of both the behaviourist and the psychophysiological schools. Explanatory mechanisms, they say, need not be neurological. By this they (merely) mean that the gap between psychological theory and neurological knowledge is so great that for the foreseeable future there is little hope of any useful interaction. Clearly Newell and Simon do not advocate a return to 19th century dualism, but it can be argued that even an operational dualism is not only unnecessary, but a hindrance to future research. Neurophysiological hypotheses can of course create artificial boundaries to psychological speculation, but at the same time the hard facts of comparative neuroanatomy form constraints which should be acceptable to scientists in a different discipline. Admittedly there are few absolutes and a good theory may be excused for disregarding observations that are not fully substantiated. However, the essence of a good theory is that it forces a reassessment of established data which it cannot accommodate. It follows that a psychological theory which is incompatible with the accepted paradigms of neurology, neuroanatomy and neurophysiology is trivial in the everyday meaning of the word unless it compels a reassessment of those paradigms.

However even hard data is often surprisingly soft and psychology and the social sciences are not the only disciplines to suffer from fashions and violent swings of opinion. Not many years ago man's intellectual pre-eminence was attributed by neuroanatomists and anthropologists to an evolutionary selection for the expansion of the associative areas of the prefrontal cortex. Recently it has become main line to see this development as relatively incidental and − perhaps with less justification − to relate man's intellectual pre-eminence to the development of the hippocampal areas of the limbic system. Clearly one of the most intriguing questions facing research workers on thinking is whether a human cerebrum contains any novel systems or components or whether there is any qualitative difference between human and subhuman thinking. At one time psychologists and anthropologists argued that language was the prerogative of man, but it is now generally agreed that language cannot usefully be defined in so limited a way. However language with its power of symbolic condensation and the facilities it provides for communication and cooperation between individuals greatly augments the intellectual power of a species, and it would certainly appear that this effect is several orders of magnitude greater for man than for any other known species.

4

It is likely but not yet proven and certainly not a logical necessity that the development of language has followed or been followed by the development of specialised neuronal structures. Certainly it is well established that speech centres are localised and early work by Kakeschita and Blinkov (quoted by Blinkov and Glazer, 1968) which has recently been confirmed by Norman Geschwind, indicates that there has been an expansion of neuronal tissue associated with the development of a language centre in the dominant hemisphere. There is however no reason to believe this development is based on the evolution of any novel computational components. There is as far as we are aware no cytoarchitectural evidence that speech and language are dependent on any particular or specific arrangement of neuronal elements. Such evidence as there is indicates that major trauma to the left hemisphere early in life will result in a take-over of speech and other intellectual functions by the right hemisphere (see for example McFie, 1961).

A recent relevant and interesting study here is that of Levy (1969) who claimed that left handed subjects of graduate ability had a more diffuse organisation of speech functions which impaired their non-verbal intellectual skills. Although few nowadays would accept Lashley's theory of the equipotentiality of neuronal learning there is very considerable evidence that the higher computational skills show great variety and plasticity in the manner in which they are organised. Few would deny that the differences, both in kind and degree, between the intellectual power of one man and another are at least partly genetic in origin, but it must be admitted that neuroanatomy has so far been able to find only the most general correlations between structure and intellectual skills.

However, although the high hopes that the early neurological and neurophysiological studies of Broca, Fritsch and Hitzig, Ferrier, Herchl, Munk and Schaeffer engendered for the early development of a cortical map of intellectual function have not been fulfilled, the recent and continuing neuropsychological studies of Benton, Hecaen, de Renzi, Zangwill and many others have done much to establish a consensus that there is a very real macro- and micro-structure for the neurological basis of human thinking.

Computer science is sometimes described as the science of data or information processing. The mammalian central nervous system is undoubtedly a special purpose computational device and the theoretical aspects of information processing are as applicable to biological computing systems as they are to computational machines. Their application in this area has in fact had a very stimulating effect on psychological theory. Treating the human central nervous system as an information processing device has led both to useful experiments and to theoretical advances.

In his ability to select biologically relevant signals from a massive bombardment of irrelevant stimuli, man is extremely efficient. However, this preset selection using highly specialised sensory receptors and special purpose analysers contrasts sharply with the extremely slow rate at which man processes relatively small amounts of data in a systematic logical manner. Several studies in this last area are included in the symposium.

As a less happy by-product of the application of information theory to psychology, *black box* psychologists came to regard human beings as single channel information processing devices equipped with a central processor of limited capacity. Although some of the early experimental results (e.g. Elithorn and Lawrence, 1955) were incompatible with this interpretation and despite the apparent bilaterally symmetrical structure of the human brain, an attractive theory was, as is usually the case, able to ignore intransigent data. However, the more recent observations on subjects with therapeutic sections of the *corpus callosum* (split brain subjects) have shown that there are at least two sensory-motor systems each capable of independent even if limited information processing (e.g. Gazzaniga and Sperry, 1966). Other recent studies (e.g., Dimond, 1970) have confirmed the earlier findings that independent processing can occur in the two hemispheres in intact human subjects. The concept of a little homunculus sitting somewhere in the central nervous system and taking the final decision has always had attractions for philosophers and psychologists. However most neurologists and neuropsychologists have for many years been adherents of the view that a variety of psychological decision systems are independently localised, that man like modern computing systems has evolved as a multichannel multiprocessor device.

Cultural Components of Thought

Defining human thinking solely as a function of the human brain is in the ultimate analysis accurate enough. Nevertheless such a bald attribution conceals the role played by experience and vicarious learning. It is found in the laboratory as in the market place that human intelligence is in part determined by exposure to the influence of Goethe's Faust, Shakespeare's sonnets, Barlow's tables, the syllogism and first grade mathematics. In other cultures the influences are different but even in the most primitive culture, thought is determined not only by the structure of the language, but also by the rhymes and myths of oral tradition. As Le Bovier de Fontenelle expressed it in the 18th century — "An educated mind is composed of all the minds of preceding ages." John Locke whose psychological perceptiveness was both accurate and acute spoke specifically of the furnishings of the mind which he saw as a *tabula rasa* much as the compiler writer sees the machine and the programmer sees the compiler. The paradigms, theories and prejudices which form part of our education together with the books, journals, conferences and personal interchanges which form part of our on-going experience are together as much part of man's intellectual armamentarium as the compiler and program are an essential part of the intelligence of the machine.

Human thinking — the human thinking apparatus — is not just a brilliant piece of biological engineering, it is a system which comprises both hardware components, and compilers and programs. The latter are acquired both didactically by precept and by personal and vicarious experience and provide a *compote* of algorithms and heuristics which have been accumulating since before civilisation began. In informational terms we may regard culture as programmed and dictionary type variables. The hardware component is a general processing capacity.

Although Cattell (1943) and many other psychologists distinguish between the cultural (crystallized) and non-cultural (fluid) aspects of intelligence, the role which the cultural milieu plays in man's intellectual functioning is in general ill-understood and consequently is both over- and under-estimated. Moreover, because the two aspects of intelligence are so closely interwoven it is difficult to devise good experiments differentiating learned skills from basic computing power. Unfortunately the issue of nature versus nurture still tends to be divisive rather than creative; a source of political heat rather than of experimental inspiration. Indeed it still leads to extreme standpoints. For some, all men are born with equal intellectual potential. For them social fac-

7

tors are the *only* determinants of school attainment and measured intelligence. For others the genetic endowment is paramount.

The child's experience up to five may be of jesuitical importance; it may also be true that no great violinist is created after seven, or a first class cricketer after ten, and that many uneducated people would have been very much more intelligent if they had been exposed to the stimulus of rich environments. On the other hand there is a great deal of evidence — from such examples as Itard's wolf child, Victor, Helen Keller and Laura Bridgeman down to Catharine Mason's Isabelle and Koluchova's twins — that inherently intelligent individuals can show a very marked recovery following extremely severe environmental and cultural deprivation (Koluchova, 1972; Clarke, 1972). On the other hand the role of experience in influencing the development of basic intellectual skills is equally well established even if ill understood (Berry, 1966; Drever, 1967). At present the arguments can still swing from pole to pole and there is far too much truth in Doran's (1971) pessimistic view about our understanding of brain function. Comparisons between man and machine readily become too facile. The analogies between artificial and human thinking suggest that in human systems analysis it is important, for example, to distinguish between hardwired programs, compiler fixation, program availability and program compiler compatibility. Is this kind of jargon a new insight? Does it herald a change in psychological paradigms? Or is it merely new words for old ideas?

Artificial Intelligence

Artificial intelligence is machine intelligence in a comprehensive sense which includes simulation but on which there is no restriction that either the mechanisms or achievements should be limited by human capacities. Simulation or simulated intelligence is often confused with artificial intelligence. Strictly simulation is the description in machine terms of the ways in which man thinks: a succession of acts or operations which a man could himself carry out are in the event carried out by a mechanical alternate.

Simulated intelligence and the wider field of artificial intelligence not only provide totally new fields of research, but themselves form important techniques for research into human intelligence. These are extremely exciting new areas of endeavour which are already making a major impact on research into human intelligence, an area which, as Doran and many others emphasise, has been very much in the doldrums (see, for example, Reeves, 1965; Butcher, 1968; Doran, 1971 and Elithorn and Telford, 1970). As Doran points out, although so little is known about its mode of operation, the human brain is by far the most intelligent machine so far developed. However Doran also claims that during the next few years the major information flow in research into intelligence will come not from the brain sciences, but from the machine intelligence field. This is a provocative challenge but research on machine intelligence is certainly a lusty infant.

In a recent paper Sandewall (1971) highlights two approaches to the development of Artificial Intelligence. The first which he himself has been pursuing is to plunge headfirst and hopefully into the world of real problems. In this paper he presents a set of general conventions for representing natural language information in a many-sorted first order predicate calculus. Sandewall contrasts this with the "monkey-banana" approach in which a particular problem area is selected and the attempt is made to write down a notation and a set of axioms which will handle this environment. The trouble with the first approach is that the generality is such that the mechanics of the calculus may be too complex to implement. The disadvantage of the second is that the problem of generality is ignored. Neither of these disadvantages are absolute and both lines of research will no doubt be prosecuted vigorously with advantage. However, one hardly needs a Royal Commission or a Congressional Committee to tell one that the key problem which faces the scientific community today is the choice between research problems. Not only must we ask which problems are most ready to yield up their solutions, but also we must ask the more difficult question about which solutions are those most needed.

Sandewall as well as other workers on A.I. must answer both these questions but it is possible that to some extent the first shock wave of A.I. has already spent itself and that a period of digestion and absorption has arrived. Many ingenious and highly sophisticated ideas have been put forward but the failure to develop in practice a novel or even a first class chess playing program stands in striking contrast to the application of computational skills to the more practical mathematical and algorithmic problems of space travel.

The problems of artificial thinking are essentially problems of scale. Man experiences directly and vicariously an enormous body of data. From this he inefficiently but effectively selects and inefficiently but effectively processes an infinitesimal proportion. In Samuel Butler's words, man is adept at drawing sufficient conclusions from insufficient premisses. To replace man's inefficient but effective skills with stand-alone automata which can be guaranteed to be more effective in anything but a circumscribed area is almost certainly beyond the range of the computational and intellectual resources likely to be available in the immediate future.

For the time being at least, hopes for major developments would seem to lie not with artificial intelligence but with machine-aided intelligence. This term now widely accepted, symbolises the symbiotic interaction of man and the computer. Strictly speaking, there is nothing new or novel about machine-aided intelligence. The papyrus, printing and the library have long fortified man's memory. The abacus was only the first of an equally long line of computational aids. Now that the circumscribed areas are increasing and the technical resources so much more powerful we may expect an explosive advance in the development of man's machine-aided intelligence. Such an increase in intellectual power will greatly augment our ability to solve problems of social organisation but at the same time, as Andrew Wilson (1968) has made abundantly clear, it can catalyse man's ability to make catastrophic mistakes. It is worth reiterating therefore that the crucial question for science is not how to apply scientific discoveries in a socially beneficial way but which lines of research are those most likely to lead to scientific advances with a high social potential. Research on research tends to be rather a neglected topic. Recently however the problem of creativity as related to intelligence has been tossed around a great deal but so far it has been more evocative of discussion than productive of experiments.

Creativity

Creativity is neither an infinite capacity for taking pains nor is it a large capacity for novel ideas. Creativity is the ability to generate novel concepts *and* either to know that they will work or to find someone who shows that they will work. Feedback, criticism and selectivity whether the source is internal or external are essential components of creativity. Indeed how to distinguish important advances from trivial or catastrophic mistakes is the central problem of creativity. At the present time it is fashionable to discuss the qualitative aspects of cognition under the semantic umbrella of cognitive style. Intellectual performances such as adventurous thinking and thinking within closed systems (Bartlett, 1958) are currently called divergent and convergent thinking. Such dichotomies and the more pejorative split between creative and non-creative intelligence can be stimulating or they can be divisive rather than divergent. Creativity is not all or none and almost any interesting problem solving involves both creative thinking and ad hoc computation. It is true that highly creative problem solving such as the more imaginative scientific research and creating permanent art forms calls for complex intellectual processes which are ill understood, but the fact that some human thinking is quite unlike computer computation as we know it at present does not mean however that in due course computer programs will not be creative. Computer poetry, at present a very suspect art, has produced some interesting poems by processes not dissimilar to the human system. We too readily forget that a great deal of bad human poetry is produced and rejected firstly by the poet, secondly by the publisher's reader and finally by the verdict of the public at large. We have chosen computer poetry as an example not because we believe that computers are poetic or even necessarily creative, but because poetry illustrates very well the importance of distinguishing between content and source. Is poetry poetry because it represents a distillation of the suffering or happiness of one man, or because it conveys a universal truth? How important are elegance, style and — *pace* Walt Whitman — form?

Perhaps we too readily forget the cultural random, selective, and developmental processes which determine the creation of new art forms, inventions and felicitous ideas.

Leibnitz has equal claim to Newton for the discovery of the calculus, and Hooper (1949) maintains that Napier's invention of logarithms was the only really novel event in the history of mathematics. Some of Napier's other inventions — tanks, submarines and death rays — were however less successful. In the biological sciences poor Lord Monboddo thought up evolution far too early and was laughed to scorn for his pains. Later when Darwin and Wallace simultaneously rethought the idea more thoroughly, Wallace was upstaged by Darwin partly because of Darwin's greater scientific output and partly because of his powerful friends.

A Comparative Psychology

Man may or may not be king of the solar system but he is unlikely to be the most intelligent organism thrown up by the big bang or evolved during the steady state. On the other hand it is possible that man is among the more conceited organisms. This may well be because he does in fact form the intellectual elite in the world as he has known it so far. Consequently a comparative psychology which deals only with biological organisms may tell us something about the neurophysiological basis of mind but relatively little about how man invented the syllogism, logarithms or a commune. Man may well be right in believing that the human brain is a beautiful piece of biological equipment, but he tends to forget that in computing terms his central nervous system is primarily an on-line computing device evolved not for list processing, theorem proving or the evolution of logical calculi, but for the integration and concatenation of simple stimulus response units. These it achieves with highly sophisticated and sensitive feedback and visual predictive mechanisms. The playing fields of Eton may or may not have helped at Waterloo, but as computing machinery man is more impressive on the centre court at Wimbledon than he is in the classroom or laboratory.

Shorn of his cultural cloak man has a very limited capacity for searching systematically through relatively small problem spaces. Thus in the laboratory, experiments by de Soto, London and Handel (1965) on linear syllogisms involving only 3 terms and other experiments by Wason and his associates (e.g. Wason, 1969) have shown that subjects of above average intelligence (undergraduates at Harvard and University College respectively) have great difficulty in applying a small and conceptually simple calculus to an equally small data base. Wason's experiments have aroused considerable interest and some controversy. In the present symposium, Bree, using the technique of protocol analysis, reports further work along similar lines. Bree's paper shows the source of the difficulty is not perhaps quite as simple as the original experiment suggested. The experiments of de Soto, London and Handel show that subjects of good intellectual level who are unable to apply a syllogistic calculus tend to operate a paralogical spatial transfer of the given rules. This approach to the analysis of illegal thinking is carried forward by Dorner who relates the phenomena to the bizarre logic found in patients suffering from schizophrenia. One inference from these and many similar experiments is that man makes fairly gross errors at a level of logical complexity which is well within the competence of existing computational devices. Consequently it is possible to develop models which not only can compete effectively but whose performance within a limited calculus (Halma is one example, chess a more complicated one) can be compared in detail with the performance of human subjects under similar constraints.

The development of the comparative study of human and machine thinking is an area of great social significance. As indicated above it will provide an increasingly effective way of studying human intelligence. It also at least in the early stages must catalyse the development of intelligent automata. Finally it is an essential field of study for the development of machine-aided intelligence since the effective interaction between man and machine and the use made by man of mechanical computing power will depend on determining which contributions are best made by the two components of the man-machine system.

The concept of an intelligent automata is one that some physiologists and psychologists find difficult to swallow. Electronic computational power, in so far as it is merely a servo mechanism for the human mind in the same manner that mechanical power forms a servo mechanism for human muscle, is more comprehensible and acceptable. *Au fond,* the problems are the same. Psychologists now realise that intelligence is not an unitary function. Mathematicians and logicians agree with this and point out that no organisms or automata (not even man!) could be an optimal problem-solver for all universes of problems.

Man's claim to being an interesting problem-solver rests in part on his versatility and adaptability and in part on the fact that man's problem solving skills are geared to the survival motive. Fortunately it is reasonable to believe that however powerful intelligent automata may become, the choice of problem areas will remain with man unless he deliberately (or inadvertently) programs machine or system survival into a machine or a system.

The Future

As far as human intelligence is concerned there can be no doubt that the development of computer techniques will catalyse the development of our understanding of the human mind in a way that will be comparable to the way in which the technological developments of the industrial revolution gave a giant's stride to the physical sciences. We have already emphasised the contribution that computers can make by modelling and by stimulating the evolution of alien types of intelligence and the development of hypotheses about the nature of human intelligence. In particular we have stressed the value of the comparative psychology of man and machine. At a more practical level, a number of papers in the symposium point to the importance of the small laboratory computer and illustrate some of the more imaginative ways in which these inexpensive *aides de recherche* can be used by experimental psychologists working on human thinking. It is clear that computer techniques provide real hope for rapid advances in our understanding of human intelligence. Can we also hope that continued thinking about thinking will also improve man's powers of rational decision making?

This problem of linking computer power to social goals that are desirable was a common link between all the participants. Taken up initially in Bernard Meltzer's opening paper, it forms a main theme in de Zeeuw's closing summary. The questions posed are not easy ones.

Although much of man's culture is a common heritage, we in western societies tend to dismiss as primitive those cultures which are markedly at variance with our own, particularly when they are less technologically advanced.

However, many of man's social problems involve what psychologists call value judgments. An increasing number of people, for example, would, like Auden and Isherwood (1936), question whether the lot of a suburban housewife or for that matter that of a lower rung minor civil servant is either exciting, or satisfying: whether either is a better answer to the problem of being, than that of a Hausa woman trader or a Maoist coolie involved in promoting a cultural revolution.

14

Dialectical materialism is currently returning to fashion. Perhaps there may be some part-truths in the Buddhist concept of recurring historical patterns, and the related Marxist-Hegelian doctrine that evolution is achieved by the continuing intermingling of contradictory ideas. Most scientific advances may either destroy or contribute to human happiness. A nuclear holocaust would certainly put the cultural clock back. On the other hand a computer explosion might enable us to retain cultural satisfactions that are at present disappearing. Socially computer techniques can contribute to a tighter control by a smaller oligarchy. Equally, by virtue of its power to process and disseminate information, Artificial Intelligence could contribute to a wider, more integrated democracy. If man could understand better his intellectual and emotional needs, he might meet these best with what Rattray Taylor (1949) has called a paraprimitive society. Using computer techniques to help man think sensibly about man is perhaps a research area equal in importance to that of high energy particle physics.

1. Programming Thought

A symposium of this type does not easily lend itself to a fully logical grouping of papers. In the hope of making life easier for the reader we have therefore, in preparing the Proceedings for publication, deviated somewhat from the order in which the papers were presented. In this first section, we start with Bernard Meltzer's paper on the programming of induction and deduction and have grouped with this the contributions of Pohl, Hayes, Banerji and Wetherick. The coordinating theme is clearly the substance of artificial intelligence. Although this section contains some of the most stimulating papers presented during the meeting, some may well be tough going for psychologists and behavioural scientists unfamiliar with the field of A.I. However, although most of the authors are computer scientists rather than psychologists, their style of presentation is such that the key ideas and concepts come through clearly to anyone with a high school knowledge of mathematics and logic. In presenting these papers first, we have taken account of the fact that Meltzer's paper was, in fact, the opening contribution to the symposium. However, the decision is also a shock tactic which reflects the fact that artificial intelligence is a key, if relatively novel, concept for our general understanding of intelligence. These papers, although specialized in content, between them give a sound introduction to the problem of devising logical statements about thought processes which are sufficiently precise to lead to a practical outcome in terms of a computer program which models these processes.

The fact that most of these papers make original contributions to a newly established field does not make them any less valuable for the behavioural scientist relatively ignorant of the technical problems involved. They have been written with an interdisciplinary audience in mind and they deal essentially with conceptual problems with which the student of human problem solving is already only too familiar. Thinking about machine thinking is not conceptually different and, at the present level of development, not appreciably more difficult than thinking about primate or subprimate thinking. As we stressed in our introduction, the development of a new comparative psychology will catalyse both the development of A.I. and the study of man.

There is, however, perhaps more than a grain of truth in some of the criticisms put forward during the meeting (echoed, suitably muted, in Professor Barton's preface). It does all seem delightfully logically sound and logically simple. Why then are computer programs still of relatively little assistance in making the decisions that dog mankind from day to day? Perhaps, after all, day to day problems present a problem of scale rather than a problem of logic. A data base that is far too large nevertheless provides insufficient premises. In contrast man is able to draw from these his own conclusions, not because he has a high central processing capacity, but by virtue of selective sensory and memory mechanisms which are essentially goal orientated. The way in which he does this is one secret that both psychologists and A.I. workers very much need to unravel. That the latter have not yet done so cannot in equity be held against them. Indeed, as the papers grouped in this section show, work in the A.I. field is not only contributing to our general understanding of thought processes but also beginning to make progress towards this important goal.

BERNARD MELTZER*

The Programming of Deduction and Induction

Summary

The programming of deductive processes has been based much more on the findings of symbolic logic than those of psychology, even though individual designers of programs may use heuristics suggested by introspection. The methods have in the main been syntactical ones, embedded in the framework of Robinson's resolution logic, but the need for supplementation by semantic procedures has been recognised. Very little progress has yet been made on the incorporation of powers of drawing analogies or learning. The development of inductive programs has been more unsystematic and special-purpose, a proposal for a suitable standard inductive logic for computer implementation having been made only recently. The deductive methods have found application in, and interacted with, many other areas of artificial intelligence such as information retrieval of the more sophisticated type, robot planning and automatic proofs of properties of programs.

Introduction

As a scientist with no professional competence in the subject of human thinking, such as is possessed presumably by many psychologists, I was most surprised when asked to contribute the "key-note" paper to this symposium. For such competence as I have is in the construction, study and development of computer programs to carry out certain intellectual tasks, and while these tasks are ones which

* University of Edinburgh

human thinking also accomplishes, the methods employed are not guaranteed to be the same as those used by people. But further reflection suggested what are probably good reasons why psychologists and the like might be even keenly interested to know how things in my field are done. Namely, it is often the case that understanding of a subject only really gets off the ground when it becomes *comparative*: for instance, evolutionary biology could only have been initiated by the careful and systematic comparison of different animal and plant species. I take it that the progress of psychology has been hampered by the lack of other really suitable conscious systems to compare the functioning of our own minds with: the only candidates for a long time have been other animal species, but we are unable to obtain of their mental activities the kind of knowledge we obtain by introspection of our own. Now for the first time — in the young and vigorous discipline of artificial intelligence — systems are coming into existence which carry out mental tasks, are different from human minds and, even more importantly, can have their functioning studied to any degree of detail in program and print-out. In the years to come comparison with these systems should boost the study of human thinking. A subsidiary but perhaps very important bonus in the future might be the development of programs which, working in interactive mode, would take over some of the chores of applied psychologists and psychiatrists, such as conducting certain kinds of interview.

I propose to give here an interim report on some of the work that has been done in very recent times on the programming of deduction and induction. It is not surprising that induction, the generation of hypotheses to explain facts, and deduction, the drawing of logical conclusions from premises, should have much engaged the attention of workers in the field of artificial intelligence. In a sense, induction is much the more important, since it is the source of our general knowledge, obtained by abstracting, generalizing or otherwise theorizing from the data of our experience; from this point of view, deduction is just the following out of the implications of such knowledge, merely — so to say — putting it in another form. It may therefore seem surprising that so much more work has gone into the computer programming of deduction. This is partly due to the existence of a much larger body of knowledge about its logic than that of induction, and also perhaps to there being a quite powerful philosophical prejudice against the notion that a machine can do anything so "creative" as generating new knowledge. But I shall later suggest that perhaps the boot is on the other foot: that the real basis of the kind of intelligent activity we are considering is the deductive process, and that a machine which can carry this out with some degree of adequacy is thereby empowered in a sense to carry out induction.

Early Work on Deduction

The first published work in this field came out about ten years ago. Wang (1960) designed programs which proved large numbers of theorems in Russell and Whitehead's *Principia Mathematica* with remarkable efficiency. Newell *et al.* (1963) developed a "General Problem Solver" which was applied to proof of theorems of propositional logic — it used a hierarchy of subgoals. Gelernter (1963) designed a program which solved problems in elementary plane geometry — it made heuristic use of figures for greatly reducing the number of subgoals pursued.

This early work already showed a branching of effort in two directions: that using standard inference systems of mathematical logic, exemplified by Wang, and that using methods suggested by introspection and observation of problem-solving behaviour, exemplified by Newell *et al.* and Gelernter. The mainstream effort since then has been in the first direction, the "logical" one, and it is only quite recently that serious consideration came to be given to developing methods which combine the two approaches. The early work was also important for the invention of the first list-processing programming languages, such as IPLV and LISP, which are almost indispensable for handling the manipulation of symbols rather than doing arithmetic.

Deduction: Syntax and Interpretation

Modern work stems from the phenomenal developments of logic, which — prophesied by Leibniz — were carried out in the nineteenth and twentieth centuries by Frege, Pierce, Russell, Hilbert, Gödel and others. I shall briefly review the language and interpretation of the version of predicate logic mainly used in present-day deductive programs.

It is a language of relations and properties. Thus

"Mary is good"

might be written

$G(m)$,

where G is a name for a property, in this case "goodness", and m is a name for an individual, in this case "Mary".

"Mary is a daughter of Jane"

might be written

$D(m,j)$,

where D is a name for a 2-place relation "being a daughter of", and m, j again are names of individuals. Similarly, one might have 3-place or more-place relations as e.g., in "Mary gave Jane an orange".

The only explicit logical constant in the language is a symbol $\neg$ for "not".

The sentences of the language are *sets* of elementary assertions of properties or relations of individuals, without or with "not". An example might be

$\{\neg D(m,j),\ G(m)\}$

which is interpreted as semantically equivalent to

either $\quad \neg D(m,j) \quad$ or $\quad G(m)$.

In the above interpretation, this would mean "Either Mary is not the daughter of Jane, or Mary is good", which is the transcription in elementary logic of "If Mary is the daughter of Jane, she is good".

Such a set of *literals* (as they are usually called) is known as a *clause*, and is always interpreted as the disjunction, the "or" of its literals, which may, of course, be of any number.

The language as described so far is adequate for what is known as the propositional part of logic, that basic part for which validity of argument can be tested by truth-tables and the like. In it, we can talk about named individuals, but we cannot generalize, make assertions such as:

"All Jane's daughters are good", or
"Some daughter of Jane is good".

For this purpose, firstly, we need *variables* to denote unspecified individuals. The first sentence is recast, successively, as

"For all x, if x is a daughter of Jane, x is good".

and then as

"For all x, either x is not a daughter of Jane or x is good".

and so finally as the clause

$\{\neg D(x,j), G(x)\}$.

Here, x is a variable, and it will be noted that our semantics for clauses containing variables assumes that a variable is "universally quantified", i.e., the above clause is interpreted as meaning:

For all x, either $\neg D(x,j)$ or $G(x)$.

How, on the other hand, does one express "existential quantification" in this language, as evinced in the second sentence above:

"Some daughter of Jane is good",

where the reference is not to all, but to some, unspecified individual. The method used in most modern automatic deduction programs is the introduction of special names, known as *Skolem functors*. In the present simple example, we generate a name, say d, and represent the sentence by *two* clauses, viz.:

$\{D(d,j)\}$

and

$\{G(d)\}$,

which interpret as

"d is a daughter of Jane, and d is good".

Here d is an uninterpreted name — it refers to one or more definite individuals, but it is not specified which.

This is the simplest kind of Skolem functor, but we also need ones of more structure. Consider the following (unlikely!) sentence:

"Everybody has a daughter".

Providing a bare name for the daughters here will not do, since the different "bodies" concerned will have *different* daughters: the existential objects will *depend* on the universal variable. A "functor" symbol f is therefore introduced, and the sentence translates into the clause:

$$\{D(f(x), x)\}$$

which interprets as

"For all x, an object depending on x is the daughter of x".

The object is denoted by $f(x)$, in accordance with the usual mathematical notation for functional dependence.

Similarly, one may have Skolem functors with more than one argument place. For instance, the 3-literal clause

$$\{\neg P(x), \neg P(y), B[x, y, g(x, y)]\}$$

might interpret as

"For every point x and every point y, there is something lying between them".

Here g is a 2-place Skolem functor, used to denote an unspecified individual, whose identity depends on those of two other individuals, B being the 3-place "betweenness" relation.

Automatic Proof

The problem of deduction is: given a collection of sentences (the premises) does some other sentence (the conclusion) follow logically from them? According to the classical results of Gödel and Turing, no procedure is possible which would be able to solve this *decision* problem in all cases, but — and this is an equally remarkable finding of modern logic — procedures can be devised which are able to solve the *proof* problem: in all cases when the implication is logically valid, to find a proof. Such a program, when turned loose on a valid implication, will always — given enough time — terminate and supply a proof, but, when applied to an invalid one, might never terminate.

Most modern proof procedures work on the *reductio ad absurdum* principle, i.e., it is shown that the premisses with the negation of the conclusion adjoined to them yield a contradiction. Couched in the language described above, the problem a proof procedure tackles is: given a collection of clauses, prove they are contradictory; some of these clauses will be a transcription of the premises, the rest a transcription of the negation of the conclusion, all provided with suitable Skolem functors where necessary.

Thus the validity of a simple argument such as:

"Every man has a daughter or is unmarried.
There are no daughters.
Every man is married.
Therefore, there are no men",

is reduced to showing that the collection of the following four clauses yields a contradiction:

$\{\neg M(x), D[f(x), x], \neg N(x)\}$
$\{\neg D(x, y)\}$
$\{\neg M(x), N(x)\}$
$\{M(a)\}$

Here the first three clauses express the premises, the last the negated conclusion, M denoting the property of "being a man", N that of "being married", D as before, while a and f are Skolem functors.

It is instructive to consider how one might show that these clauses are contradictory. Remembering that x, y are interpreted as "universally quantified" variables, we may logically assert instances of these clauses arising from the substitution of constants for the variables; in this way, we may judiciously use the two constants a and $f(a)$ to yield the following special instances of the four clauses, written out here with the implicit "or"s included:

$\neg M(a)$ or $D[f(a), a]$ or $\neg N(a)$
$\neg D[f(a), a]$
$\neg M(a)$ or $N(a)$
$M(a)$.

It is easily seen, by means of (an 8-row) truth-table or any other Boolean method, that these are contradictory.

What has been done here is an application of a version of the fundamental theorem of logic discovered by Jacques Herbrand (1930), which is at the heart of modern automatic deduction methods. This states, in effect, that the definitive test for the contradictoriness of a collection of clauses is the existence of such substitutions of constants for variables, which yield a *finite* collection of instances of the clauses (so-called *ground* clauses) that are contradictory in the truth-table sense (and therefore, in principle, easily checked).

In this simple example, the choice of substitutions was quite easy to find, but in more complex arguments (of mathematics, for example) the discovery of just those substitutions which will do the job is the central and usually most difficult task of the proof. Of course, one might attempt to do this by an exhaustive procedure, trying out all possible substitutions in sequence, and this is just what early pioneering automatic proof procedures (Gilmore, 1960; Davis, 1963) did. But computing time and space are very soon exhausted on quite simple deductions, and significant progress came only as the result of a suggestion by Prawitz (1960) for limiting the substitutions tried, in such a way as to exclude a vast number which could not possibly contribute to a proof. His idea is incorporated in the resolution method of Robinson (1965a), which is the framework within which modern automatic proof procedures are designed.

Resolution Logic

It is clear that the proof procedure has essentially to do two things: find appropriate substitutions and test the clause instances for contradiction. Robinson's logic provides a framework for carrying out both tasks simultaneously by means of a *single* rule of inference. The idea can be illustrated by considering again the last example. First, suppose one wished to show the contradictoriness of the four clause instances we had

$$\neg M(a) \quad or \quad D[f(a),a] \quad or \quad \neg N(a) \tag{1}$$
$$\neg D[f(a),a] \tag{2}$$
$$\neg M(a) \quad or \quad N(a) \tag{3}$$
$$M(a) \tag{4}$$

in a more straightforward way than by working out a truth-table in full.

Because (2) contains the negation of one of the literals in (1), one would infer from (1) and (2) the clause

$$\neg M(a) \quad or \quad \neg N(a) \tag{5}$$

Similarly, from (5) and (3) one would infer

$$\neg M(a) \tag{6}$$

Then (6) and (4) yield an immediate contradiction, and one could, in fact, — by formal analogy with what was done before — infer from (6) and (4) the so-called *empty* clause.

Essentially the same thing was done in each step of this process. Two clauses are examined to see if they contain complementary literals (i.e., a literal in one which is the negation of a literal in the other); if they do, a new clause is inferred which is the set of all the remaining literals — one just unites the two clauses after eliminating the two complements. And a proof is obtained when the clause inferred is empty.

But Robinson's method, surprisingly, avoids actually generating the instances; it operates at the general level, using clauses with variables, but providing a proof which mirrors exactly the proof at the level of ground instances. Thus, in our example, it takes as input the four general clauses; although not essential, but to save confusion, primes are used to indicate that the different clauses have different variables:

$$\neg M(x) \quad or \quad D[f(x), x] \quad or \quad \neg N(x) \tag{7}$$
$$\neg D(x', y') \tag{8}$$
$$\neg M(x'') \quad or \quad N(x'') \tag{9}$$
$$M(a) \tag{10}$$

One now looks not merely for complementary literals but for literals which might be made complementary by applying an appropriate substitution to the variables. Thus in (7) and (8), if we make the substitutions $x' = f(x)$, $y' = x$, we can infer — in just the same way as before — the general clause

$$\neg M(x) \quad or \quad \neg N(x) \tag{11}$$

Then, in (11) and (9), make the substitution $x'' = x$, yielding the clause

$$\neg M(x) \tag{12}$$

Finally, in (12) and (10) make the substitution $x = a$, giving the empty clause and so, termination of the proof.

As this example shows, resolution procedures do not make substitutions "blindly" but are guided by the clues of potentially complementary literals. And the heart of the procedures is the so-called "unification algorithm" which computes the most economical substitution required to make the appropriate literals complementary.

Proof Procedures

Resolution is a complete inference system in the sense that there are proofs in it for every logically valid implication. But by itself it is not a proof *procedure*, for it is only permissive in character: it specifies what inferences, "resolutions", may be made, not which shall be made.

Its conversion into a proof procedure is normally done in two stages. The inference system itself is modified, or "refined", by imposing constraints of a general character on what resolutions are to be permitted, thus cutting down the extent of the search space. (The search space, for any given input collection of clauses, is the collection of clauses which can be generated from them by permissible inferences.) For example, such a refinement (known in the literature as P_1-deduction – cf. Robinson, 1965b) results by imposing the condition that one of the parent clauses in every resolution should be "positive", i.e., contain no negations. The refinements chosen for proof procedures usually result from logical studies which establish that in spite of its – often very drastic – reduction of the search space, the refinement is still logically complete. Other examples discussed in the literature are: set-of-support (Wos *et al.*, 1965), linear (Loveland, 1968), SL (Kowalski and Kuehner, to be published).

The refinement having been chosen, it determines a search space, and a search strategy must be selected (or designed) to explore this space for a proof, i.e., effectively to find an empty clause. A search strategy is essentially a prescription for inducing an ordering on the clauses of the search space. Examples of search strategies described in the literature are unit-preference (Wos *et al.* 1964) and diagonal search (Kowalski, 1969).

A proof procedure is thus essentially an inference system plus a search strategy and its efficiency is very much determined by its search strategy. A beginning has been made on the general study of this central

28

issue of efficiency of proof procedures (cf. Kowalski, 1970; Meltzer, 1971), and it overlaps to some extent with studies of heuristic search and some parts of operational research (cf. Hart *et al.,* 1968; Pohl, 1970).

Limitations and Perspectives

The methods discussed have serious limitations, and active efforts are being made to overcome these. Only a brief survey is possible here:

Firstly, the very logic used is less than appropriate for many purposes. For example, its handling of that relation which is the mainstay of mathematics − namely, equality − is usually very clumsy and redundant, and proposals have been made for modified or alternative inference systems for this purpose (cf. Sibert, 1969; Robinson, 1968; Darlington, 1968; Robinson and Wos, 1969; Morris, 1969). Then, too, the restriction of variables and quantification to individuals, so that one cannot directly generalize over properties and relations as well as individuals, can be overcome in the logic but by so clumsy and inefficient a method (the inclusion of axioms of set theory in the premises) as to put it out of court; hence proposals for the use of higher-order logics, which have not got this restriction (cf. Gould, 1966; Robinson, 1969; Darlington, 1968). The use of larger inference steps and "larger" relations (i.e., ones compounded from the basic ones of the language) has been suggested (cf. Robinson, 1965b; 1967; Pitrat, 1966; Meltzer, 1969). For applications to "real-life" situations rather than mathematics, the use of modal logics has been considered (cf. McCarthy and Hayes, 1968). One of the most interesting very recent developments is Plotkin's "normalized logics" (1971b) which provide a systematic means of tailoring the inference system to the subject matter.

Possibly the most serious defect of the methods used is their purely "syntactic" character: they do not in any direct way make use of what the symbols "mean". Gelernter's early geometry program (1963), referred to in the Introduction, made good use of figures as well as formal inferences, and very recently Winograd (1970) in a deduction system of a rather novel character has incorporated the exploitation of semantic information, but we still know very little of how to do this well.

Possibly equally serious is the clean-slate feature of present methods:

every new deduction problem is tackled *ab initio,* as if the program had had no previous experience of related or similar problems. Of course one can add to its data store any results it has obtained and so create a library of possibly useful theorems. But one then quite soon faces exacting problems of retrieval from a large data base with inadequate criteria of relevance. Some of these retrieval problems have been considered by Darlington (1969) and Green (1969a).

A start has been made in the supplementation of the logic-based procedures by heuristics such as the use of a hierarchy of subgoals by, for example, Bledsoe (1971) and Kowalski and Kuehner (to be published). A notable breaking of new ground of crucial importance is a study of ways of using analogy by Kling (to be published). Until a fuller understanding and successful exploitation of analogy is obtained, there is not much hope of developing useful learning programs.

Can Induction be Programmed?

It is surprising that very distinguished modern philosophers and scientists like Popper and Medawar have taken the view that, unlike deduction, induction must contain an "irrational" element and therefore cannot be done by rules. Thus Popper (1959):

"... there is no such thing as a logical method of having new ideas, or a logical reconstruction of this process. My view may be expressed by saying that every discovery contains an 'irrational element'..."

And Medawar (1967):

"...although one can put oneself in the right frame of mind for having ideas and can abet the process, the process itself is outside logic and cannot be made the subject of logical rules."

The first answer to assertions such as these is that successful induction programs have already been written, e.g., for inferring chemical structures from mass-spectograms (Buchanan *et al.,* 1969); for inferring criteria of wins in games (Plotkin, 1971); for inferring an approximation to the axioms of group theory from a small collection of facts about particular groups (Meltzer, 1969).

But perhaps it is more interesting to accept the challenge in the quoted philosophical views, and ask whether a general logic of induc-

30

tion is possible comparable to that for deduction, by means of which theory construction can be carried out by a program. This can indeed be done, on the following lines:

Assume that we have to explain some fact (or conjunction of facts) A expressed as a sentence in a suitable logical language such as some version of lower predicate logic. That is to say, we are looking for a sentence B which deductively implies A. But that is not the only requirement on B, because B also has to be compatible with the existing body of knowledge of the subject domain we are concerned with. Let this body of knowledge be expressed by the consistent sentence (or conjunction of sentences) S; then a second requirement on B is that B and S shall be compatible with each other, i.e., that their conjunction should not (deductively) imply a contradiction. Thus the validity of an inductive inference, from A to B, is *relative* to a body of knowledge S. This account corresponds to practice, for in the development of knowledge S alters, either as a result of the discovery of new facts or the modification of old ones; so that what was previously a valid inductive inference might now cease to be one, e.g., when a new fact contradicts some other deductive implication of B.

This exhausts the logical account of non-probabilistic induction, although other less well-understood non-logical criteria, e.g., of simplicity, degree of falsifiability and explanatory power (cf. Popper, 1959; Buchanan, 1966; Plotkin, 1971b) might also be imposed on the selection of B from all those sentences satisfying the two logical criteria.

The important feature of these two conditions, namely (i) B implies A, (ii) B and S are compatible, is that — while characterizing validity of inductive inference — they are themselves deductive in character. Hence one may expect to be able to use deduction programs for carrying out inductive inference.

Condition (i) may be implemented (cf. Meltzer, 1970) by taking any deductive system and *inverting* its inference rules; the resulting system applied to A will generate sentences which will be candidates for B. If the deductive system is complete in the sense of being able to generate all logical implications of its input sentences, then this inverted system will also be complete in the sense that it can generate all hypotheses, expressible in the language, which imply A. For the satisfaction of condition (ii) each candidate for B has to be submitted to a deductive program which checks whether the conjunction of B and S leads to a contradiction. If the result of the test is negative, B is a valid inductive inference.

Thus, provided one uses an appropriate logical language, induction can be carried out by deduction programs. Recently Morgan (to be published) has even shown that to obtain the candidate-inductive hypotheses B, one does not even have to invert the deduction inference system, but can apply the latter directly, together with a certain simple transformation of the input data and output sentences!

Some Applications

The language of predicate logic – of properties, relations and quantification – is of such power and generality that a great deal of the reasoning not only of special scientific disciplines but of ordinary natural-language discourse can be translated into it. Hence deduction and induction programs can be applied to a great variety of subject matter.

Most existing deduction programs were designed for the proof of theorems of mathematics, but they have already had notable other uses. Green (1969b) introduced an ingenious small technical modification of resolution-type procedures, which enabled them – when proving a theorem – to generate as a side-product a construct which answers a question. So, by way of a simple example, one might have a program dealing with kinship relations, which when set to prove the theorem

"Mary has a grand-daughter",

would not only prove this existential quantification, but give a constructive description of the individual or object stated to exist, thus:

"Yes, and she is a daughter of Jane."

This is achieved essentially by keeping track and record of the substitutions carried out by the unification algorithm in the course of the proof. Many interesting uses can be made of this device (cf. Green 1969a), and resolution programs incorporating it are an essential part of the reasoning and planning system of what is probably the most advanced existing robot, that developed at the Stanford Research Institute (cf. Nilsson, 1969). This approach has been further developed by Luckham and Nilsson (1971). As indicated earlier, similar work is also going on elsewhere on information retrieval systems of a sophisticated kind, which find not only facts in store but their logical implications too.

The problems involved in assimilating natural-language arguments into the framework of predicate logic for the purpose of using automatic inference procedures have been considered by a number of investigators, e.g., McCarthy and Hayes (1968), Sandewall (1971) and Palme (1971).

A beginning has been made on what may turn out to be one of the most significant and useful applications of inference procedures: proofs of the properties of programs and automatic writing of programs to perform to given specifications. The mathematical theory of computation, initiated by McCarthy (1963) and now in vigorous development (cf. London, 1969), has opened up the possibility of proving properties of programs like correctness, termination and equivalence (cf. Manna, 1969). It does not require much imagination to foresee the impact of techniques which would substitute in many cases for the uncertain art of debugging scientific, automatic diagnosis and correction. Even more impressive in its effects would be the further development of methods, which − given a general description of the input and required output of a program − *generates* the program. This has already been done on a pilot small scale both by the use of Green's device (cf. Green, 1969a) and in related ways (cf. Manna and Waldinger, 1970). The main hold-up inhibiting more useful applications of these possibilities is the relative inefficiency of even the best inference procedures implemented in programs to date.

IRA POHL*

Syntactic Models of Cognitive Behavior

Summary

The steps a problem solver takes can be written as a sentence of a phrase-structure grammar. Both the problem behavior graph (PBG) notation of Newell for recording protocols and Quinlan's Fortran Deductive System (FDS) are examples. The relation of this formulation to the state space approach and the interaction of syntax and semantics are discussed.

Introduction

In studying human cognitive behavior, major impetus has been given to psycholinguistics by the phrase-structure models of Chomsky (1957, 1968). He himself has sharpened his interest in psychology and now sees linguistics, psychology and philosophy intimately related. A major criticism he levels is,

Psychology conceived as 'behavioral science' has been concerned with behavior and acquisition or control of behavior. It has no concept corresponding to 'competence', in the sense in which competence — competence in this use, means a grammar reflects the observable linguistic behavior of the native speaker — is characterized by a generative grammar (Chomsky 1968).

This criticism is right on target and is the major incentive to theorize

* University of California at Santa Cruz and Stevenson College

using information-processing models. Competence is unequivocal when a chess program (Greenblatt *et al.,* 1967) beats you, or when a pattern recognition program discriminates and names human faces correctly (Kelley, 1971). I quote Chomsky here for several reasons:

(1) Phrase-structure grammars have been used now to model high-level cognitive behavior in non-linguistic areas, such as pattern recognition (Miller and Shaw, 1968) and deductive problem solving (Quinlan and Hunt, 1968).

(2) Their use, to my thinking, is not adequate in modeling performance, and in this artificial intelligence has a more advanced viewpoint in trying to model the use of knowledge or semantics necessary for adequate performance (Minsky, 1968; Nilsson, 1971).

(3) Chomsky makes the mistake of considering artificial intelligence as a member of a family of theories in the empiricist framework which are dogmatic and inadequate.

This paper will examine syntactic models of problem-solving behavior in order to explore questions arising from (1) and (2). In the course of this exposition objection (3) will be illuminated as a misconception, which unfortunately is widely held.

A phrase-structure grammar or production system conventionally operates as a string rewriting model. Example 1 is a grammar for bracketing:

$A \rightarrow (a \, o \, A)$
$A \rightarrow a$

strings $a, (a \, o \, a), [a \, o \, (a \, o \, a)], ...$

The first production is read as string "A" is rewritten to string "$(a \, o \, A)$". Example 1 may be interpreted as a right-to-left association (bracketing) of a binary operator. Several mathematicians have devised rewriting systems, most importantly the Russian, A.A. Markov (1951) and the American E.L. Post (1936). While in appearance they seem limited and simple, they are not, but instead are equivalent to the Turing formulation of universal computability. Hence, Chomsky's demonstration of expressing natural language within this context is not so surprising. Furthermore, they are more descriptive and natural in expressing behavior than other computational schemas, such as Kleene's (1952) Recursive Functions. The units represented as an alphabet, with the productions representing transformations, may be matched to a particular cognitive domain.

Newell: Problem Behavior Graphs

The bulk of the early work in cognitive simulation was done at Carnegie, see, for example, Newell *et al.* (1959). Newell and his co-workers looked at many deductive problem-solving tasks and attempted to have a computer produce a trace of its problem-solving steps analogous to human protocols for the same problem. In this way they showed how a general search mechanism with limited evaluative capability (mostly a matching procedure) could, guided by a primitive operator-difference correspondence, solve tasks adequately and with a surface correspondence to human problem solvers.

To produce a more rigorous description of the problem-solving subjects trials, Newell proposed encoding the verbal protocol as a problem behavior graph (PBG) (Newell 1966, 1967). These graphs are closely related to game trees and path exploration graphs (Pohl, 1970), which are computational techniques used to solve these problems. The PBG is distinguished from these by illustrating the sequential history of the problem solver's attempts. The nodes represent the problem states and arrows to the right point at successor states. The arrow is labeled by the operator used to generate the successor node. If the problem solver returns to a given state to try a new operator, the state is redrawn below its old appearance. Therefore time moves to the right and down. In Fig. 1 we illustrate the analysis of a mate in four by a PBG.

The next step is to take the PBG and induce a "production" scheme which would generate these PBGs as instances. However these production schemes are not rewriting systems on strings, but instead act on states. They resemble a conditional calculus of the form:

if $P(q)$ then $f(q)$, i.e., if state q satisfied predicate P then change it by using operator f.

The attempts to automate the induction of grammars are still in their early stages (Feldman, 1967; Plotkin, 1971). It continues to be more fruitful to have human experts derive these micro-theories for specific tasks where a performance model is desired (Feigenbaum *et al.*, 1971).

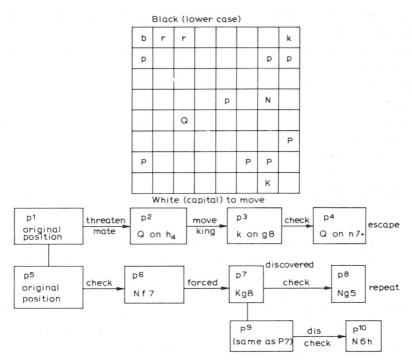

Fig. 1. Partial hypothetical PBG for analysing a mate in four. The reader might like to compare the solution plus his own PBG.

While production schemes for generating PBGs are not strictly syntactic, this work inspired J.R. Quinlan to develop a purely syntactic problem solver. Quinlan (later in collaboration with E.B. Hunt) developed a problem solving system, akin to the General Problem Solver (GPS) of Newell *et al.* (1959), using production-driven transformations. He called this system the Fortran Deductive System (FDS) (Quinlan and Hunt, 1968).

A problem is defined by two strings *s* and *g*, the starting state and the goal state, with rewriting rules being the legal moves. If the problem has a solution, then the grammar is capable of generating string *g* starting with string *s* — a compiler for a programming language does the inverse task by reducing *g* to *s* (program). A matching procedure automatically extracts syntactic correspondence by matching operands and operators by precedence (in ordinary arithmetic multiply has higher precedence than add as in $a + b \times c$ meaning $a + (b \times c)$ not $(a + b) \times c$), and applying a production which reduces any found difference. FDS has two advantages over GPS. It is a uniform scheme for representing deductive problems, where GPS was *ad hoc* in its representations. It has an automatic means of extracting the operator-difference correspondence, where GPS was given this information. However, a pure syntactic procedure like FDS, as its authors point out, has no facility for discriminating among alternate derivative strings. These issues will be illuminated in the following example.

A Yardstick Problem

Much of the progress in artificial intelligence, as in other fields, revolves on approaches to "yardstick" problems. Some are elementary, such as the missionaries and cannibals problem (Amarel, 1968) or the monkey and bananas problem (McCarthy, 1963); others are very difficult, such as the travelling salesman problem (Ore, 1963) or the mutilated checkerboard problem (Newell, 1965, 1967). Elementary problems provide cheap tests of new ideas and have pedagogical value because of their simplicity. Difficult problems measure the power of new methods and direct attention to weaknesses in our understanding.

The pail problem, used by Fikes (1969) as a problem for his nondeterministic programming system REF−ARF, is a useful addition to these examples. It stands somewhere in the middle of a hypothetical "difficulty" rating scale.

The two-pail problem

You are given two pails of capacities C_1 and C_2 gallons and you wish to exactly measure out C_3 gallons into a barrel. A tap provides you with an unlimited supply of water, and the barrel has capacity greatly in excess (formally unbounded) of C_1, C_2 and C_3.

Example 1
Pails of 7-gallon and 9-gallon capacity with the problem of obtaining 15 gallons in the barrel.

Solution

Fill the 9-gallon pail four times from the tap, pouring each into the barrel. Remove 7 gallons three times from the barrel, leaving 15 gallons.

An alternate solution involves six fillings with the 7-gallon pail and three removals with the 9-gallon pail.

What types of questions pertaining to artificial intelligence and computation, for the two are never far apart in our view, are of interest in this problem?

(a) For a given set of capacities and a desired goal for the barrel, when is a pouring sequence possible?

(b) When is there a minimal solution, i.e., fewest pourings?

(c) Can these answers be computed efficiently (or intelligently)?

The general problem

Given k integers $P_1, P_2, ..., P_k$ $(P_i \neq P_j)$ and a target integer T, obtain coefficients $a_1, a_2, ... a_k$ such that

$$\sum_{i=1}^{k} a_i P_i = T, \quad a_i \text{ integral} \tag{1}$$

$$T \geqslant 0.$$

A solution to (1) is called feasible solution to the k-pail problem. It is optimal if

$$\sum_{i=1}^{k} |a_i| \tag{2}$$

is a minimum over all feasible solutions.

The interpretation of this as k pails of capacities P_i, with T the desired amount in the barrel is obvious. Condition (2) is a solution requiring the minimum number of water pourings.

Let us attempt to answer our three questions.

Lemma 1

A solution exists if and only if $T = m^* \text{ GCD } (P_1, P_2, ... P_k)$; where GCD means greatest common divisor.

Euclid's algorithm for finding the GCD (see Appendix for more discussion) provides a construction for a sequence of pourings to achieve

T. If *T* is not a multiple of the GCD then it is relatively prime to the GCD and no sequence of additions or subtractions could be used to obtain it.

The GCD algorithm only answers question (a). Obviously the method is of no use for (b). Consider pails of capacity 7 and 9 gallons again. GCD would have

$$18 = 18 \times (4 \times 7 - 3 \times 9)$$

which would involve 156 pourings.

A syntactic restatement of the problem (for two pails)

Given the language L,

$V_t = (t, P_1, P_2, b)$ and the finite state grammar
$S \rightarrow S\,T \mid \phi$ (null string)
$T \rightarrow t\,P_1 \mid t\,P_2 \mid P_1 P_2 \mid P_2 P_1 \mid P_1\,b \mid P_2\,b \mid P_1\,t \mid P_2\,t \mid b\,P_1 \mid b\,P_2$

and a pouring machine M which interprets (executes) terminal strings in this language, the following procedure will solve the pail problem.

M has 3 integer registers (a, b, c). Registers a, b and c keep track, respectively, of the contents of pail 1, pail 2 and the barrel. M reads two symbols at a time and performs the following operations on its registers:

$t\,P_1$: val (b) := cap (P_1)

This is read as, "the value of register a becomes capacity P_1 gallons." Some typical other state transitions are:

$t\,P_2$: val (b) := cap (P_2)

$P_1 P_2$: excess := min [cap(P_2), val (a) + val (b)]
   val (a) := *if* excess = val (a) + val (b) *then* 0
            else   val(b) − cap (P_2) + val (a)
   val (b) := excess
$P_1 t$: val (a) := 0 "spill out pail 1"
$P_1 b$: val (c) := val (c) + val (a);
   val (a) := 0
$b P_2$: excess := cap (P_2) − val (b)
   if val (c) ⩾ excess *then*

$\{$val (c) := val (c) − excess; val (b) := cap $(P_2)\}$
else
$\{$val (b) := val (b) + val (c); val (c) := 0$\}$

The other state transitions are defined appropriately and M is a simple arithmetic processor.

Lemma 2
There exists an algorithm for finding an optimum sequence of water transfers (enumeration).

Proof
Generate terminal strings of L in order of length; i.e.,

ϕ, tP_1, tP_2, P_1P_2, ..., bP_2, $tP_1 tP_1$, ..., $tP_1 bP_2$, $tP_2 tP_1$, ...,
$tP_2 bP_2$, ..., $bP_2 bP_2$, ...

As each string is produced run it on M, and see if register C ends up with the desired number of gallons.
Halt on the first instance of this occurring.   Q.E.D.

The algorithm is obviously correct. It will only be run after the GCD algorithm ascertains that a solution exists. However, it is exponential in the number of steps it requires. Now we have answered our first two questions. A generate and test approach, ordered in length of steps, suffices to obtain a solution. A decision procedure, which discovers if the target capacity is relatively prime to the GCD of the pails, allows an always terminating algorithm. This latter understanding of the problem is not a simple "general problem solver" type operator, but represents complex knowledge of number theoretic theorems. It is analogous to understanding parity in the mutilated checkerboard problem (Newell, 1965) or the fifteen puzzle (Pohl, 1969).

As an investigation of the problem progresses, we see that productions should be selectively applied for a more efficient attempt at a solution. Now FDS is such a system, but it only allows selection on syntactic features. String matching is not useful here, as the form (sentence) of the solution is unknown. A solution possesses the semantic property; namely, its interpretation by M leaves target capacity in register c. This "deep" property cannot be determined from the syntactic structure of a well-formed sentence in the pail language. Hence, a use of M to ascertain progress in the deep or semantic sense is necessary.

Consider the case cap $(P_1) \geqslant$ cap (P_2), then no solution can take fewer than $\dfrac{t}{\text{cap }(P_1)}$ pourings. In fact $\dfrac{t - \text{val }(c)}{\text{cap }(P_1)}$ is the least number of steps a partially full barrel requires. In this sense the Heuristic Path Algorithm, HPA (Pohl, 1970) can select a next operator (production to apply). HPA is a path-finding algorithm guided by a heuristic function which attempts to measure progress to a goal state. The heuristic function would look at val (c), with $g(\alpha)$ the length of string α, and val (c) the computed (by M) value of gallons currently in the bucket.

It could be a function

$$f(\alpha) = g(\alpha) + \left[\frac{t - \text{val }(c)}{\text{cap }(P_1)} \right]$$

This satisfied admissibility and still provides feasible solutions. It is a more intelligent solution and models a problem solver's desire to take large steps that get within reach of the solution.

Some Concluding Remarks

The elementary non-redundant trial and error search will solve the pail problem. The REF−ARF system has done this within the context of the non-deterministic search language. In a much subtler way, the search may be expedited by a HPA algorithm provided with the previously mentioned notion of progress. The syntactic component describing the search can never provide appropriate *prägnanz* − the good gestalt or insightful organization. This instead must come from epistemological machines, like M, organized to handle knowledge applicable to the problem. (See Appendix for a systematic reorganization of this problem as an elementary ordered search for the solution of a diophantine equation.)

The mind has the ability to organize trial and error search, analogous to linguistic generative capabilities. Possibly the innate abilities the Cartesianists postulate are a general ability to induce grammars for ordering experience. This, in itself, is insufficient to explain "knowledgeable" problem-solving behavior. Artificial intelligence performance programs (examples are chess, spectrographic analysis, medical diagnosis, pattern recognition, symbolic mathematics) include as much organized knowledge as the programmer can efficiently cram into his system. Certainly, no one familiar with the Greenblatt chess program, would make Chomsky's error of calling A.I. mistaken in its *tabula rasa* approach to modeling cognition. The modeling of knowledge, not the modeling of adaptation is the foremost pursuit of research in artificial intelligence.

Appendix

A moderately efficient enumerative search

Euclid's algorithm for the greatest common divisor may be expressed in pseudoalgol as:

comment $m \leqslant n$;
$i := 1; a_0 := n; a_1 := m;$
while n mod m $\neq 0$ *do*
$\{i := i + 1;\quad a_i := n \bmod m;$
$c_{i-1} := n \; div \; m;$
$n := m; m := a_i\}$
$GCD := a_i; c_i := n \; div \; m;$

For extensive discussion of this algorithm see Knuth (1971).

When the GCD algorithm halts, it will have some value k for i with a_k the greatest common divisor. The following recurrence formula will be satisfied:

$$a_{i-1} = c_i a_i = a_{i+1} \qquad 1 \leqslant i < k$$

or

$$a_{i+1} = a_{i-1} - c_i a_i$$

by working backwards from a_k we can use this schema to obtain an integer diophantine equation of the form

(GCD) $a_k = b \, m + c \, n$

(b, c integers one of which must be less-than-or-equal-to zero).

A feasible pail-pouring sequence is then

rb pourings of the m gallon pail
rc pourings of the n gallon pail

where

$r = T/a_k$.

Solutions can only occur along the straight line $mx + ny = T$, with a known solution (rb, rc). This simple equation need only be searched for $- |rb| < x < |rb|$, and even this can be searched systematically for the best results first. Namely, enumerate and test in the order $x = 0$, $x = \pm 1, ..., x = \pm |rb|$.

The example of 7, 9, 15 worked out.
The *GCD* algorithm and recurrence give

$GCD\ (7, 9) = 1$
$1 = 4.7 - 3.9$
$15 = 60.7 - 45.9$ (1)

$$7\,x + 9\,y = 15$$

$x = 0$	$y = 1.67$	$x = -3$	$y = 4$
$x = 1$	$y = -0.89$	(integral)	
$x = -1$	$y = 2.44$	must still check positive	
$x = 2$	$y - 0.11$	x-axis until $|x| + |y| > 7$	
$x = -2$	$y = 3.22$	$x = 4$	$y = -1.44$
$x = 3$	$y = 0.67$	$x = 5$	$y = -2.22$
		$|x| + |y| = 7.22 > 7$	
		can stop.	(2)

Note: $|x| + |y|$ provides both a stopping criterion and guidance for whether the positive x values should be pursued more vigorously.

PATRICK J. HAYES*

The Frame Problem and Related Problems in Artificial Intelligence

Summary

The frame problem arises in attempts to formalise problem—solving processes involving interactions with a complex world. It concerns the difficulty of keeping track of the consequences of the performance of an action in, or more generally of the making of some alteration to, a representation of the world. The paper contains a survey of the problem, showing how it arises in several contexts and relating it to some traditional problems in philosophical logic. In the second part of the paper several suggested partial solutions to the problem are outlined and compared. This comparison necessitates an analysis of what is meant by a representation of a robot's environment. Different notions of representation give rise to different proposed solutions. It is argued that a theory of causal relationships is a necessity for any general solution. The significance of this, and the problem in general, for natural (human and animal) problem solving is discussed, and several desiderata for efficient representational schemes are outlined.

Introduction

We consider some problems which arise in attempting a logical analysis of the structure of a robot's beliefs.

A *robot* is an intelligent system equipped with sensory capabilities, operating in an environment similar to the everyday world inhabited by human robots.

* University of Edinburgh

By *belief* is meant any piece of information which is explicitly stored in the robot's memory. New beliefs are formed by (at least) two distinct processes: *thinking* and *observation*. The former involves operations which are purely internal to the belief system: the latter involves interacting with the *world*, that is, the external environment and, possibly, other aspects of the robot's own structure.

Beliefs will be represented by statements in a formal logical calculus, called the *belief calculus* L_b. The process of inferring new assertions from earlier ones by the *rules of inference* of the calculus will represent thinking (McCarthy, 1959, 1963; McCarthy and Hayes, 1969; Green, 1969; Hayes, 1971).

There are convincing reasons why L_b must *include* L_c — classical first-order logic. It has often been assumed that a moderately adequate belief logic can be obtained merely by adding *axioms* to L_c (a first-order theory); however I believe that it will certainly be necessary to add extra rules of inference to L_c, and extra syntactic richness to handle these extra rules.

One can show that, under very general conditions, logical calculi obey the *extension property*: If $S \vdash p$ and $S \subseteq S'$ then $S' \vdash p$. The importance of this is that if a belief p is added to a set S, then all thinking which was legal before, remains legal, so that the robot need not check it all out again.

Time and Change

For him to think about the real world, the robot's beliefs must handle *time*. This has two distinct but related aspects.

(a) There must be beliefs *about* time. For example, beliefs about causality.

(b) The robot lives *in* time: the world changes about him. His beliefs must accommodate in a rational way to this change.

Of these, the first has been very extensively investigated both in A.I. and philosophical logic, while the second has been largely ignored until very recently: it is more difficult. The first is solely concerned with thinking: the second involves observation.

The standard device for dealing with (a) is the introduction of *situation variables* (McCarthy, 1963; McCarthy and Hayes, 1969) or *possible worlds* (Hintikka, 1967; Kripke, 1963). Symbols prone to change their denotations with the passage of time are enriched with an extra argument place which is filled with a term (often a variable) denoting a *situation* which one can think of intuitively as a time instant; although other readings are possible. In order to make statements about the relationships between situations, and the effects of actions, we also introduce terms denoting *events*, and the function R (read: *result*) which takes events and situations into new situations. Intuitively, "$R(e,s)$" denotes the situation which results when the event e happens in the situation s. By "event" we mean a change in the world: "his switching on the light", "the explosion", "the death of Caesar". This is a minor technical simplification of the notation and terminology used in McCarthy and Hayes (1969) and Hayes (1971). Notice that all the machinery is defined within L_c. The situation calculus is a first-order theory.

Using situations, fairly useful axiomatisations can be obtained for a number of simple problems involving sequences of actions and events in fairly complicated worlds (Green, 1969; McCarthy and Hayes, 1969).

The Frame Problem

Given a certain description of a situation s — that is, a collection of statements of the form $\phi \llbracket s \rrbracket$, where the fancy brackets mean that *every* situation in ϕ is an occurrence of 's' — we want to be able to infer as much as possible about $R(e,s)$. Of course, what we can infer will depend upon the properties of e. Thus we require assertions of the form:

$$\phi_1 \llbracket s \rrbracket \ \& \ \psi(e) \supset \phi_2 \llbracket R(e, s) \rrbracket \tag{1}$$

Such an assertion will be called a *law of motion*. The frame problem can be briefly stated as the problem of finding adequate collections of laws of motion.

Notice how easily human thinking seems to be able to handle such inferences. Suppose I am describing to a child how to build towers of bricks. I say "You can put the brick on top of this one onto some other one, if that one has not got anything else on it." The child *knows* that the other blocks will stay put during the move. But if I write the corresponding law of motion:

$$(\text{on}\,(b_1,b_2,s)\ \&\ \forall z.\ \neg\text{on}\,(z,b_3,s)) \supset \text{on}\,(b_1,b_3,R\,(\text{move}\,(b_2,b_3),s)) \quad (2)$$

then nothing follows concerning the other blocks. What assertions could we write down which would capture the knowledge that the child has about the world?

One does not want to be obliged to give a law of motion for *every* aspect of the new situation. For instance, one feels that it is prolix to have a law of motion to the effect that if a block is not *moved*, then it stays where it is. And yet such laws — instances of (1) in which $\phi_1 = \phi_2$ — are necessary in first-order axiomatisations. They are called *frame axioms*. Their only function is to allow the robot to infer that an event does *not* affect an assertion. Such inferences are necessary: but one feels that they should follow from more general considerations than a case-by-case listing of axioms, especially as the number of frame axioms increases rapidly with the complexity of the problem. Raphael (1971) describes the difficulty thoroughly.

This phenomenon is to be expected. Logically, s and $R(e,s)$ are simply different entities. There is no *a priori* justification for inferring any properties of $R(e,s)$ from those of s. If it were usually the case that events made widespread and drastic alterations to the world (explosions, the Second Coming, etc.), then we could hardly expect anything better than the use of frame axioms to describe in detail, for each event, exactly what changes it brings about. Our expectation of a more general solution is based on the fact that the world is, fortunately for robots, fairly stable. Most events — especially those which are likely to be considered in planning — make only small local changes in the world, and are not expected to touch off long chains of cause and effect.

Frame Rules

We introduce some formalism in order to unify the subsequent discussions. Any general solution to the frame problem will be a method for allowing us to transfer properties from a situation s to its successor $R(e,s)$; and we expect such a licence to be sensitive to the form of the assertion, to what is known about the event e, and possibly to other facts.

Consider the rule scheme FR:

$$\chi, \phi[\![s]\!], \psi(e) \vdash \phi[\![R(e, s)]\!]$$
$$provided \, \aleph(e, \phi, \psi) \, .$$
(FR)

where $\aleph$ is some condition on e, ϕ and ψ, expressed of course in the metalanguage. We will call such a rule a *frame rule*. The hope is that frame rules can be used to give a general mechanism for replacing the frame axioms, and also admit an efficient implementation, avoiding the search and relevancy problems which plague systems using axioms (Green, 1969; Raphael, 1971).

One must, when considering a frame rule, be cautious that it does not allow contradictions to be generated. Any addition of an inference rule to L_c, especially if not accompanied by extra syntax, brings the risk of inconsistency, and will, in any case, have dramatic effects on the metatheory of the calculus. For instance, the deduction theorem fails. Thus a careful investigation of each case is needed. In some cases, a frame rule has a sufficiently simple $\aleph$ condition that it may be replaced by an *axiom scheme,* resulting in a more powerful logic in which the deduction theorem holds. This usually makes the metatheory easier and implementation more difficult.

Some Partial Solutions Using Frame Rules

The literature contains at least four suggestions for handling the problem which are describable by frame rules. In each case we need some extra syntactic machinery.

Frames

Following McCarthy and Hayes (1969), one assumes a finite number of monadic second-order predicates P_i. If $\vdash P_i(h)$ for a non-logical symbol h (predicate, function or individual constant) then we say that h is in the *i*th *block* of the frame. The frame rule is

$$P_{i_1}(h_1), ..., P_{i_n}(h_n), \phi[\![s]\!], P_j(e) \vdash \phi[\![R(e, s)]\!]$$
(3)

where $h_1, ..., h_n$ are all the non logical symbols which occur *crucially* in ϕ, and $i_k \neq j$, $1 \leqslant k \leqslant n$. Here *crucial* is some syntactic relation between *h* and ϕ; different relations give different logics, with a stronger or weaker frame rule.

Causal connection

We assume (Hayes 1971) that there is a 3-place predicate $\rightarrow(x,y,s)$ (read: *x* is connected to *y* in situation *s*) which has the intuitive meaning that if *x* is not connected to *y*, then any change to *y* does not affect *x*. It seems reasonable that $\rightarrow$ should be a partial ordering on its first two arguments (reflexive and transitive). The frame rule is:

$$\phi[\![s]\!], \neg \rightarrow (h_1, e, s), ..., \neg \rightarrow (h_n, e, s) \vdash \phi[\![R(e, s)]\!] \tag{4}$$

where (i) ϕ is an atom or the negation of an atom; (ii) $h_1, ..., h_n$ are all the terms which occur *crucially* in ϕ.

If we insisted only that $\neg \rightarrow (h_i, e, s)$ is not provable (rather than $\neg \rightarrow (h_i, e, s)$ *is* provable) then the rule is much stronger but no longer obeys the extension property. This is analogous to PLANNER's method below.

MICRO-PLANNER

The problem solving language MICRO-PLANNER (Sussman and Winograd, 1969) uses a subset of predicate calculus enriched with notations which control the system's search for proofs. We will ignore the latter aspect for the present and describe the underlying formalism. Its chief peculiarity is that it has no negation, and is therefore not troubled by the need for consistency.

Following MICRO-PLANNER we introduce the new unary propositional connective *therase*. Intuitively, *therase* ϕ will mean that ϕ is "erased". We also introduce the notion of a *transition*: an expression $\langle e: \phi_1, ..., \phi_n \rangle$. This means intuitively "erase $\phi_1, ..., \phi_n$ in passing from *s* to $R(e,s)$". The frame rule is:

$$\chi, \phi[\![s]\!], \langle e: \phi_1, ..., \phi_n \rangle \vdash \phi[\![R(e, s)]\!] \tag{5}$$

where (i) ϕ is an atom; (ii) ϕ contains no variables (other than *s*); (iii) χ, *therase* $\phi_1, ...,$ *therase* $\phi_n \nvdash$ *therase* $\phi[\![s]\!]$. Notice the negated inference in (iii).

The problem-solving system STRIPS (Fikes and Nilsson, 1971) uses the full predicate calculus enriched with special notations ("operator descriptions") describing events, and ways of declaring certain predicates to be *primitive*. We can use transitions to describe this also. The frame rule is:

$$\phi[\![s]\!], \langle e: \phi_1, ..., \phi_n \rangle \vdash \phi[\![R(e, s)]\!] \tag{6}$$

where (i) ϕ is an atom or the negation of an atom; (ii) ϕ contains no variables (other than s); (iii) the predicate symbol in ϕ is *primitive*; (iv) $\phi[\![s]\!]$ is not an instance of any ϕ_i, $1 \leqslant i \leqslant n$. Notice the similarity to (5). *Primitive* can be axiomatised by the use of a monadic second-order predicate, as in (1) above.

These four rules have widely divergent logical properties. Rule (3) is replaceable by an axiom scheme, and is thus rather elementary. It is also very easy to implement efficiently (theorem-proving cognoscenti may be worried by the higher-order expressions, but these are harmless since they contain no variables). Variations are possible, e.g., we might have disjointness axioms for the P_i and require $\neg P_j(h_k)$ rather than $P_{i_k}(h_k)$: this would be closely similar to a special case of (4).

Retaining consistency in the presence of (3) requires in non-trivial problems that the P_i classification be rather coarse. (For instance, *no* change in position *ever* affects the colour of things, so predicates of location *could* be classed apart from predicates of colour.) Thus frames, although useful, do not completely solve the problem.

Rule (4) is also replaceable by an axiom scheme, and the restriction to literals can be eliminated, with some resultant complication in the rule. Also, there is a corresponding model theory and a completeness result (Hayes, 1971), so that one can gain an intuition as to what (4) *means*. Retaining consistency with (4) requires some care in making logical definitions.

Rules (5) and (6) have a different character. Notice that (6) is almost a special case of (5): that in which *therase* $\phi \vdash$ *therase* ψ if ψ is not primitive or ψ is an instance of ϕ. The importance of this is that instantiation, and probably primitiveness also, are *decideable,* and conditions (iii) and (iv) in (6) are effectively determined solely by examining the transition, whereas condition (iii) in (5) is in general not decidable and in any case requires an examination of all of χ: in applications, the whole set of beliefs. MICRO-PLANNER uses its ability to control the theorem-proving process to partly compensate for both of these problems, but with a more expressive language they would become harder to handle. Notice also that (5) does not satisfy the extension property, while (6) does, provided we allow at most one transition to be unconditionally asserted for each event.

Maintaining "consistency" with (5) is a matter of the axiom-writer's art. There seem to be no general guidelines. Maintaining consistency with (6) seems to be largely a matter of judicious choice of *primitive* vocabulary. There is no articulated model theory underlying (5) or (6). They are regarded more as syntactic tools — analogous to evaluation rules for a high-level programming language — than as descriptive assertions.

A (Very) Simple Example: Toy Bricks

$$\neg above\,(x, x, s) \tag{A1}$$
$$x = Table \lor above\,(x, Table, s) \tag{A2}$$
$$above\,(x, y, s) \equiv.\, on(x, y, s) \lor \exists z.on(z, y, s)\,\&\,above(x, z, s) \tag{A3}$$
$$free(x, s) \equiv. \forall y\,\neg on\,(y, x, s) \tag{A4}$$

To enable activity to occur we will have events $move(x,y)$: the brick x is put on top of the brick y. Laws of motion we might consider include:

$$free(x, s)\,\&\,x \neq y.\, \supset on\,(x, y, R(move(x, y), s)) \tag{A5}$$
$$free(x, s)\,\&\,w \neq x\,\&\,on(w, z, s).\, \supset on(w, z, R(move(x, y), s)) \tag{A6}$$
$$free(x, s)\,\&\,w \neq x\,\&\,above(w, z, s).\, \supset above(w, z, R(move(x, y), s)) \tag{A7}$$
$$free(x, s)\,\&\,w \neq y\,\&\,free(w, s).\, \supset free(w, R(move(x, y), s)) \tag{A8}$$

Of these, (A6–A8) are frame axioms. (In fact, (A7) and (A8) are redundant, since they can, with some difficulty, be derived from (A6) and (A3), (A4) respectively.) (A5) assumes somewhat idealistically that there is always enough space on y to put a new brick.

Rule (3) cannot be used in any intuitively satisfactory way to replace A6–A8.

Rule (4) can be used. We need only to specify when bricks are connected to events:

$$\rightarrow (x, move(y, z), s) \equiv . \; x = y \lor above(x, y, s) \tag{A9}$$

Using (A9) and (A3), (A4), it is not hard to show that

$$free(x, s) \;\&\; w \neq x \;\&\; on(w, z, s). \supset . \neg \rightarrow (w, move(x, y), s) \;\&\;$$

$$\neg \rightarrow (z, move(x, y), s)$$

and thus, we can infer $on \{w, z, R[move(x, y), s]\}$ by rule (7). (A7) and (A8) are similar but simpler. (One should remark also that (A4) is an example of an illegal definition, in the presence of (4), since it suppresses a variable which the rule needs to be aware of. It is easy to fix this up in various ways.)

Rule (5) can also be used, but we must ensure that *therase* does a sufficiently thorough job. Various approaches are possible. The following seems to be most in the spirit of MICRO-PLANNER. In its terms, *on* and *above* statements will be in the data-base, but *free* statements will not. The necessary axioms will be:

$$therase \; free(x, s) \tag{A10}$$
$$therase \; on(x, y, s) \;\&\; above(y, z, s) \supset therase \; above \, (x, z, s) \tag{A11}$$
$$free(x, s) \supset \langle move(x, y): on(x, z, s) \rangle \tag{A12}$$

To infer statements $free[x, R(e, s)]$, we must first generate enough $on[x, y, R(e, s)]$ statements by rule (5), and then use (A4), since by (A10), rule (5) never makes such an inference directly. (We could omit (A10) and replace (A12) by

$$free(x, s) \supset \langle move(x, y): on(x, z, s), free(y, s) \rangle . \tag{A13}$$

This would, in MICRO-PLANNER terms, be a decision to keep *free* assertions in the data base.)

Notice that MICRO-PLANNER has no negation and hence no need to *therase* such assertions as $\neg on(x, y, s)$. If it had negation we would replace (A12) by

$$free(x, s) \supset \langle move(x, y): on(x, z, s), \neg on(x, y, s) \rangle \tag{A14}$$

and add

$$therase \; \neg on(x, y, s) \;\&\; above(y, z, s) \supset therase \; \neg above(x, z, s) \tag{A15}$$

53

Notice the close relations between (A3), (A11) and (A15).

Rule (6) can be used similarly to (5), but we are no longer able to use axioms such as (A11) and (A15). The solution which seems closest in spirit to STRIPS is to declare that *on* is primitive but that *above* and *free* are not, and then simply use (A14). The "world model" (Fikes and Nilsson, 1971) would then consist of a collection of atoms *on* (a,b), or their negations, and the system would rederive *above* and *free* assertions when needed. This is very similar to MICRO-PLANNER's "data-base", and we could have used rule (5) in an exactly similar fashion.

Implementing Frame Rules

Some ingenuity with list structures enables one to store assertions in such a way that

(i) Given s, one can easily find all assertions $\phi[\![s]\!]$.

(ii) Each symbol denoting a situation is stored only once.

(iii) The relationships between s and $R(e,s)$, etc., are stored efficiently and are easily retrieved.

(iv) To apply a frame rule to s, one need only:

(a) Create a new cell pointing to s.

(b) Move two pointers.

(c) Check each $\phi[\![s]\!]$ for condition $\aleph$: if it holds, move one pointer.

In the case of a rule like (5) or the variation to (4), where $\aleph$ is a *negative* condition ($\nvdash$), we need only examine those $\phi[\![s]\!]$ for which the condition *fails*, resulting in greater savings.

Space does not permit a description of the method, but MICRO-PLANNER and STRIPS use related ideas. (The authors of these systems seem to confuse to some extent their particular implementations with the logical description of the frame rules, even to the extent of claiming that a logical description is impossible.)

Consistency and Counterfactuals

Frame rules can be efficiently implemented and, in their various ways, allow the replacement of frame axioms by more systematic machinery. But there is a constant danger, in constructing larger axiomatisations, of introducing inconsistency. An alternative approach avoids this by transferring properties ϕ from s to $R(e,s)$ *as long as it is consistent to do so*, rather than according to some fixed-in-advance rule.

Suppose we have a set χ of general laws which arc to hold in every situation, and a description of — a set of assertions about — the situation s: $\{\phi_1[\![s]\!],...,\phi_n[\![s]\!]\}$. Using laws of motion we will directly infer certain properties $\psi_1,..., \psi_m$ of $R(e,s)$: the set of these constitutes a partial description of $R(e,s)$. To compute a more adequate one, we add assertions $\phi_i[\![R(e,s)]\!]$ in some order, *checking at each stage for consistency with χ*; if a $\phi_i[\![R(e,s)]\!]$ makes the set inconsistent, it is rejected. This continues until no more ϕ_i can be added. In this way we compute a maximal consistent subset (MCS) of the inconsistent set

$$\chi \cup \{\psi_1, ..., \psi_m, \phi_1[\![R(e, s)]\!], ..., \phi_n[\![R(e, s)]\!]\} \; .$$

There are two big problems: (1) Consistency is not a decidable or even semi—decidable property. Thus for practicality one has to accept a large restriction on the expressive power of the language. (2) There are in general many different MCSs of an inconsistent set, and so we must have ways of choosing an appropriate one. In terms of the procedure outlined above, we need a good ordering on the ϕ_i.

This procedure is closely similar to one described by Rescher (1964) to provide an analysis of counterfactual reasonings ("If I had struck this match yesterday, it would have lit", when in fact I didn't.). Rescher is aware of the first problem but gives no solution. His major contribution is to the second problem, which he solves by the use of *modal categories*: a hierarchical classification of assertions into grades of law-likeness. One never adds $\phi_i[\![R(e,s)]\!]$ unless every ϕ_j with a lower classification has already been tested. This machinery is especially interesting as in (Simon and Rescher, 1966) it is linked to Simon's theory of causality (Simon, 1953). One puts ϕ_i in a lower category than ϕ_j just in case ϕ_i *causes* ϕ_j (or $\neg\phi_j$), more or less. Space does not permit a complete description of this interesting material which is fully covered in the references cited. In spite of its appeal, the first problem is still unsolved.

In unpublished work at Stanford, Jack Buchanan has independently worked out another version of the procedure. The first problem is handled by accepting a drastic restriction on the language. Every ϕ_i is an atom or the negation of an atom — c.f. frame rules (7), (8) and (9) —

and, more seriously, χ contains only assertions of the form $t_1 \neq t_2$ or of the form $P(t_1,...,t,...,t_n)$ and $P(t_1,...,u,...,t_n) \supset t = u$. Under these constraints, consistency is decidable and can even be computed quite efficiently. Moreover, MCSs are unique, so the second problem evaporates. However, it is not clear whether non-trivial problems can be reasonably stated in such a restricted vocabulary.

Conclusions

In the long run, I believe that a mixture of frame rules and consistency-based methods will be required for non-trivial problems, corresponding respectively to the "strategic" and "tactical" aspects of computing descriptions of new situations. In the short term we need to know more about the properties of both procedures.

One outstanding defect of present approaches is the lack of a clear model theory. Formal systems for handling the frame problem are beginning to proliferate, but a clear *semantic* theory is far from sight. Even to begin such a project would seem to require deep insight into our presystematic intuitions about the physical world.

Observations and the Qualification Problem

We have so far been entirely concerned with thinking. The situation calculus is a belief calculus for beliefs *about* time. Observations — interactions with the real world — introduce new problems. We must now consider the second aspect of time (b,p.   ).

Almost any general belief about the result of his own actions may be contradicted by the robot's observations. He may conclude that he can drive to the airport; only to find a flat tire. A human immediately says, "Ah, now I cannot go". Simply *adding* a new belief ("the tire is flat") renders an earlier conclusion false, though it was a valid conclusion from the earlier set of beliefs, *all of which are still present.* Thus we do *not* assume that the robot had concluded "*If* my tires are OK, *then* I can get to the airport" since there are no end of different things which might go wrong, and he cannot be expected to hedge his conclusions round with thousands of qualifications (McCarthy and Hayes, 1969).

Clearly this implies that the belief logic does not obey the extension property *for observations*: to expect otherwise would be to hope for omnipotence. However, we are little nearer any positive ideas for handling the inferences correctly.

John McCarthy recently pointed out to me that MICRO-PLANNER has a facility (called THNOT) which apparently solves the problem nicely. I will translate this into a slightly different notation.

We introduce a new unary propositional connective *proved*, which is supposed to mean "can be proved from the current collection of beliefs". Then we can write axioms like the following:

flat (*tire*) $\supset$ *kaput* (*car*)

$\neg$*proved kaput* (*car*) $\supset$ *at* {*robot, airport, R*[*drive*(*airport*), *s*]} (A17)

from which *at*(*robot, airport*, ...) should be concluded *until* we add:

flat (*tire*) (A18)

at which point the $\neg$*proved*... becomes false. ($\neg$*proved* is PLANNER's THNOT).

To make this work we could try the following rules of inference.

$\phi \vdash proved\ \phi$ (P1)

$\chi \vdash \neg proved\ \phi$ (P2)

where $\chi \nvdash \phi$.

(P2) fails the extension property, as expected. (It also has the difficulties of effectiveness which worry frame rule (5), but we will ignore these.)

Unfortunately, (P1) and (P2) are *inconsistent.* Suppose $\chi \nvdash \phi$, but that ϕ is consistent with χ. Then by (P2), $\neg proved\ \phi$. But if we now add ϕ (an observation: the flat tire), then by (P1) *proved* ϕ: an overt contradiction. MICRO-PLANNER avoids this by denying (P1) and treating "ϕ and $\neg proved\ \phi$" as consistent. But this is a counsel of despair, since it clearly is not, according to the intuitive meanings.

The logical answer is to somehow make *proved* refer to the set χ of antecedents. The direct approach to this requires extremely cumbersome notation and a very strong logic which partly contains its own metatheory, thus coming close to Gödel inconsistency. Fortunately we do not need to *describe* sets χ of assertions, but only to *refer* to them, and this can be done with a very weak notation, similar to situation variables.

Assume that every belief is decorated with a constant symbol called the *index*: we will write it as a superscript. Indices denote the robot's internal belief states just as situation terms denote external situations. Observations are analogous to events. Assertions *proved* ϕ now have an extra index which identifies the state of belief at the time the inference was tested. The above rules of inference become:

$$\phi^s \vdash proved^s \phi^s \qquad\qquad\qquad\qquad (P1')$$

$$\chi \vdash \neg proved^s \phi^s \qquad\qquad\qquad\qquad (P2')$$

where $\chi \nvdash \phi^s$ *and every member of* χ *has index s.*

In applications we now insist that:

(i) in applying P2', χ contains *all* beliefs with index s;

(ii) whenever an *observation* is added to the beliefs, every index s is replaced by a new one s', *except* those on *proved* assertions.

This is just enough to avoid inconsistency; it clearly does not involve any Gödel-ish difficulties; and (ii) can be very efficiently implemented by frame-rule methods (see section Implementing Frame Rules). Indeed, more complex versions of (ii) which allow for direct contradiction between beliefs and observations can be similarly implemented.

The logic of these indices is trivial, but extensions have some interest. For instance, if we identify indices with situation terms, then expressions of the form $\phi[\![s]\!]^s$ become legal, with the intuitive meaning "ϕ is true *now*".

Seen this way, the qualification problem is closely linked with the frame problem, and one expects progress in either area to help with the other.

Acknowledgements

This work was supported in part by the Advanced Research Projects Agency of the Office of the Secretary of Defense (SD−183), and in part by the Science Research Council.

I am also grateful for comment, criticism and contributions from Jack Buchanan, Richard Fikes, Malcolm Newey, Nils Nilsson, John

Rulifson, Richard Waldinger, Richard Weyrauch and from John McCarthy, to whom I am also grateful for the invitation to visit the Stanford Artificial Intelligence Project, where this paper was written. Most of all, I thank my wife, Jackie, for improving my English; controlling my verbosity, and typing innumerable drafts of the manuscript.

N.E. WETHERICK*

The Computer Simulation
of Inductive Thinking

Summary

Computer simulation of the behaviour of an organism requires a model of internal operations which issue in observable behaviour resembling behaviour that has actually been observed in or outside the laboratory. An inductive model is proposed on *a priori* grounds in which rules are derived from instances and used to predict the presence of goal attributes of importance to the organism by the presence of other attributes more easily observable. Variability between organisms is attributed to differences (between individuals and between species) in the number of attributes that can be manipulated simultaneously, in the range of possible goal attributes and in the efficiency of memory.

In order to simulate the behaviour of an organism it is necessary to hypothesise an internal structure for the organism which could have the effect of generating given observable responses in given environmental situations. The structure hypothesised should enable the organism to learn as it has been observed to learn and make the kinds of mistake it is observed to make. It should be capable of taking on either relatively simple forms for the simulation of organisms low on the phylogenetic scale or relatively complex forms for the simulation of human organisms without the need to introduce qualitative differences at any level. (This last requirement follows from acceptance of a physical monist

* University of Bradford (Present address, University of Aberdeen)

solution to the Mind/Body problem and from the fact that the neural substance that makes behaviour possible is similar in appearance in organisms at all phylogenetic levels.) It is also a requirement that the structure should be consistent with what we know of neurophysiology although at the present time this is not to say very much since, despite advances in our knowledge of microscopic and sub-microscopic phenomena (derived from studies of the single nerve cell) and of macroscopic phenomena (derived from neurosurgery and ablation studies), little progress has been made in the intervening region which is of most interest to the psychological theorist. What is required is what I have called elsewhere (Wetherick, 1970a) an "internal event of lesser complexity" than the overt response (in the same sense that the atom is an "event of lesser complexity" than the molecule) which would in its turn be capable of explanation in terms of neurophysiological events. Harré (1971) hints at a similar requirement which he calls the "second tier" which is "likely to be a system feature of the mode of organisation of the nervous system". Twenty or thirty years ago the S—R bond was seen in this role but for a number of reasons this cannot now be maintained. The deliberate neglect of theory which psychologists have until recently tried to parade as a virtue has meant that the position remained unfilled but although it may be true that psychology can get along without "second tier" concepts, there is no doubt that computer simulation studies cannot.

For 2,500 years philosophers have maintained that we owe to induction our knowledge of contingent truths about the real world. I propose that, for the purposes of theory development, the inductive judgment be accorded status as the required "internal event of lesser complexity". I shall employ an idiosyncratic definition of the term "inductive judgment" as a 3-term proposition of the form "All A's that are B are C". A proposition may be explicit (i.e., verbal) or implicit. A human subject taking part in an investigation of concept attainment might formulate the explicit proposition "All cards (A) that are white (B) are positive (C)". A rat taking part in a similar experiment (it would be called discrimination learning) formulates the implicit proposition "All doors (A) that are white (B) have a food pellet behind them (C)". A here stands for one or more attributes that define the context of the proposition — it is about "cards" or "doors". C stands for a goal attribute of importance to the organism which may however

61

be difficult or dangerous (or, in an experimental situation, impossible) to observe directly. B stands for a set of one or more attributes that has been found to predict C in A's. In the proposed theory the inductive process takes something like the following form: The organism becomes aware that a distinction may be made between A's that are C and A's that are not-C. C however is difficult or dangerous to observe directly. Predictors of C are clearly required. A's will exemplify a number of attributes in addition to the set that defines them as instances of A, and C or not-C. It may be that some of these attributes singly or jointly predict C, either because they are the cause of C, or because they are the joint effect with C of a more remote cause, or perhaps merely because they are contingently associated with C in the instances of A which the organism happens to encounter. If this is the case these attributes will serve as B attributes in the proposition.

Implicit in the view that this inductive process is the fundamental mode of knowledge acquisition is a view of the nature of organisms which is necessarily speculative. Nothing in it is, however, either wholly lacking in experimental support or in direct conflict with any widely accepted body of experimental evidence. The organism postulated is conceived to sample the evidence available from its environment at discrete, regularly spaced time intervals. Its sensory capacities only permit the sample to be of a given maximum size which will certainly vary both between organisms at different phylogenetic levels and between different individual organisms at a given level. Kristofferson (1965) provides evidence in support of periodic sampling and proposes 50 milliseconds as the time interval. Others have suggested different time intervals, but there is a measure of agreement that organisms may function in this way and it is reasonable to conjecture that both the organism's body and the information held in its long-term memory store may for this purpose be considered as part of the environment; though all the experimental work has had, for obvious reasons, to concern itself with that part of the environment that is external to the organism. Precisely what kind of information is directly sampled is another matter of conjecture, but Hubel and Wiesel (1962) and others working at the level of the individual visual receptor have shown that the majority of these are concerned with contour, change of direction of contour and direction of movement of contour, indicating that the visual system is, at the first level of analysis, concerned mainly to distinguish object from background. Let us call these successive data samples "Observations". Any organism will be capable of sampling a wider range of data than can actually be sampled in any given observation. What data are sampled will be determined by chance, or by the salience of a particular datum for a particular organism, or by the internal state of the organism. The observation "That is a postbox" requires the application of an inductively derived general proposition "All A's (physical objects) that are B (red, cylindrical, etc.) are C (called "postboxes") which requires the application of further general propositions justifying "That is a physical object", "That is red", "That is cylindrical", etc., each of which depend in their turn on implicit primitive general propositions derived from sensory experience. There is evidence that some low-level propositions may be innate in some organisms (i.e. Fantz (1957) has shown that chicks have, at hatching, an innate preference for pecking at round, seed-like objects) but, if not innate, these propositions are at least derived during the very early life of the organism and are fundamental to subsequent learning.

New learning requires the derivation from experience of a new general proposition enabling the organism to predict C (a name, a desirable goal) from observations of B and thus make life easier for himself. The organism must however have goals. Fantz's chicks demonstrated their preference for seed-like objects by pecking at them ten times more frequently than at angular objects, and indeed most organisms seem to have an innate tendency to approach some states of the real world and avoid others. Thus the organism may have an innate tendency to approach food on which may be superimposed a tendency to approach "black" rather than "white" if black has been associated as a predictor with food in the organism's experience, and so *mutatis mutandis* with an innate tendency to avoid shock. As a result of experience one may learn either to approach (or avoid) some state of the real world which was not previously approached (or avoided) or to cease approaching (or avoiding) some state that was previously approached (or avoided). In learning to do something one would not otherwise have done, an outcome is predicted and the prediction verified. In learning not to do something one would otherwise have done, an outcome is predicted but the prediction is falsified. Consider four animal learning situations: In the first two, the animal is in a box in which there is a shelf above floor level and in which the floor may be electrified, the naive animal prefers the floor to the shelf and will normally jump down if put on the shelf.

(1) The floor is electrified and the animal learns to jump onto the shelf (i.e., to do something it would not otherwise have done).

(2) The animal is put on the shelf and when it jumps down, gets a shock from the floor. It learns to stay on the shelf (i.e., not to do something it would otherwise have done).

(3) The animal learns to press a bar by obtaining a food reward for so doing (i.e., to do something it would not otherwise have done).

(4) Having learned 3, the animal now learns to stop pressing the bar because food is no longer forthcoming (i.e., not to do something it would otherwise have done).

Call what happens in 1 and 3 above Type I learning and what happens in 2 and 4, Type II learning. There is experimental evidence (e.g., Gray, 1970) that organisms possess both a reticular and a limbic arousal system. Blocking limbic activity abolishes Type II learning but not Type I learning. Driving limbic activity facilitates Type II learning without affecting Type I. Reticular activity is clearly more fundamental (and perhaps phylogenetically more primitive) since blocking it results in coma or death. Driving reticular activity however facilitates Type I learning.

Type I learning occurs, as we have seen, when a prediction is verified. The animal sees "white", predicts "food", approaches white and finds food. This type of learning is fully compatible with S—R behaviour theory though no S—R theorist would be likely to characterise the process in these terms. In Type II learning however the animal sees "black", predicts "food", approaches black and finds no food. The animal learns to avoid "black" but how can food which is not there affect the animal's behaviour in any way? The obvious answer would appear to be that the animal has some kind of mental representation of what it hopes to find and thus knows when it has failed to find it. But this possibility is incompatible with basic behaviourist assumptions. The alternative for the behaviourist is either to treat "black" as an aversive stimulus because it is not associated with food (which is unconvincing because almost everything in the animal's environment will then be "aversive" on the same grounds) or to adopt a Pavlovian-type construct system. Pavlov's own system has achieved a pervasive influence at the theoretical level, but I am not convinced that there is satisfactory evidence for reactive or conditioned inhibition in Pavlov's sense. In favour of the obvious answer there is the fact that it seems more likely to make possible the development of a satisfactory account of animal and human behaviour outside the laboratory, which is something no behaviourist has yet succeeded in doing.

Any real life learning situation will involve a discrimination between A's which are predictably C and A's which are not-C. At the outset the organism will have some tendency to approach (or avoid) both and, in learning to approach (or avoid) one only, both Type I and Type II learning may be required. On certain assumptions, learning might be accounted for by using Type I methods only but these assumptions are not likely to be satisfied except in the laboratory. For example, presentation of a series of positive instances (A's which are C), where no discrimination is required, might result in the selection of B-attributes since they were present on every trial whereas others were sometimes present, sometimes absent. In a task requiring discrimination it would however, be necessary to suppose that the relationship between number and incidence of positive and negative trials and between the size of learning increment resulting from a positive trial and the rate of decrement resulting from passage of time was precisely such as to result in selection of B attributes from the irrelevant, randomly varying attributes also sampled. I suspect that choice of any particular values for size of increment and rate of decrement would restrict the possibility of learning much more closely to particular sequences of positive and negative trials than appears to be the case in real life.

The computer model was programmed by my colleague Dr. K.D.C. Stoodley: only a segment of the structure hypothesised actually figures in the program but there are no major difficulties in the way of an attempt to stimulate the whole. The program first generates a real world in which there is one C-attribute and up to fifteen potential B-attributes, each attribute being two-valued (either present or absent). For each problem a series of states is generated such that in each state, if C is present, a set "B" of one, two or three other attributes is also present and, if C is absent, at least one member of set "B" is also absent, other attributes being present or absent at random. A real organism might be capable of detecting the presence or absence of more than fifteen attributes but, in a given problem situation, fifteen may not be too far from the number actually employed. (The computer model in its present state may be thought of as a model of an organism set to solve a particular problem.) Similarly, a real organism will be likely to seek at least three different types of goal but in a given problem situation only one type will be operative.

The simulated organism is set to have as many memory stores as there are attributes of the simulated real world. In successive observations, these stores are incremented or decremented as a result of "experience" and the resulting store values determine which attributes will be sampled in subsequent observations. In each observation between two and five attributes may be sampled (clearly, in the program as it is, the need for A attributes does not arise since problem situations can only be simulated one at a time) and between each observation store values are decremented to simulate short-term loss (but stores do not take negative values). Learning is said to have occurred when a store reaches an arbitrary pre-set value (usually 3.00).

Currently we are simulating organisms at three levels of complexity. At Level 1 an increment of 1.00 is added to the memory store corresponding to any attribute observed to be present if the C attribute is also present on that trial (the Level 1 organism is capable of Type I learning only, lacking the capacity to "envisage" the goal which would enable it to learn from negative trials). At Level 2 memory stores are additionally decremented by 1.00 when the corresponding attribute is observed present and the C attribute is absent (the Level 2 organism has the capacity to envisage the goal and is consequently capable of both Type I and Type II learning). At Level 3 additional "hypothesis" stores are opened for every set of one, two or three attributes observed present when the C attribute is present. These hypothesis stores are not subject to the short-term decrement and are incremented if the set is subsequently present when the C attribute is present and deleted if the set is present when the C attribute is absent (the Level 3 organism can envisage other sets of attributes as well as the goal attribute).

Fig. 1 presents the results of setting the same series of twelve problems to simulated organisms at the three levels just considered, with perceptual capacities (PC) of two, three or four attributes per observation and short-term memory decrements (MD) of 0.45, 0.30 or 0.10 per trial. (Since at best the organism can gain an increment of 1.00 on every C trial and C and not-C are equiprobable, the maximum mean increment per trial is 0.50. A decrement of 0.45 per trial therefore

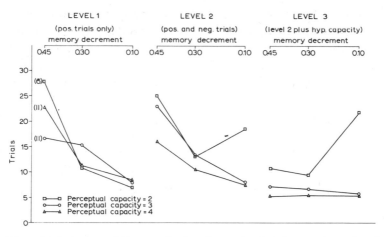

Fig. 1. Mean trials to an arbitrary criterion for a simulated organism; showing the effects on performance of level of complexity (1, 2, 3), perceptual capacity (2, 3, 4) and memory decrement (0.45, 0.30, 0.10). The same series of 12 problems was attempted under each combination of conditions. Points represent the mean of 12 values except where marked. (In the case of Level 1, MD = 0.45, the organism failed to solve some problems.)

corresponds to a relatively poor memory and 0.10 to a relatively good one.) Each problem was terminated when the value in the store corresponding to the B attribute reached 3.00, or after 100 trials. The results for Level 1 indicate that PC does not make a great deal of difference but MD does; in fact this difference is underestimated by the mean values shown since, with PC = 2 and MD = 0.45, only half the problems were solved in 100 trials. The results for Level 2 look much the same as for Level 1 but the graph does not reveal a difference which would be of major significance in a simulation of the total organism. In a Level 1 organism, stores corresponding to attributes other than the B attribute tend to contain significant values, whereas in a Level 2 organism only the B attribute store is likely to do so, since the rest will have received decrements as well as increments. For a Level 1 organism several attributes may therefore be equally likely to be predictors whereas for a Level 2 organism there will be only one contender. The results for Level 3 are uniformly good, as might be expected since the hypothesis capacity may be equatable with the capacity to develop language (see Wetherick, 1970b). The relatively poor performance of Level 2 and Level

67

3 organisms with *PC* = 2 and *MD* = 0.10 depends upon the fact that when an organism with poor perceptual capacity and a retentive memory latches on to a wrong attribute it takes some time to realise its mistake!

There is space to consider briefly two further developments of the theory and the associated computer model. The first of these was an attempt to simulate some of the findings of Bitterman (1965) on the comparative behaviour of different animal species. As a first approximation, Bitterman's results may be said to show that, in a discrimination-learning task, fish (mouth-breeders) match probabilities whereas rats maximise rewards and that, given successive reversals, rats improve their rate of learning whereas fish do not.

The former result appears when the animal has to choose between "black" and "white", where "black" is rewarded 70 percent of the time and "white" 30 percent of the time. The fish, over a period of time, learns to distribute his responses at random but in the proportion 70/30, whereas the rat learns to choose "black" on every trial. This looks very much like the difference between a Level 1 and a Level 2 organism. If we assume that on any given trial the likelihood that an attribute will be employed as a predictor is directly proportional to its associated store value (which seems to be the assumption of minimum complexity), then a Level 1 organism will, after a time, match probabilities, but a Level 2 organism will have a store value only in the store associated with "black", since only in that store will there have been a surplus of increments over decrements. This difference between species only appears where a correction procedure is employed (the animal has another go at the correct stimulus if he chooses wrong first time). If a non-correction procedure is employed both rat and fish maximise but this too is consistent with our model, since it can easily be shown that a Level 2 organism will have a store value for "black" only whether a correction or a non-correction procedure is employed, whereas a Level 1 organism will have values in the ratio 70/30 under a correction procedure but values approaching 100/0 under a non-correction procedure. (If the organism begins by choosing "black" and "white" with equal probability this will generate store values in the ratio 70/30, but if these values determine the response in accordance with our assumption this will generate values in the ratio $70^2/30^2$ and so on ....) Unfortunately, some of Bitterman's other results do not fit so neatly. His second major finding requires a new development of the theory. It is possible to get an organism at Level 1 or Level 2 to improve its rate of learning under successive reversals by incorporating a "leakage" factor. In computer terms this means that "black" and "white" are regarded as linked so that an increment to one store generates a smaller increment to the other. In neuro-physiological terms this could be taken to imply the existence of a connecting circuit constituting the precursor of the neural correlate of "brightness" in higher organisms. This improvement in rate of learning can be brought about in animals (if at all) only by prolonged training but a similar phenomenon may be observed in the normal course of human development between the ages of 6 and 8 (see Kendler and Kendler, 1962).

The second development is in the field of human personality, and space does not permit more than an indication of the extent to which the model proposed provides an account of learning in general into which an account of personality in Kellian terms may very easily be fitted (Kelly, 1955). Only the level of complexity of the attributes employed needs to be changed.

In terms of the theory advanced here, neurosis has its origins in the fact that learning may modify either approach or avoidance behaviour. If we predict that some state of the world is to be approached, we approach, and if our prediction was wrong we find out. If however we predict that a state of the world is to be avoided, we avoid, and may never find out whether our prediction was right or wrong. Even the mother/child relationship in infancy may be seen as the locus of the child's decision that people are in general predictable or unpredictable. If the child concludes for predictability he will interact with confidence with people, believing that he can in principle learn to anticipate their demands on him. If not, for his own protection he can only either withdraw or try to impose his will on the environment by aggressive self-assertion.

RANAN B. BANERJI*

Simplicity of Concepts, Training and the Real World

Summary

It has been pointed out that concepts which are useful in the description of many real phenomena tend to be considered simple by virtue of repeated use. The simplicity of description of a phenomenon has a strong influence on the amount of data needed for establishing confidence in the description. A statistical hypothesis is suggested for the explication of confidence in useful simplifying concepts.

Some Initial Disclaimers

One of the hardest things to do in interdisciplinary proceedings like the present one is to come to a communality of background. One is afraid to write about things well known in one's own area in detail, for fear of seeming naive. If one gets over this kind of egocentricity, one falls into the trap of making a mountain discussing something in one's area of secondary competence, boring the reader about a molehill.

Another problem lies in the line of citations. In an interdisciplinary proceeding, bibliographies can become rather voluminous. This is not too bad for the reader who can do his own filtering, but for the author it becomes a back-breaking job putting it together, with very little added to the content of what he has to say.

Faced with these dilemmas, I have decided to do the following. I

* Case Western Reserve University

shall present what I want to say as informally as I can, hoping that the reader assumes a modicum of intellectual honesty on my part, and I assume that my readers are reasonably well-read laymen. I shall not assume any great specialized knowledge on anybody's part, including mine. If there is any need to introduce some specialized ideas, they will be introduced *ab initio*. References to general ideas in any field will not be cited.

This sort of "fire-side chat", I believe, will still retain enough scientific and technical content. Those who would like to pursue further any of the material discussed here can pick up references from friends and colleagues in the corresponding field of specialization. Background material for the specific references can also be obtained this way. The rest of this paper is written in the belief that a paper written this way will be acceptable.

A Paradox on Simplicity and Insights from One Possible Resolution

There was a paradox going around among inductive logicians and philosophers of science a few years ago (Goodman, 1955). It went somewhat as follows.

"We shall define a thing to be "Grue" if it is green till the end of 1960 and turns blue after that. We call it "Bleen" if it is blue till the end of 1960 and turns green after that. It appears that these are very complex definitions. But it is really Green which has a complex meaning. What we call Green is really something that is grue till the end of 1960 and turns bleen afterwards."

The paradox is quoted to show that there is no essential measure of simplicity. The puzzlement arises only because we assume that there ought to be an absolute measure of simplicity. Perhaps there is (I shall discuss this later), but the complexity of the concepts Green and Grue are so great compared to the basic ones, that comparing them with one another is like comparing 10^{30} and $10^{30}+1$: something much more important than mere complexity takes over here.

In the above paragraph I have promised to comment on basic simplicities, on the relation between green and grue and a consideration more important than simplicity. Let me comment on what might possibly be the most simple concept when the area of discourse is limited to visual images. A basic concept — the simplest, perhaps, because of the hardware of the eye — would be the set of all images which excite a specific retinal cell. This concept, then, would be expressed by an English sentence like, "The cone at (x,y) is excited". The set of all images which makes this sentence true would be a simplest recognizable concept. There would be one such concept (or set of images) for each point (x,y) of the retina where there is a cone or a rod. Any image class is then some sort of a set theoretical combination of statements of this form.

Even the brain is not capable of using concepts of this simplicity when dealing with the real world. Experiments on the frog's retina (Lettvin *et al.*, 1959) indicate that within a few cellular layers of the retina the firing of a neuron does not stand for "this cone has received light" anymore. It stands for things like "there is a curved object projected on the retina" or "a shadow of some sort is moving across the retina". To a frog, then, "curved object" or "moving object" are basic simple concepts.

Compared to this, Green is a rather complex concept. It does appear to us that Grue is more complex, and that is why our paradox is a paradox. However, a point is that when we say, "Grue is Green before 1960 and Blue afterwards" we are *assuming* that Green is a simple concept. Alternatively, we could *assume* that Grue is a simple concept and make the paradoxical statement. If simplicity of concepts has to be understood in physiological terms as I have done above, then neither of the assumptions are true.

What then, makes us feel that Green is simpler than Grue? Perhaps I should recall a story. One evening a fellow engineer and I were strolling in the park and in the course of some discussion I said, "For instance, the Complement of the Transitive Closure of the Complement of a Transitive Relation is Transitive". At this time, a nice young gentleman passed, with his arm around the waist of an even nicer young lady. They heard us, and we heard the young gentleman say in an exasperated, very audible whisper, "Oh, my gosh!"

One can ask why it was so simple for my friend and me to concatenate the very sophisticated set theoretical concepts so fast while the very use of such technical terms was so repulsive to these young people. The answer, I believe, is obvious. There is something in the human mind which, given constant exposure to a concept, however complicated, makes it simple. Or, as they say in Yogic circles: "The metal of the mind, on constant polishing, becomes the mirror of divine intuition and reflects the light of truth."

If we take this to be true, then Green is simpler than Grue because there are more green things around than there are grue things. This is where the real world has to get into our theory. In the next section we try to discuss this in greater detail.

Simplicity and the Real World

Let us assume as the initial view in this section that a few statements are given to the mind as predefined, i.e., they are easy for the mind to store and also easy, given a sensation, to know which of these sentences are true for that sensation. For our present purposes, it does not matter whether these simple sentences are like "There is light on cone (x,y)" or "I am sucking my thumb". We shall only assume that, whatever they are, they are not so complicated that any simple logical combinations of them (with "and", "or", "not", "there exists one such that" and similar connectives and modifiers) would yield adequate descriptions of considerations like, "Since Mr. Jones did not seem to like my last report, this is not a good time to ask for a raise".

Let us also assume that there is a measure of simplicity associated with all sentences built up from the basic simple sentences. We want this measure to satisfy two criteria, the second of which I shall unfold as the time comes. Meanwhile, I shall assume that the complexity of a sentence is measured by the minimum number of "or"s we would have to use if we want to express its meaning with the basic simple sentences.

To give intuitive justification to what I am doing here, I will have to go a little deeper into technicalities. Suppose there is a sentence "A" which can be expressed as "B or C or D". I shall assume that the storing mechanism of our mind is not trained yet to store A as a simple concept. It is forced to store it as the three sentence B,C,D and some indicator that these are combined by "or". Storing A takes three times as much effort as storing B or C or D. One may measure simplicity of a concept as the amount of effort needed to store the concept.

Let us now assume a mind to which B, C and D are simple concepts and his experience tells him "If *B* or *C* or *D* occurs (i.e., is true) then I should hide myself". If this reason for hiding occurs repeatedly, he would give a name "*A*" to the above sentence "*B* or *C* or *D*" and store the experience "If *A* occurs, then I should hide myself".

Somewhere, however, one will again have to store the fact that "*A*" is the same as "*B* or *C* or *D*". Is this storage justified if the only reason for this lies in the simplification of the wisdom "If *A* occurs, then I should hide myself"? If such extravagance is not believable, then to what shall we ascribe the propensity for storing simplifying definitions? Such a propensity there is. Anybody who remembers his or her childhood or has a grade-school child has seen the transition from adding on fingers to multiplying on paper to the day when the child can ask with perfect facility, "Gee mom, why is it 'no' ninety percent of the time?"

"Percent" is the name of a concept which has a very difficult description in terms of counting on fingers. The fact that this concept is retained by the child is because it helps him to do lots more than argue with his mother. He can keep track of his grades, can argue vociferously about national economy, can figure his gains on the odd lot of shares he bought last summer from his lawn-mowing money.

A concept, then, becomes simple and takes on a name when it is useful for many purposes, so when its description is stored, the description of many other concepts becomes simplified. This kind of simplification has another unusual effect on the confidence with which one generalizes on experience. Let us take an example, perhaps somewhat contrived.

A person is asked to classify two-digit numerals into two sets, "Good" and "Bad". He has been shown 10 samples of good and bad numerals as follows:

11 bad	32 good	57 bad	74 good
26 good	43 bad	58 good	85 bad
99 bad	20 good		

If our subject is concentrating only on the last digit he knows that each last digit has occurred only once. 2, 4, 6, 8 and 0 have turned out good and the others have been bad. Now if he sees 72 how sure is he that he is seeing a good number?

In case the readers have already seen through my ruse, let me state at this point that the person in question does not have the concept of an even number. All he knows is that he has seen one case where the last digit is 2 and it is good. He has seen other last digits other than 2 and some have been good and some bad.

So, how does one guess that 72 is good? Because to us "even" and "odd" are simple concepts. Using those simple concepts we find that every one of the 5 odd integers has been bad in the past and every one of the 5 even integers has been good. This increases our confidence to a very great extent that 72 is good.

What I did in the two cases above is known as contingency table analysis by statisticians. My conversations with my statistician friends seem to indicate that in both these cases I did a valid analysis. In the first case, statistical analysis indicates insufficiency of data. In the second, the conclusion is clearly justified by ordinary statistical criteria.

This brings me to the "consideration more important than simplicity" that I mentioned in the last section. In a way, this consideration is again a paradox, dealing with reality and our perception of it. It can probably be stated best in terms of the experiment above. It will be noticed that our first numerically naive person could not conclude from the data that 72 was good. "We", on the other hand, could. What is disturbing about this phenomenon is that the same data are being used in both cases. All that is changed are the basic sentences used and what we consider to be simple concepts. Would we be satisfied with an experimental result where all 5 good numerals were "blinky", where "blinky" was defined to be "cases where the sum of the two digits were divisible by 3 in those cases where the first digit was odd and the second digit was 7 and where the difference of the digits was divisible by 2 in those cases where either the first digit was divisible by 4 or the second digit was odd"? Five observations, clearly, would not be sufficient to justify such a complicated explanation, which we would summarily reject as contrived. In the next section I shall make an effort at trying to axiomatize away this paradox and give my view of training.

What in the Real World Allows Training?

If anything is to be learned from what has gone before, it seems to be the following.

(1) A concept which is useful in describing many phenomena takes on a name and eventually is considered to be a simple concept.

(2) The confidence with which a phenomenon is understood depends heavily on the concepts in terms of which the phenomenon is described.

Before going further, let us remove a small lacuna that may bother the discerning about (2) above. Let us suppose that we are studying a phenomenon and that, in terms of all the concepts we know, the description of the phenomenon as seen so far turns out to be complex. As a result, observations do not seem sufficient to warrant any reliable description of the phenomenon. What prevents us at this point from giving the phenomenon itself a name with the complex description obtained so far and thereby gaining confidence that we have understood the phenomenon?

Most people have seen such pseudo-understandings occur. In the U.S. it is described as "If you don't understand it, give it a name". Many a technological and social mistake is attributable to this. Most men of discernment would object to such "attachment of names" to new concepts by interpreting point (1) above to mean that a concept deserves a name only when it allows simple descriptions of many phenomena. Hence, if no concept can simplify a phenomenon, then one does not attach a name to the new phenomenon and makes it a concept − one rearranges the whole set of basic concepts to accommodate the new phenomenon. One does not say "The Newtonian and Maxwellian theories are correct except for the Michelson−Morley experiment". One says, "Phenomena are ruled by relativistic mechanics and field theories".

This somewhat lays the ghost except for one little doubt. Suppose one has, on the basis of previous observations of phenomena, come up with a simplifying set of concepts. Suppose a new phenomenon is being studied and the first few observations seem to be simply described in terms of these. One could, at this point, describe the phenomenon in a very complex way in terms of some more primitive concepts and demand further observation. What actually happens, however, is that one makes (formally or conceptually) a contingency table based on the simplifying concepts (so the phenomenon can be described with very few "or"s and hence very few cells in the contingency table (Fisher, 1928)) and is satisfied with a few observations.

Basically, however, there is no reason for being confident that concepts developed in view of past phenomena should be useful enough for future phenomena to be used with confidence. It just happens. Indeed, if it did not, i.e., if the real world was not one regulated by a number of basic principles which are universally true, life would have been impossible, since it takes a long period of experience to develop the basic concepts and so there would be no way of keeping up with the vagaries of the real world. The very fact that we are alive, then, seems to point to a basic law of nature, i.e., that laws of nature exist. More specifically, there is a small set of concepts in terms of which all natural phenomena have simple descriptions.

The process of training, by this view, then, comes to the following. The mind to be trained comes equipped with certain concepts which, to it, are simple. Its observations on the real world are only describable in terms of these concepts. If the part of the real world with which it is concerned yields phenomena which are already simple in terms of these concepts, then there is no training needed. (To the frog "bugginess" is simple and that's all it wants to see.) If, however, phenomena do not show simple descriptions, then a very large amount of observation is needed before the adequacy of the description can be established. The untrained mind often does not go into this phase of further observation. Instead, simple descriptions are made and adhered to by stopping further observation. Our fictitious person could have believed after seeing 32 that all numbers greater than 30 are good. Many believe that only lazy people are poor. However, with an adequate training sufficient data are accumulated before believing a description, simple or complex.

If many descriptions of different phenomena turn out to be complex, efforts are made to develop new concepts which simplify these descriptions. These simplifying concepts are then used when further phenomena are observed. Because of our assumptions about the real world, the chances are greater that many of the new phenomena will have simple descriptions. If the concepts developed do not match the actual simplifying concepts, further concepts have to be developed and the older ones modified.

One does not quite know how this formation and modification of simplifying concepts can be done. If one considers the space of descriptions for an algebra of some sort — pattern recognition people use polynomial rings (Sebesteyen, 1962), logicians use boolean and polyadic algebras (Halmos, 1962) — then the problem of simplifying concepts can be posed as follows: "Given a set of generators for the sub-algebra of a given algebra, find another set of generators for the sub-algebra which are simpler". The definition of "simple" is not well specified here — nor are good solutions for the above cases known for many algebras. In the case of free groups, a solution is known if by simplicity of a generator one means the number of symbols of the original free group whose subgroup is under consideration (Magnus *et al.*, 1966). It is a far cry from here to polyadic algebras!

Conclusions

The last thing I seem to have said is "I do not know how a mind trains itself to make sense out of observed data". We do know, of course, that simplifying concepts can be introduced from outside. That is what we do in school to the young minds — continuously expose new concepts to students which we believe simplify their decision making in life.

I hope that what I have been able to do in this paper is to indicate what the most important and useful aspects of the training process are. This may give some insight into "how to train" and perhaps "how to train to learn" as opposed to "how to indoctrinate" or "how to instill a faith". It is the contradiction between what we teach and what happens which cause the young to dislike their teaching institutions. At times it is also the fact that the concepts we teach are taught as complicated descriptions without a first view of the complexity of the phenomena whose descriptions are to be simplified. Hence, perhaps, the charge of "irrelevancy". Such thoughts may yield possible practical consequences to the above view of training.

Before ending this paper, I am going to allow myself one burst of egotism by including one reference to my own work. I have been able to convince myself that this would fall into the category of quoting detailed results. The law of nature that "laws of nature exist" can be given a mathematical form based on the idea of conditional probabilities (Banerji, 1972). The basic structure is as follows: "We are faced with a world of theories and a world of phenomena. If a specific theory is true, phenomena occur in the world which have simple explanations in the theory. Complex phenomena occur rarely. On the basis of this one can, by noting which phenomena occur, make decisions as to what theories may be true." No technical method is feasible for searching for theories, because of the computational enormities involved. I am at present looking at the algebraic formulation of the problem.

Acknowledgements

The preparation of this paper was supported by the National Science Foundation under grant GJ-1135. Parts of the research leading to it are related to the AFOSR Contract No. AFOSR-71-2110.

2. Techniques

Human beings without technical knowledge who interact with computers tend to distrust and even fear them. Yet it is the interaction between man and machine which carries the greatest potential for human benefit, since it is machine-aided, rather than artificial intelligence which is the more applicable to social problems.

The range of potential applications of computer techniques is enormous. Some avenues have been explored, but largely the area is wide open for systematic study. Of necessity, the application of a technique is an interdisciplinary problem. It is necessary to be aware of existing techniques, whether they be in psychology, education, medicine or some other discipline, and at the same time to appreciate the advantages and possible disadvantages of modifying procedures by introducing some degree of computer control. Merely replacing some human by an information-storing or decision-taking computer may well be a valuable application where the work involved is tedious or dangerous. However, this is a modest aim and applications of this sort are likely to be judged in terms of their cost effectiveness. Of far greater importance are applications where the computer makes possible the development of methods that could not reasonably be achieved by any other means. Very often it is not so much the sophistication of the program that is important as the ingenuity of the application. It is also apparent that a great deal can be achieved using relatively small and unsophisticated laboratory computers. A number of papers in this section effectively emphasize this point.

The papers which follow make up an interesting range of potential computer applications. In several of the papers the computer is used in an on-line situation e.g. in instruction, in clinical assessment, in monitoring and controlling interaction between individuals, in determining psychophysical thresholds.

The fact that few of the contributions discuss such a mundane problem as cost effectiveness does not mean that the psychologist has his head in the clouds. As Bovet's contribution emphasizes, even a minimal outlay can introduce process control techniques to the laboratory and hence revolutionise experimental procedures. In any case, it is a truism that the economics of applications at the experimental level give little indication of the economics of the widespread application of a technique. With the foreseeable increase in availability of both small computers and complex time-sharing systems in schools, hospitals and laboratories, successful techniques similar to those described here, which experience will show are truly cost effective, have every opportunity of widespread adoption.

DAVID JONES* and JOHN WEINMAN**

Computer Based Psychological Testing

Summary

The main approaches to psychological assessment are briefly described and the requirements of computer based test systems are outlined. Such systems have been developed at two levels. At the first the computer controls the sequencing of a remote visual display, and at the second the computer is directly responsible for item generation and display. Examples of the application of the second type of system are given and methods of analysis of test results are discussed. The main advantages of this approach are in allowing for serial assessment and for more detailed investigation of cognitive abilities.

Introduction

The assessment of individual differences in thought processes is an essential function of the work of the clinical psychologist. The area is a wide one, embracing traditional psychometric assessment and an awareness of the effects of social and cultural factors on perceptual and cognitive styles. With a few notable exceptions, existing computer applications in the clinical area have been confined to the use of large machine programs for the analysis of test results obtained in the standard psychometric setting. Here we are more concerned with the development of on-line procedures for the assessment of cognitive abilities

* Birkbeck College, University of London
** Medical Research Council, London

both as a supplement to existing approaches and to provide some entirely new facilities.

Traditionally there have been two basic approaches to the assessment of intellectual functioning by clinical psychologists.

(1) A rigorous psychometric approach involving strict adherence to the test administration procedures and an interpretation of results within the limits set by available normative data. The limitations of this approach are very apparent, since there is little or no information as to how items have been solved and this information is rarely used to calculate the test score. Moreover the demands of complete objectivity in administration mean that data collection is very inefficient since all subjects have to proceed through the same sequence of items.

(2) A more intuitive clinical approach which may or may not be combined with an ideographic view of personality. Here the emphasis is on the analysis of a subject's method of working and the characteristics of his performance, as much as on defining the level at which he fails.

A computer controlled system of test administration can contribute to the efficiency of both approaches and, perhaps of greater value, such a system can allow a combination of the advantages of both methods of investigation. It is fairly easy to conceive how a computer controlled system could simulate the functions of the human examiner in the administration of the majority of tests. The problems here are the technical ones of devising peripheral equipment for adequate presentation of test items and recording of subjects' responses. If the use of the computer is confined to the role of substituting for the test administrator it is questionable whether the system can be justified in terms of administrative or cost efficiency. Seltzer (1971) has recently made a similar point in regard to substitution of the computer for the teacher in such areas of instruction as routine drills. With these considerations in mind it was felt that a computer based system ought to contribute to the scope of the clinical psychologist in the following ways:

(a) Improve the data collection procedure by homing down more efficiently on any subject's optimal level of performance.

(b) Allow for sequential assessment of individual subjects at the level found above.

(c) Allow for the accumulation of more detailed information of the subject's performance, in order to determine which factors are represented in the final score of a test.

水煮玉米粒 一袋

牛肉（有哪种通道）

盐（一大瓶的那种）

油 一瓶

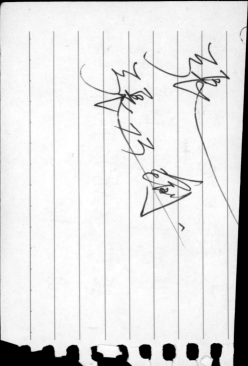

We have been pursuing these aims at the two levels of sophistication described in more detail below. At both levels it is necessary to concentrate on the principles of test construction and, in particular, on the ordering of items within the test. There is an implicit criticism here that item difficulty has been largely neglected in test design beyond the establishment of empirical levels of difficulty. The problem in each case is to isolate the objective parameters of difficulty or at least to be aware of some of the more likely variables. It is then necessary to be able to order the items in terms of these parameters. Loevinger (1957) discusses some of the problems of content validity and the concept of a possible universe of items for a test. Defining objective parameters of difficulty is a method of sampling the theoretical universe of items. Hypotheses can usually be tested when we are assessing the effects of single parameters, but prediction becomes increasingly difficult when we are confronted by the effects of multiple parameters. To take a simple example, a short-term memory test involving the ability to repeat strings of digits invariably demonstrates that length of the digit string is the primary objective parameter. Even here other parameters, like rate of digit presentation, are of importance. In contrast, defining the objective parameters of item difficulty in a vocabulary test is exceedingly difficult. Word frequency is one parameter that can be controlled but word length, concreteness, meaningfulness, pronouncibility, etc., are but a few of the possible important parameters.

Computer Selection of Test Items

At the first level of sophistication, the computer controls the administration process, and times and scores subjects' responses. This has been achieved by presenting items as single frames of a 16 mm cine film. The projector can be single-stepped under computer control and it is a simple process to skip forward by any selected number of frames. The flexibility of the present system is limited by the inability to reverse the projector under computer control. The film is projected onto a screen which is mounted behind 10 translucent flaps in two rows of five which completely cover the projection area. The flaps are hinged and activate microswitches which are connected to computer input lines. Thus stimuli can be presented in any number up to ten positions

and adjoining positions may be combined if larger display areas are required. Response requirements are a light push on the flap covering the selected stimulus. The program times and records the response and selects the next item for the subject. With appropriate test materials, the system is simple and attractive enough to use with nursery school children and yet capable of handling material sufficiently complex to tax superior adults.

At present we have adapted tests of general intelligence, spatial reasoning, vocabulary and memory for this system, and there are no problems in incorporating further tests, which can be adapted to a multiple-choice format. Such a system effectively improves test administration and, by the use of feedback, converts the test situation into a directed search for a relevant threshold of ability compared to the "blind" normative approach. In the words of another writer, this process "trades serendipity for efficiency" (Pollack et al., 1966). In considering a test score as a threshold estimate, one aim has been to increase the reliability of the measure without significantly increasing test length.

The technique we have adapted is simple and depends upon the ability to devise multiple items at each level of difficulty. Using a simple skipping procedure, the subject is presented with further items at the same difficulty level and only allowed to pass on to the next level if he is succesful. By using this simple procedure the subject is required to spend a greater proportion of his time on items near his threshold level. Control programs of this sort have been widely used in automated teaching situations and Gedye and Miller (1969) describe a similar model in testing for the attainment of concepts at different levels.

While this system certainly streamlines the data collection side of testing, at present it can do little to bring about serial assessment and the collection of more detailed information about the subject's performance. This limitation is basically due to the difficulty and impracticality of generating and storing the requisite number of test items at all possible levels of competence, and to the fact that the tests we have adapted for this system are not particularly amenable to the detailed analysis of performance levels.

Computer Generation of Test Items

At the second level of sophistication we are working with test items which possess physical parameters which can be incorporated into the computer program. These programs have been developed for a minimal PDP-8 configuration (4K store, 34D oscilloscope control), using standard laboratory oscilloscopes for the display, an external clock for timing, and either the 33ASR teletype or a purpose-built response box for the subject's responses. All the test programs allow for matched or unmatched item selection by providing a choice between the selection of test items from a previously designed store, which can be held in core or on any backing store, and the on-line generation of test items. In the second case the computer is directly responsible for the generation of test items, and because of this the tests must have the following characteristics:

(a) The tests should possess as few parameters as possible controlling complexity and these should be readily specified and capable of systematic control over a wide range of difficulty.

(b) The test should be amenable to systematic analysis and allow for the analysis of patterns of errors and other characteristics of performance.

We have also added the requirement that tasks should be suitable for serial testing since this is an area that has been seriously neglected in clinical psychology. The day-to-day fluctuations in performance levels can provide valuable information on the patient's progress. Previously this problem has been investigated using matched test items and control groups. Here we are adopting an unmatched item approach, in which the patient serves as his own control. To make this possible the tests should have the following additional features:

(i) Relatively large families of homogenous test items should be readily available at any level of complexity.

(ii) The tasks should be relatively interesting and therefore not prone to rapid boredom effects.

(iii) The tasks should be sensitive to small changes in mental status.

The tests we have developed have these characteristics and provide measures of perceptual scanning, span of attention, coding and visual memory. Two of these tests have been used more frequently and will be used to demonstrate this approach.

Perceptual maze test

This test described by Elithorn *et al.* (1963) consists of a triangular lattice of tracks with large target dots situated at selected intersections, as illustrated in Fig. 1. The task is to find the pathway, from the

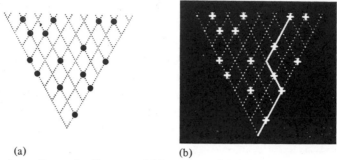

(a)   (b)

Fig. 1. An item from the Perceptual Maze Test: (a) paper and pencil version; (b) computer generated version displayed on a cathode ray oscilloscope, together with a solution path.

bottom to the top of the pattern, which goes through the largest possible number of target dots . There are two rules: the subject must keep to the tracks and must go forward at each intersection. An early study by Elithorn *et al.* (1964) showed that size, or number of rows in the matrix, and the saturation, or proportion of targets dots to intersections, are both related to subjective difficulty. Further work has indicated a number of other parameters that also correlate with subjective difficulty, such as the number of dots in the solution pathway, the number of high value non-solution pathways and various perceptual grouping factors (Lee, 1965). The test provides a measure of spatial ability, but also correlates quite well with more general intelligence tests and has been found to be very sensitive to ageing (Heron and Chown, 1967) and localised cerebral impairment (Archibald *et al.* 1967).

In the on-line situation, the computer generates patterns within defined size and saturation parameters from a random generation routine and displays them on an oscilloscope. Further restrictions on pattern generation may be made by limiting the size of the solution path and the number of dots in any string. Subjects respond by using separate

Left and Right tracking keys and a complete record is kept of the subject's pathway, the solution time and the number of dots found, together with the maximum possible on that pattern.

Digit span test

This is a test of immediate memory span, which is included in many intelligence test batteries and is very sensitive to fluctuations in concentration. In the on-line situation the computer generates digit strings from a random number generator and filters these to avoid "easy" sequences, prior to displaying them sequentially on an oscilloscope. Responses are typed in using teletype digit keys. Digit string length and presentation rate are both capable of systematic variation.

With both tests, testing commences with easy items and proceeds by increasing the difficulty after each success and by decreasing it after failure. Thus the test procedure resembles Taylor and Creelman's (1967) PEST (Parameter Estimation by Sequential Testing) technique for estimating psychophysical thresholds. Since this system has a potentially huge number of items available at all levels of competence, it provides a very flexible approach to data collection by allowing for different rates of progress by different subjects. Whereas the traditional psychometric approach terminates testing as soon as this threshold is found, here testing can be readily continued to look at various additional characteristics of performance in a single session or over a number of test sessions for comparative purposes.

Applications

We have taken advantage of these facilities for serial testing in the routine assessment of individual patients recovering from brain surgery, undergoing electro-convulsive therapy and in various drug trials.

One of these applications has been concerned with assessing performance of patients undergoing L-dopa treatment for Parkinsonism. In addition to monitoring changes in motor speed, short-term memory and problem-solving skills, it was felt important to examine for improvements in speed of problem solving, which might be indicative of a reduction in mental "akinesia". Fig. 2 shows the relative changes in one

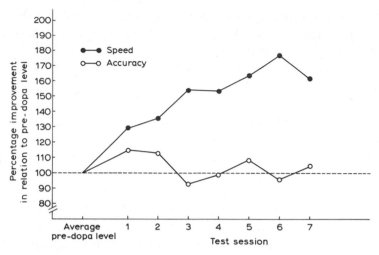

Fig. 2. Percentage improvement in speed and accuracy on the Maze test of a Parkinsonian patient on a trial of L-dopa.

patient's speed and accuracy levels in comparison with a pre-L-dopa level of performance. From this one can see a clear improvement in speed, which is not accompanied by any overall increase in accuracy level.

Serial assessment with the digit span test has revealed a number of important points. Patients can be seen to vary enormously in the extent to which they show learning, are susceptible to day-to-day fluctuations, and benefit from a slower presentation rate. Results like these have emphasised the need to look in more detail at the characteristics of performance to understand factors contributing to changing perform-ance levels. This problem has been tackled in two distinct ways.

Analysis

Off-line approach

This approach consists basically of the *post hoc* analysis of responses or errors made in one test situation. This may be carried out on the PDP-8 or more usually by large machine programs. In the case of the Maze test a complete record is kept of the pathways taken by each subject. These pathways are later analysed to build up a picture of a number of characteristics of the subject's problem-solving skills. At present programs have been developed to look at immediate and long-term gain tendencies, straight-line or perseverative tendencies and directional biases. Using these, the effects of differing degrees of planning ahead and learning on performance have been examined and error patterns associated with age changes and with localised cerebral lesions have been classified.

Off-line analyses with the Digit Span Test have so far been limited but are envisaged in terms of classifying error patterns, particularly to differentiate those due to auditory or visual confusion from those due to decay.

On-line approach

Here the test situation is structured to investigate particular cognitive or non-cognitive aspects of performance. With the Maze test subjects are assessed on a speed stressed and an accuracy stressed version of the task at their "threshold" level. Each decision change (rubout) is recorded and each binary decision is timed, making it possible to look at the relative amount of time spent by subjects on different parts of

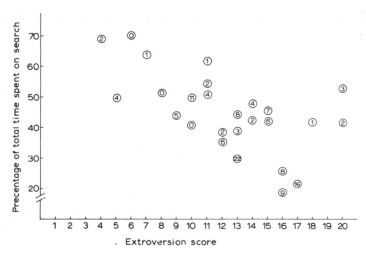

Fig.3. Extroversion and search time on the Maze Test. (Digits show number of decision changes made by each subject.)

the pattern. Thus one can see the amount of time spent planning, prior to the first decision, and the nature of subgoals later on.

In order to get more information about the factors associated with these indices of performance, an experimental study with a relatively homogenous group of 26 young adults was carried out. The general finding of the relation between extroversion and speed preference was confirmed and it was found that this involved a greater impulsiveness, and an increase in careless errors. Fig. 3 shows the relation between extroversion, search time and decision errors, revealing the diversity of "non-cognitive" styles in this group.

With the number span test, two separate presentation rates are used routinely for each patient. One of these (1 item per 2 seconds) allows time for inter-item rehearsal strategies and the other (2.5 items per second) makes this far less likely. Evidence from a study of approaching 50 subjects shows that it is not really possible to make a simple statement about the effects of presentation rate on memory span, since it can be seen that the ability to develop rehearsal strategies is a function of age, intelligence and personality factors.

Conclusion

Some clinicians might take the view that this is too mechanistic an approach to testing. It must be emphasised that we are not seeking to replace the psychologist, but to supplement his skills. Our experience and that of other workers has been that most patients respond readily to such a system, and there is good evidence to suggest that some groups of subjects prefer a situation in which they are removed from face to face contact with an observer. The latter point is particularly true of the serial testing situation.

It has not been possible to do more than outline a few examples of computer-controlled testing in the space available. The full potential of such a system depends upon the development of a battery of tests sampling a wide range of cognitive abilities. However sophisticated the system may be, the validity of the measure depends upon the validity of the test being used. We have been working on a variety of tests with an awareness that detailed standardisation will only be possible when the procedures are more widely implemented. However, even at this early stage we can see the potential of computer techniques in combining the psychometric and experimental approaches to the study of cognitive abilities.

J.A.M. HOWE*

Individualizing Computer-Assisted Instruction

Summary

Computer-Assisted Instruction is classified into three categories: drill-and-practice systems, tutorial systems, and dialogue systems and the advantage and disadvantage of each discussed. Various theoretical and practical problems are made explicit, drawing particularly from experience gained from the C.A.I. project at the Bionics Research Laboratory, Edinburgh University. Emphasis is placed on the need to devise constructed response systems, and also full dialogue systems, if the goal of individualizing instruction is going to be achieved.

The term computer-assisted instruction (C.A.I.) is usually applied to methods and systems developed *to control* learning. (I purposely exclude from this definition the use of the computer as a calculating device, simulation apparatus or management tool.) These can be classified according to the complexity of the pupil—system interaction.

Drill-and-Practice

At the simplest level are systems which present a fixed linear sequence of problems — usually referred to as "drill-and-practice" systems. These have been developed to supplement classroom instruction. Proba-

* University of Edinburgh

bly the best known centre for this work is Stanford University where Suppes (Suppes and Morningstar, 1970) has devised a series of arithmetic programs which have been extensively used by children in California, in Kentucky and in Mississippi. Questions organized in concept blocks are presented to the pupil via a teletype, the time allowance per problem being selected by the pupil at the start. Each concept block is spread over a 7-day period and consists of a pre-test drill and review drills and post-tests. For each day of drill, five drills of varying difficulty are available. The pupil's performance on the pre-test determines the level of difficulty on the first day of drill, and the difficulty of each successive drill is determined thereafter by performance level in the preceding day's drill. If 80 percent or more, the difficulty level is increased by one step, and if 60 percent or below it is decreased by a step.

What about the adequacy of this method of teaching? Perhaps the most important criticism is that it is based on the over-simplified view that reinforcement of the correct answer is sufficient for learning. Hammond (1971) refers to this as "stupid learning" — even when learners do learn they are frequently unable to give an explanation of what it is they have learned. Being provided with the correct answer is not useful as feedback since any one answer can often be produced by various combinations of components or cues, and a long series of trials would be necessary to distinguish between what is nearly regular in a task and what is wholly accidental. In view of this, it is not entirely surprising that the results of the Stanford drill-and-practice experiments are no better than those from children taught in a more conventional way (Suppes and Morningstar, 1969). To develop effective learning, we must discover how to take account of differing abilities, aptitudes, motivations and so on. These are aspects of the problem with which the drill-and-practice approach cannot deal.

A major practical difficulty is design of lesson material. In the case of arithmetic, it is possible to construct hierarchical sequences of presentation and to devise varying levels of difficulty within units of sequences, although validation is a time consuming and expensive iterative process. However, it is not clear how we can deal with less readily structured material, e.g., foreign languages, in other than a trivial way.

Tutorial Systems

These allow pupils of varying ability to follow different paths through lesson material according to their individual performances. There is little doubt that this ought to be a more effective teaching method than drill-and-practice — the fast learner is not bored by needless repetition and the slow learner progresses only as fast as he can grasp the material.

With this branching technique the design of lesson material is also a difficult problem. The method most often used is known as "task analysis". In a nutshell, learning objectives are laid down and lesson material is arranged into a series of steps to be covered in attaining the objectives. A major problem is how to choose criteria on which to base decisions about the best route for a given individual. Atkinson and Paulson (1970) and Smallwood (1970) have emphasized the importance of developing a theory of instruction with mathematical models for optimizing learning on the basis of a pupil's past history. The magnitude of the problem is put thus by Smallwood: "If there are five instructional alternatives at each decision node in the tree and if there are two possible responses by the student for each instructional alternative, and if we desire to calculate the optimal instructional alternative based on these paths by the student that extend ten presentations into the future, then this will require the consideration of 10 billion possible student trajectories for each decision." Clearly the problem must be reduced to manageable proportions. This involves the devising of procedures to compare the values of alternative paths, relative to the purpose of the instruction. The values assigned to each path must be weighted by the probability that the pupil will traverse that path in the tree. For this, a model of pupil behaviour is required that allows a calculation of the probability that a pupil will produce a particular response to the presentation of an instructional alternative.

The weaknesses of this approach at present are several. We have yet to devise ways of accurately representing the state of knowledge of a pupil at a given time. It requires suitable models of learning, but the models in use so far are too simple to be helpful — they ignore such factors as motivation and previous learning. Moreover, most important of all, it assumes that all individuals should be brought to the same state of knowledge, but is this what individualizing of instruction is really all about?

Due to the above difficulties, branching is usually employed as a simple extension of the linear technique, to deal with particular difficulties encountered by a pupil. As Cronbach (1967) has pointed out, this is a hole-filling procedure to bring an individual back to the norm. But thinking of ways in which a pupil may go astray as he progresses is not a trivial task. Even if the author realises that a particular difficulty may arise and wishes to provide remedial material, he may not realise that a given error response can result from different trains of thought. If he does anticipate alternative thinking strategies, he may not know how to select between them. Either way, the pupil may be puzzled or even misled by the remedial material provided. This problem is similar to that faced by any teacher in the classroom. Instead of carrying out a post-mortem and attempting to find exactly where the pupil has made his error, it may be more productive to identify what the pupil does know and to get him to use this to discover the difficulty and/or the correct response. This is the approach which we have followed in part in devising an arithmetic teaching program which generates the questions to be presented (Howe, 1971).

Bunderson (1970) suggests that C.A.I. curriculum development projects, especially those involving considerable text and display authoring, can require 200, 300 or more hours of work to produce a sequence that would take a pupil only one hour to complete! From this, we may conclude that it is unlikely that individual teachers will attempt to develop their own material, or even adapt to their own needs the material provided by others.

What about the pupil's attitude to controlled learning? In the course of our research in Edinburgh using a branching program we have attempted to assess the attitudes of the groups of boys (both experimental and control) who participated in the experiments (Delamont and Atkinson, 1971). When asked to describe both the ideal teacher and the computer, using a check list of 20 items, considerable differences were revealed on some 6 items:

97

	Ideal teacher	*Computer*
5. Allows me to offer my own ideas and suggestions	Yes	No
7. Is prepared to wander off the subject	Yes	No
10. Makes me feel at ease	Yes	No
12. Always keeps to the point	No	Yes
14. Allows me to ask questions	Yes	No
17. Sticks to the syllabus and does not digress	No	Yes

It is clear from these results that the boys would prefer a dialogue situation, in which they would be able to ask questions and to digress from the topic under consideration.

A method for reducing the complexity and difficulty of preparing lesson material has been proposed by Simmons (1970). It also has the merit that it satisfies at least one of the requirements made by the boys.

The aim is to construct a language processing program to check the pupil's response to determine if it is an equivalent paraphrase of a stored answer. The pupil's answer is expected to vary widely in vocabulary and phrasing from the stored answer, and the language processor has to determine in what ways the meaning content of the pupil's answer corresponds to and differs from the content of the stored answer. The pupil's response may be completely correct, completely incorrect and irrelevant, partially correct with some incorrect or irrelevant information, or entirely correct with additional irrelevant material. Decisions about what questions to put next will be based on the classification of the response in the above five ways. So instead of having to present for each question all categories of possible response from the pupil and decide in advance what to do for each (as in branching), the author of the material can concentrate on the main line of lesson content.

Dialogue Teaching Systems

While, from a teaching point of view, Simmons' system might be more effective since the constructed response requires the pupil to generate statements to express the meaning of what he has been told, it would not answer the boys' request for a system which will answer their questions. Recent advances in artificial intelligence techniques for language processing and comprehension, for the storing of knowledge and for the use of stored knowledge to answer and generate questions suggest the possibility that a radically different type of C.A.I. system might be devised — a system capable of maximizing interaction between pupil and computer. A significant gain would be elimination of the need to prepare lesson material.

Carbonell (1970) has described a prototype system which he has devised to maintain a mixed-initiative dialogue with a pupil, with questions asked by either side and answered by the other. The dialogue takes place in a subset of English and it is directed to reviewing a pupil's knowledge of the geographical facts of South America. The program is more interactive than other C.A.I. programs, but does have limitations. In practice, it asks questions until interrupted by a question from the pupil. It then promptly answers his question and requests an answer to its own previous one.

Carbonell's system is founded on a data-base of facts, concepts and procedures. The components are called units which define words and events in the form of multi-level tree-lists. For example, the units are concepts such as country, continent, latitude, or examples of concepts such as Venezuela, mining. The lists consist of other words which point to their respective units, and so on. Information is therefore stored hierarchically downwards in a collection of trees, with connections between trees.

A pupil's question can be input in "wh" form or various standard forms such as "Is it true that...", "Tell me about...", "Tell me more about...". "Wh" type questions use words "what", "where", "which", also "how many", "how large". The only verb allowed is the verb "to be", so relationships are expressed in a possessive form by using "of" and other prepositions. Answers are generated with similar simple sentences, though a few verbs are allowed. In reply to a "Tell me about..." question, the computer may provide a succession of several short sentences, sometimes linked by pronouns. Embedded clauses are not dealt with.

Carbonell found that it is much more difficult for the system to interpret the pupil's answers to questions when any reply is allowed than it is to generate questions. The difficulty lies with understanding whether they are correct or not. He resorted to using closed questions in any of three ways: (a) true or false questions; (b) fill in the gap questions, and (c) multiple-choice questions.

One of the main working features of the program is that of keeping the discourse connected by using contexts. A context is similar to a discussion topic. When a context is set up it becomes the topic of a discourse and questions are generated from knowledge about that context. Within the discussion of a context sub-contexts can be found, so the length of time a context is discussed depends on how deep it is in the tree and the time available. This way of dealing with contexts is not adaptive since contexts are picked probabilistically with reference only to the data-base and not to the pupil.

In Edinburgh, we are investigating the problems which arise when attempting to write a program of this type (also using a geography data-base). We are concentrating on the problem of controlling the interaction between pupil and system. As Suppes (1971) points out, we do not have a good model of the interaction between a tutor and his pupil due to our lack of understanding of the character of a successful dialogue. But we do have some intuitive ideas to guide our initial efforts. As noted previously, the mixed-initiative of Carbonell's system is restricted to dealing with a single question interposed either by the machine when the pupil is putting the questions to it, or vice versa. This type of interaction may be more frustrating than useful if it abruptly interrupts a train of thought. While the system is dealing with aspects of a *particular* topic by making statements and asking questions, it may be better to make it difficult for the pupil to change the subject if the questions he puts are not sufficiently clearly related to the topic under consideration. While they are relevant, however, it would leave control in the hands of the pupil. If the issue under discussion is a *general* one (involving several topics) it will be difficult to assess the relevance of different questions unless the system can define a work-space or context. To constrain the dialogue within a limited part of the data-base is not a solution to this problem. It is only by defining aims, by keeping a record of the course of the dialogue, and by relating these to the pupil's history, including his state of knowledge, that an effective dialogue can be created. It is, however, important that the system should take the initiative when errors are detected. Usually errors will be made in response to questions presented by the system, but errors may also occur when the pupil is questioning the system, such errors being due to misunderstandings, and misinterpretations, of a pupil's questions.

We have already referred to the need to characterize individual pupils. No existing program uses information about a pupil's aptitude, ability, interests, attention, and so on, because of lack of information about how these factors affect learning. Clearly they are relevant, and for a dialogue to be successful the system must build up a model of each pupil in which at least some of these parameters are quantified. Control of the extent to which the system will digress, and the extent to which it provides hints, additional explanations, and so on depends upon adequate interpretation of the individual pupil's strategies. Until we attain some success with this particular problem we cannot claim that we are able to individualize instruction.

J.L. GEDYE *

The Use of an Interactive Computer Terminal to Simulate Decision Making Situations

Summary

This paper describes an interactive computer terminal designed for direct use by untrained operators. It allows users sitting down at the terminal for the first time to operate it — in accordance with the particular requirements of the situation — within a few minutes. The terminal has been used for a number of "information gathering" applications and one — which involves the use of the terminal to simulate a general practice clinical decision making situation — is described in some detail. Attention is drawn to some of the implications of the work for research on human thought processes.

Introduction

Computing, looked at as a human activity, provides a set of concepts in terms of which it is possible to discuss various aspects of the psychologist's activities in studying human behaviour, including thinking. We can, for example, on the one hand liken the act of instructing a human being to carry out a given task to the act of instructing a computer to execute a given program, and, on the other, liken the act of instructing a human being *how* to carry out a task to the act of writing a computer program to do likewise. It is not difficult, of course, to draw attention to dissimilarities between the two activities: we might, for example, try

* University of Essex

102

The machine now is becoming cleverer and cleverer, will it some day really think like human? Many Scientifics spend their whole life on making a real thinking machine. It is not about the possibility, ~~it is~~ but the dream which ~~they~~ people cannot stoped seeking.

History

This paper does not talk about ~~the~~ a ~~practice~~ how to make an intelligent ~~reseach of~~. machine, it just involve to the discussions of the

No.

Date

to express one of the most obvious of these by saying that the human being, as opposed to the computer, lacks a "well-defined instruction set". Nevertheless, it is the very fact that the attempt at a comparison focuses attention on such differences, and provides a language in which to express them, that makes the exercise worthwhile, and this paper is, in a sense, concerned with an attempt to deal with some of the implications of the difference between "man" and "machine" illustrated by the example above.

In general, experiments on thinking seem to involve the psychologist in situations in which subjects are presented with information and required to process it in some way to meet stipulated demands. Such experiments can usefully be thought of as belonging to a class of situations in which a contract exists between two people — an "employer" and an "employee". The employer specifies the task that is to be carried out by the employee, and the employee undertakes to carry it out. If he fails to do what is required of him he has "broken his contract", and may be called upon to "defend himself against a charge of negligence".

The value of this *jurisprudential* approach is that it provides a framework within which it is possible to carry out an examination of the set of possible defence arguments, and the circumstances in which they would be acceptable. These range from claims of the form "I failed at the task because the employer did not explain it to me adequately", on the one hand, to claims of the form "I failed at the task because I was suffering from a lack of oxygen" on the other. In an earlier paper (Gedye, 1964) it was argued that the study of the effects of oxygen lack on human behaviour in task situations could be regarded as a systematic attempt to accumulate evidence which would allow defence arguments of the latter kind to be evaluated, and the problem of protection against oxygen lack could be regarded as one of determining under what circumstances such forms of defence would be inadmissible, and taking steps to ensure that such circumstances would always prevail in practice.

In the present context the approach is useful because it draws attention to the importance of employer—employee communication in setting-up the contractual relationship which underlies the experimental situation, and underlines the possibility of task failures (as judged from the standpoint of the employer) being attributable to failures of employer—employee communication, consequent on the lack of a "well-defined instruction set".

This approach to experiments on human thinking implies, therefore, a process of at least two stages:

(1) A stage of setting-up a contractual relationship between the experimenter and subject, which can be likened to writing a computer program.

(2) A stage of implementation of the contract, which can be likened to running a computer program.

The Active Interface

So far, we have only considered computing as a source of terminology for describing certain aspects of human task behaviour in a relatively novel, and, hopefully, stimulating, way. It is, however, possible to go further and consider computing as an activity which is *itself* directly relevant to the two-stage process of setting-up and implementing contractual relationships of the type described above. More specifically, we may consider the process of "instructing a computer 'how' and 'when' to instruct a human being 'how' and 'when' to carry out a task".

In the system we are considering the experimenter communicates with the subject through an intermediary *active* interface (Gedye, 1969) as opposed to a situation where, from the present point of view, the interface plays an essentially passive role in the communication process, for example: face-to-face communication by means of a video-phone. In the present situation the interface plays an active part in the communication process by acting as the experimenter's *delegate* in his interaction with the subject.

Systems of this type have recently been implemented in the U.K. by Questel Limited as dual terminal configurations linked through the Post Office Datel 200 service to a remote DEC tss 8 time-sharing computer in London. Whilst there are, undoubtedly, many other ways of implementing such a system, this arrangement has the advantage of allowing experiments to be run almost anywhere there is a telephone, and so "the experiment can be taken to the subject" — an important consideration if one is interested in applying the approach to real-life situations such as one might find in schools, hospitals and industry. With this arrangement, the experimenter can, through his own terminal, by writing and observing the running of a program, use the computer to control and study the way in which a subject using another terminal interacts with the program.

In recent years we have been particularly concerned with the problems of designing interactive computer terminals for direct use by untrained operators (Gedye, 1969). A fundamental requirement has been that it should be possible for a user to sit down at the terminal for the first time, and to be operating the system in accordance with the particular requirements of the situation within a few minutes. In practice this has meant that the first assignment of the active interface in any specific interaction has been for it to teach the user how to operate the terminal, and to check that he has acquired sufficient skill to be able to cope with what is to follow.

Looked at from the experimenter's point of view, this process of teaching the user, through the terminal, how to use the terminal is an essential first stage in establishing indirect communication with a subject, as subsequent possibilities are very much dependent on what can be achieved at this stage. There is a sense in which the experimenter has an "instruction set" defined for him, which is determined jointly by the behaviour of the terminal and the subject's behaviour in response to it, and his task becomes one of using these "behavioural elements" to create the situation he is interested in.

In the Questel system the experimenter can normally use one of two programming languages. The first, QUASIC, is a specialised form of Essex BASYS, a greatly extended form of the original Dartmouth College BASIC (Gaines *et al.*, 1971) which contains special processors for the control of the subject's terminal and provides a quick and powerful means of writing programs to control subject-terminal interaction and to analyse the results and present them to the experimenter in an appropriate form. The second, a special tree-structured language, will be used in this paper for illustration as it shows the nature of subject-terminal interaction particularly well. In this case source programs are assembled to produce a highly efficient core-resident object program for multi-terminal operation on the tss 8.

The terminal consists of a visual display and a keyboard, as illustrated in Fig. 1, comprising 2 large response keys labelled A and B; 4 keys labelled ENTER, CANCEL, RUB OUT and HELP; and a single

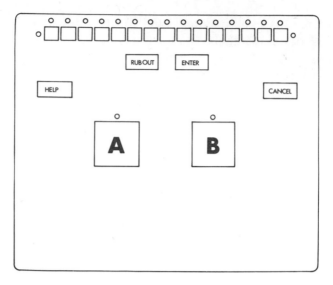

Fig. 1

row of 15 small response keys. In the display, images, 21 cm high by 30 cm wide (A4), are generated by static back-projection of single frames from a 16 mm casette-loaded colour microfilm. The operation of the keyboard can best be understood from a description of the terminal's operating cycle from the subject's point of view. At the start of the cycle a shutter opens to display the current frame of the microfilm, and at the same time the keyboard is put into one of three possible states:

(1) Autoadvance – all keys are inactive, and the current frame is displayed for a predetermined time interval, at the end of which the shutter closes and the film is moved to the next frame, ready for the next cycle to begin.

(2) Binary response – the response keys A and B are activated, this state being signalled to the subject by the lighting-up of a small lamp above each key. Response is by depression of either key which terminates the display cycle by closure of the shutter, and moves the film to the next frame.

(3) Multiple response – the row of 15 small response keys is activated, this state being signalled to the subject by the lighting-up of a small lamp at each end of the row of keys. Response is by depression of up to 15 of the small keys, followed by depression of the ENTER key, which terminates the display cycle, as described in (2) above.

In addition HELP and CANCEL keys provide alternative means of response, for use in emergency conditions.

In order to illustrate the kind of facilities provided for the experimenter in this system, two frames from an initial instructional sequence which has been found to work satisfactorily in practice will be discussed in some detail. Imagine that a subject with no previous experience is seated in front of the terminal, and that a frame with the following text is displayed:

Below this screen you'll see two
keys labelled A and B

Press either key A or key B

The relevant source program segment might look like this:

```
/INS901    FRM       4
KEY        SHT
AK         INS003    BK      INS004    TIM    INT001
HLP        1         CAN     1                ;
```

The "/" and the ";" are delimiters which indicate the beginning and end of a *node specification* respectively.

"INS901" is the node name, which may be up to 6 characters, typically 3 alphabetic characters followed by 3 numerical characters (this allows whole program segments to be copied and incorporated in new programs by use of a single string substitution editing command).

"FRM 4" causes the 4th frame from the reference end of the microfilm strip to be shown.

"KEY" sets the keyboard with the "A" and "B" keys active.

"SHT" sets a timeout facility to a predetermined "short" value of, say, 30 seconds.

"INS003" "INS004" and "INT001" are the next nodes according to whether the "A" key (AK) or the "B" key (BK) are pressed, or there is a timeout (TIM), that is 30 seconds elapses without a response from the subject.

"HLP 1" and "CAN 1" specify subroutines to be called if the "HELP" or "CANCEL" buttons, respectively, are activated.

It will be seen that the language allows the experimenter to specify what he wants to happen under each terminal condition that may occur. The subject's interaction with the terminal generates a record of the form:

.

.

| INS901 | AB | SHORT | B | 1.102 |
| INS004 | AB | SHORT | B | 1.127 |

.

.

which can be operated on by analysis programs. In the listing shown above each line is generated by an interaction controlled from a single node, and the contents contain, in addition to the node name, a brief description of the keyboard state, the timeout setting, and the subject's response and the latency of the response in seconds.

The next example illustrates the use of the multiple response facility of the keyboard. Imagine that the following frame from the initial instructional sequence, say the 19th on the filmstrip, is displayed to the subject:

Below this screen you'll see a row of fifteen
grey keys, and, below these, two larger white
keys labelled RUBOUT and ENTER

Press some grey keys, and then press ENTER

The relevant source program segment might look like this:

```
/INS216   FRM 19
SCALE     USE      1 — 15   LSC     1 — 15   LNG
NDST      1        RPST     1
AK        INS116   BK       INS117  TIM      SCATIM
HLP       I        CAN      I        ;
```

"SCALE" (as opposed to "KEY") sets the keyboard with the row of 15 small keys active.

"USE 1–15" specifies "allowed" response configurations by instructing the interface to accept responses from any of the 15 keys. If the experimenter wished to exclude, say, key 15 he would write "USE 1–14" and, in addition, would, by writing BAD 1, say, specify a subroutine to be entered in the event of the user including key 15 in his response. The subroutine called BAD 1 might show a caption of the form:

```
You set a pointer outside
the relevant range

When you are ready to try again
Press either key A or key B
```

and return to INS216.

"LSC 1–15" specifies the subset of allowed responses that are to be regarded by the interface as the "left" (AK) (as opposed to the "right" (BK)) set. In this example the right set contains only the response in which none of the keys 1–15 is pressed. This facility can be used to detect null responses and is used routinely as the first stage of the response-filtering process.

"LNG" (as opposed to "SHT") sets a timeout to a predetermined "long" value of, say, 90 seconds.

"NDST 1" puts the address of the current node, that is INS216, into a store called "nodestore 1", thus providing a return address if a jump has to be made to a subroutine which is being addressed from more than one node in the program.

"RPST 1" puts the subject's response into a store called "responsestore 1" where it remains until overwritten by a subsequent "RPST 1" instruction. This allows decisions to be made on the basis of information obtained from the subject in response to frames displayed prior to the current frame.

"INS116" and "INS117" indicate the addresses of the next nodes according to whether the response configuration satisfies the "left" (AK) or "right" (BK) condition.

"SCATIM" is the name of a counter which counts the number of timeouts and initiates appropriate activity if this exceeds a critical value.

If the subject follows the instructions on the display, and provided that RUBOUT has not been actuated, the interface will accept the set of keys which have been pressed when the ENTER key is pressed as the subject's response.

A typical record might appear as follows:

.

.

INS216   SCALE   LONG   6,9   5.038
.

.

indicating that the keys 6 and 9 were pressed and that ENTER was pressed after 5.038 seconds.

If the subject does not respond within 90 seconds the shutter will close, and a subroutine will be entered which may, for example, show an autoadvance frame to remind him that a response is required, and then return to INS216. If this cycle is repeated too often a critical SCATIM count will be reached, and appropriate action taken.

In addition to the facilities for controlling the behaviour of the subject's terminal, the language allows nodes to be specified which will carry out such functions as "masking" and "counting" on current and stored information derived from the subject's interaction with the terminal, and thus provides the experimenter with a full range of facilities for the design of interactive structures.

These brief examples convey some idea of what is involved in instructing an active interface in an elementary situation, and of what was being hinted at when it was suggested earlier that one could think of the experimenter using "behavioural elements", jointly determined by the behaviour of the interface and of the subject, to achieve his purpose. It has been possible to write an initial instructional teaching program that works with a range of "average" subjects using the "behavioural elements" provided by the system. The approach was modelled on that used by Newman and Scantlebury (1967) in an automated guidance program designed to allow unskilled people to carry out repair operations. The use of controls is taught by giving instructions to operate the controls and observe their effects, and then providing the subject with a description of what he has just done and observed in a way in which he can assimilate it verbally.

For example, after a successful response to Frame 19 above, the subject is presented with the following:

Good, you will have noticed that when you press a
grey key a lamp is lit just above it, so that the
lamps give you an indication of which keys have
just been pressed.

Now, press some grey keys, press RUBOUT, and then
press ENTER

---

and then

Good, you will have noticed that when you press RUBOUT
you extinguish all the lamps that have been lit — so
if you have made any mistakes you can start again.

The action of lighting a lamp by pressing the grey keys
just below it will be called "setting a pointer". Set
pointers to indicate the positions of the crosses (X)
at the bottom of this screen, and then press ENTER

X – – – X – – X – – – – X – X X X X X X X X X X X X X X X

---

and so on.

A Simulated Clinical Decision Making Situation

Having seen something of the facilities which can be made available to the experimenter who wishes to delegate his interaction with a subject to an active interface, it will be useful, in order to bring out some of the possibilities for research on human thinking, to describe briefly a program designed as part of a study of decision making by medical practitioners.

111

The aim, in the program to be described, is to try to get the practitioner to play a "game" which will reveal useful information about his decision making processes. After being taught how to use the terminal in the manner discussed above, he is invited to play the "game". He is shown a photograph of his patient, given some preliminary information about him, and then invited to ask for further information about the history and physical examination. After each "move" of the game he is allowed a choice of either asking for further information (up to a predetermined limit) or of making a diagnosis. Having made a diagnosis, he is invited to outline his proposals for managing the patient and to prescribe treatment.

One of the most interesting aspects of such a study is likely to be the information gained about the relative priorities given to different sources of diagnostically useful information by different practitioners, so an attempt was made to create the impression that it was desirable, consistent with being "correct", to reach a decision with as little information as possible. As it was recognised that, with this approach, there was always a danger of antagonising the practitioner by appearing to put too much pressure on him, steps were taken to get his acceptance of the situation in advance.

This is done in the program by asking him to study a description of "the general practitioner's job" and to prepare himself to decide whether or not he is in broad agreement with the viewpoint expressed. Having done so, he is asked to accept it as "a fair description of at least one aspect of his role as a general practitioner". Having gained acceptance of the job description, which was modelled on that given in Part One of Dr Keith Hodgkin's book *Towards Earlier Diagnosis* (2nd Ed., 1966), it is pointed out to the subject that practice according to the precepts he has just accepted implies trying to make as accurate a diagnosis as possible as early as possible, but the problem is that the earlier in the natural history of the disease one tries to diagnose the harder it is to be accurate. As a contribution to research on this problem he is then invited to participate in a "game" designed to study how he might handle a common clinical situation on the basis of limited information.

The game itself was designed by taking as a "target" diagnosis the condition which, according to Hodgkin's 1955—59 practice statistics, provides the commonest infective illness for which an antibiotic might be prescribed. This is "Acute Bronchitis", with a quoted "suspected" incidence rate of 119.1 per 1,000 National Health Service patients and a "confirmed" incidence rate of 101.2 per 1,000 National Health Service patients, the difference giving a measure of the difficulty of the diagnostic problem involved and leading Hodgkin to classify it as a "common problem of recognition". "Cough", with an incidence rate of 113.0 per 1,000 National Health Service patients per year was chosen as the presenting symptom. Lists were then made of the symptoms and signs of both the target condition and the conditions with which it was most likely to be confused in practice, and these were used as a basis for drawing up the lists of questions that the subject could ask. The answers were chosen to be consistent with the typical picture described by Hodgkin for the target diagnosis. When the subject is ready to make a diagnosis he is asked to choose the diagnostic label that comes closest to what he has in mind from a list including all the conditions used to generate the symptom and sign lists.

Insufficient experience has been had with the program to date for it to be possible to draw any firm conclusions about clinical decision making. It is, however, possible to state that the approach works — in the sense that practitioners learn to use the terminal in less than five minutes and take the game seriously; and, in spite of the way in which it was designed, it does not seem to be too easy. One gets the impression that subjects approach the game in a way that reflects attitudes to real-life clinical problems, illustrating the point, discussed previously in another context, that one may be able to learn quite a lot about a highly skilled person's behaviour patterns by studying how he deals with simple problems (Benson and Gedye, 1963), provided that he can be led to treat them "professionally".

Acknowledgements

The work reported in this paper was carried out in the Department of Electrical Engineering Science, University of Essex, during the academic year 1970—71, under a research grant from Questel Limited for work on automated questionary techniques.

My thanks are due to R. Aish (Design), S.W.S.J. Curry (Software) and T.C.S. Kennedy (Hardware), for their contributions to the project.

ROULETTE W. SMITH*

The Ombudsman: A Computer Model of Dialogue in Instruction and Conflict Mediation

Summary

A novel application in the computer simulation of human thinking is the mediation of conflict in dialogues involving two or more parties. This paper describes a program, the OMBUDSMAN, which monitors and simulates participants in dialogues. The paradigm used is easily extended to provide a generalized model of classroom instruction and interaction. This model suggests that classroom instruction involves the avoidance, mediation and resolution of social and curricular conflicts. The teacher counsels, advises and instructs according to the model. A simple but formal language is developed, using the three-letter common nouns from the English language. A syntax of discourse is described enabling two or more participants to engage in dialogues using this language. Despite its simplicity, the language provides a unique opportunity for investigating cognitive, affective and social variables in dialogues. The weaknesses and advantages of the present research are discussed together with its applications in education and computer-assisted instruction.

Introduction

This paper will focus on two central problems. The first concerns techniques for explicating some of the subtle and often highly elusive issues related to dialogues among men (or, by inference, men and machines). In addressing this concern, the main emphasis will center

* University of California, Santa Barbara

around the method of computer simulation of cognitive, affective and social variables in dialogue.

The second concern is the development of an actual, albeit elementary, model of dialogue. This model is intentionally simple because of the equipment and facilities available. The model is also primitive since several important issues are either ignored or are not capable of being subsumed in the model. The central aim is to show that one need not construct large, unwieldy computer simulations of natural language dialogues in order to develop an appreciation for some of the deeper issues related to dialogue.

The specific model that is discussed is called the OMBUDSMAN. Although this model operates at present on a 8K word (16 bits/word) PDP-11 computer, it is sufficiently general to allow a more theoretical investigation of dialogues in examples of conflict and instruction.

Despite the usefulness of the OMBUDSMAN for discussing some matters related to dialogue, the present paper does not add to some of the linguistic issues affecting dialogue. That is, the present discussions purposefully avoid many of the syntactic and semantic questions directly related to dialogue. A subsequent paper will deal with these issues.

Before proceeding with a description of the OMBUDSMAN, it is perhaps worthwhile to review my own research interests and some of the related contributions by others. The central problem leading to the present research concerns the nature and importance of classroom dialogues as a determinant of learning and instructional behaviors. Anyone familiar with lecturing in a classroom environment may recall being impressed (or depressed) by the various dialogues that arise in the classroom. These dialogues are most frequently among the teacher and several students. The teacher occasionally encounters dialogues solely among students too. One concern is therefore to provide answers to the following questions. "Can one isolate and discuss in meaningful theoretical detail the contributions of interpersonal dialogues in an instructional environment? Can one further infer that individualized tutorial instruction — meaning an interaction between one student and a teacher — need not be more effective than an interpersonal interaction among two (or more) students and a teacher? If the latter is a distinct possibility, what might be an optimal class size?"

The relevance of these problems to the stated purposes of this symposium should be clear. It is to describe an aspect of human thinking and problem solving, to wit, understanding and communicating with others. But more important, the methodological approach of computer simulation, employed in the manner to be described shortly, opens up a range of research approaches not considered in any serious detail in the extant literature.

Computer simulation, as an approach to some social and behavioral science problems, has been considered widely and employed effectively. This technique has been applied in investigations of the problem of dialogues. Colby *et al.* (1966) and Weizenbaum (1966) are familiar examples of researchers employing this approach, although these citations by no means capture their most recent contributions. There are several problems that emerge as a result of their investigations, however. One problem is that the dialogues are usually "non-directed". Few specific objectives or constraints are established. Their systems are not effective in exhibiting assertive behaviors that invoke learning, although these, in part, may be characterized as teaching behaviors. The course of many of their dialogues often moves in different directions at the whim of the human interacting with the computer system.

Another problem is that their research is frequently too specialized to be easily replicated. My point here is not to demean their methods and strategies. Rather, the point is that other researchers, seeking not to verify, but to further develop their models, are often hampered because of equipment and staff requirements.

A third problem with the earlier research is that the construction of dialogues is very often not amenable to detailed statistical analysis. Their approach rests largely on the appreciation and acceptance of a protocol of a man—machine dialogue by human observers and interpreters. Another objection is that earlier models avoid considering the tendencies of man to generate and accept ambiguities which are corrected or reconsidered at some subsequent point in the dialogue. They also overlook some of the significant cognitive, affective and social behaviors such as listening, becoming "excited", withdrawing, interrupting and dominating.

Other researchers have considered many of these issues. Schelling (1963) describes many of these variables when considering strategies of bargaining in conflict situations. Schegloff (1967) describes some of the rules and activities associated with opening dialogues in telephone conversations. Their approaches lack the appeal and much of the theoretical elegance provided by computer simulations, however.

The remainder of this paper is devoted to a discussion of several computer programs which attempt initially to listen and ultimately to interact in dialogues among two or more persons. An ultimate goal is for these programs to remain undetected (as a non-human performer) and maintain some degree of credibility as a conversationalist and effective participant in a dialogue. In this sense the program aims to pass a modified Turing test in the sense that the computer model remains undistinguished from man. The other goal is to use the computer model to direct the dialogue of the participants, thus exhibiting the leadership often ascribed solely to mankind.

There is also an interesting theoretical consequence of this treatment of the OMBUDSMAN as a simplified model of some of the classroom teaching behaviors. The OMBUDSMAN may be viewed as a simple model of the classroom teacher. The model postulates that the teacher's role, in large measure, is to engage the students in dialogues in order to avoid or resolve social and curricular conflicts. Curricular conflicts, in this context, are meant to imply that the student and/or teacher are in disagreement with facts or beliefs pertaining to a specific subject matter.

A Description of the OMBUDSMAN

The OMBUDSMAN is a computer program operating, in part, on the PDP-11 computer at the POLIS (Political Science) laboratory of the University of California. The program has recently been translated to operate on the PDP-10 computer.

The program and its participants communicate using a language, L, consisting of the three-letter words (TLW) in the English language, excluding proper nouns and abbreviations. The reason for the latter restriction will become apparent later. A set of more than 650 such TLW's has been compiled after consulting the Webster's Seventh New Collegiate Dictionary.

Each three-letter word (TLW) is called a sentence, each character of the TLW being analogous to a word in an English language statement. Similarly, each TLW is analogous to a sentence of natural language.

(Some of the pitfalls of this analogy are discussed in the concluding remarks.) The analogy continues by regarding subsequences of the TLW's as thoughts or paragraphs. Obviously, only those subsequences contained in an individual's protocol are considered in this case.

It is readily apparent that the set of three-letter words forms a formal language. A discussion of the semantics of this language is deferred for a subsequent presentation. What remains is to describe the syntax of discourse, and how the language can be used in two- (or more) party dialogues.

The rules for the syntax of discourse are the following:

(1) A participant may use a TLW by changing one and only one character such that the resulting TLW is also in L.

(2) All participants are informed of an initial TLW.

(3) Each participant is given a target TLW (called a belief) which is known only to that participant.

(4) It is a goal of any participant to use rule 1 in getting from the initial TLW to his belief.

(5) A participant should assume that other participants are interested in his belief as well as the intermediate TLW (beliefs) leading to the terminal one. But more important, each other participant wants to be helpful by articulating a sequence of TLW's which will lead to a common terminal belief, if the latter exists.

The control of discourse is determined in the following way. Each participant can type a number 0 to 5 inclusively. These numbers may be typed at any time and will have the following meanings:

"0" The participant presently in control wishes to release control. He has nothing more to contribute at this time.

"1" The participant wishes to interrupt the dialogue (and gain control).

"2" The participant (possibly the one in control) wishes to gain control or not release control (by overriding a level "1" control request).

"3" The participant insists on gaining control.

"4" The participant threatens that if he does not receive control he will terminate his participation in the dialogue.

"5" The participant terminates his participation in the dialogue. He decides that there is no further basis for further communication between himself and other participants.

118

```
JLM:    YOUR TARGET WORD IS . . . ZAX. THE COMMON WORD IS . . . ADZ
JLM                         KEB
ADZ                         ADZ
                          1 ADD
                            AID
                            BID
                      0

1 BUD
  DUB
                          1 TUB
                            TAB
                            TAX
                            WAX
2 ZAX
                      5
GREAT . . . WOULD YOU LIKE TO TRY ANOTHER DIALOGUE? (Y OR N)
N
GOODBYE . . . JLM
```

Fig. 1. Protocol of a dialogue between JLM and KEB.

A sample dialogue is provided in Fig. 1. This protocol shows two individuals, whose initials are JLM and KEB, using the common TLW "ADZ" and both attempting to derive the TLW "ZAX". The computer is not one of the conversationalists in this dialogue. (The program, OMBUDSMAN-I, is primarily a monitor and medium for communications using the TLW language. It does not attempt to use the TLW language to communicate with the participants. That program does attempt to form a model of a participant's usage of the language. In this example, it would attempt to predict the sequence of TLW usages for one of the participants.)

The present research is primarily directed at modeling and predicting TLW usage for a given subject. I am certainly aware of the many other problems related to this paradigm that are of equal interest. The goal at the moment, however, is to have a model of dialogue and interaction which incorporates a model of an individual's usage of language L.

The OMBUDSMAN-I is designed for this challenge. It consists conceptually of two subprograms, the supervisor and the model. The central responsibility of the supervisory subprogram is the coordination and formatting of information to and from a participant's teletype-writer. The supervisory subprogram also checks on spelling and the availability of a word in its dictionary.

The principal concern of the modeling subprogram is to predict TLW and control character usage. These predictions of TLW's depend on several presently rather simplistic considerations. They include:

(1) The position(s) of the vowel(s) in a TLW.

(2) The character position for which changes occurred most frequently.

(3) The character position for which changes occurred most recently.

(4) The order that characters are used in any character position for which changes occur (e.g., the vowels A, E, I, O, U as opposed to the consonants B, C, D, F etc.).

(5) Cycles of TLW's (e.g., ADD, AID, *BID, BUD, BID,* BIN, SIN, SIX, FIX, PIX, PAX, ZAX).

(6) The frequency and length of a sequence of redundant TLW's (e.g., ADD, AID, BID, *BAD,* BUD, ...).

(7) the number of attempted TLW's which are not a part of the vocabulary. The success of this aspect of the program is encouraging, but does require additional effort. The main problems center around introducing mechanisms for explaining phonetic and alliterative generation of TLW's. Another concept not adequately treated is the tendency to plan and look ahead.

The prediction of control character usage is somewhat less than satisfactory. For some individuals, the model of the usage of the control character "0" is found to depend on the number of TLW's in a subsequence. This may exhibit an individual's concern for having participants enter the dialogue.

Other factors used in attempting the prediction of control characters include:

(1) Cycles in the protocol caused by the interactions, not by an individual.

(2) The number of TLW's in the vocabulary beginning with the same letter as the first character of the last TLW entered.

(3) The number of TLW's in the vocabulary beginning with the same letter as the first character of the target TLW.

(4) The presence of one or more cycles in an individual's subsequence.

(5) The presence of one or more redundant TLW's in an individual's subsequence.

(6) The order that characters are used in a particular position and the availability of TLW's in the vocabulary having those characters in the corresponding position.

(7) The presence of an attempted TLW which is not in the vocabulary.

(8) The latency between TLW's and control characters.

(9) The increase or decrease of latencies between successive TLW's.

There are several important observations to be made regarding the problems of modeling an individual's protocol in contrast to simulating an individual in dialogue. (The OMBUDSMAN-I program is an example of the former.) In modeling an individual's protocol, one needs to know the target TLW, the common TLW, and the sequence of TLW's used by all participants. It also is important to know the contribution of that individual to the sequence of TLW's. A simulation of an individual participating in a dialogue does not require the knowledge of all target TLW's or the specific information concerning an individual's performance.

A simulation model, called OMBUDSMAN-II, is being developed. Its purpose will be supervisory in the same sense of the OMBUDSMAN-I. But more important, I hope that it will be able to infer the target TLW's used by the participants and generate a strategy for leading or directing the participants to these target TLW's. The strategy must be sensitive to the need for the usage of control characters by any of the participants (including itself). It should predict, with reasonable accuracy, where those controls should be used in order to avoid reducing the size of its audience or destroying its credibility. The program certainly should not dominate a dialogue either.

Remarks and Conclusions

The model of dialogue characterized in the OMBUDSMAN-I provides several contributions to the discussion and investigation of some of the social, affective and cognitive variables in dialogue. Perhaps most important is the notion of monitoring man—man dialogues instead of simulating man's contributions by means of man—machine dialogues. This is not intended to denigrate studies using man—machine dialogues for the OMBUDSMAN-II is one of these. The intention is to supplement those investigations with an equally attractive methodology. This method permits a closer scrutiny of actual language usage. The distinction here is that man very often alters his strategy of generating language according to his perception of his listener's ability to generate and accept language. Thus, by monitoring man—man dialogues, the likelihood of detecting subtle changes and developments increases. There does not appear to be sufficient evidence that these subtleties are captured in present simulations of language usage. Perhaps the ideal methodology is to have systems which both simulate and monitor language usage.

The strategy employed may be thought of as an on-line, dynamic protocol analyzer. This is in contrast to the usual procedures of protocol analysis, an example of which is Newell's analysis of the Cryptarithmetic task (1967). Important data from these procedures are often lost or may be contaminated due to prompting, etc. One's ability to analyze complex protocols on-line is still a "pipe-dream", however.

Another feature of the OMBUDSMAN paradigm concerns its simplicity. The program can be subjected to close scrutiny. The protocols may be replicated and subjected to rigorous statistical analyses.

This emphasis on simplicity is not without its problems. In the current example dealing with TLW's one is concerned about the analogies between a TLW and a sentence in natural language. The fact that there is no correspondence between noun phrases and verb phrases is a specific but important example. There also are difficulties in defining an appropriate notion of semantics for the language.

There are other attractions and weaknesses of the particular implementation of the OMBUDSMAN-I. One significant weakness is that each TLW must be derived from the preceding one. A more general procedure could be implemented permitting the entry of any TLW, although the connections between it and other TLW's would have to be justified. This procedure is tantamount to relaxing some of the restrictions on the "syntax of discourse".

Two rather significant attractions concern the usage of the vocabulary and one's knowledge of the language. By having participants pursuing similar target TLW's, one has a naive example of consistency in belief without real conflict. If the target TLW's are different the participants are clearly in conflict. The second attraction concerning the usage of the vocabulary stems from the presence of words not easily derived from others. "USE" is an example of a TLW which is difficult (if not impossible) to derive from other TLW's. "URN" is difficult if the participant does not have the word "ERN" in his TLW vocabulary. The paradigm is therefore important when considering mechanisms for investigating the qualitative and quantitative effects of a vocabulary on language usage.

One might reasonably inquire about the future of these models and the particular paradigm. I have commented earlier that a model, the OMBUDSMAN-II, is in the offing. This model, if successful, will embody important aspects of human thinking. These include the mechanisms of understanding and misunderstanding information, and, in particular, subjective information. The model also seems to account for a frequently undiscussed aspect of instruction theory. This is the importance of peer feedback on learning and instructional performance.

There are two longer term goals of this research. One is the formulation of a small set of requirements for instructional languages in order that they should effectively handle pedagogical strategies employing social (peer) learning.

A second goal of this research is the development of a program to teach its participants to play chess. This goal includes the development of a chess-playing program along with an OMBUDSMAN-like model for interacting with student chess players at those points where an interaction is advisable. The actual implementation of this program will probably be similar to the implementation of the OMBUDSMAN-II. Chess moves would be represented as three-letter symbols (TLS) of the form XXN, where X is a unique name for each chess piece (e.g., GF6 might describe a move of KN to KB6).

A student, Robert Reynolds, and I have already developed an algorithm which plays an encouraging game of chess. The focus of this effort will not be on teaching "chess for the sake of chess". It is to discover, among other things, the concepts of good game-playing strategies and their mathematical properties. We also expect to answer a few of the important questions concerning the effectiveness of instruction by (good and bad) experience.

An added advantage of the "chess teaching" OMBUDSMAN is that the subtle problems of semantics cannot be ignored. Although the "syntax of discourse" is considerably more restricted, the "semantics of discourse" can be dealt with effectively.

The present description of the OMBUDSMAN paradigm and its relationship to natural language dialogues can be questioned because of its "game-playing" characteristics. This may be attributed to the lack of a clear-cut semantics. If this is indeed true, it will be useful to examine dialogues of very young children for similar game-playing behaviors, since the semantics of natural language is probably not clearly defined for them.

Acknowledgements

In addition to help from Robert Reynolds I am grateful for further assistance from Messrs. Phillip Karlton and Douglas Marsh.

I also wish to acknowledge the unfunded usage of the PDP-11 computer at the POLIS Laboratory of U.C.S.B.

PIERRE BOVET*

A Psychophysical Experiment
With a Dependent Experimental Rule

Summary

The extent to which very small laboratory computers can increase the power and sensitivity of psychological experiments is still not widely appreciated. In particular, process control techniques mean that stimulus parameters can be progressively "tailored" for each subject during an experiment. This greatly reduces errors of interpretation due to individual differences between subjects which are irrelevant to the hypothesis being tested.

The experiment presented here is part of a psychophysical study oriented towards a mathematical model of psychology in which the mechanism involved in the identification of time intervals will be related to various probabilistic models. Such a study, founded on experimental comparison of models, requires both extensive and reliable data suitable for a variety of statistical treatments. The automation of the experimental procedure described here aims at collecting such data under optimal conditions of reliability and accuracy. The use of a small computer not only avoids any mistakes in transcription and recording, but also lessens the accidental occurences of "technical hitches" during the experiment and, in particular, facilitates an extensive control of the schedule of the various events occurring during the experiment.

Perhaps more important, the use of the computer in real time enables

* Laboratoire de Psychologie Expérimentale et Comparée, Paris

us to achieve another kind of experimental improvement. With the realisation of a "dependent experimental rule", we reach a new order of experiments, which are original not only by their time-saving properties but also by new "on-line" adaptative processes which they make possible.

We call a dependent experimental rule a rule according to which the choice of the stimulus to be presented at every trial depends on what happened during the previous trials. By taking into account the subject's responses to the previous stimuli in order to choose the following stimuli, one can study accurately certain response mechanisms which it would not be possible to study without such a procedure. In particular the psychological mechanisms at work in absolute judgments of durations can be closely studied with models fitting to such a dependent experimental rule. The experiment presented in this paper illustrates such a study.

Experiment

Aim

To determine the individual ranges of time durations allowing subjects to transmit equal amounts of information.

The determination of the homogeneity of individual performances on any particular skill is essential to the question of the validity of the models used in experimental psychology and particularly to the validity of probabilistic models. Thus the identity of individual mechanisms may be concealed because of apparent inter-individual heterogeneity in a given aptitude.

Being interested in the general mechanisms involved in absolute judgments of durations (Bovet, 1969), we have attempted in this preliminary study to determine individual experimental conditions which, by taking into account inter-individual differences in discriminative ability, allow a more meaningful comparison of data from a number of subjects.

Method

Each subject made 200 judgments of the duration of a single tone (900 Hz) presented through earphones. The theoretical framework suggested, and the results of previous experimental studies on absolute judgments determined, the choice of the following experimental characteristics. Five different durations were used. These were varied according to a geometric progression, the geometric mean being constant at 1 second. Each stimulus was presented to the subject following a controlled random sequence leading to an equal frequence of each stimulus. Once the stimulus was heard, the subject responded by pushing one of the five keys, which correspond to the correct response. Two experimental conditions were used. In the first, the "without information" condition, a subject's response ended a trial and he was not given any knowledge of the correctness of the response. In the other, the "with information" condition, subjects were informed of the correctness of the response by the illumination of the appropriate response button.

The presentation of the stimuli was controlled by a 4K PDP-12 computer configuration. The tone was created by a generator (LEA) switched by an electronic switch (Grayson Stadler) and transmitted to the subject by earphones. The program was written in FOCAL 8 with two PAL-III and LINC subroutines for testing sense-lines and relays which controlled the presentation of the tone and the recording of the subject's responses. Full details of the program, or a printout, can be obtained from the author, but it is perhaps worth making one or two points.

For each trial, the change of geometric ratio of stimuli was an increment or decrement of 0.004 according as to whether the transmitted information was < 1 or > 1. The formula used to calculate the amount of information transmitted (Q) on the basis of the 25 previous trials was:

$$Q \times N = N \log_2 N + \sum^i \sum^j n_{ij} \log_2 n_{ij} - \sum^i n_i \log_2 n_i - \sum^j n_j \log_2 n_j$$

where n_{ij} was the number of occurrences of the response j to the stimulus i, n_i the number of occurrences of stimulus i, n_j the number of occurrences of response j, and N the number of previous trials over which the amount of information was calculated. Note that the calculation of Q requires a table of $n\log_2 n$ which is given to the computer during the initialisation.

Eight well-trained adults were subjects for the experiment. Their training consisted essentially of previous experimental sessions of the same type (with or without knowledge of results) as that recorded here. Four subjects were working with knowledge of results and four without.

Results

Evolution of the statistic Q (Fig. 1)

It will be recalled that, at each trial, the amount of transmitted information Q between stimuli and responses was computed on the

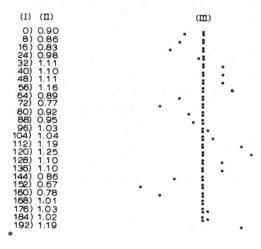

(I)	(II)
0)	0.90
8)	0.86
16)	0.83
24)	0.98
32)	1.11
40)	1.10
48)	1.11
56)	1.16
64)	0.89
72)	0.77
80)	0.92
88)	0.95
96)	1.03
104)	1.04
112)	1.19
120)	1.25
128)	1.10
136)	1.10
144)	0 86
152)	0.67
160)	0.78
168)	1.01
176)	1.03
184)	1.02
192)	1.19

Fig. 1. Example of evolution of Q (subject J). I. Trial number, II and III: Q value.

basis of the 25 previous trials. It is noteworthy that, for every subject, the value of Q throughout the trials varies on either side of 1. This shows the operational validity of the regulation procedure used. Thus, when this procedure is annulled for some subjects, the variations of Q throughout the trials are systematically below 1, and for others they are systematically above 1.

Mean values for the final geometric ratio for individual subjects

The geometric ratio used to determine the stimulus duration was initially 1.10 for all subjects. This value determines a set of given stimuli with the values 0.83, 0.91, 1.00, 1.10 and 1.21 secs., while increasing the value e.g. to 1.20 gives the series 0.69, 0.83, 1.00, 1.20 and 1.44 secs. For each presentation the change in the geometric ratio was an increment or decrement of 0.004.

Table I gives the mean values and standard deviations for each of the eight subjects. They are calculated from the last 100 trials and are an estimate for each subject of the geometric ratios required to equate the perceptual performance of subjects under the conditions of the present experiment.

TABLE I

Estimates of geometrical ratios of stimuli required to equate each subject's rate of information transmission

	Without knowledge of outcome				With knowledge of outcome			
Subjects	B	O	C	N	J	M	G	F
Mean value of geometric ratio	1.12	1.14	1.17	1.18	1.08	1.09	1.10	1.15
Standard deviation	0.035	0.040	0.032	0.047	0.038	0.042	0.032	0.032

Confusion matrix (Table II)

A special FOCAL program was written to compute the confusion matrix from the individual paper-tape punched data. These matrices show two noteworthy results. Firstly, the mean category scales obtained are close to linearity. In conjunction with our previous studies (Bovet, 1968) this means that for the perception of duration a geometrical progression of stimulus duration leads to a more regular discrimination than does an arithmetic progression.

Secondly the marginal distribution of the responses is, as usual in absolute judgments, arch-shaped. That is to say that the extreme categories of responses appear less often than the medians. But this effect is less when the subject is given knowledge of his results.

TABLE II

Stimulus response Confusion Matrix for subject 0 (without knowledge of results)

	$R1$	$R2$	$R3$	$R4$	$R5$	Σ	$m(R)$
$S1$	10	25	3	2	0	40	1.93
$S2$	3	13	21	3	0	40	2.60
$S3$	0	6	26	8	0	40	3.05
$S4$	0	2	14	21	3	40	3.63
$S5$	0	0	5	20	15	40	4.25
Σ	13	46	69	54	18	200	

Discussion

This experiment, which is part of a larger study designed to develop probabilistic models of psychological mechanisms, would have been impossible without on-line computer control. It is worth emphasising that this implementation was achieved with an inexpensive minimal laboratory computer: a PDP-12 with 4K memory and no oscilloscope display. Although the consequent absence of the DIAL compiling system limits the flexibility available to the programmer, it was relatively easy to develop a powerful and effective program using FOCAL which is an interpretative language. Consequently it was possible to automate the experiment completely, including the control of the randomisation of the stimuli and the recording of data, the progress of the experiment, including the value of amount of information being transmitted (Q), and the subject's responses, continually throughout the experiment. The recording of data on papertape means that it was possible to make an immediate and complex computer analysis without any intermediate manual transcription. More important than the facilitation of presentation recording and analysis which the laboratory computer provides is the facility it gives the experimenter to implement experiments such as that described here, which require as immediate feedback an analysis of the subject's response. In this case the control in a geometrical ratio of the scale of stimuli presented produced, as predicted, a real regulation of our subject's performance when these departed from either side of the set standard. The complexity of computational formulae of the amount of transmitted information which determines the regulation would have been impossible without the use of a computer.

Acknowledgements

This experiment was conducted in collaboration with D. Lepine and H. Rouanet at Centre d'Etude des Processus Cognitifs et du Langage. M. Kubryk kindly wrote the input—output machine language subroutines.

RICHARD M. FENKER, JR.*

The Use of Multivariate Statistical and Distance Models in the Study of Schematic Concept Formation

Summary

Multidimensional scaling techniques were used to study how humans discriminate and encode patterns belonging to statistically defined classes. Similarity judgments were obtained for pairs of patterns both visually and from memory. For the three sets of patterns having an underlying class structure, the visual and memory solution spaces were highly congruent, with the dimensions denoting sources of between- and within-class variance. The results suggest that information processing strategies for both discrimination and encoding are largely dependent on the statistical characteristics of the pattern sample. The utility of multidimensional scaling as a method for investigating the organization of patterns in memory was also demonstrated.

Introduction

Most information processing models of human behavior assume that the immediately apparent properties of an object represent the salient perceptual parameters as well as the bases for encoding or inferential judgments (Garner and Felfoldy, 1970; Fenker, 1971). A property or cue achieves the status of a dimension when enough objects are compared with it to define some sort of order. Cue dimensions can be dichotomous or many valued, but in either case they reflect the degree to which objects possess the corresponding property.

* Texas Christian University

Although the literature on perception is replete with studies establishing the relationship between a limited set of physical dimensions and perceptual responses (Zusne, 1970; Evans, 1970), there is a paucity of research concerned with the process by which humans select certain dimensions as useful in certain situations. Also, while it is assumed that the perceptually relevant properties of objects can be represented as dimensions, there has been little experimental work which deals with the question of whether or not objects are encoded in terms of these dimensions.

The Selection of Cue Dimensions

I am proposing that the selection and weighting of cue dimensions is a process dependent on three interrelated components: the "statistical regularities" present in the stimulus variation, the information processing requirements associated with particular perceptual tasks, and the learned relationships between the statistical regularities and particular task requirements. According to Brunswick (1956), perceptual experience consists of associations formed between object values on a set of cue dimensions and inferences made about the objects. After one encounters a sufficient number of objects related to a particular cue dimension, it becomes possible to estimate a frequency distribution for that object property. Moreover, since the perception of the cues generally takes place within the context of a particular task, the distribution of cue values becomes associated with inferences required by the task.

There is evidence to suggest (Beach, 1964) that in classification tasks in which subjects are presented with the value of an object along a cue dimension they will choose the class that has the greatest relative frequency of association with that cue value. In the case of discrimination tasks, Cornelius (1971) showed that subjects learned to select cues on the basis of their variance within the given sample. What these studies (and many others) indicate is that, through experience with a collection of objects, the distributions of the objects along the cue dimensions are learned, and that the associations between these distributions and various inferential tasks determine the corresponding information processing strategies.

Statistical Regularities

The term "statistical regularity" refers to any distribution of objects along a cue dimension (or dimensions) which provides a source of information relevant to a particular perceptual task. There is evidence that such distributional properties can be learned without specific instructions or feedback (Peterson and Beach, 1967; Shipstone, 1960). This suggests that the regularities reflect the structure imposed on a probabilistic environment by our information processing mechanisms. Also, because the task-related statistical regularities represent an important part of the information encoded about the objects, these regularities should be reflected in the organization of the objects in memory.

In this report, the statistical regularities of interest are those which permit objects to be grouped into classes or schema families. The orderliness in this case is defined by the redundancies present in a collection of objects belonging to the same class. These redundancies can be represented mathematically as a set of covarying cue dimensions defining a cluster of points in a multidimensional space. Since in most situations the association between object values on a cue dimension and that object's class membership are probabilistic, a subject may require the "redundant" information present in several dimensions in order to make an equivocal decision.

Multidimensional Scaling

In order to study the influence of the statistical regularities present in a sample of stimuli on both the discrimination and later encoding of the stimuli, a methodology for obtaining information about the underlying cue dimensions is needed. Multidimensional scaling analysis (MDS) is especially useful in this respect because it provides a means for obtaining estimates of these dimensions directly from human responses rather than indirectly through correlation of the responses with physical measures. Also, it provides a unique methodology for investigating the encoding and retrieval of nonverbal materials. The judgments required for a MDS analysis are estimates of the degree of difference or similarity between two stimuli. Such judgments can be the result of a verbal analysis of the stimuli or a highly intuitive perceptual comparison. The important point is that the nature of the task, similarity estimation, has not predisposed subjects to use one or the other type of analysis for their judgments. They are free to respond on the basis of whatever strategy best reflects their visual impression or memory of the stimulus material.

Multidimensional scaling procedures transform the similarity judgments into "distances" between the stimuli in a psychological space and then determine the coordinates of the stimuli along the dimensions of the space. These dimensions are assumed to represent the important attributes of the objects. This procedure of recovering the axes underlying perceptual judgments has been applied with enormous success to a large variety of stimulus domains, including schematic faces, words, attitudes, personality characteristics, nations, colors, geometric patterns, and many others. Recently Dansereau *et al.* (1970) and Shepard and Chipman (1970) have used this procedure to study memory phenomena.

Now, granted that it is possible to get people to estimate the similarity or difference between two objects, and also that their judgments may be based on several cue dimensions: how does the similarity data tell us anything about those underlying subjective dimensions? To illustrate how MDS procedures extract information about subjective dimensions from estimates of the similarities or differences between stimuli, consider the following example. Suppose I showed you three photographs of women, one of whom had a beautiful face (A), another of whom had an outstanding figure (B), and a third with neither of these blessings (C). When you estimated the degree of difference between the photographs your judgments were: $AB = 5$; $AC = 4$; and $BC = 3$. Now if these judgments were actually based on a single underlying subjective dimension, then it should be possible to position the pictures along this dimension in such a way that the distances match the judgments. Fig. 1 illustrates this problem.

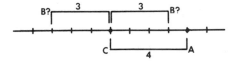

Fig. 1. A one-dimension representation of three points with the following interpoint distances: AB = 5, AC = 4, BC = 3.

If we take the first two distances AC and BC as fixed and assume that B must also lie on the same subjective scale as A and C, then B can occupy one of two possible positions. These are at distances of 1 and 7 units from A. But the obtained distance AB as given by the subject is 5 units. Thus the three distances are incompatible with the supposition that the three pictures lie on the same subjective scale. In this case you can see that a two-dimensional space would be necessary to represent the difference judgments since they form the sides of a right triangle. The dimensions of the space are represented by the two axes in Fig. 2. By examining the projections of the three stimuli on these axes it would be possible to identify Dimension 1 as a cue which discriminates the pictures on the basis of facial beauty while Dimension 2 corresponds to figural goodness. Although the interpretation of psychological dimensions underlying a MDS analysis is not always so straightforward, this example illustrates the basic procedure. By determining the proper number of dimensions necessary to explain the inconsistencies in judgment data and then representing the stimuli in a space of this dimensionality, MDS procedures make it possible to discover the dimensions underlying complex judgments.

To summarize what I have said to this point, the current paper has two major objectives. The first objective is to demonstrate the importance of a type of statistical regularity, the presence of stimulus classes, on the perception and encoding of sets of stimuli. The second objective is to illustrate the use of MDS analysis as a technique for revealing the subjective cue dimensions underlying both visual and memory similarity judgments. These objectives are closely related since it is proposed that

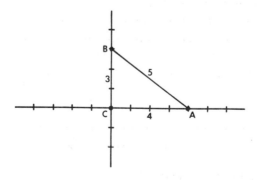

Fig. 2. A two-dimensional "beauty" space.

the class-defined regularities will influence the selection of the cue dimensions in the visual and memory tasks and hence be reflected in the distributions of the stimuli along these dimensions.

Experiment 1

In the first study that I will report (other parts of this study were previously reported by Dansereau *et al.* 1970) our goal was to determine whether the presence of statistically defined classes would influence the way subjects encoded a set of abstract patterns. Two sets of eighteen saw-toothed stimuli were constructed by mapping 14-element digit sequences into column heights, then connecting the columns. One set of patterns consisted of three different schema families generated using the VARGUS-9 procedure (Evans and Mueller 1966). Four of these patterns from two different schemata are illustrated in Fig. 3. Each family had six members. The other set of eighteen stimuli was generated by randomly permuting the elements of each of the schematic patterns.

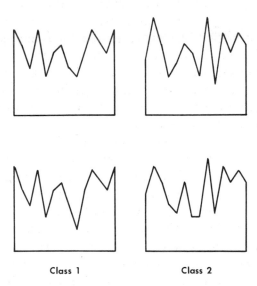

Class 1   Class 2

Fig. 3. Four eighteen-element VARGUS-9 patterns from two different classes.

137

Two independent groups of subjects were used, one for each pattern condition. Each group of subjects first estimated the visual similarity between all possible pairs of the eighteen patterns. They then learned paired associate responses (nonsense syllables) to each of the patterns. When they gave 100 per cent correct associate responses on three successive trials, it was assumed the patterns had been encoded. At this point, subjects were presented with pairs of the nonsense syllables associated with the patterns and asked to estimate the similarity of the corresponding patterns from memory.

Both the visual and memory similarity judgments for the two pattern conditions were analyzed using Kruskal's (1964) non-metric scaling procedure. The results for the schematic stimuli were quite impressive. First of all the visual and memory spaces were three-dimensional and essentially identical. When the two solutions were superimposed on the same three-dimensional plot, the congruence between the spaces was quite apparent. Secondly, while we were not able to identify any of the dimensions of the spaces in terms of physical measures (a linear combination of column heights) a more contextual interpretation was possible. The stimuli in each of the three classes varied primarily along only one dimension, each class having its respective dimension, while the three dimensions together clearly separated the classes in the multidimensional space. These results suggest that within-class comparisons were made on the basis of a single class-specific dimension. Despite the fact that no physical interpretation is available for these dimensions it is clear that each defines an ordering of the patterns which reflects discriminable within-class variance. It is interesting to note that the class prototypes always appeared in the center of the distributions of the classes on their respective dimensions.

The multidimensional scaling solution indicates that the relevant cue dimensions were associated with the statistical regularities present in the sample, the class structure, and that these same dimensions were utilized both in visual comparisons of the stimuli and in encoding as reflected by the memory comparisons. What makes these results even more interesting is that while the scaling solutions for the nonschematic stimuli were also not interpretable in terms of column height measures, there was no apparent similarity between the visual and memory solutions in this latter case. It appears that the statistical regularities present in the schematic sample provided a basis for encoding, but that when this type of salient variation was eliminated the cue dimensions employed in the visual discrimination task were not used for encoding. While you might attribute these results to random behavior on the part of subjects in the nonschematic conditions, intra-subject reliabilities and inter-subject correlations were reasonably high (> 0.60) for both groups.

Experiment 2

One question which concerned us after this first study was to what extent the pattern format had influenced these results. As a part of a second series of experiments conducted by Don Hastings and myself (Hastings *et al.*, 1971) this problem was dealt with in part.

Two groups of 20 patterns were constructed. The first group consisted of two statistically defined classes in the saw-toothed format described previously. The second set of patterns was constructed by mapping the column heights of the first set of patterns into radial lengths spaced in equal angular increments throughout 360°. When the ends of the radial lengths were connected, a polygon format resulted. The two types of patterns are illustrated in Fig. 4.

Two independent groups of subjects, one group for each pattern format, again judged the similarity of the patterns both visually and from memory. This time, however, the data were analyzed using Carroll's INSCAL[1] procedure (Carroll and Chang, 1970). In some respects, the results were quite similar to the previous study. All solutions were three-dimensional. In each case, one of the dimensions separated the two stimulus classes, while the other two represented sources of within-class variation as described above. Canonical analyses showed that, within each pattern format condition, the visual and memory solutions were highly congruent except that the patterns within the classes were clustered more tightly in the memory spaces than in the visual spaces.

---

[1] INSCAL is a multidimensional scaling program which makes stronger assumptions about the data (distances are assumed to be *linearly* related to similarity judgments rather than *monotonically* related as with the Kruskal procedure) but provides estimates of individual subject parameters (weights for the dimensions) as well as a stimulus space.

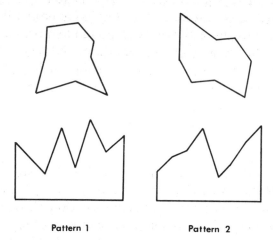

Pattern 1   Pattern 2

Fig. 4. Two patterns from different classes as they appear in polygon and saw-tooth format.

The scaling solutions make it apparent that subjects in both format conditions were using the statistical regularities associated with the class structure as the bases for visual comparisons and encoding. It was interesting to note, however, that there was essentially no correlation between the two within-class dimensions across formats. This lack of correspondence suggests that, while the distribution of stimuli along these dimensions reflects their importance in discriminating between members of the corresponding classes, there is little physical isomorphism between the dimensions across formats (for example, the format transformation preserved the statistical regularities in the sample but not any set of within-class features).

Conclusion

Considered together, these studies offer strong support for the hypothesis that information processing strategies are in part determined by the statistical regularities present in the stimulus sample. In every case where the sample continued a class structure, the underlying cue dimensions were directly interpretable in terms of the structure. There is also evidence for the influence of the perceptual task on dimension selection since all of the spaces containing classes had dimensions with distributions appropriate for both between- and within-class discriminations. Finally, the use of multidimensional scaling analysis as a procedure for evaluating the encoding of nonverbal materials was clearly successful as demonstrated by the congruence between the visual and memory scaling solutions.

Acknowledgement

This research was supported by the Department of Defense, Project THEMIS contract (DAAD05-68-C-0176), under the Department of the Army to the Institute for the Study of Cognitive Systems. Further reproduction is authorized to satisfy needs of the U.S. Government.

141

3. Games Playing and the Study of Thinking

In many countries games are not yet seen as an area of psychological research which will within the foreseeable future produce a worthwhile scientific product. This attitude is in part an example of that conceptual contamination which occurs so frequently in human thinking and which is known to psychologists as the Halo Phenomenon. Games as the average committee member recalls them are a relief from the serious aspects of life's struggle, and anything connected with them must *ipso facto* be frivolous. It is really a remarkable phenomenon that many western and eastern countries will spend very large amounts of public money on supporting sports and physical games but relatively little on intellectual games. Perhaps this is partly because in Anglo-Saxon and many European cultures concern about physical fitness preempts interest in mental health.

There are of course problems other than semantic difficulties and cultural biases. The status of psychology itself is insecure and the direction of the lines which future research will take often lies in the hands of those who are most conservative. It is also true that in the past, research into games playing has been desultory and not very productive. The work on chess by Binet (1894) and on Pegity (Go Moku, Ren-ju or Five-in-a-row) by Rayner (1958a, 1958b) are examples of lines of work which have failed to develop fruitfully. Even the now classic work of de Groot (1946) to which several of the authors in the symposium have paid tribute might have lain relatively fallow if its potential had not been pointed out by Newell, Simon, Shaw and other workers in the

United States who had independently developed a similar protocol analysis technique. Another exception perhaps is the study of the relative importance of innate and cultural factors which determined the chess skill of the players in the international tournament at Moscow in 1925 undertaken by the Russian psychologists Djakow, Petrowski and Rudik (Brannasky 1927). Their conclusions that peasants could play as well as counts and that chess playing develops and strengthens general intellectual skills, may well have had considerable influence in determining the future official Russian attitude to chess and its active encouragement within the Soviet Union.

However, even if there have been psychological reasons for the neglect of games playing as a field of research, it is also true that the complexities of the problems involved have been greater than the experimental techniques available. In the past games have been too difficult and complex to provide laboratory experimental problems and insufficiently *real* for field studies. Games have fallen between two conflicting styles of psychology. To the social psychologist games seem trivial when compared with murder, suicide, marriage and economics. To the experimental psychologist they have been too complex for the experimenter to be able to control the relevant variables. Over the past few years a number of factors have been tending to redress this balance. Although less productive than first hopes predicted, the application by Von Neumann and Morgenstern (1944) of Emile Borel's mathematical theory of games to the field of economics and politics helped to lay a sound foundation for a combined sociological and mathematical approach to games themselves. Partly because of this theoretical development and partly for other reasons, both sociologists and psychologists have come to recognize not only that games from a useful microcosm in which to study interpersonal and group behaviour, but that game "involvement" is part of the formative structure of the developing child's environment. In adult life games are no longer regarded as extracurricular activities but as an integral part of a complex adaptive survival response. Extracurricular activities, as several large corporations realize, are an important component of an individual's stability at work. Currently it is fashionable to emphasize the homeostatic role of game involvement and to see work and play as comprising reciprocal activities providing relaxation or stress as is needed (Elias and Dunning 1970). Equally valid is the approach which sees game involvement in adult life

144

as the product of the pattern with which the developing child meets social tensions and stresses (Sutton-Smith, Roberts and Kozelka 1963). In the West, games involvement is primarily physical. It is an amusing sidelight therefore on the dangers of the statistical approach to report that from a survey of 12 countries, participation for male citizens in active sport runs highest in the Soviet Union, 30% compared with between 5 and 8% in the United States and 1% in Yugoslavia. The reason being that the average Russian likes to start the day with a few exercises (Robinson 1970). He is then free to devote his time to more serious matters such as chess.

Another factor which hurries the study of games towards intellectual respectability is the development of computer programs which mimic and, in the cases of simple games such as penny guessing, surpass human skills. In games of strategy the board position is fully determined or, as with poker, has well established statistical properties. It is his opponent's mind which forms the rich data base from which the human player develops sufficient strategies from insufficient premises.

In this section the papers, not surprisingly, deal mainly with games playing programs. One, however, by Rivka Eifermann provides a welcome link to wider, more immediate sociological issues.

RIVKA R. EIFERMANN*

Rules in Games

Summary

Games are not just a convenient laboratory microcosm for studying thinking. They are an inherent part of the developmental process. The study of a current game culture and game "rules" therefore can provide us with data on the development of the child's attitudes to and the effects of formal constraints on behaviour response in well-defined problem solving situations. In the present study, which is part of a series, a classification is proposed for game rules. These are first classified as regulations and instructions. The former are subdivided into requirements, prohibitions, rules of permission and "meta" rules. Some examples illustrating the development of rules in children's games are given and the relationship of rule structure to age and sex is discussed.

Introduction

In a recent article Coleman (1969) put forward the intriguing suggestion that games may be conceived of as "time out" from life, in the same sense that "time out" is used in games when a break is announced. In other words, games are to a large extent insulated from the normal "rules" prevailing in daily life by a set of explicit rules of their own which are in effect for as long as the game continues. This insulation does not, however, mean that game-rules form a special category of rules. On the contrary, games have often been treated in philosophical

* The Hebrew University of Jerusalem

discourse as providing a convenient and compact prototype set of rules, which can serve as a model for legal, moral, or linguistic rule classifications (Mayo, 1951; Hart, 1961; Black, 1962). Indeed, they also possess generic priority in the sense that relatively early in childhood they are voluntarily embraced, growing and developing both in meaning and complexity as the child grows older. It is not surprising, therefore, that early psychological research on children's moral development was concerned with their attitudes to the rules of a game, such as Marbles (Piaget, 1932); that game-like situations are devised for various types of psychological studies on the capacity to think logically (e.g. Bruner et al., 1956; Wason, 1969; Eifermann and Steinitz, 1971), as well as for the analysis of man-computer interaction in cognitive contests (Elithorn and Telford, 1969); and that analysis of board and poker games and their computer simulations have been conducted for the purpose of studying human thought processes (Elithorn and Telford, 1970; Clarke, 1972; Findler, 1972). Indeed, employing these natural games in this manner has a special appeal: They are amenable to graded analysis of problem complexity, their rules tend to be conveniently clear-cut, and they possess the added asset that they have withstood the test of time and are, in this sense, part of human reality, adapted to human needs and attractive to those engaged in playing them. They thus do not suffer from many of the severer limitations inherent in research on problem solving, as for example in most investigations on concept identification, where highly specialized laboratory "games" are played which have little to do with human concept acquisition (Bar Hillel and Eigerman, 1971).

However, in these divergent attempts to utilize games for psychological research, the *classification* of their rules with reference to their meaning, relative importance, or functions, has hardly been attempted. My purpose herein is to offer one such preliminary classification of game rules. I shall first briefly distinguish between two major classes of rules – *regulations* and *instructions* – a distinction not always explicitly made, with the result that the role of instructions and their relationship to regulations has often been ignored, even where it is of major importance for an understanding of the behaviour studied. Secondly, I shall distinguish four types of regulations, namely: *requirements, prohibitions, rules of permission,* and *meta rules,* a classification which may, hopefully, be a fruitful basis for various hypotheses concerning the place and function of these different regulations in games and perhaps in other situations as well. Finally, I shall present the results of a test of one such functional hypothesis, viz., that rules of permission and meta rules, in contrast to requirements and prohibitions, contribute to a game's flexibility, thus making it possible for a game's challenge to fit a great variety of players, and specifically enabling younger players to engage in games played by their older peers, a constant aspiration which can otherwise be rarely fulfilled.

The examples of games quoted herein, as well as the numerical analyses included in the course of this presentation, are all derived from data gathered in a large-scale investigation of children's games in school playgrounds and on streets in Israel, conducted under my direction with the aid of some 150 observers, a few years ago. The total number of game descriptions collected exceeded 2,000, and the cumulative number of players recorded was over 100,000. Since relevant details concerning the methods of investigation have already appeared in a number of publications (Eifermann, 1970a,b, 1971a,b, 1972), I shall not repeat them here.

Regulations and Instructions

First then, I shall distinguish, in a partial adaptation of Black's (1962) classification, between two senses in which the word "rule" is used: the "regulation sense" and the "instruction (direction) sense". When "rule" is used as an approximate synonym for *"regulation"* it is meaningful to refer to it as announced, put into effect, enforced, reinstated, broken. Rules, in this sense, may also be said to have histories — they come into effect, suffer modifications, cease to be in effect, and so on. In a specific game situation, they are, however, remarkably constant and furthermore, while new games undergo extensive and quick modifications (see an example of such a game in Eifermann, 1971a, p. 54ff.), their regulations seem to change little over generations of players once stabilization has been achieved (Opie and Opie, 1969). For this reason, it may be particularly revealing to understand why some changes nevertheless do occur, and I shall discuss one such change in the following section.

Instructions, in contrast with regulations, evoke contexts in which

149

some purpose is in view and it is therefore appropriate to refer to them as useful, misguiding, or useless. Unlike regulations, of which the players of any specific game must be in full command in order to be able to play, knowledge of instructions is not essential for participation, although such knowledge may enhance success. A few distinguishing examples may be enlightening: Children playing Commander Said[1] know the regulation that players must not follow any commands which are not prefaced by the words "Commander said". However, they may or may not be aware of the instruction which endows the knowing leader with the following strategy: repeating a string of commands preceded by "Commander said" and then rapidly intercepting one omitting the formula — e.g., "Commander said, scream!" (they scream), "Commander said, stop!" (they stop), "Commander said, scream!" (they scream again) and then just "Stop!" (they stop...). Similarly, in Heavens Hopscotch a player should know that he must first throw the stone into box number 1 of the Hopscotch (a regulation); he may or may not be aware that, when playing on a pavement, he would be well advised to choose a flat stone, which will slide easily (an instruction). Again, when playing Sliding Ring (in which two groups compete in sliding the greater number of rings onto their pole), each of the groups has its own pole holder and may choose any of its members to fill this role (a regulation); but it is wise to choose the fastest and most alert player for this role, since he will be able to hold the pole in the direction of the approaching rings and thus "save" poor shots (an instruction).

Instructions

The importance of such practical instructions as quoted above cannot be overestimated, since they represent skills acquired through the individual player's practice, as well as the wisdom of experience accumulated by previous generations of players. Indeed, when children are requested to describe a game they will often spontaneously insert instructions into their descriptions. In addition to these evidently useful

---

[1] All games referred to herein are included in our research Encyclopedia of Games, a small sample of which appears in Eifermann (1971a).

instructions there are numerous others, whose usefulness may not be obvious to the nonplayer, and particularly the adult. Such are the various ritualistic and magical devices as, e.g., charming a rolling marble by chanting "Roll, roll, tootsie roll,/Roll, marble, in the hole" (Opie and Opie, 1969); saying "For life or death" so as to ensure a safe landing before, say, vaulting over a huddled group of five bending friends; or shaking a dice in the cup of one's hand, or blowing on it for good luck, before throwing it; or indeed, any other magical means of "ensuring" luck, courage or favour or, equally, of preventing catastrophe. In most cases children draw a clear distinction between what is for their own good (behaviour according to instructions) and the formal framework of the game (regulations). However, it is interesting to speculate on the possibility that, e.g., certain rituals found in games, which are required by the game's regulations, may have been integrated into the latter from their original status of instructions. Indeed, it is revealing in this connection to present the relevant part of our findings on various forms of verbalization in games: In our classification of verbal usages occurring in games, we distinguished between ritualistic, dramatic, narrative, descriptive, informative, instructional and other usages (Eifermann, 1970c[1]). In the course of this analysis we found, to our great surprise, that the numbers of those playing games requiring ritualistic verbalization, which (logically) has no effect on the game's outcome, tended to increase rather than decrease, with age! Table I gives the findings obtained from recordings of free play of rule-governed games during recess in two Jerusalem schools, one of high—middle and one of low socioeconomic levels (for details concerning these schools see Eifermann 1971a). Since the general trend in both schools was the same, the results have been combined for present purposes. The table shows that there is a significant age-related increase in the proportion of players of games involving ritualistic verbalization, out of the respective total number of players of all games analysed, both in the case of boys and girls. This rather puzzling finding can perhaps be understood as a manifestation of *role distance* — a concept adopted from Goffman (1961), which I have already discussed in another, related context (Eifermann, 1971b). We may accordingly say (with reasonable assurance), that as children grow older they become increasingly doubtful about the ef-

---

[1] I would like to thank Adrian Toma for his assistance in this analysis.

TABLE I

Number of boy players and girl players of games requiring verbal ritual and their respective percentages out of all boy- and girl-players of games requiring verbalization

	Age groups of players *			
	6–8	*8–10*	*10–12*	*12–14*
Number				
Boys	50	112	177	126
Girls	41	95	248	113
Percentage				
Boys	3.82	9.02	19.54	29.79
Girls	2.63	4.90	22.59	33.63

* The differences between successive pairs of age groups are all significant at $p < 0.01$ level, on a test of significance of difference between proportions in independent samples.

fectiveness of ritual as a contributory factor to success in games. At the same time, a faint feeling that it may help and that some chance may be missed if it is neglected may linger on. Moreover, the ritual may be enjoyable as an activity in its own right. However, while it retains the status of an instruction, i.e., something that is done because of its presumed usefulness or effectiveness, carrying it out stigmatizes the older player as one still possessed of "babyish" beliefs. Distance from such a compromising status is achieved once the instruction is formalized into a fully fledged regulation: the ritual must then be carried out simply because it is a requirement of the game. Thus the player achieves "role distance" from the naive believer in magical devices, while at the same time "playing safe", and/or with greater pleasure. In other words, the compulsion to carry out the ritual is thus transformed, at least formally, from an internalized to an induced phenomenon via the formal framework of the game. This line of thinking leads to the further speculation that if some instructions are transformed into regulations in older children's games, then the proportion of instructions out of all game-rules should be smaller among older than among younger children. A test of this possibility was conducted by examining the percentage of boy players and girl players of variants of Marbles in four schools. It was found that while the percentage of girl players of variants containing one or more instruction was 9.0 in the age range 6−10, there was a significant drop in this percentage to 5.6, in the age range 11−14. In the case of boys, however, there was a slight, though non-significant increase in the corresponding percentages, from 6.1 to 6.6 per cent. Since the number of boys playing Marbles was, on the average, far greater than that of girls and since the percentage of instructions out of all rules was altogehter small (15.1 per cent), comprising 13 instructions in all, these findings remain inconclusive.

Regulations

Requirements, prohibitions, rules of permission and meta rules, are four types of regulations which I shall distinguish here. Let me begin with the predominant type, requirements.

Requirements

Regulations form the backbone of the game. Those which are required dictate the action in the most clear-cut manner: "You must count to 100 before looking around" (in Hide and Seek); "After 'ones' comes 'twos' " (in Jack Stones); "The first player runs in, skips and says 'A', the next says 'B' etc." (in Jumprope, "alphabet" style); "Each player writes down a number" (in Bull's Eye). Since most game rules are of this type, examples could, of course, be multiplied endlessly. Indeed, as already mentioned, in the construction of simple laboratory games as well as in the analysis of man-computer interaction in play, attention has been centred largely on this type of regulation. The point to notice about such rules is that once a player has entered a game, or at least once he has selected a particular course of action in the game (see rules of permission below), it is these requirements that dictate what he will do, and how − though the extent of freedom permitted the player regarding specific modes of operation varies considerably even here.

Prohibitions

Rules of prohibition, on the other hand, dictate what should not be done, or in what manner the game should not be played: one must not tread on the line in Hopscotch; nor kick the ball out of the field in Soccer; nor should one under any circumstances laugh in War of Laughs; nor hit too hard in Black Fist.

Both with regard to requirements and prohibitions, breaking rules often, though not always, carries penalties such as loss of points (or gain for the opponent), loss of property (e.g., marbles, apricot pits, coins and the like), forfeit of a turn, or even dropping out of the game altogether. Sometimes such actions "do not count", and the erring player merely tries again. The penalties themselves are also formulated as requirements or prohibitions, though their application only comes into force if the dictates of other rules are broken. The principles applying with regard to penalties of course correspondingly apply to rewards for successful performance.

Rules of permission

In contrast to the above types of regulations, rules of permission are not only non-obligatory, but − *ipso facto* − cannot, *in themselves,* carry penalties or rewards. They are characterized by greater flexibility than those of requirements and prohibitions. Often, they offer the player alternative courses of action. Thus, in *Mor* (a variant of Marbles), players may either try to hit an opponent's marble or one lying in the *mor* (hole in the ground); in Attention − Quiet! the leader may command another player not to move (Attention!), not to speak (Quiet!) or both at once; in Tic-Tac-Toe, players may put their marks in any free square they choose; in Five Stones (a variant of Jacks), a player may combine the sub-stages of "Changes" and "Planting", a procedure granting exemption from performing either of the two sub-stages separately. Alternatively, rules of permission offer the option of making a move or refraining from action: In Five Stones, for example, after all the stones have been pushed through the "gate", one may be picked up and tossed in the air while the remainder are snatched up. Success in this manoeuvre results in credit, but it is not an obligatory move; in Rescue Tag, it is up to each player to choose whether or not to attempt to rescue prisoners; in many variants of Tag, the "it" may, but need not, announce "Ten for all" before starting off in hot pursuit, thus giving the players a chance to move away from him; again, in a great variety of games, participants may, if they so wish, forfeit their turn in favour of others, even competitors.

All rules of permission thus offer various options, between action and non-action, and between alternative modes of operation or courses of action. However, in most cases — and despite whatever other considerations may exist — players must also take into account the fact that the alternatives are not of equal difficulty and do not necessarily offer the same pay-off. We shall return to this important point presently.

Meta rules

Another kind of option, which seems to me of special interest, though I have not seen it mentioned elsewhere, lies in the possibility, afforded by some games, of enforcing a rule drawn from an available "frozen" or "spare" repertoire. Once such a rule is admitted, it modifies, or even cancels, that basic regulation (or regulations) to which it refers. It may pertain equally to requirements, rules of permission or prohibitions, and it is usually put into effect through announcement, or by consensus. Thus for example, our observations have recorded the existence of the following meta rules: "With reminding" (e.g., in Hopscotch, where the basic rule requires that a player who forgets the order of the game's stages loses his turn); "Without drawing lines" (in Knives, where such marks on the ground denote a special way of occupying an opponent's territory); "Without *pus*" (where the announcement *"pus"* means a pause in the game); "Without strangling" (in Wrestling); "With ground support" (in Leapfrog, where no such support is normally permitted after vaulting); "Without looking at the funny faces" (in Elastic, in the stage in which the player must jump "without laughing" while the other players make funny faces). Meta rules thus evidently invalidate a basic regulation, or set of such regulations, for a step or stage in the game, or even for a complete round.

Flexibility and Challenge

I have elsewhere (Eifermann, 1971a,b) proposed the general hypothesis that, in order for a game to preserve its attraction, it must offer a challenge or challenges to its players, and that these challenges must be neither too difficult nor too easy. If they are too difficult, no play is possible; if too easy, the game will soon be given up. Furthermore, because of differences in ability, players of different ages, and even of the same age, may not agree over what constitutes a challenge. Hence, the more flexible the rules make a game, the greater the range of players who will perceive it as a challenge. It is in this connection that rules of permission and meta rules — because of the flexibility they offer — have a special function, which requirements and prohibitions cannot serve. In what follows, I shall elaborate this point.

In my classification of games according to their life span (Eifermann, 1972) I have contrasted Steady Games, which are played more or less constantly at all times, with Sporadic Games which are played only intermittently, in short "waves", never reaching great intensity. Thus, the element of challenge which can be adapted to fit different ages and abilities is characteristic of Simple Tag — a Steady Game — in sharp contrast to Running Matches, for example, which tend to appear only sporadically in the playground. In the former the players are allowed considerable flexibility in their mode of operation in the game: thus, the "it" is permitted to select either an easy or a tough "catch", while the other players are allowed to vary the extent of their involvement by either staying at a safe distance, or getting provocatively close and even otherwise teasing the player who is "it". Thus, both younger and older children, as well as weaker and stronger players, can play together, each at a level fitting his abilities relative to other players.

It should be evident that it is the existence of rules of permission which give the game this flexibility. Of course, such rules may also open the way to strategic considerations as, for example, in Checkers, or in Tic-Tac-Toe, where there is often an obvious best move, even though the option to choose a less promising move also exists (the special though very interesting case of games of pure chance will not be considered here). However, as we have seen with regard to Simple Tag, it is not always and not necessarily strategic considerations alone which determine the style of play where options are the rule. Correspondingly, a player of *Mor* (a variant of Marbles mentioned above), given the choice between a "sure hit" at an opponent's marble lying very close at hand, and an attempt at another marble further removed, may nevertheless aim at the latter, not necessarily because he is recklessly daring but rather because his opponent is no serious match for him. Such a course of action is, then, the only way in which he can maintain the game's challenge for himself and, in addition, retain the respect, or even gain the admiration of, possible onlookers. For such, or similar reasons, a player may try to hit his opponent's marble from an upright position, even though it is easier to hit it kneeling down; and other examples are, of course, numerous.

Parallel to this "upward" adaptation of the challenge on the part of the more skilful player, there is also a lowering of challenge, i.e., an adaptation of the game to the abilities of the poorer player, which makes it possible for him to participate in the game, and do so without losing face. Thus, in Simple Tag, as indicated above, a player may stay at a safe distance away from a tagger who is a far superior runner; in Five Stones, a player may carry out two simple stages separately rather than attempt to combine them; in Marbles he may aim at his opponent's marble from the convenient kneeling position, etc.

Meta rules function similarly to raise or lower the level of a game's challenge. A glance at the examples given on p. 12 should make this evident. There is an important difference, however, in that while with regard to most rules of permission the decision to act on one level or another (the choice between options) is in most cases left to the individual player, meta rules, once announced, usually apply to all players with the force of requirements or prohibitions. Their function seems, therefore, to lie less in enabling children with different levels of ability to play jointly, than in making it possible for groups of children who cannot cope with the more demanding level of play, to play – nevertheless – but at a level of challenge more fitted to their abilities. By the same token, groups of skilful players, when applying meta rules which make the game more difficult, can continue to enjoy a game which they might otherwise abandon as "too easy".

I would like to propose, however, that while rules of permission and meta rules, by virtue of the flexibility they introduce into games, have an important function for all age groups, their role is more significant where younger, rather than older children, are involved. Firstly, because the former often have no choice but to resort to simplifying rules of permission and meta rules in order to be able to play at all (whereas older children *can*, if they so wish, play on a low level of challenge); and more importantly, because younger children aspire, in their games, as in every other sphere of activity, to do "the same" as their elders. This aspiration is rarely capable of realization in full-scale reality, but is often clearly reflected in unstructured, "as if" play. Games containing rules of permission and meta rules often provide just this rare chance, and they therefore have a special appeal for the younger player, with no such parallel appeal for the older player.

The findings presented below indicate that indeed, at least with regard to the games analysed (variants of Marbles), the proportion of younger children playing games with rules of permission and meta rules is significantly greater than that of older children (more younger than older children play games in which rules of permission and meta rules occur, or occur to a greater extent). Before presenting these findings I shall elaborate somewhat on the nature of our data on Marbles, to which I have already briefly referred. The analysis was conducted on 20 descriptions of variants such as Hole Marbles, Hitting Marbles, Marbles King or Slave, *Daram*, Cherkas Marbles, and *Iyne*. These games were observed and recorded, through interviews with and demonstrations by children in four out of a total of 14 schools in which systematic recordings of all players in groups were conducted for at least one year, during free recess. On the basis of the rather detailed descriptions thus obtained (see Eifermann, 1971a, for examples) a careful analysis of the rules governing each variant was conducted by two independent judges[1] (after practising on games other than Marbles, not included in the present analysis). Altogether, 243 different regulations were distinguished. Agreement between the judges was obtained in 83 per cent of the cases; in cases of disagreement, a third (practised) judge was called in to arbitrate. For present purposes, the results obtained in the four schools (three town schools, two of low socio-economic level and one of middle-high level, and one kibbutz school) were pooled, since our interest here is in the examination of general developmental trends rather than specific sub-cultural differences. The data on boys and girls are, however, presented separately, since many of the variants of Marbles were in fact played predominantly by boys.

Table II gives the total number of regulations in each of the four types, viz., requirements, prohibitions, rules of permission and meta rules, and their percentage out of all regulations.

The table also gives the number of boy- and girl-players aged 6—10 and 10—14 who played Marbles according to each of the four types of regulation, and their percentage out of all players of Marbles, separately

[1] I would like to thank Jacob Golomb for his assistance in this analysis.

TABLE II

Four types of regulation in variants of marbles and the distribution of boy-players and girl-players according to these regulations

Type of regulation	Regulations		Players							Significance of difference between age group	
			Boys				Girls				
			Age: 6–10		10–14		6–10		10–14		
	N	%	N	%	N	%	N	%	N	%	Boys	Girls
Requirements	198	81.47	4546	75.82	2357	78.80	1596	73.55	1370	77.18	*	*
Prohibitions	6	2.47	38	0.63	22	0.74	0	0	22	1.24	n.s.	*
Permission rules	22	9.06	675	11.22	291	9.73	390	17.97	249	14.03	*	*
Meta rules	17	6.99	741	12.32	321	10.73	184	8.48	134	7.55	*	n.s.

* $p < 0.01$; n.s. = not significant.

for each sex and age group. Tests of significance of difference between percentages in independent samples were conducted to compare the two age groups with regard to each type of regulation, separately for boys and girls. The results are also presented in Table II. The results indicate a decline with age in the employment of rules of permission and meta rules, and a corresponding rise in the utilization of requirements and prohibitions. This trend is statistically significant in all but two cases, where the direction is, nonetheless, the same. The distribution of the four types of regulations indicates clearly the predominance of requirements, which are the core of the game, and the relatively sparse occurrence of prohibitions. The infrequency of "don'ts" can be meaningfully related to another of our findings derived in a different context, namely, that rewards for success in performance in games far exceed punishments for failure.

Conclusions

In experimental research on human thought processes, game-like situations are often employed. Computer-aided studies of human performance in games have been largely aimed at creating accurate simulations of man's play behaviour in such games as Chess and Poker, and at analysing the hesitations and types of errors made by subjects in simple games such as Halma. In this contribution I have tried to show that in addition to the analysis of actual human performance in specific game situations, a careful examination of the types of rules which make up natural games may be highly revealing in its own right. It can provide insights into the formal and semi-formal structure of closed systems which have evolved naturally and which are recognized and accepted (as a frame of reference for limited defined periods of time) because they are regarded as both manageable and attractive coping situations. I have tried to illustrate this through an analysis of children's games played between the ages of 6–14. This developmental approach is, I believe, particularly promising, since it seems to facilitate the tracing of the evolution of the needs and preferences for various types of rules, and offers a means of clarifying their varying psychological rather than purely logical functions.

Acknowledgement

Support for the data analyses reported in this paper was obtained from the Human Development Center, The Hebrew University of Jerusalem.

ALICK ELITHORN and ALEX TELFORD*

Design Considerations in Relation to Computer Based Problems

Summary

This paper describes three halma game playing programs which can be implemented on a small laboratory computer. The logic of the programs differs in a conceptually simple way, and these conceptual differences are related to the strength of the programs. The pattern of play obtained with the machine programs interacts with the competence of the human subjects. The characteristics of the programs play and those of the human players are shown to be a function of the quality of the opposition as well as of the production rules available to the program or player. It is argued that for psychological experiments on thinking there are considerable advantages in developing interactive – game – problems in which the complexity of the simulated opponent can be controlled systematically in a way that is conceptually simple.

Introduction

The content of psychological journals and text books shows clearly that the majority of psychological research deals with mental functions such as memory, visual perception, auditory perception and attention, and relatively little with thinking, problem-solving and planning.

Obviously the identification and separate study of the component elements of thought are of major importance, but there are pressing

* Medical Research Council, London

social reasons why psychologists should study human planning skills as such. It is only by studying thinking, or problem-solving, as an integrated goal-orientated performance that we can analyse the central control mechanisms which relate the component parts together. Indeed it is probable that some of the more important features of such integrative mechanisms may be relatively independent of the characteristics of the elements they integrate.

In the past, psychologists have had considerable difficulty in devising laboratory situations suitable for the objective and critical study of plan development. From time to time they have turned to games as a source of relatively simple micro-environments in which to study planning, but in general they have found the situations too complex for an adequately controlled analysis. Although the power of computer techniques may at times have been overstated, they undoubtedly allow the use of more variables and higher levels of interaction than is otherwise possible. Consequently, psychologists can, with the aid of computer techniques, handle problems which are appreciably more complex than those which they could handle in the past. The work of Newell and Simon and their collaborators forms a good example.[1]

In productive thinking subjects proceed from a premise to a conclusion — from a given starting point to a goal with specified characteristics. Indeed, any problem can be considered as a network of pathways from which the problem solver must seek a subset which links the initial and goal states. Only in the case of very simple problems can human subjects undertake a complete search of all possible paths and choose the one which gives an acceptable solution. We argued — largely intuitively — heuristically — that a fruitful class of problems is one in which the parameters which determine the areas to be searched can be clearly defined and manipulated systematically so that a set of problems can be generated which have optimal characteristics and secondly, that there are very considerable advantages in choosing a problem which lends itself to programmed machine solutions.

There are two major classes of machine program which should be considered. Simulation programs which model the hypotheses which the experimenter has about his human subjects, and man-aided artificial

[1] A source reference published since this paper was written: Newell and Simon (1972).

intelligence programs in which the solution strategies programmed are designed to take full advantage of the capabilities of the computer hardware available. The latter type of program has three important roles to play. In the first instance, a comparison of their performance with that of human subjects will reveal classes of behaviour, e.g., the accurate storage and recall of large amounts of data — which the mechanisms subserving human thinking cannot mimic. Contrariwise they also reveal functions e.g., associative type memory, in relation to which it is the performance of the human subject which is difficult to imitate. Secondly, the responses made by such programs may assist in classifying the responses made by subjects. Finally, in studying problems which involve the social interaction of individuals, it is invaluable to have an automaton whose behaviour can be controlled and systematically varied.

We have stressed elsewhere (Elithorn and Telford, 1970) the value of being able to manipulate the parameters which determine problem difficulty in a systematic way. In the present paper we suggest that the principles apply particularly to the use of computer programs as experimental tools and that the application of these principles brings an important area of experimentation within the range of laboratories with limited computing resources.

It has been argued that the study of game playing forms a useful tool for psychologists because games are models of reality. This is an attractive half-truth. Many games are part of reality: they occur naturally and as a form of play have a function in real life. On the other hand, games which model reality differ from reality in that in the modelled situation failure does not carry the same consequences as it does in real life. However, in both Russia and Japan it has been claimed that those who exhibit mental adroitness, persistence, courage and overall competence in model war games such as chess are likely to be amongst those who are most competent in the reality of war itself. Whatever the degree of truth there is in this assertion, there is no doubt that in games of strategy the player exhibits a variety of intellectual functions.

The fundamental difference between puzzles and games and between problems in the calculus and social problems is that in the case of games and social problems the problems contain indeterminate features. These are indeterminate not because of chance or random elements but because they are determined by the unknown structure of irrational opponents, or collaborators. In this respect many games model social situations and consequently enable us to study social intelligence. In particular, games of strategy may be especially suitable for studying how man develops a planned approach to solving a problem and the way he acts and adapts when his plans are continually thwarted by a planner with a different and conflicting objective.

Board Games

The development of computer techniques has given very considerable impetus to the use of games of strategy as a vehicle for the study of human thinking. Although something useful about thinking could probably be learned from the study of most games, it seems reasonable to assume that some games may be better vehicles than others. As Eifermann points out, games of strategy and board games in particular do not suffer from some of the severe limitations inherent in the use of highly specialized laboratory games. (Bar Hillel and Eifermann, 1970, quoted in Eifermann, 1972). Some of the factors determining the choice of game have been discussed in an earlier paper (Elithorn and Telford, 1970). In this we described a problem paradigm A is B in which an initial set of cartesian co-ordinates has to be transferred under the rules of a given calculus to a defined goal set. In its simplest form, and with the introduction of an alien intelligence making alternative transformations, this is equivalent to an archetypal race game, Cain and Abel. A single simple addition to the calculus of operations gives a set of games which includes halma, grasshopper and Chinese checkers. This addition is the hop move described below.

Halma (Fig. 1) is a popular children's game which is played either on a special board or on a chess board, when it is known as grasshopper. In the latter case each player has an army of ten men located in opposite corners of the board. Each player tries to move his own army into his opponent's camp before his opponent can occupy his camp. The rules governing the movement of the pieces are very simple. At each turn a player may move his piece using the same move as the King in chess or alternatively using a hop move. This move is the same as that allowed to a King in checkers except that hops can be orthogonal as well as diagonal and there is no capture. Halma is essentially a race game and the

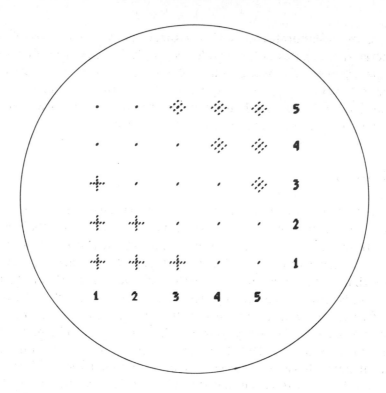

Subject 9		Subject 3			
subject's moves	program's moves	subject's moves	program's moves		
44 33:	12 34	35 34:	21 23		
33 23:	11 33	55 33:	13 24		
23 12:	21 23	53 13:	24 35		
53 52:	22 44	45 43:	23 45		
52 41:	31 51	54 32:	22 42		
41 31:	33 43	43 21:	31 22		
54 32:	34 54	32 31:	42 43		
55 33:	44 55	34 32:	22 24		
33 22:	13 53	44 22:	43 44	13 33:	35 24
35 34:	51 52	13 23:	12 54	31 13:	53 42
32 21:	43 44	32 12:	35 55	23 32:	24 35
34 24:	23 25	33 13:	24 35	22 31:	11 22
24 13:	25 35	23 33:	44 53	33 11:	42 43
45 43:	54 45	13 23:	35 24	32 23:	22 33
43 32:	52 54	33 13:	24 35	23 22:	33 44

Fig. 1. Starting positions and co-ordinate references for games of reduced halma (6 a side on a 5 × 5 board). The moves of two games from the tournament are given as examples of play. In both cases the program is L1P.

hop move creates hostile and co-operative "social" relationships between the pieces. It is the manipulation of these relationships which
comprises the halma skill and determines the rate of movement of the
whole army.

The Simulated Opponent

The fact that one can develop highly sophisticated complex games
playing programs on large and powerful computers does not necessarily
mean that it is a waste of time programming games on a smaller laboratory machine. Except for the fortunate few the difficulties and cost of
playing even relatively simple games with a large computer are prohibi-
tive. The main gist therefore of our thesis is that the right choice of
game will allow computer-based research in games playing to become a
useful tool for research, even when computing facilities are limited. We
shall illustrate this thesis by describing briefly the characteristics of
some halma playing programs which one of us (A.T.) has written for a
small laboratory computer with only 4K 12 bit core store and no
additional backing store. These programs have been written for on-line
experiments in which the human subjects interact directly with the
program. Since the same computer is used to generate and refresh the
display, to communicate with the human player through a teletype, and
to time the subject's responses, and since a small proportion of the core
is retained for operating programs, the amount of core available for
playing games is approximately 3.2K. The instruction set of about 30
instructions is small for a current 12 bit machine, but the add time at 3
microseconds is, for this generation of machine, relatively fast. These
are minor points, the main issue being that the most complicated program we describe here consists of only 2.5K 12 bit instructions. This
means that considerably more complicated programs could be implemented on the type of minicomputer which is shortly going to become
a universal and indispensable item of laboratory equipment. A further
implication is that the implementation of this approach in time-sharing
mode would allow the development of even more powerful programs.

In writing these programs the aim has not been to create a powerful
player or to simulate human players but to develop programs which
would be useful in studying human play. Basically, this means that we

needed to produce programs capable of giving an enjoyable and challenging game to players with a wide range of ability. A secondary but important aim was to produce programs with a simple conceptual structure which could be varied systematically. Such programs would allow the evaluation of an experimental subject's style in terms of a variable opponent and would also allow an analysis of his ability to perceive and respond to the strategy set which his automated opponent was using.

Structure of the Programs

The three programs described here, LØM (Level-zero Manhattan), L1M (Level-one Manhattan) and L1P (Level-one Planning) use a simple measure of distance from goal for each army as the evaluation function for move selection. This measure is sometimes known as the Manhattan distance. If a piece moves (legally) from A to B with co-ordinates (x,y) (X,Y) respectively, and B is the nearer to goal, then the Manhattan distance is:

$$D = (X + Y) - (x + y)$$

LØM (Level-zero Manhattan)

This program which was written first is the simplest of the three. Its central feature is a search routine which evaluates as described above all legal moves for the computer's own men. If there is a D value > 2 a move with the highest value is selected. For $D = 2$ a laggards routine is called which chooses a move of this length for the piece furthest from goal. If D is < 2 then a routine "sideways move" is called. This latter routine tests every legal move and finds a minimum unsigned Manhattan route to an empty goal position. In this program and in the programs described below, the program chooses between moves of equal value by taking the move that is first on the list. Currently we are developing versions in which "ties" are resolved by a randomization routine.

L1M (Level-one Manhattan)

This program looks ahead in the sense that it tests the effect of its own possible moves on the best reply by the subject. In other words it searches for all possible moves for its own men and for all possible replies by its opponent. Every legal move for the machine is evaluated and the Manhattan score (B) of these base moves is stored. For the board configurations arising from each machine move the program then computes the value D_{max} for its opponent's replies and calculates the value $E = B - D_{max}$ for each legal machine move. The program then selects the move with greatest E. If more than one move has value E_{max} that with the greatest B is selected. As in LØM, if B is zero or less the sideways routine is called.

L1P (Level-one Planning)

This is the same as L1M with the addition that when the program evaluates the subject's (machine opponent's) reply it also evaluates its own best next move, giving two quantitites $D_{max\ subj.}$ and $D_{max\ mach.}$. This latter evaluation does not however take account of the possible effect of the subject's next move. To do this would require much more machine time. The evaluation produced is now:

$$E = B - D_{max\ subj.} + D_{max\ mach.}$$

The effect of introducing $D_{max\ mach.}$ is to enable the program to plan ahead for long moves which can be generated by a current move. These, however, may be thwarted by the subject if he perceives the threat. For all these programs the time required for move generation is not very great. For the 5 × 5 board with 6 men the times are about 100 ms. for LØM and about 3 seconds for L1M and L1P.

The above programs will play halma games on boards up to 8 × 8. Apart from board size and shape — the board must be square — there are no restrictions on the army size or starting configurations. Either the machine or the subject may start. Although they are conceptually very simple, it is encouraging to find that these programs interact with human players in a way which throws light on the relative value of the production rules which determine the competences of the programs.

Evaluation of the Programs

In order to evaluate the relative strengths of the three programs a tournament was arranged between LØM, L1M, L1P and twelve adult halma players of widely varying competence. Since some of the players were relatively inexperienced and learning effects might occur, the order in which each player played the programs was randomized in two balanced blocks each of six subjects. The games were all on a 5 × 5 board with 6 men a side. The human player always had the first move.

Halma is a race game without capture and the extent of a victory or a defeat can be expressed as the minimum number of moves which would be required for the loser to complete the course. The results for this tournament are therefore presented (in Table I) in terms of wins, losses, draws and total points scored. By convention a plus sign indicates a

TABLE I

Results of halma tournament between 12 human players and the 3 computer programs *

Subject		Programs			
		L1P	L1M	LØM	Totals
Group 1	1	−1	−3	−3	−7
	2	−1	0	−3	−4
	3	0	−2	−1	−3
	4	+1	−1	−2	−2
Group 2	5	+1	0	−2	−1
	6	+2	−2	0	0
	7	+1	+1	−1	+1
	8	+1	0	+1	+2
Group 3	9	+2	0	+1	+3
	10	+1	+2	+2	+5
	11	+4	+2	+1	+7
	12	+5	+2	+3	+10
Totals		+16	−1	−4	

* The scores are the minimum number of moves required by the loser to complete the course. Computer wins +, human wins −.

computer win, a zero a draw, and a negative sign a computer loss. Both the players and the programs have been arranged in order of relative strength in terms of the outcome of the tournament. Since time prevented a tournament of all against all, a direct comparison of the players and programs is not possible. However, it is reasonable to divide the players into three groups of four: the least successful, Group 3, the most successful, Group 1, and an intermediate group, Group 2. Analyzed in this way it can be concluded that program L1P was weaker than Group 1 and stronger than Groups 2 and 3. LØM and L1M were both slightly weaker than the middle group of players, but markedly stronger than the weakest group. The order of halma competence therefore is Group 1 first, with L1P a close second. Next L1M, LØM and Group 2 are approximately equal in strength, while Group 3 is definitely weakest.

Having established relative differences in strength between the programs and different groups of players, it is relevant to ask whether the difference between programs and the differences between players represent differences in competence of a similar or different kind. The contributions which a computer program can make to analyses of this type are discussed in another paper (Elithorn and Cooper, 1972). At the present time we can only present some suggestive evidence from a simple preliminary hand analysis.

In comparing games playing programs we may usefully ask whether the patterns of play of the machine programs resemble human play and in particular whether changes in the pattern of play which relate to programs of different strength are similar to the differences which are found in play patterns for human players of different strength. Here a simple analysis which can be undertaken by hand is the distribution of moves of different lengths. Fig. 2 shows some sample histograms illustrating the pattern of moves made by the most and least competent computer program and by Groups 1 and 3 of the human players. Although there are quite marked differences between the patterns of play of the programs and of the human players, increasing competence is in both cases accompanied by an increase in the variance of the length of move generated and an analysis in terms of move length is reported below.

Game behaviour as with any interactive social behaviour needs to be evaluated both in terms of an analysis of the individual's own produc-

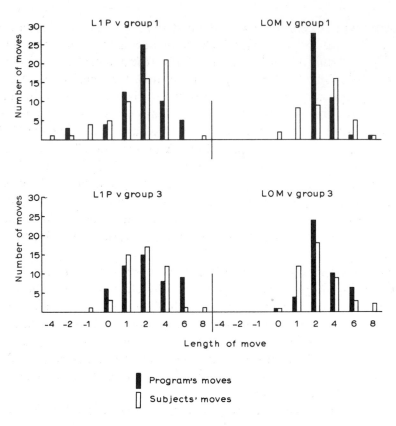

Fig.2. Distribution of moves of different lengths for games between Groups 1 and 3 and programs L1P and LØM.

tions and in terms of the effect that his productions have on his opponent's behaviour. An examination of the move profiles for each pairing of protagonists, 3 programs and 3 groups of players, suggested two simple statistics: the number of waiting moves (moves which produced no advance) and the proportion of game movement accomplished by long as opposed to short moves. Game movement is defined as the total Manhattan distance covered by an army at the time the game is won, drawn or lost. For the human player these statistics are summed over the four players in each group. For the machine programs they are summed over the four games played against each group of players. The proportion of game movement attributable to long moves is preferred

TABLE II

Analysis of each set of four games played between the three programs and the three groups of subjects

*(a) Total waiting moves **

Subjects	L1P		L1M		LØM		Total all programs	
	Moves by							
	Pro-gram	Sub-ject	Pro-gram	Sub-ject	Pro-gram	Sub-ject	Pro-gram	Sub-ject
Group 1	7	11	16	15	0	2	23	28
Group 2	13	13	4	2	0	0	17	15
Group 3	6	4	8	2	1	1	15	7
Total all groups	26	28	28	19	1	3	55	50

*(b) Percentage long move ratio ****

Subjects	L1P		L1M		LØM		Mean all programs	
	Moves by							
	Pro-gram	Sub-ject	Pro-gram	Sub-ject	Pro-gram	Sub-ject	Pro-gram	Sub-ject
Group 1	53	69	50	63	51	80	51.3	70.7
Group 2	59	60	54	50	53	65	55.3	58.3
Group 3	67	56	60	50	59	59	62.0	55.0
Mean all groups	59.7	61.7	54.7	54.3	54.3	68.0		

* Number of waiting moves ("Zwischenzug") (i.e., moves which produced no forward movement).
** Percentage long move ratio (i.e., ratio of distance travelled in moves of length 4 or more/distance travelled in moves of 2 or less × 100).

to the proportion of long moves since it gives an appropriate weight to different length moves. It appears from inspection that a suitable cutting point would be the ratio of moves producing an advance of four,

173

six or eight units related to moves of one or two units. In Table IIa this statistic is presented as the percentage of longer moves to all forward moves. Table IIb presents the number of waiting moves for the same sets of games. Looking first at the totals for the three groups of human players, it is clear, as would be expected, that increasing competence is accompanied by both an increase in the long move ratio and by an increase in waiting moves. At the interactive level, increasing competence on the part of the human players tended to produce a reduction in the long move ratios of all the programs and also an increased tendency for the latter to produce waiting moves.

The differences between the programs were almost equally consistent. Programs L1M and L1P produced an approximate equal number of waiting responses (28 and 26, respectively) whereas LØM produced only one waiting response. Similarly LØM and L1M produced virtually identical long move ratios which were affected in the same sense and to the same degree by the competence of the human players. Program L1P had a higher long move ratio than the other two programs, but this was also affected in the same way by the human players. With regard to interactive effects, both L1M and L1P stimulated the production of waiting moves by their opponents, the effect being more marked with Groups 1 and 2 than with Group 3. Both L1M and L1P produced a reduction in the long move ratio for the human players in relation to LØM but the effect was much more pronounced with L1M than with L1P.

The changes in performance shown by the human players in relation to their three levels of competence are entirely consistent with the hypothesis that increasing competence is associated both with an increasing ability to generate long moves and also with an increasing ability to thwart the development of long moves by an opponent. This being the case, it is difficult at first sight to see why the introduction of a blocking routine which represents an increase in a whole level of look-ahead should have so little effect on program strength, while the introduction of a smaller additional amount of look-ahead which ignores possible replies to the first move should have a much more marked effect. This is the more surprising since the introduction of the blocking routine does have quite a marked effect in reducing the long move ratio of the human players.

There are two areas of explanation. The first lies in the nature of the game structure and the second in the strategies of the human players. To take the latter point first, it would appear that the three subgoals of: find the longest move, prevent long replies, and plan a long move next time, are not introduced by the human subject in a serial or hierarchical fashion but are implemented with less or greater effects by players of lesser or greater competence. It also seems clear that the human players are not particularly good at finding the longest moves. Consequently the blocking strategy fails to work effectively with the less efficient human players because it is in effect deployed against moves that they would not have taken in any case. This interpretation receives some support from the fact that the effect of adding the blocking routine is most marked in play against the best group of subjects. Game structure is important in that it appears that a systematic blocking routine is of far less value than a limited amount of forward planning aimed at generating good moves.

The above analysis in terms of the pattern of moves made has been undertaken on the basis of a very elementary hand analysis. It seems likely that purpose-built analytic programs would allow more direct tests for specific production rules. Such a program has in fact been written and reported in another paper (Cooper and Elithorn, 1972).

Conclusions

The main aim of the paper has been to pursue the thesis that the study of human thinking will be facilitated by designing problems — experimental micro-environments — which are well defined and which maximise the utilisation of the facilities which even limited computer techniques bring to psychology.

No claim is made specifically for halma as an experimental game. It is, however, argued that there are great advantages in designing or selecting games which not only have a simple structure but which also lend themselves to simulation programs in which a variety of conceptually simple production rules can be embedded. The experimental results obtained support this viewpoint.

Acknowledgements

We are grateful to the Medical Research Council for the facilities provided and to many colleagues for their constructive criticism and in some cases their willingness to play "childish" games.

NICHOLAS V. FINDLER*

Computer Experiments on the Formation and Optimization of Heuristic Rules

Summary

First, a short review is given of a complex programming system that has been used to study a variety of aspects of human decision making within the framework of the game of Poker. This system is flexible enough to incorporate techniques aimed at discovering and improving heuristic rules. A detailed description of these techniques and the results obtained is followed by an outline of present and future research efforts.

Introduction

It is very rare indeed that a human decision maker relies exclusively, or even predominantly, on algorithmic processes. Further, the heuristic rules used instead are highly specific to the task and often difficult, if not impossible, to express precisely enough so that the researcher in psychology, political science or economics can formulate them in a computer program for further study. It is, therefore, a highly desirable objective to create a program that, having been put in the proper task environment, can discover useful heuristics, possibly in a parametrized format, and improve these on the basis of experience. One has to be careful of course, not to provide too much or too little guidance to the

* State University of New York at Buffalo

learning program in order to stay within a reasonably realistic and economic range of activity.

A few of us have been engaged in a long-term effort that aims at this goal. It is necessary here to give a short review of the basic system that is being adapted in this manner. A detailed description of it can be found in Findler et al. (1971), to which frequent references will be made.

The Basic System

The overall objective of our investigations is to find out how the decisionmaker's environment (real or assumed), his goal structure and value scale are combined by some cognitive program to result in a particular choice behavior. We stated in Findler et al. (1971):

"A realistic approach to study the problems of decision making seems to be to select a reasonably complex and rich environment, in which the relevant variables are easy to identify and relatively small in number. This idea will hopefully lead to the construction of a computer program that may serve as a rigorous model and theory, with high descriptive, explicatory and predictive power, of the information processes involved. One would expect to draw, on this basis, some conclusions of fairly universal validity, concerning decision making in general."

The reasons for selecting Poker as the domain of the experiments, a description of the decision processes in Poker, a qualitative and quantitative discussion of the information available to the players, and a summary of various game theoretical (mathematical) and computer models of the game are given in the earlier paper (Findler et al., 1971). Let it suffice to say here that Poker represents a social environment with elements of both risk and uncertainty. The stochastic components of the game contribute to situational variables as well as personality variables. The lack of perfect information lends to the game the most interesting aspects of "buying" information from the opponents and "selling" misleading information about oneself. The assessment of other players' characteristic style over past games, their current betting behavior, and one's own hand result in an expected outcome of the game and thereby prescribe a quasi-optimum decision sequence within the

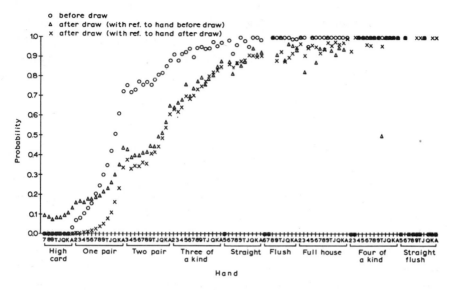

Fig. 1

framework of an individual strategy. The multilevel decisions thus made have both an immediate, tactical effect on the current game and a longer lasting strategical effect in projecting a certain image of the player. This will be discussed in detail later on.

In the first set of experiments, we tried to identify human decision making techniques by means of empirical investigations, to formulate these as explanatory hypotheses, and then to express them precisely as computer programs. An executive routine was written that assumes the banker's role and performs various housekeeping duties. Two series of Monte Carlo calculations (7 players in 10,000 games and 5 players in 30,000 games) were then carried out to estimate the probabilities of being high before and after draw, across the whole range of possible hands. The results of the 5-player run are shown in Fig. 1. This presents three types of information:

(1) The probability of being high before the draw with reference to the hands dealt (o).

(2) The probability of being high after the draw with reference to the hands dealt (△).

TABLE I

Partition	Range with	
	5 players	7 players
< low pair	all	all
low pair	2−8 (incl.)	2−10 (incl.)
high pair	9−A (incl.)	J−A (incl.)
2 low pairs	3−9 (incl.)	3−10 (incl.)
2 high pairs	10−A (incl.)	J−A (incl.)
low triple	all	2−9 (incl.)
high triple	all	10−9 (incl.)
more	all	all

(3) The probability of being high after the draw with reference to the hands held after the draw (×).

We arrived, by visual inspection, at the following partitioning of hands for the sake of heuristic rule generation in respective domains (Table I).

Within each partition, a straight line approximates the "experimentally" obtained points very well. We have thus structured, and can submit to analysis, a problem space that has been the sole domain of experienced judgement or, as is often referred to, "intuition". The role of "chunking", as defined by Miller (1956), is clearly indicated, both as a mnemonic device and as an information encoding scheme. A good decision maker's first task is to discriminate between strategically different stimuli after having set up relevant categories of the search space. The second task, to arrive at an optimum choice in each category, is discussed later.

A number of heuristic rules of strategical and tactical import can be derived from these results. These can be formulated in a flexible manner and further refined under various game-environmental conditions, such as:

(a) the ratio of people staying in the game after paying the ante;

(b) seating arrangement (number of players before and after the player in question);

(c) the number of raisers and checkers;

(d) odds offered by the pot;

(e) the nature of selected opponents and of the games played so far (conservative, fair, liberal, wild, etc.), and so on.

It is very important to find out which variables are "active" at given stages of the game, both from the psychological/descriptive and abstract/normative points of view. The human player is a limited capacity information processor. The size of his memory active at given times and his data processing ability are manifested in his search and decision making behavior. The second series of experiments served for the purpose of learning more about this.

Teams of two students in a course on List Processing Techniques supplied strategies of varying sophistication. As a first, somewhat crude, way of evaluating these, we simulated an "evening of play" among them, each having the same amount of money initially. In spite of some statistical fluctuations, very good and very poor players became clearly separated after a couple of hundred games. We then picked for further studies six players that had the most interesting (but not necessarily the best) strategies.

In order to eliminate the effects of good or bad hands and of a permanent seating arrangement, we adopted a practice similar to the one used in Bridge tournaments. We deal six hands that are then randomly assigned to the players, who in turn are randomly seated around the table. There are, therefore 6!5! = 86,400 different hand-player-seat

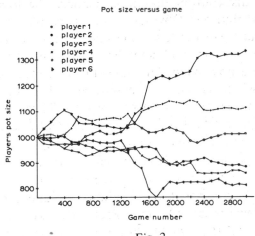

Fig. 2

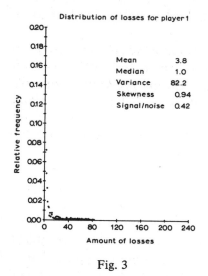

Fig. 3

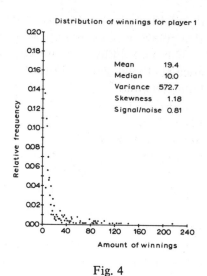

Fig. 4

arrangements (one player can be considered anchored to a constant seat). A *tournament* in our terminology consists of 300 games, each with a different arrangement. The arrangements are randomly selected from the 86,400 without replacement.

Ten tournaments have been played. The financial status of each player vs. games played is shown on Fig. 2. The most characteristic evaluation is based on the following ideas. Let us form for each player two probability distribution functions, namely the loss per game and win per game distributions. Obviously, for a good player the mean value of the first would be in the low-value region (close to that of the ante, which is one unit in our case) since he must realize very soon that he cannot win with a poor hand. The opposite is true for his win per game distribution — when he wins, he makes sure that the opponents are carried as far as possible in the betting process. These two distributions are shown on Figs. 3 and 4 for one of the players, Player 1. (Note that each of the four figures were computer generated.)

We have also pooled the above statistics for the "complement" of each player, i.e. for the other five players, in order to obtain a good contrast. We have computed the median (m) and mean (μ) values, the standard deviations (σ), the Pearson's skewness coefficients $[s = 3(\mu - m)/\sigma]$, and the signal-to-noise ratios (μ/σ) for the $6 \times 4 = 24$

distributions. The usual statistical techniques can be used for quantitative comparisons between different players.

The need for exact comparison is emphasized, particularly with reference to the learning aspects of the project to be described below. One indeed cannot state how efficient various learning processes are unless one proves it quantitatively by rigorous statistical methods.

Various Approaches to Learning

(a) *How to assess the opponent's playing style and current hands on the basis of their past and present behavior*

Bluffing is a multifaceted activity in Poker. It has two distinct objectives whether the player under-represents a strong hand ("sandbagging") or over-represents a weak one. Firstly, there is the direct monetary objective of winning as much as possible in the current game, which is a short-term goal. Secondly, it is related to the long-term goal of maximizing overall profit by keeping the channels of communication sufficiently noisy. Namely, a good player always raises doubt with his opponents regarding the motivation for his actions. An optimum bluffing strategy would necessarily depend on the game environment, i.e., on the playing style of the opponents, and on the past history of all hands.

A reasonably promising way of characterizing a player is to relate his subjective probability scale, which includes also bluffing, to objective probability values. After each showdown, the program compares the player's mathematically fair chances with his actual betting behavior. Both his average bets and its variability (cf. certainty of assessment, variance preference) are characteristic of the player, over the whole range of possible hands.

Without going into much detail about the system that creates an image of a given player, the following should be noted:

The total range of all possible hands is subdivided into 22 partitions in each of which the probability of being high (after the draw) can be taken constant. Statistics are collected in these partitions about the distribution of the so-called Personality Factor. The latter is defined as the ratio between the actual and fair bet. So, in the ith partition, for player j, in the kth cycle of betting, we have

$$F(i, j, k) = \frac{B_a(j, k)}{B_f(i, j, k)} \tag{1}$$

where $B_a(j, k)$ is the actual and $B_f(i, j, k)$ is the fair bet. The latter can be computed from

$$p_{i,j} \cdot B_0(j, k) = (1 - p_{i,j}) \left[\sum_{m=1}^{k-1} B_a(j, m) + B_f(i, j, k) \right] \tag{2}$$

It means that the expected value of winning (probability of winning $\times$ the opponent's contributions so far) is equal to the expected value of losing (probability of losing $\times$ the player's own contributions including the current bet). Here, $p_{i,j}$ is the probability of player j's winning in the ith partition; $B_0(j,k)$ is the total contribution of player j's opponents to the pot up to the kth betting cycle; $B_a(j,m)$ is player j's bet in betting cycle m.

As games are played and whenever showdown takes place, new data are added to the *image table* of the still live players. These include the new Personality Factor value, the number of observations, the updated mean, $\bar{F}(i,j)$, and standard deviation, $\sigma_F(i,j)$, of $F(i,j,k)$, all in the relevant ith partition to which player j's hand belonged. Finally, the Personality Factor averaged over all partitions is updated,

$$\bar{\bar{F}}(j) = \frac{1}{22} \sum_{i=1}^{22} \bar{F}(i, j) = \frac{1}{22n_i} \sum_{i=1}^{22} \sum_{k=1}^{n_i} F(i, j, k) \tag{3}$$

All the above is public information that can be made use of by different techniques. We are currently experimenting with various versions of the following idea.

We wish to ascertain, from the past and present betting behavior of a certain player, what his most likely hand can be. Basically three distinct cases have to be discussed;

(i) No history of past games is available: A fair bet will be assumed from which the probability of being high and, indirectly, the actual partition can be computed.

(ii) Most of the partitions have less than two observations: The overall average Personality Factor $\bar{\bar{F}}$ is used to calculate the most likely fair bet. Then the method described above, under (1), is followed.

(iii) Most of the partitions have more than two observations: We mark those partitions for which the following predicate is true

$$\left| \frac{B_a(j, k)}{B_f(i, j, k)} - F(i, j) \right| \leqslant c_i \cdot \sigma_F(i, j) \tag{4}$$

Here, $B_f(i, j, k)$ is the bet that would be fair for player j if his hand were in partition i, in the kth betting cycle; c_i is a constant of which more is said below.

If no partition seems appropriate, i.e., (4) is not true for any i, the c_i values have to be increased across the whole range. If there is one satisfactory partition, that is the best estimate for the hand. If the hand can be "fitted" into an unbroken sequence of partitions, the respective probabilities of winning in these have to be averaged. The same applies if there is a gap in between satisfactory partitions that is shorter than the sequences of satisfactory partitions on the two sides of the gap.

The values of c_i can be optimized by a simple learning process as follows: After finding out what the actual hand was, we see if the hand was placed in one or several wrong partitions. If so, reduce the c_i for these and increase c_i for the correct partition. The steps in c_i are not to be too small (cf. speed of learning) or too big (cf. effect of erratic playing style).

Further refinements take into account the number of cards drawn and the player's contribution to the pot so far. The latter is important in view of the fact that more risk is usually accepted when more is at stake. Also, immediate past events must be given greater weight since playing styles do change accidentally or deliberately.

We are also considering certain pattern recognition techniques that would discover betting sequences of low or high bluffing levels. Simple extrapolations in this kind of time series could contribute to a planning process, which may well surpass the human approach to the game in responding to a given situation.

(b) *How to make use of a player's image?*

The questions arise: how long does a player have to build up an image before a given opponent "buys" it and how many opponents have to believe in his image before he can make use of it by suddenly changing his playing style?

It seems plausible to assume that a conservative player would be more cautious and take longer in accepting the image of another player than an extravagant one. Also, the farther away from the mathematically fair the image is the more convincing the seller has to be. We are putting these ideas in parametric forms and trying to draw some quantitative conclusions.

Experiments are planned to find out whether the majority of all, or just the best couple of opponents, have to buy a certain player's image in order to make the change-over in strategy profitable.

Although the concepts described here appear easy to verbalize, their formulation in computer programs is a formidable task. To capture, for example, the human economy in pattern encoding and recognition, to discover the concept of similarity between patterns, to establish powerful "chunking" techniques, etc. represent major problems. The language AMPPL-II (Findler and McKinzie, 1969; Findler, et al., 1972) should be of great help in accomplishing these tasks.

A by-product of the studies described under (a) and (b) is the possibility of testing experts' recommendations saying that a player's style should match, in the statistical sense, that of the majority of opponents. Some mathematical models, however, lead to different conclusions. Also, the optimum frequency and intensity of bluffing could be approximated under a variety of game conditions.

(c) To develop a "Bayesean" player

The relevant strategy here must be an extremely flexible one. It is continually readjusted by comparing the actual outcome of events with the one previously anticipated. This should be done in two ways. First, by systematically modifying parametric values built in the contributing heuristics, and second, by ordering the heuristics in a hierarchy according to their frequency of successful employment. Waterman's experiments (1970) are highly relevant in this context.

One could interpret our approach by saying that the value scale guiding our inborn "rationality" is made better (and more refined) on the basis of experience.

H.A. Simon has re-introduced the old English word "satisficing" into the realm of decision making. It stands for a "good enough" choice in a given situation, which requirement is then adjusted on-line, so to speak, as a function of the current aspiration level. It should be interesting to study how the players' financial status and possibly other factors affect their monetary goals.

Conclusions

Our research objectives cover both descriptive and normative aspects, in a deliberately combined manner. As our experiments provide more and more results, the two areas of inquiry may diverge somewhat. Besides adopting the attitude of the cognitive theorist in formulating and testing hypotheses embedded in computer programs, we also aim at discovering optimum rules of behavior in the game playing environment. It should be informative to find out why some of these rules are not used by human players or are used in a less than optimum way.

The model constructed is very flexible and capable of making inductive and deductive inferences. The multitude of learning modes clearly show how complex a task environment must be in order to shed light on real-life problems.

As stated elsewhere (Findler et al., 1971):

"The psychological "insight" acquired by Poker experts may be interpreted as their ability of placing themselves into the opponents' role, reversing their reasoning processes by inferring from the opponents' actions their status in the game, and act accordingly. This Bayesean-type inference making is based on the interaction between the usual human egocentrical viewpoint, 'how would I have done in this situation?' and the opponent's 'image' as a decision maker. Our ultimate objective is to capture this phenomenon, which is so common in our everyday life."

Hopefully, we shall have made by then a few more steps towards understanding human behavior.

Acknowledgements

The work reported here was partially supported by the National Science Foundation, Grant GJ-658. Many of the ideas and results described were arrived at in collaboration with my co-workers Heinz Klein, William Gould, Alexander Kowal and John Menig. Besides expressing my indebtedness to them, I must undertake the responsibility for the errors and omissions to be found in this paper.

M.R.B. CLARKE*

Some Ideas for a Chess Compiler

Summary

A brief survey of chess programming is given, and some points of difficulty identified. It is suggested that chess programming requires a problem oriented language, and an illustration is given of such a language based on the syntax of Algol.

Introduction

Programs to play chess have been written and discussed almost as long as computers have been in existence, and a critical summary of what has been achieved in these twenty years has been given recently by Levy (1971). The two strongest programs, that of Greenblatt et al. (1967) and that of Slate and Atkins (1969) play at about the level of the 500th best player in Britain. They are both *tours de force* of machine code programming designed specifically to play chess, and work on the by now familiar principles initiated by Shannon (1950). In the position to be analysed a few moves, usually between four and seven, are selected on the basis of some rather *ad hoc* coding of a few chess heuristics. The tree of possible variations is grown, pruned at a fixed depth or when the position becomes quiet in some sense, and a numerical evaluation function computed for the terminal positions, usually as a weighted sum of more chess heuristics. These values are then backed

* Institute of Computer Science, University of London

up the tree by some efficient minimaxing procedure, such as the alpha-beta algorithm, to select the variation for which the highest possible terminal value can be forced. This procedure reached its ultimate development with Samuel's (1967) draughts (checkers) program which was also a learning program in the sense that the program itself rather than the writer of the program varied the weights in the evaluation function in the light of its experience.

Samuel's program plays draughts at nearly world championship level. Similar programs for simpler games, such as kalah (Slagle and Dixon, 1969), are probably unbeatable by human players. One of the difficulties of using simple games that are not often played by people is that it is sometimes hard to see exactly what has been achieved. If chess was hardly ever played the two programs mentioned above would probably be considered unbeatable. As it is, there is an extensive chess culture and their performance can be seen to fall short of good human play in many respects.

Comparison of Machine and Human Play

In an interesting series of experiments De Groot (1966) measured the ability of both experts and non-experts to reproduce chess positions after being shown them for only a few seconds. He found that success in doing this was highly correlated with chess ability, indicating that the experts had developed a particularly efficient mental representation of the position. Unfortunately his results in that paper were purely quantitative and I have been unable to trace a subsequent paper. It would have been interesting to know what kind of relationships between the pieces were reproduced correctly by the experts in order to give some clue as to what representation of a chess position they used. De Groot also found that good players think that they consider on average less than two moves as at all playable in analysing a position during play. In other words there are on average less than two branches from each node in the tree of variations to be analysed, compared with between four and seven for the chess programs. This, of course, enables the good human player to look at least twice as far ahead for the same amount of work.

A second, related, reason for the comparative weakness of chess

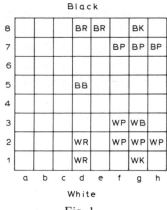

Black

	a	b	c	d	e	f	g	h	
8				BR	BR		BK		
7						BP	BP	BP	
6									
5				BB					
4									
3						WP	WB		
2				WR		WP	WP	WP	
1				WR			WK		

White

Fig. 1

programs is their lack of ability to make use of and collate the results of "local" analyses in order to deduce new moves worth analysing. Chess programs usually start with a wide selection and reject by brute force; people seem to start with a small selection of moves and add to it on the basis of what they find. As an illustration consider the simple chess position shown in Fig. 1.

The human player as White might begin by thinking 1. Rd5 won a piece. On analysis he would see that 1. Rd5 Rd5 2. Rd5 Re1 is mate. This would prompt him to try 1. h3 to give the king some room, a move that without some analysis appears motiveless as Re1 is not an immediate threat. Apparently Black can now save his piece, but further analysis shows that the bishop is pinned and cannot be protected. The machine using a numerical evaluation function would also try 1. Rd5 and find 2. − − − Re1 mate, but it would then reject this line completely and try the apparent second best at the top of the tree, perhaps some irrelevant "threat" such as 1. Bh4. If 1. h3 was tried at all, it would be as a result of some general "king-safety" heuristic rather than by reasoning from a specific line of play. To simulate reasoning of this kind, a qualitative description of the position must be maintained throughout analysis in terms similar to those of the human player. This description must be backed up the tree as the result of the analysis and used to suggest further lines of play. It is interesting to note that the example given above would present even harder problems to the machine if Black was to play, because he would have to realise that 2. h3 is a real threat on White's part, forcing him to play 1. − − − Rd7 2. h3 Red8 to save the bishop.

191

One recent approach to this problem of specifying a good description of a position is that of Botvinnik (1971) who constructs what he calls the mathematical map of a position based on the squares that the pieces can attack in one or more moves. The rest of this paper is concerned with a more conventional approach, that of suggesting that chess programs should be written in a problem oriented language which, because the syntax is based on Algol, will be called Algol 64.

Description and Examples of the Language

A program written in Algol 64 is an algorithm for finding a move in a given chess position. Hopefully the design of the language is such that a good player will be able to write a better algorithm to find a better move than a bad player. The basic idea is that, just as in Algol 60 the user can give names to variables of different types such as integer, real, or boolean, and manipulate them in expressions, so in Algol 64 he can give names like KINGSQUARE or CAPTURE to variables of type square and move. A list of types and their range of values is given below. The algebraic chess notation is used with abbreviations for the pieces, WN for white knight and so on.

Type	*Range of Values*
rank	1 – 8
file	a – h
square	a1 ––– h8
move	all combinations of 2 squares
position	all board configurations
piece	WP, WN, BK etc. or free (unoccupied)
colour	White, Black
integer	0, ±1, ±2 –––
predicate	true, false

In addition to these, lists of variables of the same type can be formed, referred to as *squarelist, movelist* and so on, and there is one other type, *vector*, a list of mixed types for describing positions. Syntax is Algol-like for procedure declarations, blocks, conditional expressions and transfers of control, but to improve legibility assignment is denoted by *becomes*, equality by *is* and iteration through the elements of a list by

for < variable name > *in* < list name > *do*

There are no arithmetic operators, where necessary arithmetic is done by procedure call. In the examples, user defined names will be in upper-case, constants in lower-case, and reserved words in italicised lower case.

It will be clear that not all move constants represent legal moves in a given position. The basic system procedure for testing this is *predicate-procedure* POSSIBLE (POSITION, MOVE) and the corresponding *movelistprocedure* MOVES (POSITION). Other system functions, procedures of general use incorporated into the compiler, are required for dissecting moves and finding pieces moved, namely

squareprocedure FROM(MOVE)	the square from which a piece moves
movelistprocedure MOVESTO(SQUARE,POSITION)	the moves to SQUARE in POSITION
squarelistprocedure PATH(MOVE,POSITION)	the squares over which MOVE goes
colourprocedure COLOUR(PIECE)	self explanatory
colourprocedure OTHER(COLOUR)	the other colour
pieceprocedure PIECE(SQUARE,POSITION)	the piece on SQUARE
colourprocedure CPT(MOVE,POSITION)	the colour of the piece on the square MOVEd to

To enable these to be implemented efficiently there is an internal representation of a position as a set of linked lists — for each square a list of all moves to it, from it and through it, for each move a list of all squares that it moves through. In this context all pieces are considered to move to the edge of the board regardless of pieces in the way. This implies that the legality of moves is dealt with by explicit programming in the source language, ALGOL 64 itself, as are anomalous moves such as the double pawn move, *en passant* capture, castling and promotion. The presence of rank, file and square constants makes these complications relatively easy to incorporate. Other important consequences of using this wide class of moves are that pins and discovered attacks can be readily detected by dissecting move paths and that the side effects of making a move are well defined below source level, a fact which is important when we come to consider the question of efficiency. Some examples are now given to illustrate how a legal move generator could be coded. Thus, a move will be called feasible if there are no pieces in its path, and a procedure for testing whether this is true or false could be written as follows:

```
predicateprocedure FEASIBLE(MOVE,POSITION)
move MOVE; position POSITION; begin
if IN(MOVE,MOVES(POSITION)) is false then FEASIBLE becomes false;
else begin square ASQUARE;
    FEASIBLE becomes true
    for ASQUARE in PATH(MOVE,POSITION) do
    if PIECE(ASQUARE,POSITION) isnot free then FEASIBLE becomes false;
    if CPT(MOVE,POSITION) is CPF(MOVE,POSITION) then
    FEASIBLE becomes false;
end else; end feasible;
```

In a similar way, by examining the paths of moves through FROM(MOVE) a *predicateprocedure* PINNED(MOVE,POSITION) could be defined.

A list of legal moves for one side could then be set up by

```
movelistprocedure LEGALS(POSITION,COLOUR)
position POSITION; colour COLOUR; begin move AMOVE;
LEGALS becomes null comment sets up the null list;
for AMOVE in MOVES(POSITION) do if PINNED(AMOVE,POSITION) is false
and FEASIBLE(AMOVE,POSITION) and CPF(AMOVE,POSITION) is COLOUR
then LEGALS becomes ADDTOLIST(AMOVE,LEGALS); end legals;
```

The four procedures that follow show how a minimal chess program could be written, where the moves analysed at each level are checks and captures or, if in check, moves out of check, and the evaluation of a position is solely in terms of mate and material. INFORMATION is a procedure that for a given position and colour computes the required predicates and movelists. DESCRIPTION combines these into a move generating procedure, MOVESWORTHANALYSING, and an evaluation procedure, VALUE. BETTER is a predicate for comparing two evaluations. EVALUATE is a minimaxing routine that calls itself recursively — a more sophisticated version would employ the alpha—beta algorithm. Apart from the position and colour of the side to move the arguments of this procedure are as follows. VARIATION is a movelist leading to the terminal position that EVALUATE finds is the best that can be forced, and EVALUATION is the result of VALUE being applied to this position. DESCRIPTION and BETTER are the procedure names mentioned above, so that the rules for move generation and comparison of positions can be made arguments of EVALUATE. It can now be seen why type *vector* is necessary — if it did not exist then EVALUATE would have varying numbers of arguments as the number of elements in the evaluation was changed.

    procedure INFORMATION(POSITION,COLOUR,CHECK,MATE,MATERIAL,
                INCHECKFROM,CHECKS,CAPTURES,
                ANTICHECKS);
   position POSITION; *colour* COLOUR; *predicate* CHECK,MATE;
   integer MATERIAL; *squarelist* INCHECKFROM;
   movelist CHECKS,CAPTURES,ANTICHECKS;
   begin move AMOVE; square ASQUARE;
      CHECKS *becomes* CAPTURES *becomes* null;
       for AMOVE *in* LEGALS(POSITION,COLOUR) *do begin*
         if CPT(AMOVE,POSITION) *is* OTHER(COLOUR) *then*
         CAPTURES *becomes* ADDTOLIST(AMOVE,CAPTURES);
         if IN(TO(MOVE),CHECKSQUARES(POSITION,OTHER(COLOUR),
         PIECE(AMOVE),POSITION))) *then*
         CHECKS *becomes* ADDTOLIST(AMOVE,CHECKS);
       end AMOVE loop;
      comment IN is the list membership predicate, CHECKSQUARES is a proce-
dure giving the list of squares from which a king of given colour can be checked with a given piece;
     INCHECKFROM *becomes* null;
     MATERIAL *becomes* 0;
     for ASQUARE *in* SQUARES(POSITION) *do begin*
     piece PIECEONIT; PIECEONIT *becomes* PIECE(ASQUARE,POSITION);
     MATERIAL *becomes if* COLOUR(PIECEONIT) *is* COLOUR *then*
     PLUS(MATERIAL,VALUE(PIECEONIT)) *else*
     MINUS(MATERIAL,VALUE(PIECEONIT));
     comment PLUS and MINUS are the arithmetic operators, VALUE is a lookup
for the value of a piece, queen equals nine pawns, etc. which can be set by the programmer;
      if IN(ASQUARE,CHECKSQUARES(POSITION,COLOUR,PIECEONIT) *then*
      INCHECKFROM *becomes* ADDTOLIST(ASQUARE,INCHECKFROM);

end ASQUARE loop;
CHECK *becomes if* INCHECKFROM *isnot* null;
if CHECK *then comment* here would come a block to
generate ANTICHECKS, moves to escape check, using the information in
INCHECKFROM. There are three possibilities, capture the checking piece, inter-
pose or move the king. If INCHECKFROM contains more than one square it is
double check and only king moves are legal;
MATE *becomes if* CHECK *and* ANTICHECKS *is* null;
end information;

procedure (DESCRIPTION(POSITION,COLOUR,MOVESWORTHANALYSING,
VALUE);
value POSITION,COLOUR; *position* POSITION; *colour* COLOUR;
vector VALUE; *movelist* MOVESWORTHANALYSING;
begin predicate CHECK,MATE; *integer* MATERIAL; *squarelist* INCHECKFROM;
movelist CHECKS,CAPTURES,ANTICHECKS;
INFORMATION(POSITION,COLOUR,CHECK,MATE,MATERIAL,
INCHECKFROM,CHECKS,CAPTURES,ANTICHECKS);
MOVESWORTHANALYSING *becomes if* CHECK *then* ANTICHECKS
else UNION(CHECKS,CAPTURES);
VALUE *becomes* MATE,MATERIAL;
comment this is a new kind of assignment for making up lists from elements;
end description;

predicateprocedure BETTER(AVALUE,BVALUE);
vector AVALUE,BVALUE
comment HEAD,TAIL are the usual list dissectors;
begin if HEAD(AVALUE) *then begin* BETTER *becomes* false; *goto* OUT; *end*;
if HEAD(BVALUE) *then begin* BETTER *becomes* true; *goto* OUT; *end*;
BETTER *becomes if* HEAD(TAIL(AVALUE)) *ge* HEAD(TAIL(BVALUE));
OUT:
end better;

procedure EVALUATE(POSITION,COLOUR,VARIATION,EVALUATION,
DESCRIPTION,BETTER);
value POSITION,COLOUR; *position* POSITION; *colour* COLOUR;
vector EVALUATION; *movelist* VARIATION; *procedure* DESCRIPTION;
predicate procedure BETTER;
begin vector VALUE; *movelist* MOVESWORTHANALYSING
DESCRIPTION(POSITION,COLOUR,MOVESWORTHANALYSING,VALUE);
if MOVESWORTHANALYSING *is* null *then*
begin EVALUATION *becomes* VALUE; VARIATION *becomes* null; end;
else begin move AMOVE; *vector* VALUE; *movelist* PATH;

196

EVALUATION *becomes* WORSTPOSSIBLE;
comment this is an initialising vector than which all others are better;
for AMOVE *in* MOVESWORTHANALYSING *do begin*
EVALUATE(MAKEMOVE(POSITION,AMOVE),OTHER(COLOUR),
        PATH,VALUE,DESCRIPTION,BETTER);
if BETTER(VALUE,EVALUATION) *then begin*
   EVALUATION *becomes* VALUE;
   VARIATION *becomes* ADDTOLIST(AMOVE,PATH); *end*;
  end AMOVE loop;
 end else block;
end evaluate;

It will now be clear that an Algol-like language such as this provides the facilities needed to tackle the example given above. For suppose that if the MATE predicate is found to be true in *procedure* INFORMATION a *movelist* ANTIMATES is generated, moves that would make MATE false in the final position. These can then be passed back up the tree in EVALUATE, as EVALUATION is, and any that are legal in the current position, POSITION, given as arguments to EVALUATE to perform a further analysis. Black now has another move and can try to generate moves that avoid loss on d5, of which there are none, the bishop being pinned. It is perhaps worth noting here that moves to prevent an opponent's move, MOVE, can be generated quite easily. They are either captures on FROM(MOVE), pins of FROM(MOVE), interpositions on one of the squares in PATH(MOVE), or moves that protect TO(MOVE). As a threat is defined by a list of moves, VARIATION, representing the result of a local analysis, this provides a general method of dealing with threats. Whether it works at all well in practice is something that can only be settled by running the program.

Comments and Conclusions

As the title of the paper implies these proposals have not yet been implemented. The plan is to write a preprocessor which converts a program in ALGOL 64 into ALGOL 60*. The names of variables are retained, but substitutions are made for type declarations, assignment, conditional and *for* statements. Type *predicate* becomes *boolean,* types *move* and *position* integer arrays, and the rest integers. In the case of

* This has now been completed using the language BCL. M.R.B.C.

lists the integer is a pointer to a reserved area of store. List assignment statements are substituted by calls to list processing procedures, and *for* < variable> *in* < list>*do*, by statements of the form *for* next in list *while* next not null *do*. The ALGOL 60 compiler deals with the labels, procedure calls, block structure, recursion and so on.

It can be seen therefore that this ALGOL-like language specifically designed for chess programming retains the elements of ALGOL associated with procedures, block structure, recursion and transfer of control, but substitutes variable types and operations related to chess. This should provide a convenient framework for simulating a way in which people think about chess positions, particularly with regard to the deductions which can be made from the results of several local analyses.

One important advantage of such a specialized chess programming language is that it can facilitate the description and communication of chess algorithms, and thus greatly reduce the duplication of effort which occurs at the present time. It should perhaps be emphasized that the aim of the proposal is essentially to facilitate the systematic description of chess procedures. The proposed language does not contain any specific facilities for the programming of learning or concept formation. It seems premature to attempt to do this until one knows in some detail what a chess program is trying to learn.

Acknowledgement

I would like to acknowledge the help of David Till and Derek Brough in many helpful discussions.

RICHARD COOPER and ALICK ELITHORN*

The Organization of Search Procedures

Summary

The concept that problem solving is primarily the organization of heuristic search procedures is illustrated in relation to the three phases of chess. The value of board games as experimental tools for the study of thinking is discussed and it is argued that this area of research would be greatly facilitated by the choice of games which are conducive to the development of suitable analytic programs. The results of a preliminary analysis of games of reduced halma using such a program are briefly discussed.

Introduction

Thinking can be considered as composed of a set of internal responses. In studying thinking we try to externalize and evaluate as many of these responses as possible. To some extent this can be achieved indirectly by recording the subject's introspective comments on his internal behaviour or by asking him to record certain intermediate steps of the problem itself. However in either case we may alter materially the character of the problem solving process. Nevertheless, even though some distortion inevitably follows externalization, this can be an extremely valuable experimental technique (see for examples De Groot, 1965; Newell, 1967). Fortunately in many problems frequent external

* Institute of Neurology, London

responses are an intrinsic part of the problem solving process. In such problems the pattern of these responses may not only provide clues about the nature of the problem solving activity but it also provides a physical set of markers which form a track through the problem space. As a reasonable first assumption it may be argued that the more closely a simulation follows such a track the more likely it is that the simulation is a good one.

In choosing a board game to study thinking, we have been influenced considerably by the opportunity that this offers to record operations by the subject on a mechanical system which is part of the problem structure. Since the problem requires the subject to make a series of sequential choices from subsets of possible moves we can use an analysis of the subsets and the choices he makes from them to test hypotheses about his thinking processes. Moreover as these externalized responses are an integral part of the problem then it cannot be argued that recording them objectively will interfere with the internal aspects of the problem solving activity. An additional advantage of board games is that they can be presented in puzzle format as well as a competitive interaction. Rather surprisingly board games have rarely been used experimentally (see for examples Binet, 1894; De Groot, 1946; Rayner, 1958; Newell and Simon, 1965; Reeves, 1965; Sutton-Smith and Roberts, 1967) primarily perhaps because the need for an opponent introduces an uncontrolled variable into the experimental situation.

Computer techniques can greatly facilitate the use of board games experimentally in two ways. Firstly even a very small laboratory computer can be programmed to provide opponents with a variety of different but fully defined playing characteristics (Elithorn and Telford, 1970, 1972). Secondly a computer can be programmed to implement a set of production rules within the calculus of the game and thus to produce a subset of moves which can be used as a template to analyse the moves made by human players (Newell, et al., 1959).

Problem Solving as Search Behaviour

Human problem solving is a search procedure. Theoretically the "space" to be searched can be considered as a set of interconnected states which can be described formally either as a tree or as a directed graph or net. The nodes of the tree or net represent the possible states, and the arcs joining the nodes represent the permissible operations which change one state into another. In the tree the operations are represented as being unidirectional. In the net they may be uni- or bidirectional. In games the search requirements differ from those required in theorem proving and puzzles. In the latter the subject sets out to find a single solution route — there may be only one or there may be many to choose from — which meets certain defined criteria and which forms a path through the problem from initial state to goal state. In the games situation the subject still seeks a route from an initial state to a terminal goal — preferably to a win position — but the route to be taken is in part determined by one or more other players who seek an alternative route. Conventionally in many games two persons choose nodes alternatively. In such a situation each subject or player seeks not a single pathway but rather a set of routes forming a sub-tree of the whole game tree. At the next move he remains passive and it is then his opponent who chooses a subtree which he believes to be most favourable to him. Subtrees of decreasing size are chosen alternately in this way by the two players until the search space is small enough for one player to discern a path to a forced win or until a draw is conceded, or the game abandoned. At each node the decision as to whether a particular choice is favourable or not will depend on the subject's assessment of possible outcomes. This assessment will be based on a search of the proximal areas of the trees between which he must choose and partly on his evaluation of the skills of his opponent. In many situations this last consideration reduces to the concept of the optimal or perfect opponent. When a game tree is relatively large, moves must often be made in the absences of any certain knowledge as to whether progress is being made towards or away from goal. In this situation the development of subgoals may reduce the game to a series of puzzles in which the presence of the opponent is largely immaterial since each move is made in terms of a set of evaluation rules.

Concept Development in the Control of Search Behaviour

As Vergnaud (1972) points out, the concepts used in the analysis of thinking are often overlapping and confusing. Here we are concerned with the concept of search and of the heuristics which control search behaviour within defined problem spaces. Any search heuristic other than a random one or a systematic exhaustive one involves a presumption that certain areas of the problem space are more likely to contain a solution pathway than are others. In other words search heuristics are a condensation of past experiences of past searches through similar problem spaces. Foresight, in the sense of prediction, is a form of negative memory − a method of projecting into the future the experience of the past.

A heuristic, or more generally a concept or a set of concepts, forms a condensation of experience which in a game playing or problem solving situation provides an effective short cut way of weighting the balance of a decision process.

For example, in the middle game in chess the choice of move is determined by various concepts which can be classified in a variety of ways. Thus a move will be chosen because it increases mobility, helps dominate the centre, threatens an unguarded piece or because it defends the king or other important piece against a threat. Certain classes of move such as *forks* and *pins* may be dignified with special names.

In the opening phase of the game most of these concepts are still valid, but the method of play is quite different. At this stage the game tree consists of sign-posted routes. Some are well-beaten tracks, e.g., the Ruy-Lopez, some are trails which are used only infrequently, e.g., Philidor's defence, others are rejected or neglected pathways, e.g., Steinitz's gambit. Of the twenty possible opening moves only 5 are used with any frequency. This selection is not the immediate outcome of an over-the-board analysis. During the first part of the game there is for every move a set of well-established conventional − ritualised − responses, almost all of them with an eponym. Clearly in the opening phase a memory for statistical analysis of the outcome of past games is of great importance.

In chess terminology the "end game" is not synonymous with the end part of the game. Paradoxically the game frequently ends well before the end game phase is reached; either one player exploits an advantage of material or position sufficiently to give checkmate, or else the balance of advantage and disadvantage gained is manifestly so great that one or other player resigns. In chess an end game position is reached when there are few pieces on each side — 2 to 4 is the usual number — and yet the outcome is by no means obvious. Here the ability to undertake over the board what amounts to an almost complete analysis is essential for first class play. Such an analysis, however, is helped by concepts such as the opposition, the move, triangulation and the king's master square. These concepts are algorithmic rather than heuristic in that they provide a definitive answer about the outcome of a search in a specific limited situation. Although simple once defined, such concepts are the fruit of many years of analysis. Indeed, such an apparently trivial situation as Greco's position[1] defied analysis for over two hundred years. The history of the end game in chess as well as the popularity of two move problems illustrate very well the difficulty that the human problem solver has with forward searches.

It is well recognized in chess circles that the three phases of chess require different psychological skills and that some chess masters excel at one phase rather than another. Capablanca was brilliant in the middle game but loath to bother with opening theory and Alekhine was most at home in the end game, whereas Staunton and Tarrasch were walking encyclopaedias of the opening "culture". This psychological distinctiveness for different phases of the game applies to many games, including halma. In the reduced form of halma which we have considered here the distinction is blurred and, except possibly for the first and the last two or three moves, the search problems are essentially those of the middle game. However, in halma algorithmic and concept development can be important and this is illustrated later in relation to the halma variant of the A is B puzzle situation (Elithorn and Telford, 1970).

The Attributes of the Move

In evaluating a move in a game, psychologists are interested both in its evidence as to the subject's skill — his ability to select good moves —

---

[1] Greco's position, an end game problem of King and 3 pawns against King and three pawns (4k3, 5 ppp, 32, PPP 5, 4K3), dating from the late 17th century or earlier was believed drawn until Szen showed conclusively at the beginning of the 19th century that it was a win for White whoever had the move (Walker, 1840).

and also in the evidence it provides as to the strategies or production rules that the subject is using. Such an analysis must always be a statistical one since, even if a complete analysis is possible and it can be shown that the subject's move is the best one, this move may still have been selected by chance or for the wrong reasons.

In the absence of a complete analysis, a move may be evaluated in terms of moves chosen from a similar position by players (human or simulated) of varying degrees of competence. Alternatively, given a defined evaluation function, a chosen move may be ordered in terms of this evaluation in relation to other available moves which were not chosen. For example in terms of better moves missed.

Computer programs can implement a simple strategy rigorously and completely. Such programs can be used as powerful analytic tools since in each situation each legal response can be classified in terms of a set of attributes each of which represents whether or not the move would be generated by a particular strategy. For economic reasons such an analysis would best be limited to the move actually chosen and the better moves missed.

In analyzing problem solving it is necessary to consider not only the strategies of the problem solver but the way the problem is represented or presented. In the case of board games and human players, this involves an analysis of the perceptual characteristics of the display. It is true that many grand masters play chess very effectively blindfold, but the analyses undertaken by Binet and by De Groot (see De Groot 1946) make it clear that even in blindfold play visual imagery can be important. In sum, therefore, a psychological classification of moves needs an analysis at three levels or more properly in three dimensions. Firstly it may be robustly assumed that the player chooses the move he believes to be best. Consequently the move chosen partitions all legal moves into better moves missed, equal moves not chosen and less good moves not chosen.

Secondly it can be assumed that production rules which would select better moves missed have not been systematically implemented. Finally it is assumed that perceptual factors are one element which determines how effectively a production rule is implemented. A move in any game therefore can usefully be classified in terms of its perceptual characteristics, the production rules which could have selected it and the number and character of the better moves which could have been selected.

Human performance at chess has been analysed along these lines for hundreds of years, but the automation of such an analysis for chess presents formidable problems. The perceptual factors, although relatively unimportant, are complex. More important are the difficulties involved in delineating a sufficiently accurate evaluation function and programming appropriate strategies. These limitations apply to many other games besides chess. Indeed, although there is a plethora of games playing programs for a large variety of games, relatively few programs have been developed for the *analysis* of games playing. In part this reflects the fact that the emphasis has been on the development of programs which play a strong game. However, it is also true that the majority of the games programmed have not been selected because their characterisation makes them suitable for experimental psychological analysis.

In reduced halma we have a race game without capture in which it is practical to give numerical values to each player's distance from his goal. Consequently we can develop hierarchical sets of evaluation functions which evaluate a move in terms of the maximum rate of movement which this permits for varying degrees of forward search. These functions can be calculated either separately for each player or in terms of the interaction of the two players. Combined with a laboratory situation in which the experimental subject plays a programmed opponent with specified characteristics, (see Elithorn and Telford, page 165) this type of analysis would appear to be potentially a powerful one.

In halma a player is required on each move to produce the maximum advance not just for one man but by implication for the army as a whole. At each move there is in general a choice between moving one of several men each with a variety of possible moves. At each turn there is then a set of moves which is optimal in the sense that, given perfect play on both sides, each member of the set gives the player the fewest possible moves to goal. Even with a small board size and few men (e.g., 6 men on a five by five board) a complete forward search, except during the last few moves, is impracticable for human subjects. As with chess, therefore, the human subject's partial search through the game tree is directed by a hierarchy of heuristics. However, an important factor in determining the outcome of the subject's selection heuristics is the fact that some moves are perceptually more difficult to see than others.

In playing halma, subjects may use a number of strategies or sub-goals. These include:

(1) Finding the man who can make the longest move.

(2) Finding a positional move, i.e., a move which, while not immediately advantageous, contributes towards the development of a position which gives an advantage at a later date.

(3) Not letting any man lag too far behind.

(4) Finding a move which blocks one's opponent.

With optimal play any one move will often be over-determined in that it fulfills more than one strategic need. Nevertheless a great deal can be learnt about a subject's strategy from an analysis in such terms.

The Analytic Program

The assessment of moves in terms of the strategies with which they are compatible is an important first step in determining the production rules a subject is actually using. It seemed worthwhile therefore analysing play at halma in terms of forward search strategies which could be related to the sub-goals described above. Consequently one of us (R.C.) wrote a FORTRAN program which will evaluate all legal moves at varying levels of look-ahead. For each level the program prints out the moves which are as good as or better than the move selected. The evaluation function used is the decrease in distance from goal. At level O (first move) the evaluation applies only to the player's own move; at level 1 the evaluation takes account of the opponent's best possible reply; at level 2 all possible second moves by the player are considered and the best moves evaluated in terms of the total advance which would be obtained with optimal play for the next two moves. In the program written by Alex Telford (Elithorn and Telford, 1972) the evaluation distance from goal was calculated in terms of the aggregated Manhattan walks needed for all men to reach base. The present program will use either this function or the mean squares of the geometrical distances from goal. This latter function which was used in the analysis presented below has the advantage that it favours moves by the more backward men.

The above program even when, as in the present instance, it is limited to three levels, provides quite a complex classification of moves which allows detailed conclusions to be drawn about the strategies being used. Obviously it is limited in many ways. It is not for example logical to conclude that a move which is not best at any of the three levels of analysis is necessarily a bad move. The analysis presented below, however, suggests that the limitations are not in the first instance very serious ones and in any case the program is a prototype and there are many ways in which it can be improved.

Move Analysis

The analysis which is described briefly in order to illustrate the general principles is based on a preliminary study of 29 games. Of these 22 were played against computer programs. Of these 10 were played by 10 inexperienced players and the remaining 12 by 5 relatively experienced players. The remaining 7 games were played between two human players, both of whom were also members of the second group.

Except for the fact that the games between the two experienced human players contained a significantly higher proportion of blocking moves than did the games of the same players played against the computer, the responses of the two experienced groups were very similar. For the analysis presented here therefore, the results of these two groups have been aggregated and the comparisons made are between experienced and inexperienced players.

En passant it is worth just noting that there were marked differences in the opening moves chosen by the experienced and inexperienced players. The latter distributed their choices fairly evenly over six of the nine tactically different possible opening moves. The experienced players chose the move (1,1) to (3,3) in 15 out of the 19 games.

With regard to the main analysis, only the human moves have been analysed and the total material therefore consists of 424 moves played in 36 half games. Of the 113 moves made by the inexperienced group only 30% (36) were as good as the best of the control moves found by the program using a look-ahead of three moves (level 2). Three of these 36 moves (3% of the total) were moves which would not have been found without look-ahead at level 1 and a further 3 (3%) were moves that required look-ahead at level 2. The corresponding figures for the experienced subjects were 60% (178 out of 311) as good as any found by the program, and of these 13 (4% of the total) required a look-ahead of at least one move (level 1) and 23 (7% of the total) a look-ahead of two moves (level 2).

The conclusion that the experienced players were both using more look-ahead and also carrying out a more effective search at level 0 (no look-ahead) is borne out by the analysis of better moves missed given in Table I. Here the average number of better moves missed by the inexperienced group increases steadily as the level of analysis is deepened whereas for the experienced group it decreases. This indicates for the latter group that in the majority of cases in which a long first move was not taken this was not because it was overlooked but because a move of greater potential had been selected.

Table II shows that perceptual factors besides look-ahead were important in determining the difficulty that the inexperienced subjects had in selecting good moves. For this analysis these moves made have been classified as single step moves, straight hops and hops which involved a change in direction. In addition to analysing the actual moves made the analysis program has been used to classify the longer moves which were not taken.

The observation that the experienced players apparently missed proportionately far more single step moves which were better — at level 0

TABLE I

Average number of "better" moves missed *

Subjects	Level of look-ahead analysis		
	0	1	2
Inexperienced	3.04	3.54	3.92
Experienced	1.93	1.82	1.54

* The mean number of better-valued moves found by the Halma Analysis Program are given for the two groups, for the first three values of look-ahead — note that the last two moves of every game are not included.

TABLE II

Perceptual characteristics of moves *

Character of move	Moves taken		Moves not taken	
	Inexp.	Exp.	Inexp.	Exp.
Step moves	42	125	15	74
Straight hops				
Single	57	134	42	63
Double	4	9	8	0
Angulated hops				
Forward	10	27	16	5
Sideways	0	10	12	1
Backwards	0	6	2	0
Totals	113	311	95	143

* The first two columns show the characteristics of the moves actually taken by the two groups (inexperienced and experienced subjects) and the last two columns show, for each group, the number of occasions on which each type of move occurred among the longer moves not taken.

— than the moves actually taken indicates that this group made a higher proportion of sideways moves aimed at obtaining a positional advantage as opposed to an immediate gain. The table also shows clearly that the inexperienced players had considerable difficulty in perceiving hop moves which involved an initial move either sideways or backwards. Of the better moves missed by the inexperienced group 15% fell into this category, the figure for the experienced group being less than 1%.

The above preliminary observations illustrate some of the advantages which can be gained from the use of analytic programs of this type. However, they do not adequately reveal some of the deficiencies. Our experience so far suggests that programs of this sort should be quite powerful in evaluating search strategies related to clearly defined goals. The present program which can certainly be extended considerably is powerful enough to evaluate the subject's competence in a systematic search for all base moves at level 0, his ability for selecting blocking moves (moves directed at holding up his opponent) as revealed by the frequency of moves which are optimal with a look-ahead of one move (level 1), and his ability to plan positional moves (moves which give a delayed advantage) as revealed by the presence of level 2 moves. However, it would appear that some of the good moves made by the better subjects are misclassified as inferior because the level of analysis has not been taken deep enough.

Concept Development in Halma

Although the depth of search of the program can be extended both absolutely and by sacrificing some of its breadth, it is clear that it will help little if at all in determining how human problem solvers develop the concepts of play which define subgoals. This limitation is in the present instance minimised by the use of a small board. Blocking the enemy and using short moves for a later advantage are, it is true, prototype subgoals, but they are a pale shadow of the combinational play which is so characteristic of chess and which is an equally important feature of halma played on a larger board. The most important combinational features of halma are the open and closed ladders. As Elithorn and Telford (1970) pointed out, the open ladder represents a very simple algorithm — a repeatable sequence of 3 moves — which provide a maximum rate of movement parallel to the leading diagonal for an army of any size $n(n > 2)$. There is surprisingly one unexpected exception when $n = 4$. For $n = 3$ there is a closed ladder algorithm which is just as fast as the whole army moves at an average of 2/3 of a vector unit (1,1) per move. For $n = 3$ therefore the choice of algorithm will depend on the arrangement and symmetry of the starting and goal positions. For $n = 4$, however, a ladder algorithm exists which will give a faster rate of movement (3/4 of a vector unit per move). This algorithm and the problems of reflection and symmetry it raises are illustrated in Fig. 1.

Once found, the fours algorithm is simple to implement but the whole problem of discovering the appropriate concepts is very similar to the problem of discovering the concepts of triangulation, opposition to the move and the King's master square in relation to King and Pawn endings at chess (Mott-Smith, 1946).

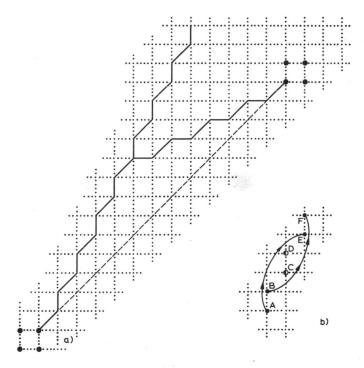

Fig. 1. *Note on the 4-man algorithm.*

The fastest advancing procedure for the special case of 4 men, consists of repeating the pattern ABCD — (b) in the Figure — by means of the two moves A to E and B to F. This, effectively, translates the army by (1,2) steps. On its own the procedure takes the army away from the leading diagonal, but employing a procedure, which is merely the reflection of the basic procedure in the transverse diagonal, will return the army to the leading diagonal. These two procedures, together with an unfolding algorithm (to move the army from the square initial position — (a) in the Figure — to configuration ABCD), an infolding algorithm to finish and a connecting procedure of 4, 5 or 7 moves [depending on the board size, r, (modulo 3)] which joins the basic procedure to its reflection by effectively reflecting the army in the transverse diagonal, constitute an algorithm which will move the army across a board of any size $r > 6$, in the fewest number of moves. This algorithm, which is symmetric, because the unfolding and infolding procedures are reflections of each other and all the three connecting algorithms are symmetric, is re-stated below in symbolic form:

211

Shortest move algorithm is

begin
$j = [(r-6)/3]$;
$k = r-3*[r/3]$;
   unfold;
      basic(j);
         connect(k);
      rbasic(j);
   infold;
end

unfold is $(1,1)$ to $(3,3)$; $(1,2)$ to $(3,4)$; *end*

infold is $(r-3,r-2)$to$(r-1,r)$;$(r-2,r-2)$to(r,r); *end*

basic(j) is
  for $i = 1, j$ *do* begin
         $(1+i, 2i-1)$ to $(3+i, 3+2i)$;
         $(1 + i, \ 2i)$ to $(3+i, 4+2i)$;
      end; *end*

rbasic(j) is
for $i = 1, j$ *do* begin
      $(r-3-2i, r-2-i)$ to $(r+1-2i, r-i)$
      $(r-2-2i, r-2-i)$ to $(r+2-2i, r-i)$

connect(k) is *do* one of three distinct procedures, according as $k = 0$, 1 or 2 and not here described which all have the effect of:

begin for $i = 1$, 4 *do* man$_i = (r + 1, r + 1) - $ man$_j$; *end*

Conclusions

It seems to us that the study of games reveals three fundamentally distinct human problem solving skills. The first which we can simulate effectively and at which computers already can sometimes excel, is the implementation of a concept directed search. The second is the acquisition of concepts by vicarious experience. The third and most important is the development of these concepts. That is to say the development from personal experience of production rules together with recognition rules which define the situations in which these production rules are applicable. This third skill is one which psychologists understand very little and computer scientists can simulate hardly at all. Computer programs sometimes seem very clever, but this cleverness is often inbuilt human ingenuity. Even at this level Levy (1971) has expressed pessimism about the development of ad hoc chess programs. Is it unreasonable to challenge computer scientists to produce a program which will discover rather than acquire vicariously some of the simple concepts that arise when such simple problems as A is B are systematically elaborated?

Acknowledgements

In addition to contributions from many colleagues we are particularly grateful to Professor R.A. Buckingham of the Institute of Computer Science, London and to Professor I.M. Khabaza of Queen Mary College, London for the provision of computing facilities.

DIRK REVENSTORFF* NORBERT MAI*
ROMAN FERSTL* and WOLFGANG GRUDE*

Effects of Simulated Opponent in an Experimental Game

Summary

The literature shows that simulated opponents in two-person non-zero-sum games are generally unsuccessful in influencing a subject's behaviour, whereas interaction appears in games with two human subjects as players. A computer program was designed, which reacts to some extent contingently on subject's choices. A hundred subjects were run in four experimental groups, which refer to sex and two different simulated counterparts. The data have been analysed by the conventional and also by new classes of game parameters using combination scores of the subject's choice and his expectation. The latter reveal some interpretational advantages. The results indicate that the subject's behaviour can be influenced by simulated opponents, reacting contingently on the subject's responses.

Introduction

In recent years there has been considerable interest in experimental games, especially in the two-person non-zero-sum games. To many psychologists and game theorists these games seem to be a tool to study conflict and conflict resolution by quantitative methods. The most frequently used games (Prisoners' Dilemma and Chicken) are two-choice games in which the outcome depends on the decisions of two persons. Consider the following example of a Chicken payoff matrix.

* Max-Planck-Institut für Psychiatrie

	Opponent	
	C	D
Subject C	50, 50	−30, 80
D	80, −30	−60, −60

On each trial the subject chooses between rows C and D and the opponent between columns C and D (a choice of C is usually referred to as "cooperative" and a choice of D as "non-cooperative" or "defective"). After each trial the two persons receive the payoffs shown in the cell of the matrix which is defined by their joint choices. The first number in each cell refers to the first subject (row player), the second to the opponent (column player).

The validity of experimental games in reflecting social interaction processes is often accepted at face value. As Kubicka (1968) has pointed out, there is some danger "that step by step, the subject's behaviour in the experimental game situations may become the reality one is interested in". One approach to the validity problem could be to demonstrate that the behaviour of the subject is systematically influenced by the "Other's" behaviour. The influence of the players upon one another has been investigated with real subjects for both as well as with one player simulated.

In experiments with real subjects for both players, mutual influence is demonstrated, e.g., by the high correlation (0.9 − 1.0) between the C-frequencies of the two subjects over pairs of players, which is consistently found when long sequences of games were run (Rapoport and Chammah, 1965). Further the same authors found correlations about 0.5 between the subject's choice and the immediately preceding choice of the "Other".

Secondly there are studies where the subject plays against a stooge or simulated opponent, whose strategy is to choose a specified proportion of C-moves. Here, generally there was no difference between groups which played against simulated move-sequences with C-proportions between 15 and 85 per cent (McClintock et al., 1963; Phelan and Richardson, 1969; Bixenstine et al., 1963), although there is some evidence that shifts in C-probability of the simulated opponent, within a sequence, against the same subject are more influential (Sermat, 1967; Oskamp, 1970).

Comparing the two types of experiments, with and without simulated opponent, the clear lack of correspondence in the results may be explained by the fact that in the studies reported the simulated opponent "acted" completely unresponsive to the subject's behaviour (c.f. Halpin and Pilisuk, 1970). Therefore the situation may have appeared clearly artificial and of little relevance to the real interaction process in games.

On the other hand simulated opponents have obvious advantages over experiments with two real subjects, insofar as there is a greater possibility to control the interaction process. In the experiment reported here it was attempted to improve the realism of the simulation by devising a computer program which to some extent reacts contingently upon either C- or D-moves of the subject. We expected the subjects to respond differently to these two kinds of simulated opponents.

By expanding the subject's task slightly by asking him to predict on each trial "Other's" next choice, it is possible to derive a class of behavioural parameters by combining expectancy and choice, which may facilitate the understanding of underlying motives in the decision process.

Since Tedeschi et al. (1968) and Halpin and Pilisuk (1970) demonstrated that the task of predicting does not affect the subject's choice behaviour, we also asked our subjects what they expect their opponent to choose.

Method

The matrix employed was the Chicken matrix used as in the example above (see Harris, 1969, for classification of 2 × 2 games).

Computer simulation of the opponent

By simulation it was intended to influence the subject's choices to increase either cooperative or defective behaviour. To have a standardized reaction pattern contingent on the subject's gambling behaviour, the following simulation program was devised: the simulated opponent (SO) started out with a 50 per cent random vector. The SO took into account the last two preceding moves. He either increased or decreased reinforcement probability by 20 per cent each time a subject played two Cs or Ds in the cooperation training. If the 90 per cent or 10 per cent-level was reached, it was retained as long as the subject continued C- or D-moves respectively. In the defection training D-choices were reinforced instead of C in the same manner. Simulation and data collection was carried out on a PDP 8/L.

Procedure

The subjects played for real money; they were given 8 DM as a starting fund. At the end of the game, six outcomes were randomly selected for their total gain. The subjects were instructed that there would be a real subject sitting in another experimental room. No further information about the counterpart was provided. In the instruction it was attempted to favour neither cooperation nor defection. It was pretended that the computer served merely as a data-collecting device and communication unit between players. The subjects were told that the experiment would be a study of decision processes under restricted communication conditions. Sixty-six consecutive trials were announced. After initial instructions, the subjects were brought to the experimental room and seated in front of a teletype. The experimenter explained the necessary response keys and indicated that the outcome of each trial would be printed out. The pay-off matrix was presented to the subject during the session. The subjects were required to make their prediction of the opponent's next choice as well as their own choice, after which a brief interruption by the SO-program simulated different reaction times of the opponent. Next, opponent's choice as well as the win or loss of both players were printed. After ten training trials in which the SO played randomly 50 per cent C, the actual 66 trials were run. For all 66 trials, the subject's predictions and choices were recorded. Subsequent to the game procedure they were asked to fill out a semantic differential describing their opponent. Furthermore they had to fill out questionnaires on extraversion, neuroticism, and need achievement; the Nufferno Intelligence Test was also given.

Design

A 2 × 2 design was employed: sex and two training conditions. Under each condition 25 subjects were run (students from 18 to 27 years old).

Results

Behavioural indices

Five classes of indices were derived from the game behaviour of the subject and compared with regard to their dependence on training conditions. All indices are frequency counts.

(1) C-moves [$M(C)$] and C-expectations [$E(C)$].

(2) All possible combinations of moves and expectations: $ME(CC)$, $ME(CD)$, etc. The first letter in the brackets refers to the move, the second to the expectation or prediction of Other's move in this trial.

(3) C-moves, conditional to the four possible states of the game in the immediately preceding trial, e.g., $M(C/CC)$, which means a C-move after both played C in the preceding trial. In the same way $M(C/CD)$, $M(C/DC)$, $M(C/DD)$ are constructed.

(4) C-expectations conditional in the same way as (3): $E(C/CC)$, $E(C/CD)$, etc.

(5) All move expectation combinations conditional in the same way as (3) and (4). There are 16 possible indices of the form: $ME(CC/CC)$, $ME(CC/CD)$, ... $ME(DC/CC)$, etc.

Of these indices two classes are considered as personality variables in the literature: the unconditional ME-scores (2) by Tedeschi et al. (1968) and the conditional C-frequencies, "propensities" (3) by Rapoport and Chammah (1965). Variables which can be regarded as stable individual parameters and personality correlates should at least be independent of situational variations, which in our experiment means independent of the two training conditions. Neither the Rapoport nor the Tedeschi indices qualify in this respect. Most of the 30 indices show significant mean differences (5 per cent level) with the following exceptions: $ME(CD)$; the four respective conditional scores ($ME(CD/CC)$, $ME(CD/CD)$, $ME(CD/DC)$, $ME(CD/DD)$); and three of the four conditional predictions ($E(C/CD)$, $E(C/DC)$, $E(C/DD)$), the latter four indicating special kinds of optimism. These along with the other indices however seem to have little relevance to personality assessment by means of sex differences and correlations with questionnaire variables.[1]

---

[1] Full data are available on request.

Training effects

Several mean differences in the two training conditions are considered in Table I. Overall number of C-moves is different in both groups as one would expect (row 1). Change in C-frequency from first to second 33 trials shows opposite direction in both training conditions (row 4). As evident from the number of C-moves by the computer, which serve as reinforcement, learning is approximately equal in the two training conditions (row 2). Δ-reinforcement (row 5, computed analogously to the values in row 4) indicates an equal increase in re-

TABLE I

Analyses of variance for the effects of the two training conditions *

		Mean (S.D.)	Mean (S.D.)	F-value	p-value
1	Number of subjects's C-choices M(C)	27.29 (9.5)	40.8 (10.3)	50.25	0.001
2	Number of computer's C-choices (reinforcements)	40.9 (8.2)	44.9 (11.1)	8.6	0.004
3	Number of subject's predictions E(C)	39.5 (10.4)	42.5 (13.0)	3.6	0.07
4	Increase in subject's C-choices M(C)	−2.9 (1.1)	1.7 (1.2)	42.2	0.001
5	Increase in computer's C-choices reinforced	2.3 (6.0)	1.8 (6.2)	0.04	0.83 NS
	Combinations of subject's move (M) and prediction (E)				
6	ME(CC)	17.7 (8.5)	30.7 (13.7)	38.1	0.001
7	ME(DC)	23.2 (18.0)	14.2 (5.9)	23.8	0.001
8	ME(CD)	9.6˙ (6.6)	10.1 (6.3)	0.02	0.88 NS
9	ME(DD)	15.5 (8.0)	11.0 (7.8)	13.7	0.001

* Columns 1 and 2: means: defection and cooperation training respectively.

inforcement. In two cases (rows 6 and 7), the combined move- and prediction-scores show significant differences in the expected direction: to expect C and to choose C should be more frequent in a program which trains to cooperate. On the other hand to choose D and to expect C as reinforcement should be more frequent under a training for defectiveness. Number of C-choices combined with predicted Ds showing no difference can be interpreted as loss minimization, which seems to prevail with some of the subjects irrespective of training conditions. Therefore the treatment difference in C-moves (row 1) can be reduced to the difference in pure cooperativeness, that is joint choice and prediction of C (row 6). Different numbers of C-moves obviously imply different numbers of D-moves as complements, and these can be of two sorts: (1) in combination with prediction of C, it is "exploitation", and (2) in combination with prediction of D, it could be "maximization of gain difference". Both motivational components seem to be more pronounced in the defection training.

Images of the opponent rated on a semantic differential (Krieger, 1964) were different for the sexes (Mahalanobis D^2, $p = 0.01$), however, there was no difference for the description of the simulated opponents in the two training conditions.

Time course

The 66 trials were divided into six blocks of 11. Time course of subjects' C-moves $M(C)$, predictions $E(C)$ and their combinations are plotted in Figs. 1 and 2. In the defection training, male subjects learn faster than females. In the cooperation training females show no progress in the beginning, but are quite successful afterwards. Male subjects learn immediately but decrease their C-rates substantially at the end. This impression is corroborated by the significance of the sex $\times$ treatment $\times$ blocks interaction effect in the resulting analysis of variance (Table II). An understanding of the underlying motivation is enhanced by consideration of the subject's predictions as additional information. Looking at the $ME(CC)$ plot, the females show distrust at the beginning of the cooperation training — there is a decrease in C-moves and C-predictions at the same time. Similarly, the consideration of $ME(DC)$ is helpful in the discussion of the behaviour of males in the cooperation training. Increase in D-choices at the end [complement to $M(C)$] is generally accompanied by C-predictions and not by D-predictions. This suggests

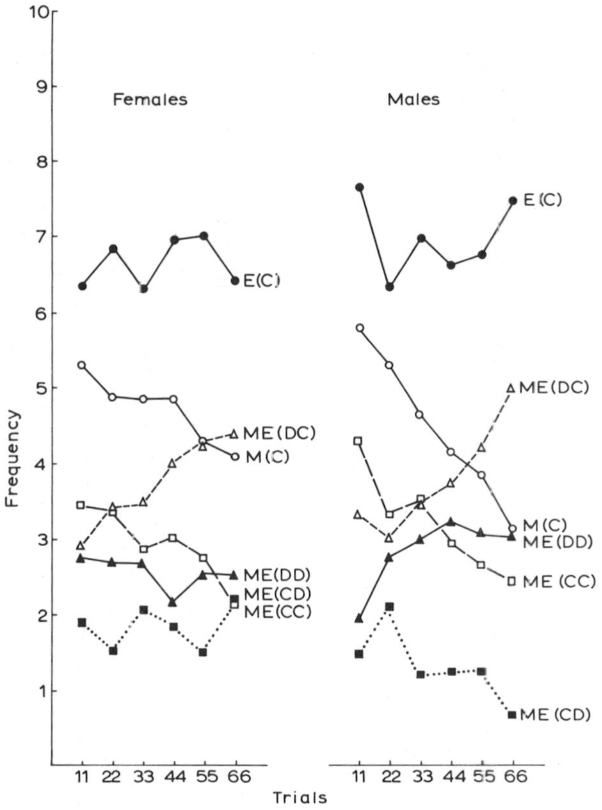

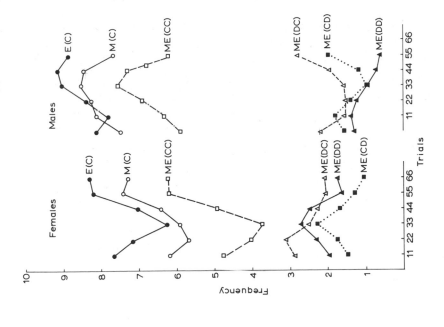

Fig.1. Defection training. Time course over six blocks each of 11 trials of the behavioural parameters: frequency of C-moves [M(C)], C-expectations [E(C)] and their four combinations [ME(CC)], ME(DC), ME(CD), [ME(DD)] are plotted.

Fig.2. Cooperation training. Time courses as for Fig.1 of the parameters: [M(C)], [E(C)], [ME(GC)], [ME(DC)], [ME(CD)], and [ME(DD)].

TABLE II

Analysis of variance for $M(C)$ for the four treatment conditions and six consecutive blocks

Source of variation	Sum of squares	DF	Mean squares	F	p (%)
between subjects	2892.17	99			
A = sex	36.51	1	36.51	2.06	15.47
B = treatment	1056.03	1	1056.03	59.51	0.00
A × B	96.00	1	96.00	5.41	2.21
subjects within groups	1703.64	96	17.75		
within subjects	2199.00	500			
C = blocks	42.89	5	8.58	2.09	6.56
A × C	60.45	5	12.09	2.94	1.25
B × C	115.65	5	23.13	5.63	0.00
A × B × C	8.20	5	1.64	0.40	84.94
C × subjects within groups	1971.80	480	4.11		
within cells	3675.44	576			
Total	5091.17	599	8.50		

that male subjects tended to exploit their opponents at the end of the series after they had learned that their partner consistently cooperated.

In the defection training the increase in D-moves is accounted for by concomitant expectancy of "Other's" cooperation ($ME(DC)$), which leads to the conclusion that the aim of the SO behaviour is generally recognized.

Discussion

A simulation program which reacts contingently on the subject's behaviour turned out to be effective in changing cooperativeness in either direction. The influence of simulated "Other" was found not only in the usual index of C-frequencies but also in the more informative parameters of game behaviour. Except for the state-conditioned expectancies, most parameters seemed to vary with training conditions, including those which are generally considered as relatively independent of the interaction processes (i.e., the "propensities"). The distinguishing feature of the simulation employed here, compared with related studies, was that the reinforcement schedule was changed depending on subject's behaviour. This might help to mask the computer as a real counterpart. It is supported by the fact that in the final interview only 3 out of 100 persons suspected a computer simulation. For these reasons we feel that the critique of Vinacke (1969) does not hold in our case. Vinacke objected, that "there is little value in the artificial technique in which a stooge, experimenter, or computer takes the part of one player. By this procedure, one only eliminates what is perhaps the most important feature of the game". In contrast, we think that what is needed is more sophisticated simulation programs whereby more specific aspects of the interaction process in a controlled situation can be investigated.

4. Model Building and Psychological Theory

The relationship between psychology and mathematics is more symbiotic than parasitic. Just as some sceptics define intelligence as that which psychologists test, so others define mathematics as that which mathematicians do. Mathematics is in fact primarily concerned with what can be accomplished by reason. This after all is what psychologists test. There can be no doubt that mathematics has played a key role in the development of man's reasoning abilities and his subjection of nature. An eclipse is no longer a frightening, capricious event but rather evidence that nature is predictably as punctual and reliable as a Victorian cleric. Unfortunately, in spite of this analogy, mathematics has been considerably less effective in contributing to man's knowledge of his own mind. The prediction of human behaviour remains at best statistical rather than precise — some Victorian clerics led extremely bizarre and unpredictable lives. Nevertheless mathematicians as well as psychologists still hope that research on mathematical models may yet make large contributions to our understanding of both social problems and psychological events. Unfortunately, once we get away from relatively trivial generalities, we find that individual differences in human behaviour are so complex that we must either complicate our equations to an extent which defies analysis and computation, or else we must simplify our assumptions to a degree that makes any resemblance between the behaviour and its model coincidental rather than explanatory. To take a completely nihilistic view of modelling, however, would be to neglect unjustifiably the major role that model building plays in the testing and modification of psychological theory. This is an aspect of modelling brought out in the papers grouped together in the next section. These illustrate very clearly the advantages that can occur when psychologists learn a formal language which enables them to express psychological concepts in terms which are readily susceptible to mathematical manipulation. As Kline (1962) has pointed out, mathematics is essentially a device for applying reasoned argument to empirical data. It is also an international language for the communication of ideas. Moreover the discipline involved in reducing a psychological hypothesis to a series of equations or to a set of FORTRAN statements can, in Johnson's words, "concentrate the mind wonderfully."

Models as we have implied are sometimes a vainglorious attempt to express complex fundamental psychological ideas in an all-comprehending equation. Alternatively, they can be a rewarding intellectual exercise which sharpens the perception of the modeller and encourages self criticism, and also facilitates the communication of his ideas not only to his colleagues but to workers in other disciplines. Computer models have the advantage over conventional models in that as programs they can be tested on a wide range of data. Models of this type are widely used for predicting future events by extrapolating from a known body of past experience. Weather, stock market predictions and war gaming are well known examples. These have been less successful than might have been expected, the last example according to Andrew Wilson (1968) often disastrously so. These failures partly reflect the real difficulties of the technique but also its misuse, in particular the gay abandon with which, in the model, ignorance is replaced by what are euphemistically known as reasonable assumptions. In psychological theory the main danger is quite different. Here the temptation is to give excessive weight to a model's success. Perhaps the greatest danger of modelling is the temptation to regard a mathematical statement as more reputable and trustworthy than its psychological precursor.

M. FUAT TURGUT *

An Evaluation of Computer Simulated Models of Human Problem Solving

Summary

The role of models in the advancement of sciences and the logic of analogy from the models are discussed and some criteria developed for the evaluation of computer simulation techniques as models of scientific inquiry. Some of the computer simulation research is then critically examined.

Models: Their Role and Validity in Scientific Study

Human thinking and problem solving have been the subject of research in psychology for a long time and various methods of study have been used (Davis, 1966). However, the use of computers to model human thinking has a short history.

The word "model" is used in various connotations (Apostel, 1961; Suppes, 1961). The variation in the meaning of the word is so great that Apostel (1961, p. 36), after examining various types of models used in "non-formal" sciences, says, "We can not hope to give one unique structural definition for models ...." This diversity of meaning is caused by the fact that models have different functions in different areas of usage. A small scale and imperfect replication of an aircraft is called a "model airplane". An arrangement of plastic spheres forms a "model of a molecule". A mechanical gadget may be a model of the solar system.

*Hacettepe University, Ankara

These examples, and many others, can generally be termed *material analogues*. A material analogue is usually created to represent some important aspects of a real system which is difficult to study directly.

Sometimes the word model is used synonymously with the word "theory". Mathematical theories of learning, Gestalt theory, the statistical theory of parametric inference, and the like are called models. Any formal theory, whether it is mathematical or not, may be called a *conceptual model*.

The simulation of human thinking by means of computers does not fit well into either of these two categories of models. In the first place, the machine with its electronic circuits and related hardware is *not* intended to be an analogue of the human brain. However, every computer works by a set of instructions which is called a "program". Is it the program that should be considered as the model of human mind? The answer to this question cannot easily be affirmative or negative. No computer looks like a human brain, yet the functioning and especially the outputs of computers resemble some of the products of human mental activity.

Let us take symbol manipulation processes as an example. The computer reads, writes, erases, copies a symbol; or compares two symbols and takes a different course of action according to the result of the comparison. If the researcher considers the computer as a model of such basic symbol manipulation processes, his aim is to find an ordered sequence of those basic processes and to write a set of instructions (the program), so that the computer will produce some results which will be indistinguishable from the behaviour of human beings provided with comparable information. Thus, "the sequence of ordered processes" in symbol manipulation of the computer is taken as an analogue of "human mental processes" in manipulating comparable symbols.

The aim of a technician is to find some "sequence of ordered processes" that fits his technical aims and he may not be interested in the similarity with "human mental processes". However, a psychologist is primarily interested in those "human mental processes". He wants to know more about them. He will be interested in the computer, or in its program, only if it helps him to understand the human mental processes better. Therefore, a computer may be a model for the real system he wants to study.

When the real system to be studied is too complicated for a full analysis it may be simplified and idealized in a model. Models are often approximations of the real systems. Since models are built by the researchers, they can be made to any desired degree of approximation within the limits of the techniques available. Usually some characteristics of the system are isolated and studied for a given purpose. Everything that is irrelevant or trivial for the purpose of study is omitted in the model. Sometimes the real system is exaggerated on the model. This is also an approximation. Thus, models, whether material or conceptual, are means of simplification and idealization. A further, perhaps the most important, role of a model in scientific inquiry is to help *generate experimental hypotheses*. That is, the model suggests some hypotheses about the real system; then, such hypotheses are tested.

One cannot think of a model for a completely known system. The real system is usually partly known; and, by inductive reasoning, one can build a model of it. Then, the model is studied and by *analogy* inferences are made about the real system. The validity of the inference will depend upon the validity of the analogy. Hence it is essential that the relevant crucial elements of the real system are accurately represented in the model. Similarity may also be required between structural elements, functional relations, processes, input—output relations, and the like. An element in the real system which has an analogue in the model is called a "positive" analogue. Both the real system and its model may have elements that are not related to the characteristic under study. Such elements may be called "neutral" elements. They are irrelevant to the characteristic under study. A third type of element may be found either in the real system or in its model only. Such an element may be relevant or even crucial to the characteristic under study, and is called a "negative" analogue (Hesse, 1966).

The existence of positive analogues and the degree of similarity between them increases the validity of reasoning by analogy. The existence of neutral elements cannot invalidate reasoning by analogy. However, the presence of negative analogues invalidates reasoning by analogy to the extent of their effect on the characteristic under study. Since the real system is only partly known, and since the model is strictly controlled by the researcher, the negative analogues are more likely to be found in the real system.

The second stage of analogical argument is that a relationship found in the model is inferred to exist in the real system as well. The analogical reasoning does not provide a rigorous proof. An analogy, by the nature of its logic, is just a hypothesis. More detailed discussions about the validity of inferences drawn from models can be found in a number of reviews (e.g., Apostel, 1961; Hesse, 1966).

Criteria for Evaluation of Models Used in Scientific Study

The model should be *internally consistent*, i.e., the model should reproduce the same responses under the same conditions. The internal consistency of a model can be used as a criterion in evaluating its usefulness in a scientific inquiry. Models can be tested for their internal consistency.

The model should be precise to the degree of tolerable measurement errors. The precision of a model can be used as another criterion in evaluating its usefulness. The precision of a model can be measured on the data produced by the model.

The model should in some sense be *isomorphic* to the real system. However, the isomorphism between the real system and its model has to be only partial. If a model replicates some of the known elements of the real system, but does not have any element, relation or function which is different from the real system, it would have no value in scientific inquiry; because all of the facts deducted from such a model would be already known on the real system. The elements, relations or functions which exist in the model, but are not known to exist in the real system, make the discovery of new facts possible. Therefore partial and relevant isomorphism should be a requirement for the model.

Given a real system and a model of it, one can test the isomorphism between them by several methods. Turing's test (Turing, 1950) is usually applied for this purpose. Data are gathered from the model and from the real system separately, then the two sets of data are compared (Hunt *et al.*, 1966, pp. 133, 144).

If a model is to be useful in scientific study, it should *generate testable hypotheses* about the real system.

If a hypothesis is deduced from a model, tested independently on the real system and confirmed, then one may say that the model has predictive power. Here one finds the fourth criterion for the evaluation of a model.

230

Alternatively, a hypothesis may be deducted from the real system, and then tested on the model. The conclusion reached through such testing will again only be valid to the extent of the validity of the analogy.

Secondly, one should not discredit a model if a hypothesis deduced from it is shown to be false on the real system. Rejection of a hypothesis adds to our knowledge too. However, if most of the hypotheses deduced from a model turned out to be false when tested on the real system, one should look at the model with suspicion.

Thirdly, one should not credit a model if the hypotheses generated by it may also be deduced from the real system alone. In this case the model might be replicating the real system without any new element relevant to the characteristic under study.

Evaluation of Computer Simulated Models of Human Thinking and Problem Solving

In the first section we have suggested that the human mind with its processes and products in thinking and problem solving be considered as a real system, and that computers with their programs should be considered as models of this real system. Computers and their programs have been developed mainly for technical purposes and the simulation of such mental activities as classification, computation, decision making, etc., is largely incidental. Neither the machines nor the related programs were created to be models of human mind and human mental activities. Consequently, some writers maintain the view that computers should not be taken as models. For some writers (Neisser, 1963) the discovery of even better computers may not teach us anything about human problem solving. Such machines are technical aids or, as sometimes called, devices of "artificial intelligence". Fogel et al. (1966, p. 8) say that "artificial intelligence is realized only if an inanimate machine can solve problems that have, thus far, resisted solution by man, not merely because of the machine's sheer speed and accuracy, but because it can discover for itself new techniques for solving the problem at hand". However, even though machines demonstrating artificial intelligence were not built as models of human intelligence, a careful study of their methods of problem solving can nevertheless suggest hypotheses about the problem solving processes in human beings.

In many studies on computer simulation of human thinking it is in fact not clear whether the aim was to develop artificial intelligence or to build a model in order to learn more about human thinking. To mention a few examples, one can cite the earlier works on chess and checker playing programs and the automatic question answering machines (Feigenbaum and Feldman, 1963, pp. 39–105, 207–16). This type of research may pass the first two criteria mentioned above, that is the programs may be consistent and precise. But it is doubtful whether their isomorphism is relevant and whether they contain new relevant characteristics. Certainly, they do not all suggest new hypotheses about human problem solving.

More fundamental mental activities which are essential for human thinking and problem solving have also been simulated. For example, pattern recognition programs may simulate certain aspects of visual perception although they may not simulate other cognitive processes which immediately follow perception (Selfridge and Neisser, 1963; Uhr and Vossler, 1963). Perception in human beings inevitably results in the classification of stimuli, but this in turn frequently involves concept formation and higher orders of learning. In general computer models of pattern recognition try to simulate these mental processes only to the extent of processing and classifying the data which are fed into the computer. For example, in a recent study Runge et al. (1970) constructed an electronic model capable of replicating optical-to-electrical transformations of human vision. Such a system with a data processing component may suggest some hypotheses about the processes of visual perception in human beings. Simon (1967) for example tried to explain some perceptual phenomena by information processing principles used in computer programs. More recently Simon and Barenfeld (1969) proposed a theory to explain some of the known phenomena which are seen at the beginning of problem solving behaviour, in terms of information processing principles. The theory was tested on a chess player's eye movements during the first five seconds in choosing a move. The computer simulated data were consistent with the data gathered from the chess players. These studies show that some of the fundamental processes of cognition can successfully be simulated.

Another group of studies is concerned with the simulation of concept learning. Feigenbaum's Elementary Perceiver and Memorizer (Feigenbaum and Feldman, 1963, pp. 297–309 and Hunt *et al.*, 1966 Concept Learning System) are examples of such simulation programs. The essence of these studies is that the stimuli fed to the machine are evaluated by sequential decisions and classified according to their major characteristics. The claim of such studies is that they simulate inductive thinking, or at least some fundamental processes involved in it. Again here the machines and the programs may be consistent and precise, but the similarity between the processes used in simulation and the inductive thinking of human beings seems to be quite weak. It is doubtful whether generalization of concepts in human beings follows systematic sequential decisions like computer programs. One gets the impression that the aim of these studies was to develop programs that enable computers to do things which human beings do. Thus, these studies, by just sheer imitation of some human abilities, do not contribute significantly to our knowledge of human thinking. Simulation programs differ according to the problems that they purport to solve with the computer. However, a general characteristic of many programs is that the problem is solved by the programmer and this solution is translated into computer sequences. Of course, the solution has to be in such a form that it fits the capabilities of the computer. Many types of problems have been solved by computers and even a "problem finding machine" has been described (Klugh, 1969). With the computers of our day, identification, classification, comparison, computation, decision making and similar basic operations can be carried out. Thus, any problem that can be reduced to some of these basic operations in its solution can be handled by computers.

Now we can take up the main question of this paper. Can these problem solving machines and their programs be taken as models of human problem solving processes? We shall try to give an answer to this question by applying the criteria discussed above.

The first criterion is that the computers and their programs be consistent and precise in problem solving operations. One may say that they are just too good in this respect. The machines and their programs are so consistent and precise that this very consistency and preciseness mean that they do not approach isomorphism with human mechanisms. There are several sources of differences.

Firstly, there are inevitable differences which may be a source of negative analogy. Secondly, sources of human inconsistency and human error are often not represented in computer programs, and these also may cause negative analogies. As George (1970) has emphasized, "human logic is less efficient than computer logic". The third important difference between computers and human problem solving is seen in the principles of functioning of the machine and human brains. Computing machinery can be based on two principles — digital and analogue. The existing computers on which the majority of simulation studies have been carried out are purely digital machines. The human nervous system apparently works by both analogue and digital principle (Von Neumann, 1956; Egawa and Haga, 1966). The mixed character of the human thinking process is likely to be the greatest source of negative analogy when digital computers are used as models of human thinking.

There is ample evidence that computers are quite different from the human thinking processes in many respects. Is there any element in the computer that is relevant to the problem solving processes but does not seemingly exist in human beings? Here the speed and accuracy of the computer memory contrasts with the slow but wide-ranging power of the associative memory of man.

Do computers generate new hypotheses about human problem solving? Certainly they have done so but many of the hypotheses are not testable. Unfortunately for the theoretical psychologist, many studies are designed primarily to exploit the problem solving power of computers rather than to develop models of human thinking which will allow him to generate testable hypotheses which will enable him to learn more about human thinking and problem solving. It appears that many of the early models stopped short at the "successful" imitation of human problem solving without further consideration. However the techniques developed will allow psychologists to build models for the specific purposes of scientific inquiry.

Little can be said on the final criterion, i.e., that the simulation studies should generate experimentally testable hypotheses. It is a personal view that most models are at the stage of simulating known human characteristics and few important hypotheses have been generated.

P.O. WHITE*

A Mathematical Model for
Individual Differences in Problem Solving

Summary

A mathematical model for individual differences in problem solving is described. This relates the latency of a subject's response to an item and the probability of the response being correct, to the speed, persistence, and accuracy level of the subject and to the difficulty level and discriminating power of the item. The model leads directly to a likelihood function which provides a basis for the computation of joint maximum likelihood estimates of all subject and item parameters.

Introduction

Traditional tests of cognitive abilities are of two main types. Some, exemplified by the Thurstone tests of primary mental ability, include problems which span a broad range of specific types of ability. These tests typically yield single scores for each of the ability types (such as verbal, numerical and perceptual, for example) and a single, global score for what is usually called "general ability". Other tests, exemplified by the Advanced Progressive Matrices (Raven) include items which, though differing in difficulty, are all essentially of the same type. Tests of this sort also tend to yield but a single global score for "general ability".

It is clear (as many vocal opponents to the testing movement in psychology so readily point out!) that, for either type of test, such

* Institute of Psychiatry, London

single scores obscure much, if not most, of the fine grain in the confrontation between test and subject, in the sense that different individuals may achieve identical scores for quite different reasons. On the one hand, a slow accurate worker will attempt fewer problems but may correctly solve a high proportion of those which he attempts. A fast but inaccurate worker, though attempting many more problems, will make a low proportion of correct responses. On the other hand, one individual may achieve a low score by virtue of his particular speed-accuracy configuration, while another individual, though fast and accurate, may achieve a low score by abandoning problems, which, given greater persistence, he may well solve.

Thus the single score obtained by an individual on a traditional test is some unknown function of his speed, persistence and accuracy. The present model provides for the determination of separate scores for each of these logically distinct components. Practical application of Furneaux' (1963) model has already demonstrated significant improvements in predictive accuracy of academic achievement by utilizing such separate measures of speed, persistence and accuracy.

In this paper we present a mathematical model for individual differences in problem solving. The model relates the latency of a subject's response to an item and the probability of the response being correct, to the speed, persistence, and accuracy level of the subject and to the difficulty level and discriminating power of the item. The model stems more or less directly from a conceptual model for problem solving reported by Furneaux (1960) and from a logistic latent trait model for test scores reported by Birnbaum (1968). The model reformulates Furneaux' conceptual model in statistical terms and extends Birnbaum's statistical model to include speed, persistence, and response time variables. The model yields an expression for the likelihood of a subject's response pattern to a number of different items. It thus leads directly to an expression for the likelihood of the set of response patterns of a number of different subjects to the same set of items. This function provides a basis for the computation of joint maximum likelihood estimates of all subject and item parameters. In the following section we present a concise mathematical statement of the model and derive the likelihood function. In a final section we discuss some of the practical problems anticipated in fitting the model to empirical data and comment on a possible theoretical difficulty with the model.

Mathematical Statement of the Model

Notation

x_{ji},y_{ji} observable discrete random variables
s_i,a_i,p_i unobservable continuous random variables
t_{ji} observable continuous mathematical variable
d_j,D_j unknown item parameters
X_{ji},Y_{ji} realization of the observable random variables x_{ji} and y_{ji}
T_{ji} observed value of the mathematical variable t_{ji}
c unknown model parameter
$\hat{s}_i,\hat{a}_i,\hat{p}_i$ estimates of the unobservable random variables s_i,a_i,p_i
$\hat{d}_j,\hat{D}_j$ estimates of the item parameters d_j and D_j
$\theta[z]$ cumulative logistic function with argument z

Model

Subject i is presented with item j. After some time $t_{ji} = T_{ji}$ he responds to the item. His response is either to abandon the item or to put forth an attempt at its solution. If he abandons the item, the random variable y_{ji} assumes the value $Y_{ji} = 1$; otherwise it assumes the value $Y_{ji} = 0$. If he makes an attempt to solve the item, then his attempt is either correct or it is incorrect. If the attempt at solution is correct, then the random variable x_{ji} assumes the value $X_{ji} = 1$; otherwise it assumes the value $X_{ji} = 0$. Thus, for each item we have two observable discrete random variables x_{ji} and y_{ji} with realizations X_{ji} and Y_{ji}, and an observable mathematical variable t_{ji} with observed value T_{ji}. For a subject we assume three unobservable random variables a_i,s_i,p_i (accuracy, speed and persistence); and, for the item, we assume two unknown parameters d_j and D_j (difficulty level and discriminating power).

$$Pr[Y_{ji} = 0 \,|\, t_{ji} = T_{ji}] = \theta[c(p_i - T_{ji})] = \alpha_{ji} \tag{1}$$

$$Pr[X_{ji} = 1 \,|\, Y_{ji} = 0, t_{ji} = T_{ji}] \tag{2}$$
$$= \theta[D_j(a_i\{1 - \exp(-s_i T_{ji})\} - d_j)] = \beta_{ji}$$

Eq. (1) defines the probability that a response yielded at some time T_{ji} will be an attempted solution rather than an abandonment. This probability is a function of the subject's persistence (p_i) and of the time (T_{ji}) since the presentation of the item.

Eq. (2) defines the conditional probability that an attempted solution (yielded at time T_{ji}) will be a correct solution. This conditional probability is a function of the speed (s_i) and accuracy (a_i) of the subject; of the difficulty level (d_j) and discriminating power (D_j) of the item; and of the time (T_{ji}) since presentation of the item.

In Eq. (1), c is an unknown model parameter. The notation $\theta[z]$ indicates the cumulative logistic function, defined in Eq. (3):

$$\theta[z] = [1 + \exp(-z)]^{-1} \tag{3}$$

From the above definitions, Eq. (4) to (7) follow directly:

$$Pr[X_{ji} = 0, \ Y_{ji} = 0 \,|\, t_{ji} = T_{ji}] = (1 - \beta_{ji})\alpha_{ji} \tag{4}$$

$$Pr[X_{ji} = 0, \ Y_{ji} = 1 \,|\, t_{ji} = T_{ji}] = (1 - \alpha_{ji}) \tag{5}$$

$$Pr[X_{ji} = 1, \ Y_{ji} = 0 \,|\, t_{ji} = T_{ji}] = \alpha_{ji}\beta_{ji} \tag{6}$$

$$Pr[X_{ji} = 1, \ Y_{ji} = 1 \,|\, t_{ji} = T_{ji}] = 0 \tag{7}$$

Eq. (4) expresses the joint probability that a response elicited at time T_{ji} will be an attempt at solution and that the attempt will yield an incorrect solution.

Eq. (5) expresses the joint probability that a response elicited at time T_{ji} will be an abandonment, and thus not a correct solution.

Eq. (6) expresses the joint probability that a response elicited at time T_{ji} will be an attempt at solution, and that this attempt will yield a correct solution.

Eq. (7) expresses the joint probability that a response elicited at time T_{ji} will be an abandonment and that a correct response will be given. It merely reflects the obvious fact that a correct response to an abandoned item is impossible.

Eq. (4) to (7) may conveniently be combined into the single equation:

$$Pr[x_{ji} = X_{ji}, y_{ji} = Y_{ji} \,|\, t_{ji} = T_{ji}] = 1_{ji} \tag{8}$$

$$= [\beta_{ji}^{X_{ji}} (1 - \beta_{ji})^{(1 - X_{ji} - Y_{ji})} \alpha_{ji}^{(1 - Y_{ji})} (1 - \alpha_{ji})^{Y_{ji}}] [1 - X_{ji} Y_{ji}]$$

Eq. (8) expresses the likelihood of any particular observed response pattern ($x_{ji} = X_{ji}$, $y_{ji} = Y_{ji}$) as a function of the speed (s_i), accuracy (a_i) and persistence (p_i) of the subject; of the difficulty level (d_j) and discriminating power (D_j) of the item; and of the response time ($t_{ji} = T_{ji}$) to the item.

Assuming local independence over items and independent sampling across subjects, we may write the likelihood function:

$$L = \prod_{j=1}^{n} \prod_{i=1}^{N} 1_{ji} \tag{9}$$

Eq. (9) is the likelihood of the set of response patterns of N different subjects to the same set of n items, expressed as a function of the $3nN$ observed quantities (X_{ji}, Y_{ji}, T_{ji}; $j = 1, 2, ..., n$; $i = 1, 2, ..., N$); of the $3N$ unobservable subject variables (a_i, s_i, p_i; $i = 1, 2, .., N$); and of the $2n$ unknown item parameters (d_j, D_j; $j = 1, 2, ..., n$).

The likelihood function defined in Eq. (9) provides a basis for the computation of joint maximum likelihood estimates of the unobservable subject variables and of the unknown item parameters, given the observed values.

Practical Aspects

The solution for the maximum likelihood estimation problem cannot be given in explicit algebraic form. However, the use of iterative numerical techniques can determine a solution to some specified accuracy. For large-scale problems of this sort, computational requirements are massive (both in terms of computer storage requirements and computational time). Furthermore, effective solution of such large-scale problems requires a flexible system of sub-programs for a variety of optimizing procedures, each utilizing sophisticated numerical techniques. Mathematical analysis of the statistical model detailed below indicates several ways in which the magnitude of the estimation problem may be reduced by minimizing with respect to subsets of the variables. We do not go into specific details here. However, such a device would reduce computer storage requirements to about one-half of that required by explicit use of the likelihood function defined above and could possibly reduce computer time by a factor of about four.

One possible problem with the model stems from the fact that each time we add another subject to our sample we add three new parameters (i.e., for speed, accuracy, and persistence) to be estimated. A possible consequence of this is that the maximum likelihood estimates for the item parameters (i.e., difficulty level and discriminating power) may not have the "consistency" property usually associated with such estimates. This may be quite disturbing to most statistical readers. However it should be borne in mind that the important parameters from the psychological point of view are the subject parameters: the key issue is whether the estimates of these parameters relate reliably to significant non-test performance. This is an empirical problem and can ultimately be settled only on an empirical basis.

Current Status

At the time of writing, computer programs have been prepared for fitting two very simple special cases of the model to real data. These programs have been thoroughly tested on artificial data but have not yet been applied to real data. A program for fitting the full model with speed, accuracy, and persistence parameters for each subject and difficulty level and discriminating power parameters for each problem has been prepared but has not yet been adequately tested.

This paper, then, is very much a report on progress to date rather than a final report on a completed program of research. Its main function is to put on record a formal statement of the model. Technical details on the procedure for fitting the model, on the computer programs involved, and on the substantive findings will appear in later reports.

JEAN-FRANCOIS RICHARD* and DOMINIQUE LEPINE**

Strategies in Concept Identification

Summary

Two types of hypothesis testing models applicable to unidimensional concept identification tasks are formulated. Their goodness of fit to empirical data is examined with simulation programs. Of the two models tested, that which includes both attention and learning processes gives the better fit.

Introduction

Unidimensional concept identification tasks are usually analysed within the framework of hypothesis testing models (e.g., Restle, 1962). In this type of model, a set of hypotheses (including the correct one) is assumed to be available to the subject. On each trial, a subset of these hypotheses (possibly reduced to one single hypothesis) is tested; then, each hypothesis is either retained or rejected, with a certain probability, which depends on whether it was confirmed or disconfirmed on that trial through reinforcement. If every hypothesis tested is rejected, a new subset of hypotheses is sampled in the next trial. Only when the correct hypothesis alone is retained, is the problem considered solved. Although the testing mechanism is of major importance in these models, one notices that the idea that the differing attributes of the

*Laboratoire de Psychologie, University of Paris
**Laboratoire de Psychologie Experimentale et Comparée, Paris.

objects may be unequally salient is either disregarded as part of that mechanism or is introduced in only a subsidiary manner.

We compare here a model of this type with a second model in which the hypothesis sampling mechanism includes an attention process and a learning process, both of which operate on each attribute. In this respect it resembles the "attention models" developed for discrimination learning situations.

Experimental Procedure

In the present paper, using data from an experiment by M. Levine (1966), we compare the ability of the two models to predict, as closely as possible, the subjects' behaviour during the learning process. In Levine's experiment the stimuli (letters of the alphabet) were four-dimensional: the dimensions being form (upper or lower case letter), colour (white or black), size (large or small), and position (left or right). The response to the two types of trials in the experiment — reinforced trials and non-reinforced (blank) trials — were used to infer the subject's current hypothesis.

Each set of trials defining a problem was constructed as follows: 1 reinforced trial (trial 0); 4 blank trials, used to infer the first hypothesis (H_1); 1 reinforced trial (trial 1); 4 blank trials, used to infer the second hypothesis (H_2); 1 reinforced trial (trial 2); 4 blank trials, used to infer the third hypothesis (H_3); 1 reinforced trial (trial 3).

Eighty adult subjects were trained on 16 problems each, giving a total of 1,280 problems. Each dimension was relevant for about one-quarter of the problems. There were relatively few cases — about 5 percent[1] — in which the pattern of response in the 4 blank trials was not consistent with one hypothesis, and these were dropped from the analysis.

[1] If the responses were given at random, there would be 50 per cent inconsistent patterns.

242

The Attention Model

The model assumes that:

(a) On each trial each attribute A_i is either observed or not observed: the subject's observation state on a given trial is then defined by a four-element vector, with each element having two possible values:

(i) observed ($A_i \in O_n$),

(ii) not observed ($A_i \notin O_n$). (If k is the number of attributes, there are 2^k observation states in the case.)

(b) Each attribute is in one of three possible conditioning states:

(i) the unconditioned state (z_i^0)

(ii) conditioned to the value (') (z_i')

(iii) conditioned to the value ('') (z_i'')

The set Z of the conditioning states is the product $Z = \Pi_i z_i$.

(c) At the beginning of each problem, each attribute is observed with a probability c_i, and all the attributes are in the unconditioned state.

(d) On each trial the subject has a leading hypothesis (H_1), which is the basis for his response. If, for instance, his hypothesis is "white", he will choose the stimulus that is white, whatever values it may have for the other attributes.

(e) If the response given at the current trial is positively reinforced, the same hypothesis is retained as leading hypothesis for the next trial. If it is not reinforced, a new leading hypothesis is chosen at random from a set of "tested" hypotheses, which are defined as follows: For each attribute A_i that is not observed, there is no tested hypothesis belonging to that attribute. If the attribute A_i is observed and not conditioned (z_i^0), the two hypotheses of this attribute h_i'' and h_i' are in this set. If the attribute is observed and conditioned to the value (') (z_i'), there is one tested hypothesis (h_i') for this attribute. If the attribute is observed and conditioned to the value ('') (z_i''), there is one tested hypothesis (h_i'') for this attribute.

The evolution of the subject's observation and conditioning states may be described as follows:

(a) If the attribute A_i is observed on trial $n (A_i \in O_n)$ and it is in the unconditioned state ($z_i = z_i^0$), the attribute is still observed on trial $n + 1 (A_i \in O_{n+1})$, and it becomes conditioned to the reinforced value of the attribute with probability θ_i.

(b) If the attribute A_i is observed on trial n and it is already conditioned to the value that is reinforced at the end of the trial n, there is no change in either the observation state or in the conditioning state.

(c) If the attribute is observed on trial n and it is conditioned to the value that is not reinforced, the attribute becomes non-observed for the next trial with probability c' and independently with probability θ_i, the attribute becomes conditioned to the opposite value, which was reinforced.

(d) If the attribute A_i is not observed and there is no other attribute A_j which is observed — and is either unconditioned or conditioned to the reinforced value — the attribute A_i becomes observed at the next trial with probability c_i.

(e) If there is another attribute that is observed and is either unconditioned or conditioned to the reinforced value, A_i remains unobserved, and its state of conditioning does not change.

θ_i is assumed to equal 1.00 for the attribute of the leading hypothesis. For the other attributes that are observed, θ_i has the value θ_i^+ when the response is correct and θ_i^- when it is incorrect. θ_i^+ and θ_i^- have the same value (θ^+ and θ^-) respectively for every attribute except the attribute of the leading hypothesis.

There are seven parameters in the model: c_i, c_2, c_3, c_4 (which measure the saliency of attributes); c', θ^+ and θ^-. Because each attribute is relevant roughly the same number of times throughout the entire set of problems, several statistics may be computed for all problems. We have used only one parameter value c, to obtain predictions for these statistics instead of the four c_i. For the statistics based on the problems having the same relevant attribute, differing values of c_i were re-introduced.

The Hypothesis Sampling Model

This model assumes that, on each trial, the subject tests only one hypothesis. If this hypothesis is confirmed, it is retained for the next trial. If it is disconfirmed, it is rejected, and the subject tests another hypothesis to be sampled.

The sampling scheme works as follows: With probability c, the chosen hypothesis is consistent with the information given on the last trial and with probability $1 - c$, it is not consistent with this information. Thus, with four dimensions, a value which is reinforced has a probability $c/4$ of becoming the tested hypothesis; a value which is not reinforced has a probability $(1 - c)/3$ of becoming the tested hypothesis (since the rejected hypothesis cannot come into test on the next trial). The hypothesis to be tested is chosen at random from the eight possible hypotheses at the beginning of each problem.

Results

The statistics to be considered first are of two types:

Firstly, the probability that H_2 is one of the two values that the positive stimulus can take on trials 0 and 1, given that there is a correct response on these two trials $[P(H_2 \in s_o^+ \cap s_i^+ /+ o, + 1)]$. See Table I.

TABLE I

Probability that H_2 is one of the four types of hypotheses, as a function of the pattern of reinforcement on trials 0 and 1 *

Pattern of reinforcement	$H_2 \in$			
	$s_0^+ \cap s_1^+$	$\bar{s}_0 \cap s_1^+$	$s_0^+ \cap \bar{s}_1$	$\bar{s}_0 \cap \bar{s}_1$
$+_0 +_1$	0.98	0.01	0.00	0.00
	0.99	0.01	0.00	0.00
	1.00	0.00	0.00	0.00
$-_0 +_1$	0.85	0.14	0.00	0.01
	0.80	0.20	0.00	0.00
	0.83	0.17	0.00	0.00
$+_0 -_1$	0.60	0.21	0.14	0.06
	0.62	0.16	0.07	0.14
	0.43	0.43	0.04	0.09
$-_0 -_1$	0.51	0.27	0.11	0.10
	0.58	0.24	0.06	0.12
	0.43	0.43	0.05	0.08

* Line 1, data; line 2, predictions from the attention model ($c = 0.60$, $c' = 0.80$; $\theta^+ = 0.70$; $\theta^- = 0.40$; line 3, predictions from the hypothesis sampling model ($c = 0.87$).

245

TABLE II

Probability that H_3 is one of the eight possible hypotheses as a function of the pattern of reinforcement*

Pattern of reinforcement	$H_3 \in$							
	$s_0^+ \cap s_1^+ \cap s_2^+$	$s_0^- \cap s_1^+ \cap s_2^+$	$s_0^+ \cap s_1^- \cap s_2^+$	$s_0^- \cap s_1^- \cap s_2^+$	$s_0^+ \cap s_1^+ \cap s_2^-$	$s_0^- \cap s_1^+ \cap s_2^-$	$s_0^+ \cap s_1^- \cap s_2^-$	$s_0^- \cap s_1^- \cap s_2^-$
$+_0+_1+_2$	0.94	0.03	0.00	0.00	0.02	0.00	0.00	0.00
	0.99	0.01	0.00	0.00	0.00	0.00	0.00	0.00
	1.00	0.00	0.00	0.00	0.00	0.00	0.00	0.00
$-_0+_1+_2$	0.85	0.15	0.00	0.00	0.00	0.00	0.00	0.00
	0.79	0.21	0.00	0.00	0.00	0.00	0.00	0.00
	0.87	0.13	0.00	0.00	0.00	0.00	0.00	0.00
$+_0-_1+_2$	0.61	0.16	0.15	0.07	0.00	0.00	0.00	0.00
	0.62	0.15	0.07	0.14	0.00	0.00	0.00	0.00
	0.55	0.28	0.06	0.11	0.00	0.00	0.00	0.00
$-_0-_1+_2$	0.46	0.27	0.11	0.14	0.00	0.00	0.00	0.00
	0.58	0.23	0.06	0.11	0.00	0.00	0.00	0.00
	0.43	0.43	0.05	0.08	0.00	0.00	0.00	0.00
$+_0+_1-_2$	0.44	0.14	0.19	0.07	0.04	0.06	0.06	0.05
	0.44	0.19	0.07	0.02	0.00	0.07	0.06	0.09
	0.22	0.22	0.22	0.22	0.00	0.04	0.04	0.04
$-_0+_1-_2$	0.36	0.19	0.10	0.07	0.05	0.08	0.09	0.06
	0.42	0.21	0.09	0.06	0.01	0.06	0.06	0.08
	0.22	0.22	0.22	0.22	0.00	0.04	0.04	0.04
$+_0-_1-_2$	0.29	0.12	0.16	0.17	0.06	0.09	0.07	0.04
	0.37	0.17	0.10	0.16	0.02	0.06	0.04	0.08
	0.22	0.22	0.22	0.22	0.02	0.02	0.04	0.04
$-_0-_1-_2$	0.25	0.23	0.16	0.09	0.10	0.08	0.06	0.03
	0.39	0.19	0.09	0.15	0.03	0.05	0.04	0.07
	0.22	0.22	0.22	0.22	0.02	0.02	0.03	0.03

* Line 1, data; line 2, predictions from the attention model ($c = 0.60$, $c' = 0.80$, $\theta^+ = 0.70$; $\theta^- = 0.40$); line 3, predictions from the hypothesis sampling model ($c = 0.87$).

Secondly, the probability that H_3 is the value for the positive stimulus on trials 1, 2, and 3, given that the response is correct on trials 0, 1 and 2 $[P(H_3 \in s_o^+ \cap s_i^+ \cap s_2^+/+ o +_1 +_2)]$. Table II). If $H_3 \in s_0^+ \cap s_1^+ \cap s_2^+$, H_3 is in fact the correct hypothesis, as the sequence of reinforced stimuli is such that four hypotheses are logically eliminated after trial 0, two others after trial 1 and the last one after trial 2.

These statistics are computed over all the problems and consequently do not reflect any differences in the saliency of the attributes. The attention model was studied by Monte-Carlo techniques, and the hypothesis sampling model by analytical procedures.

It is clear from the data that the probability that H_2 will be one of the two hypotheses consistent with the information in the first two trials depends, primarily, on whether the response on trial 1 was correct or incorrect and, to a lesser extent, on whether the response on trial 0 was correct or incorrect. This trend is well predicted by the observation model (see Fig. 1).

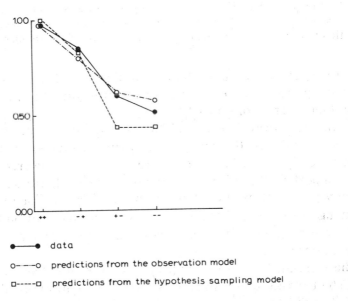

Fig. 1. Probability that H_2 is one of the two hypotheses compatible with the information of the first two trials as a function of the pattern of reinforcement on trials 0 and 1. ●————● data; o—·—o predictions from the attention model; □————□ predictions from the hypothesis sampling model.

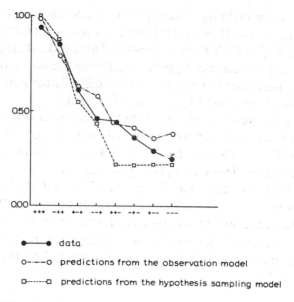

●————● data

o—·—o predictions from the observation model

□·······□ predictions from the hypothesis sampling model

Fig. 2. Probability that H_3 is the correct hypothesis as a function of the pattern of reinforcement on trials 0, 1 and 2. ●———● data; o—·—o predictions from the attention model; □———□ predictions from the hypothesis sampling model

With regard to the hypothesis sampling model, this model predicts the same performance for either correct or incorrect response on trial 0 when there is an error on trial 1.

In the same way, the probability that H_3 is the correct hypothesis depends mainly on the correctness (or incorrectness) of the responses on trials 0, 1, and 2, but to a different degree; the nearer the trial, the more important the influence of the outcome of that trial. This trend is roughly predicted by the attention model (Fig. 2). For the hypothesis sampling model, whatever the pattern of reinforcement on the first two trials, the same performance is again predicted after an incorrect response on trial 2.

The most likely incorrect hypotheses given in H_3 are those that are consistent with the information in the last trial; however, the probability that each hypothesis will be given as H_3 also depends on whether or not it was reinforced on trials 0 and 1, and whether the response on trials 0, 1 and 2 were correct or not.

The data and the predictions from the two models are given in Table

248

TABLE III

Probability that H_2 is one of the four types of hypotheses and that H_3 is one of the eight hypotheses, as a function of the relevant attribute *

		Relevant attribute			
		Colour	Size	Position	Form
$P_r(H_2 \in s_0^- \cap s_1^-$:	$- \; -$	0.049	0.048	0.043	0.036
		0.048	0.063	0.067	0.075
	$+ \; -$	0.049	0.025	0.068	0.098
		0.025	0.032	0.043	0.047
	$- \; +$	0.091	0.118	0.217	0.202
		0.117	0.145	0.173	0.185
$P_r(H_2 \in s_0^+ \cap s_1^+$	$+ \; +$	0.811	0.808	0.672	0.664
		0.810	0.762	0.718	0.688
$P_r(H_3 \in s_0^- \cap s_1^- \cap s_2^-)$	$- \; - \; -$	0.052	0.016	0.010	0.010
		0.027	0.039	0.044	0.040
	$+ \; - \; -$	0.014	0.044	0.027	0.049
		0.010	0.019	0.034	0.044
	$- \; + \; -$	0.027	0.032	0.031	0.075
		0.010	0.024	0.043	0.054
	$+ \; + \; -$	0.024	0.025	0.038	0.055
		0.004	0.006	0.006	0.013
	$- \; - \; +$	0.062	0.066	0.062	0.097
		0.050	0.082	0.107	0.129
	$+ \; - \; +$	0.069	0.066	0.131	0.149
		0.032	0.050	0.073	0.085
	$- \; + \; +$	0.117	0.130	0.148	0.230
		0.101	0.148	0.201	0.237
$P_r(H_3 \in s_0^+ \cap s_1^+ \cap s_2^+)$	$+ \; + \; +$	0.634	0.620	0.552	0.334
		0.765	0.632	0.487	0.399

* Line 1, the observed value; line 2, the predicted value by the attention model, with the following parameter values: $C_1 = 0.83$, $C_2 = 0.66$, $C_3 = 0.50$; $C_4 = 0.41$, $C' = 0.80$; $\theta^+ = 0.70$, $\theta^- = 0.40$.

II. The major weakness of the hypothesis sampling model is that it predicts the same probability for the four hypotheses that are consistent with the information in the last trial, when the response on trial 2 is wrong. On the other hand, despite some discrepancies, the attention model gives a relatively good picture of the data.

It is possible, within the framework of the attention model, to take the saliency of attributes into account. The values of c_1, c_2, c_3, and c_4 were roughly estimated from the proportion of hypotheses in H_1 that were about each attribute, given the constraint that the mean value of c_1, c_2, c_3 and c_4 were equal to the value retained for c in the preceding analysis. These values were used to predict the probability of the occurrence of colour, form, size and position in H_2 and H_3. The results are given in Table III. If one accepts the overestimation of the probability of H_3 to be correct when colour is relevant, the predictions are reasonably close to the data.

Discussion

Despite its complexity (in comparison with hypothesis models, but not with discrimination-learning models) and its rather large number of parameters, the attention model seems worth considering, because of its seeming ability to take into account the major trends of the data, with relatively few large discrepancies. This is not the case with the simpler hypothesis sampling model. Out of 128 predictions obtained from the attention model, there are 23 cases in which the discrepancy is greater than 0.05 and 4 cases in which the discrepancy is greater than 0.10, the largest deviation being 0.14. To have reasonably powerful tests of such models it is necessary to have large sets of data. It is for this reason that we have considered nearly every statistic for which it was possible to get a reasonably good estimation from the exceptionally large volume of data accumulated in the experiment undertaken by Professor Levine.

One problem encountered in the study of this model is that it necessitates using Monte-Carlo techniques, which are so time-consuming and costly that we were not able to study the whole parameter space. The values retained for the parameters are certainly not the best ones, and we do not know to what extent the predictions would be improved if a better examination of the parameters were possible. We are, therefore, now developing analytical procedures that will enable us to estimate some of the parameters more closely.

Acknowledgements

We are indebted to Professor M. Levine, both for making the raw data of his experiment available to us, and for a number of valuable suggestions. We also thank Madame B. le Roux who wrote the program for the simulation of the models.

UWE MORTENSEN*

Models for Some Elementary
Problem Solving Processes

Summary

Three models of problem solving for a defined class of problems are developed. Data are obtained from the analysis of the operations in typical water-jar problems. Model III which is based on a short-term memory interacting with a long-term memory provides the best fit to the results, and suggestions are made for its further development.

Introduction

Three models for simple problem solving processes are introduced and discussed with reference to empirical data. The problems considered belong to the class of problems characterised as follows. The problem is given by the triple $P = (Z, F, Y)$, where Z is a finite set of so-called states of the problem (e.g., the set of possible disk positions in the Tower-of-Hanoi problem or the set of possible distributions of water in a water-jar problem), F is a set of functions or mappings defined in the formulation of the problem (e.g., $f \in F$ is a certain movement of a disk in the Tower-of-Hanoi problem or the pouring of water in a water-jar problem), such that

$$f : Z_f \rightarrow Z ,$$

* University of Konstanz

where $f \in F$ and $Z_f \subset Z$ is the set of states to which f is applicable. A more detailed definition of the elements of F is given by Mesarovic (1965). $Y \subset Z$ is the set of goal states. In the following the application of a function $f \in F$ to a state $z \in Z_f$ (e.g., the "calculation" of $f(z) = z'$ $\in Z$) is called an "elementary operation" or simply an "operation". The problem is solved when a sequence of functions $f_i \in F$ ($i = 1, ..., m$) is found with

$$f_m(f_{m-1}(...f_1(z_o)...) \in Y ,$$

where z_o is the initial state given in the formulation of the problem; m is called the length of the solution. These definitions are taken from Banerji (1969). The "structure" of the problem is given by a graph, the nodi of which represent the states $z \in Z$ and the arrows connecting the nodi represent functions $f \in F$.

In order to keep the complexity of the analysis within the bounds of feasibility we shall consider here problems where the number of aspects for each $z \in Z$ is low and where there exist no difficulties of retrieving them from memory, so that each $f \in F_z$ is found with approximately equal probability. In other words, for this class of problems the set F of functions is homogenous — i.e., the elements of F are of the same sort and of approximately equal difficulty. Furthermore if $F_z \subset F$ is the subset of functions applicable to $z \in Z$ then each $f \in F_z$ is related to some aspects of z; that is to say the knowledge of the possibility of applying f to z is a consequence of these aspects coming to attention.

It is also assumed that the problem solving process can be described in terms of a sequence of discrete steps T_1, T_2, ... and that in each T_t a decision v_t is made as to what function f or sequence of functions has to be applied to the state arrived at in the last step. Since the development of models for the problem solving process necessitates the formulation of assumptions about the development and application of the mechanisms which lead to these decisions, some assumptions about such mechanisms are listed below.

(1) The function to be applied to z is chosen with equal probability from the set of functions applicable to z, independently of the number of steps already made and of the state z.

(2) A subgoal is a certain state or a certain class of states from which a goal state may be reached and which the problem solver thinks can be reached more easily than a goal state.

(3) A "loop" is constructed when the problem solver arrives at a state he has already reached by a former operation. He tries to avoid "wrong" operations, which lead into such loops, and chooses with equal probability from among the functions which he assumes do not lead into such loops.

(4) A sequence of steps is developed as follows: Starting with the state Z_m (where $z_m \in Z$), state $z \in Z$ is chosen for which a function $f \in F$ exists so that the state z_m is reached by the application of f to z'. A z'' is then chosen, such that there exists a $f \in F$ for which $f(z'') = z'$. This process is repeated until the initial state z_o is reached. This mechanism is equivalent to the principle of dynamic programming.

The above list is not exhaustive and the mechanisms described are not independent. However it serves as a useful first approximation and has led to the development of the following models.

Model I

In this model it is assumed that at each step T_t the subject draws a hypothesis from a finite set H_t of hypotheses. A hypothesis is an allocation of subjective goal distances to states $z \in Z$. A subjective goal distance may be conceived of as an ordering of states with respect to the assumed minimal number of elementary operations necessary for them to reach a state in Y. Viewed this way, the set H_t also contains hypotheses about subgoals, where a subgoal is a state not yet arrived at in the solving process but aimed at because the supposed goal distance is low for this state (in water-jar problems, for example, a subgoal may be the set of all states characterised by an approximately equal distribution of water in the pots). The following assumptions which are similar to those of Restle and Greeno (1970) for replacement learning are made.

(a) The number m of hypotheses in H_t is constant for all steps T_1, T_2 ,..., T_t ,...

(b) In each step T_t, k "old" hypotheses are exchanged against k newly developed hypotheses. k is assumed to be constant for all steps T_t.

(c) Each hypothesis in H_t is either correct or incorrect. A hypothesis is "correct" if it implies the rank ordering of some states $z \in Z$ which is equivalent to the rank ordering of these states with respect to their objective goal distance, (e.g., the minimum number of operations for each $z \in Z$ to reach a state in Y). Otherwise the hypothesis will be called "wrong".

(d) Among the k newly developed hypotheses there are k_w correct ones, and k_w is constant for all T_t.

From these assumptions it follows that the expected number of correct hypotheses in H_{t+1} in step T_{t+1} is

$$m_{t+1,w} = m_{t,w} - k \frac{m_{t,w}}{m} + k \frac{k_w}{k} \tag{1}$$

If Eq. (1) is divided by m one gets the relative frequency of correct hypotheses in H_{t+1} which can be interpreted as an estimation of the probability of choosing a correct hypothesis, that is of choosing a correct operation. Setting $a = k_w/k$ and $0 = k/m$, the solution of the difference Eq. (1) is

$$P_{t+1} = (1-\theta)^t (p_0 - a) + a , \tag{2}$$

where P_o is the probability of choosing a correct hypothesis under the assumption that all hypotheses are equally likely to be chosen. This model predicts that the probability of a correct operation increases monotonically with the number t of steps.

Model II

The foregoing model did not specify how hypotheses are developed. Here it is assumed that this process is mainly a search process which takes place only in short-term memory (STM). The STM is assumed to have a variable capacity. As in Model I it is assumed that the solution sequence is found in a number of discrete steps T_1, T_2, ... The following assumptions are made, the basis of which are the mechanisms (1) and (3) given above.

(i) In T_t several sequences of operations are performed (at least one sequence with at least one operation). If one of these sequences contains a goal state from Y, this sequence is chosen with probability 1.0. If there is no such sequence, one sequence is chosen randomly, where all sequences have the same probability of being chosen. Sequences developed in the foregoing steps $T_1, \ldots, T_{t-1}$ are assumed to be completely forgotten.

(ii) When constructing a sequence, the decision for a function $f \in F$ to be applied to the state which has just been arrived at is made randomly under the restriction that the resulting state is: (a) not already an element of the sequence which has just been developed; and (b) is not already an element of a sequence which has been developed in T_t.

This means that in each step T_t sequences of operations are constructed which contain no loops. So, if there are loops in the solution sequence they are produced by the concatenation of sequences developed in different steps.

(iii) Let L be the random variable equal to the number of operations which make up a sequence. L is assumed to have the same value for all sequences constructed in T_t. Let W be the random variable equal to the number of sequences formed in T_t. It is assumed that L takes the value k with probability

$$Pr(L = k) = p(1-p)^{k-1}$$

where p is a free parameter $(0 \leqslant p \leqslant 1)$.

W takes the value j with the probability

$$Pr(W = j \mid L = k) = f(k)(1 - f(k))^{j-1} \, ,$$

where $f(k)$ is a parameter depending on k, $0 \leqslant f(k) \leqslant 1$. $f(k)$ has to be defined such that k and j are inversely related to each other.

(iv) The capacity of the STM is defined to be $\text{Kap} = E(LW)$, that is the expected value of the product of the variables L and W.

In assumption (iii) it is postulated, that

$$f(k) \to 1 \text{ for } k \to \infty$$
$$f(k) \to c \text{ for } k \to 1, \, 0 \leqslant c \leqslant 1,$$

for the parameter of $Pr(W=j \mid L=k)$. One reasonable assumption about $f(k)$ is

$$f(k) = \frac{k}{k+1}$$

from which it follows that $c = \frac{1}{2}$. The capacity $E(LW)$ has now the value

$$E(LW) = \sum_{k=1}^{\infty} \sum_{j=1}^{\infty} kjp(1-p)^{k-1} f(k) \, (1-f(k))^{j-1} \, , \tag{3}$$

256

From this it can be shown that the capacity $E(LW)$ takes on the value

$$E(LW) = \frac{1}{p} + 1 . \tag{4}$$

Model III

As in the foregoing model, the basis for this model is the assumption that the mechanisms (1) and (3) are used. In distinction from Model II the search process is assumed to be a process in long-term memory (LTM) as well as short-term memory (STM). Model III is basically an adaptation of the memory model of Atkinson and Shiffrin (1968). Again it is assumed that for each $\Sigma \overset{\in}{\underset{\in}{}} Z$, $z \notin Y$ the function $f \in F$ to be applied to z is chosen randomly under the restrictions that f does not lead into a loop. If there are m functions $f_1, ..., f_m$ applicable to z, the probability of the decision for f_i ($i = 1, ..., m$) is assumed to satisfy

$$p(f_i) = \begin{cases} 0, \text{ if } f(z) \text{ is a state which is remembered} \\ \quad \text{as being arrived at in a former step} \\ \frac{1}{\nu}, f_i(z) \text{ will not be remembered} \end{cases} \tag{5}$$

where ν is the number of functions f_i ($i = 1, ..., \nu$) where $f_i(z)$ will not be remembered. In order to determine the probability given in Eq. (5) the following assumptions are made.

(i) In step T_t an operation is made and the resulting state enters the STM which is assumed to have a fixed capacity r, e.g., the STM may contain at most r states. A newly incoming state will take the position r and all states already in the STM are pushed down one position, so that the state in position k will take the position $k - 1$ ($k = r, ..., 2$). The state in position 1 will be knocked out of the STM and cannot be remembered again unless it has been previously transferred into the LTM.

(ii) In each step T_t a number k ($0 \leqslant k \leqslant r$) of states will be transferred from the STM to the LTM. Let Tr be the random variable equal to the number of states transferred during a step from STM to LTM. The probability that Tr takes the value k is assumed to be

$$Pr(TR = k) = Ac(1 - c)^{k-1}$$

where c is a free parameter ($0 \leqslant c \leqslant 1$) and $A = 1/[1-(1-c)^r]$ is such that

$$\sum_{k=0}^{r} Pr(Tr = k) = 1$$

It is assumed that the states in the positions 1, ..., k are transferred, which is consistent which Atkinson and Shiffrin's observation that "older" items (here the states) in STM have a higher probability of being transferred than those items which have been put into the STM more recently. A state transferred into the LTM will not be forgotten during the following process.

(iii) Let $z \in Z$ be the last state arrived at. If there exists a function $f \in F$ and $F(z) \in Y$ it will be chosen with probability 1.0. If there is no such f a function will be chosen according to Eq. (5), where for each state $z' \in Z$ resulting from an application of a function to z, (a) the STM is examined as to whether it contains z' and if z' can be remembered, a function applicable to z will be chosen randomly. States stored in the STM or LTM are found with probability 1.0.

Assumption (iii) above does not allow the subject to return to a state attained in the immediately preceding step, e.g., sequences of the form $z_i(t - 1)$, $z_j(t)$, $z_i(t + 1)$ cannot occur because z_i is already in the STM. On the other hand those operations are actually made, and so the following assumptions had to be made. The model has been examined in two versions:

(iva) *Version 1*: The probability for an operation that leads back to the immediately preceding state is d = const. for all steps. The probability for an operation which leads back to the initial state z_o is d_1 = const. for all steps.

(ivb) *Version 2*: The probability for an operation $f^{-1}(z') = z$ depends on the number t of steps already made: it will be assumed that $d = a^t$, where a is free parameter ($0 \leqslant a \leqslant 1$). The probability for an operation that leads back to z_o is set equal to zero for all t.

Version 2 is characterised by the additional assumption:

(v) Let f be a function applicable to z and let $f(z) = z'$. If the operation $f(z)$ is not actually made the state z' will nevertheless enter the STM and will take the position $j(r \leqslant j \leqslant 1)$ with probability $1/r$. The state in the position j formerly will be pushed out of the STM.

Like all the assumptions, this postulate is purely *ad-hoc* but is at least plausible because it makes it possible to explain why problem solvers know the structure of the problem better than they should according to the solution sequence alone.

Experiment

Subjects had to solve six water-jar problems which possessed the same structure. They were given notionally three pots with volumes a_1, a_2, a_3 (of water). a_1 was always the largest pot, a_2 the second largest and a_3 was the smallest pot. The a_1 pot was said to be filled and the task was to halve its contents by use of the three pots only. Starting with $a_1 = 8$, $a_2 = 5$ and $a_3 = 3$, the other problems were generated by multiplying the numbers 8, 5 and 3 with 2, 3, ..., 6 giving the problems (16, 10, 6), (24, 15, 9), (32, 20, 12) (40, 25, 15) and (48, 30, 18). To shorten the solving process, the tasks had to be solved under the restriction that the largest pot should never be emptied. The tasks were given to the subjects in a random sequence. Fig. 1 shows the graph of the problems.

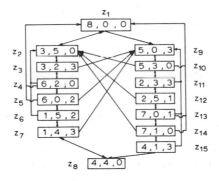

Fig. 1. Graph of the problems used. The triplets of numbers are the contents of the largest, the second largest, and the smallest pot, in this sequence.

The sequence z_1, z_2, ..., z_7, z_8 will be called the path V_1 in the following, the sequence z_9, z_{10}, ..., z_{15}, z_8 the path V_2.

Subjects were 150 pupils aged 15–18 years. The protocols of 31 subjects could not be used because these subjects gave incomplete solutions or did not work as instructed.

Procedure

Each subject was given a writing pad and instructed to write down the results of each operation and then to turn over the sheet so that he could not see the solution sequence generated. Subjects were told that the content of the largest pot in the respective problem was to be halved under the restriction mentioned earlier. The pupils were told that if they considered they were on the wrong track they were allowed to jump back to a previous state only if it were possible to attain this state by an operation or a sequence of operations. This restriction was imposed because states attained previously had to be retrieved from memory. This retrieval could have been incomplete and the following sequence of operations would then no longer be valid.

Estimations of parameters

Programs simulating each model were written in FORTRAN and the relevant parameters were estimated by minimising the function,

$$\Omega(\delta) = \sum_{i,j} \frac{h_i [p_{ij} - p_{ij}(\delta)]^2}{p_{ij}(\delta)} \tag{6}$$

with $i, j = 1, ..., n$. n is the number of states z and

$$p_{ij} = \frac{h_{ij}}{h_i}$$

is the relative frequency of the transition from z_i to z_j; $p_{ij}(\delta)$ is the relative frequency of the same transition as simulated with the computer. δ is the parameter vector. The p_{ij} were averaged over all subjects and all steps T_t. The minimum value of Ω was found by laying — for each model — a grid over the parameter space; for each combination of parameter values 1000 "artificial subjects" were generated. The $p_{ij}(\delta)$ were calculated similar to the p_{ij}-values.

Since all six problems had the same structure it was assumed that subjects would learn a certain solution sequence. As the solution processes proved to be very similar for all six problems, the description of the results is restricted to the first problem.

For Model 1 the parameter a [see Eq. (2)] was set equal to 1 for all simulations. This is plausible since it can be assumed that the probability of a correct operation converges to 1 only if the number of steps is large enough for the subjects to learn the structure of the problem.

For $\theta = 0.25$ a minimum $\Omega = 735.7$ resulted. Since the solution sequence is found quicker when $(1 - \theta)$ is small this implies that the problems were difficult. However the value of θ should be interpreted cautiously since its statistical properties are unknown; the same applies to Ω so that its value also should only be used for a first comparison of the models. However, compared with the values obtained for the other two models, Ω is rather large.

As expected from consideration of Eq. (2), the expected frequencies increase monotonically with decreasing goal distance. The observed frequencies for the transitions (z_2, z_3) and (z_9, z_{10}) are much higher than expected; since the model predicts an almost random choice of operations when the number of steps is low, operations leading back to z_o are chosen more often than subjects actually do. There is a significant drop in the observed frequencies from (z_2, z_3) to that of (z_3, z_4). It is plausible by inspection of Eq. (2), that one is not able to predict on the basis of the model the differences between the frequencies for transition from states, from which a change of path is possible (e.g., z_3 and

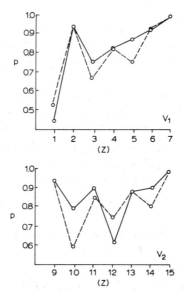

Fig. 2. Observed (———) and expected (– – –) values of transition probabilities for the paths V_1 and V_2, problem 1, model III, version 1.

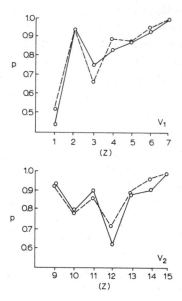

Fig. 3. Observed (———) and expected (– – –) values of transition probabilities for the paths V_1 and V_2 problem 1, model III, version 2.

z_5 in V_1 and z_{10}, z_{12} and z_{14} in V_2) and from which a jump back to the initial state of a path can be made (e.g., from z_4 and z_6 to z_2 in V_1 and from z_{11}, z_{13} and z_{15} to z_9 in V_2). Obviously a linear model cannot account for the data.

In Model II a minimum $\Omega = 166.8$ was calculated for $p = 0.25$, which gives an average capacity of 5 states for the STM [Eq. (4)]. This value of Ω is much lower than that of Model I and 5 is plausible but, as the values of the expected transition frequencies show, nor does this model explain the data in a satisfying way.

Model III seems to be most promising. For Version 1 a minimum $\Omega = 55.5$ was found for the parameter values $d = 0.063$, $d_1 = 0.056$, $c = 0.69$, $r = 7.0$.

For Version 2 the even better value $\Omega = 30.8$ was found, with the parameters $d = 0.085$, $c = 0.55$, $r = 4.0$.

Again the parameter values should not be overinterpreted, but it may be mentioned that the value for the STM-capacity, $r = 4$, in Version 2 is similar to that found by Atkinson and Shiffrin. Figs. 2 and 3 show the transition frequencies for the two versions. As can be seen, the values predicted by Version 2 are closer to the data than those of Version 1.

While it can still be said that the expected values of Model III Version 2 do not fit the empirical data adequately, this version seems worthy of further developments: for example:

(i) Altering the assumptions about the memory process.

(ii) Combining Model II and Model III Version 2, so that not only a decision about one elementary operation is made but possibly about sequences of operations.

(iii) Including the possibility of finding subgoals through (incomplete) dynamic programming.

Even though the structure of such a model is much more complicated it can be hoped that simulation techniques will make them feasible. Furthermore the experimental situation should be changed so as to make possible a stricter control of experimental variables. Problems used by Ray (1957), where the subjects have to handle switches, seem to be appropriate examples.

Acknowledgement

I wish to thank Dr. D. Vorberg for many suggestions on the problem of developing models of problem solving.

GERARD VERGNAUD *

Capacity and Limit of the Computer in the Study of Problem Solving. An Example: Solving Arithmetical Problems

Summary

The difficulties of simulating problem solving behaviour on a digital computer are discussed. One of the main points raised is the fact that, although it may be technically difficult, the simulation of a sequence of actions is quite straightforward: the notion of "rule of production" is an adequate notion that covers both algorithms and other rules. But problem solving involves some kind of "computable representation" that cannot be simulated so easily. These problems are discussed in relation to observations made with children solving arithmetical problems and simple mechanical devices.

The power of the computer in problem solving experiments comes mainly from two sources.

(1) It enables the experimenter to use complicated experimental plans for presenting items, which take into account the subject's previous responses.

(2) The ease with which it can record long sequences of the subject's actions, and the fact that it can simulate such sequences.

Experimentation

It is obvious that problem solving can hardly be studied, even in the

* Centre National de la Recherche Scientifique, Paris

simplest situations, without taking into account several variables, particularly the subject's responses. In fact these responses can be used in two different ways:

(i) As variables for determining further items during an experiment.

(ii) As data determining actual states, events and transformations of the experimental procedure.

In the first case an item can be presented according to whether the subject has failed or succeeded in a preceding one, or according to the sort of mistake he has made. Such an approach is necessary for studying arithmetic problem solving, since the structure of problems may be very different, and because solving one problem may have an influence on the solving of others. In French primary school education (6–11 years) the child learns the four arithmetical operations, or rather the four corresponding algorithms in the arabic numbering system, and he is supposed to learn to solve a fairly wide variety of problems for the solution of which these operations are needed.

The psychologist, like the educator, starts by distinguishing the adding-type problems which involve only one space of measure, from the multiplication-type problems which always involve at least two. Thus, when a problem includes both adding-type operations (additions and subtractions) and multiplication-type operations (multiplications and divisions), it is necessarily of the multiplication type and involves more than one space of measure.

Let us take for example the following problem: "I buy 10 marbles at the marble shop for 2p each and 7 from my friend at 1p each. I resell them all for 30p. How much do I gain or lose?"

This problem needs several operations, namely multiplication of the sales price of each marble by the number of marbles bought and the addition and subtraction of various sums. This is a multiplication-type problem, consequently there are several isomorphic spaces of measure – cardinal of the marbles, cost price and sales price, profit.

The analysis of the structure of such problems shows that they can be extremely varied. Here I shall consider only adding-type problems in a transformational representation, since these can be experimented with fairly completely.

There are two valid ways of representing an addition:

(i) as a binary composition: $a + b = c$

(ii) as a state–transformation–state relation $a \xrightarrow{+b} c$

The former may be useful for some problems, especially for those in which the quantities a and b play a symmetrical role. But the second is more adequate for most adding-type problems because the temporal aspect distinguishes the transformation b from the state a.

This is certainly true when b is an addition. Take the example of a bus stopping and starting around town:

before the stop a people are in the bus,

at the stop b people get in.

a and b do not have the same status: a is the state of the bus load before the stop, b is a transformation. (c is the state of the bus load after the stop.)

This is even clearer when b is a subtraction, since the only adequate representation is the second one:

state–transformation–state $\qquad a \xrightarrow{\;-b\;} c$

Thus returning to the example of the bus:

before the stop a people are in the bus,

at the stop b people get out.

b is a transformation and cannot be greater than a. a and b do not play a symmetrical role at all. The state of bus-load cannot be negative but only null or positive, because it is a measure; whereas the transformations can be negative or positive and form a group.

A simple classification of these problem types could be as follows:

(i) Problems with a single transformation, which can be represented as an initial state (IS), a transformation (T), and a final state (FS), i.e.:

$$IS \xrightarrow{\;T\;} FS$$

Here the problem may consist of finding the value of the final state (FS), given the values of the initial state and the transformation; or of finding the initial state (IS), given the final state and the transformation; or finally of finding the transformation (T) given the final and initial states.

(ii) Problems with two transformations (T_1 and T_2) and the composition of these transformations (T_3), which can be represented thus (iS being the intermediary state):

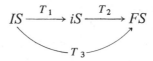

The following factors are important determinations of problem complexity:

(1) The object of the problem. Here a comparison can be made between problems which consist of finding the value of a state (FS, IS or iS) and problems which consist of finding the value of a transformation (T_1, T_2 and T_3).

(2) The information structure of the problem. Since information structure is variable, comparisons can be made, for instance whether one has information about states or not.

(3) The relative value, sign and absolute value of the transformations can lead to great variations of complexity. For example, the problem "given T_1 and T_3, find T_2", may vary in difficulty for the following values of T_1 and T_3.

$$T_1 = +4 \qquad T_3 = +6$$
$$T_1 = +4 \qquad T_3 = -6$$
$$T_1 = +6 \qquad T_3 = +4$$
$$T_1 = -6 \qquad T_3 = +4 \qquad \text{etc....}$$

(4) The content of the problem and the order and syntactical form used for its presentation. The content can alter the difficulty of the problem appreciably, according to whether, for example, it involves people getting on or off buses, winning or losing marbles or earning and spending money, etc. The same is true for the variations in the order and the syntactical forms used in presenting the problem (e.g., temporal order, or inversed order, or different order; independent or subordinate propositions; verb tenses, etc.).

When such an analysis has been completed, experimental plans can then be drawn up for the study of well-defined aspects of these types of problems and their respective difficulty for the child may be determined, considering on the one hand the problem structure itself and on the other hand the problems which the child has already solved.

Success and failure, solving time, mistakes, are elements of the subject's response which may enter into the experimental plan and which the psychologist studies.

But this is not all for the psychologist. He must also study the subject's procedures, strategies, algorithms, heuristics, rules — everything that gives rise to the behaviour he records. This puts the finger on the psychologist's main difficulty, which is asking the right questions concerning the subject's procedures and simulating those procedures. I will reserve this problem for later.

In the second case the subject's actions and responses determine the course of the actual experimental situation and the computer is used for simulating it.

It is a fact that in real life the subject's actions transform reality and that the subject often has at least partial access to the relations implied in the reality he transforms. This is a much more complex problem, as the computer cannot easily provide successive states of the reality transformed by the subject, especially when transformations are continuous (movement in space, for example).

The simplest case is where the subject's actions alone produce transformations of reality and where these transformations are discrete. The sequence of actions performed by the subject then gives rise to a sequence of reality entirely determined by the subject's actions and the preceding states of reality.

Many instrumental actions may be thus described and the rules of dependency may be written up in the computer so as to give the sequence of states in the situation. Nevertheless, the situation engendered by the computer is usually poorer and, in some cases, has hardly any relation to reality. Take, for example, the simulation conceivable in the Tower-of-Hanoi problem. It can hardly be argued that the task of a subject simulated in this way is the same as if he were working in real space where he is confronted with the spatial relations *above, below, between*, etc.

Things become more complex when reality transforms itself and the subject's actions modulate these transformations. Even if these transformations are discrete, the temporal factor is continuous when the experiment is programmed and this increases the complexity of the program even more. Moreover, a great many transformations of reality are continuous and the problem of continuous action on continuous transformations will keep psychologists busy for many a day yet.

Simulation

The way in which the subject's actions have been considered above may hardly seem relevant to arithmetical problem solving and yet, if the solution process is considered as a transformation and a composition of abstract information, it then appears, on first sight, as an example of the first and simplest case, whereby discrete transformation is entirely produced by the subject. At the present stage of work this seems re-assuring, since problem solving simulation then seems possible. Simulation is not involved in the experimentation but it is concerned with trying to replicate the sequence of the subject's mental operations and the successive states of the abstract information he is working on. Tech-nically speaking, simulating problem solving procedure is about the same thing as simulating concrete reality transformed by the subject in an experiment. Consequently, a psychologist when simulating inherits all the technical difficulties we examined above (continuity, inter-action, etc.). However, the basic theoretical difficulty is knowing what psychological concepts are implied in problem solving procedures.

Production rules

The first important concept is the *rule*, or better, the *production rule*. Without considering whether all rules are conscious or not, it can be said that the subject's sequence of actions is generated by rules which determine the actions (productions) as a function of the states of reality and past actions. This concept of the *rule* is basic to such con-cepts as *strategy, algorithm, heuristic* and *procedure* — terms widely used in problem solving theory.

Thus in my opinion the notion of *strategy* refers more specifically to chance situations than to univocally determined ones, or to situations which have been rendered uncertain through the presence of an oppo-nent or the ignorance of some relations.

The notions of *heuristic* or of *algorithm,* often considered as comple-mentary, are very important notions but are not general enough to give a correct definition of rules generating a subject's actions. A notion including both is needed.

The notion of a *procedure* is doubtless the nearest to what we are trying to define, but it more or less implies that the rules the subject follows are explicit and therefore conscious to him, which is not necessarily the case for the production rules.

The notion of *algorithm*, the most precise of all, helps to make a few important distinctions. The common definition of an algorithm is a set of rules which allows the subject, in a finite number of steps, either to find a solution if it exists or to discover that no solution exists.

The effectiveness of an algorithm is determined by the necessary relations which link it to the structure of the problems in the predetermined class of problems to which it is applicable. Few production rules have this *conscious* necessity feature, so typical of the mathematician's algorithm. And yet many production rules are effective even with a child who is not necessarily aware of the rule's effectiveness, nor even of the rule itself. This is what has led me to use the notion of *spontaneous algorithm*, and I have found some good examples of it in unlocking experiments, for example.

It is true that many production rules are not conscious. But does this mean that a subject may follow these rules without being at all aware of them, just by a conditioning process? This hardly seems possible to me and that is why I consider a second important concept in problem solving, namely "computable representation".

Computable representation

Let us consider for example, a 4-year-old's spontaneous algorithm in an experiment where he has to unlock a series of nested bars, of the type shown in Fig. 1.

The earliest spontaneous algorithm consists in trying to pull the bar the experimenter wants him to unlock, then trying to pull the one that is directly nested in it and so on, until one bar gives way. Then he starts all over again, either from the first bar he had pulled, or by pulling the series of bars in the opposite order. Obviously either rule implies the apprehension of the blocking relations between bars and of the fact that it is anti-symmetrical. The rule followed is completely deduced from this single relation. The transitivity of the blocking relation appears much later (6 or 7 years old) and gives rise to another rule.

The notion of "computable representation" is the minimum representation of the relations which convey a meaning to the rule followed. For the rule to exist, the subject must carry out a basic amount of

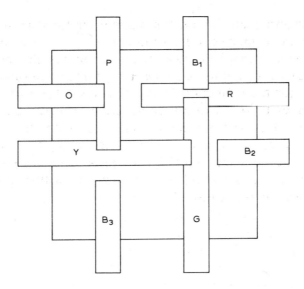

Fig. 1: An example of a nested bars problem. The subject had to pull out the bar R (Red). The other bars were different colours: B_1 = Black; B_2 = Blue; B_3 = Brown; O = Orange; G = Green; Y = Yellow; P = Purple.

Several tasks were studied: practical problem solving, with the relations between bars either visible or hidden by a screen; verbal anticipating of operations to be made; copying the device (by drawing or describing the hidden device); oral questions about the device, etc.

Take for instance the simplest task that consists of pulling out the bar R with the whole of the device visible. The sequence of the subject's actions is considered and the simulating consists of finding the rules of production which account for this sequence. These production rules include various algorithms which may be more or less economical. More often than not these may only be called "spontaneous algorithms" (see text). Despite the fact that the rules followed by the subject are determined by the properties of the relations concerned, the subject is frequently ignorant of their effectiveness and even sometimes of the fact that he is following rules.

transformation and composition of relations, with their results in actions, which is why the term "computable" is used. This of course does not alter the fact that the representation or the computation may be right or wrong. A child may have incorrect rules, coming from mistaken relations, or an incorrect computation of relations.

Although it is not always easy to record upon the computer a series of operations effected by the subject, the computer is an adequate tool for simulating production rules, especially when there are not many and when they are reapplied a fair number of times. In this sense, the computer marks a stage in experimental analysis and may be used to test production rule hypotheses against experimental results.

However, for the moment it hardly seems possible to simulate "computable representation" with hypotheses that can be tested against experimental results for two reasons. Firstly, this representation is almost completely hypothetical, since it is difficult actually to observe it in the subject's behaviour, and, secondly, a colossal number of possibilities exist, due to the different relations required with their possible transformations and compositions.

D. S. BREE *

The Interpretation of Implication

Summary

Most people fail to perform a *modus tollens* inference when asked to validate an implication rule. A previous model advanced to account for this failure is criticised in the light of new experimental data. From an analysis of some protocols of subjects thinking aloud while performing the task, an information processing model was developed. The model postulates that a person forms a simple node and link type of internal representation of the rule in memory. He then uses a pure search or a hypothesis testing strategy to select instances which are needed to validate the rule.

Introduction

In a reasoning task developed by Wason (1968), a subject is shown cards which have, for example, a letter on one side and a digit on the other. He is given an implication rule such as: *"if the letter is a vowel, then the digit is even"* which applies to 4 cards with, say, the symbols S, E, 7 and 4 visible to the subject. The subject is then asked to select only those cards that he needs to turn over to find out whether the rule is true or false. Most subjects in this *validation* task select only the E or the E and the 4, rather than the logically correct answer of E and 7. That this is the correct answer becomes obvious if the rule is expressed

* Rotterdam University

in the equivalent form: "no card has both a vowel and an odd digit".

This failure occurs not only with this particular rule, but in general with rules expressed in the form "if p then q" or "every p is q", where p and q are terms which specify the presence on the card of a member from a certain class of symbols. The logical representation of such implication rules is "$p \supset q$". From this rule and the truth value of one term, either p or q, an inference about the value of the other term is logically possible from:

p, when the hidden symbol must be q (*modus ponens*);
$\tilde{q}$, when the hidden symbol cannot be p (*modus tollens*);

but not from $\tilde{p}$ nor q. This is the situation with the cards as only one of the two symbols on each card is visible. If the rule is expressed as "if p then q" or as "every p is q" inference by *modus ponens* is readily performed by people but *modus tollens* is not. Practically everybody selects the card with p on it, but hardly anybody selects the $\tilde{q}$ card. Some even select the q card (Wason, 1969; Johnson-Laird and Wason, 1970).

This validation task is deceptively simple, even for intelligent adults. It seems that it extends the human information processing abilities beyond their limits. An understanding of how people perform this task should provide some insight into these processing limitations. In this paper the shortcomings of a previously proposed model of how people make their selections are discussed and a new model is proposed.

The Johnson-Laird and Wason Model

Johnson-Laird and Wason (1970) proposed a model to account for the results they had obtained with various versions of the validation task. They postulated that a subject retrieves the appropriate truth table for the particular rule that is presented. He then decides if the rule implies its converse. If he thinks it does (although this is logically incorrect for implication) he considers initially those cards on which appear either the antecedent or consequent terms (the p and the q in this case). Otherwise he initially considers only the card with the antecedent term (p). He then uses one of 3 progressively more appropriate strategies depending on his degree of insight. These are:

(1) With "no insight" *only* cards under initial consideration that can *verify* the rule, are selected.[1]

(2) With "partial insight" *all* cards that could *verify* or *falsify* the rule are selected.

(3) With "complete insight" *all* cards that can *falsify* the rule are selected.

The predictions of this model for different truth tables are shown in Table I. Note that whether a subject believes the rule implies its converse or not, makes no difference to his selection once he has at least "partial insight".

When explaining their results with the model, Johnson-Laird and Wason used a truth table for illative implication (Chipman, 1971) rather than the truth table for material implication. With illative implication any card with $\tilde{p}$ can neither verify nor falsify the rule, but is irrelevant to it. Based on this truth table, the majority of subjects, who choose either just p or both p and q, must have "no insight". The few subjects who select p, q and $\tilde{q}$ cards have "partial insight", while "complete insight" is required for the correct solution. So the "insight" model accounts for almost all the selections made by the subjects. However, it has two points that are intrinsically dissatisfying: the subjects who accept the converse of the rule use the same truth table as those who do not make this error, and they can reach the right answer when they achieve "complete insight".

By the converse of "if p then q", subjects presumably mean that "if q then p". Thus they should consider a card with $\tilde{p}q$ on it to falsify the rule. However, Johnson-Laird and Wason assumed that all subjects considered this card irrelevant to the validity of the rule. This was on the basis of an experiment by Johnson-Laird and Tagart (1969) in which all of the 24 subjects who were asked to evaluate cards that were completely revealed (the *evaluation* task), classified the $\tilde{p}q$ card as irrelevant. But if we look back at Wason's (1968) first experiments we find that more than half the subjects evaluated $\tilde{p}q$ as *falsifying*, a result recently confirmed by Schetagne (1970).

---

[1] In the flow-diagram version of the model these subjects would select cards that could also *falsify* the rule, but it seems that this was not the intention of the authors (Johnson-Laird, 1970, Goodwin and Wason, 1972). It makes no difference to the predictions here.

TABLE I

Predictions of the Johnson-Laird and Wason model and new model

Evaluation of:	Name			
	Illative implication	Positive equivalence	Equivalence	Material implication
pq	true	true	true	true
$p\tilde{q}$	false	false	false	false
$\tilde{p}q$	irrelevant	false	false	true
$\tilde{p}\tilde{q}$	irrelevant	irrelevant	true	true

	Inference card procedure			
	$p \ \tilde{p} \ q \ \tilde{q}$	$p \ \tilde{p} \ q \ \tilde{q}$	$p \ \tilde{p} \ q \ \tilde{q}$	$p \ \tilde{p} \ q \ \tilde{q}$
Johnson-Laird, Wason model				
No insight not converse	+ . . .	+ . . .	+ . . .	+ . . .
converse accepted	+ . + .	+ . + .	+ . + .	+ . + .
Partial insight	+ − + +	+ + + +	+ + + +	+ + + +
Complete insight	+ − − +	+ + + +	+ + + +	+ − − +
New model				
Int. representation	$p \rightarrow q$	$p \leftrightarrow q$	$p \leftrightarrow q \ \tilde{p} \leftrightarrow \tilde{q}$	n.a.
Strategy A or B	+ − − −	+ − + −	+ + + +	
Strategy C	+ − + +	+ + + +	n.a.	
Strategy D	+ − − +	+ + + +	n.a.	

+ card selected, − card rejected, · card not considered, n.a. not applicable.

It is not surprising to find that when a rule is expressed in the form "if p then q", the converse is sometimes accepted. If your spouse says to you "if you go out and buy some cream, we'll have chestnut purée tonight" and you do not go, you would be most surprised if the chestnut purée turned up after all! The converse is accepted, and $\tilde{p}q$ is not expected to occur.

If the subjects who accept the converse evaluate $\tilde{p}q$ as false they cannot be using the illative implication truth table. They might instead be adopting the "positive equivalence" or complete equivalence truth tables shown in Table I. The "insight" model predicts that whichever truth table is used, the selections of the subjects with "no insight" can equally well be just p or both p and q. Now this turns out not to be the case.

In a re-analysis of early experiments of Wason (1968) and in a series of experiments, Brée and Meerum-Terwogt (1971) found that subjects who evaluated the $\bar{p}q$ card as false usually selected both the p and the q or all 4 cards in the validation task and a related inference task, whereas subjects who thought that $\bar{p}q$ was irrelevant usually chose only the p or p, q and $\tilde{q}$ or even the correct solution (p and $\tilde{q}$). It is possible to adapt the "insight" model to take account of this relationship, but it is clear that few people have in their minds a truth table as such. What is needed is some internal representation of the rule from which the truth table is derivable. Also evidence from some protocols suggests that the processing is not as specified by the three degrees of insight.

Some Protocol Evidence

Kunst (1971) collected 12 protocols from subjects shown the 4 cards mentioned at the beginning of this paper and given the validation task. Half the subjects were given the rule: *"if on one side of the card there is a vowel, there is an even number on the other"*. The other half of the subjects had the equivalent but negative rule: *"if on one side of the card there is a vowel, there is no odd number on the other"*. Subjects had more difficulty with the negative version, but the cards they selected to turn over to "know if the rule is or is not true" did not differ between the two groups. Subjects were also asked to give the reason for their choice.

Ten of the 12 subjects *always* mentioned, either during their deliberations or when giving their reasons, that they selected a card "to see if there was a ... on the other side", or words to this effect. Most subjects try to form an hypothesis about the hidden symbol on the card, and if they succeed, they select the card. So it is not surprising that Brée and Meerum-Terwogt (1971) observed the same pattern of selections in their inference task as has been observed in validation tasks.

The 3 of Kunst's subjects who selected the E and the 4 (p and q) mentioned that the rule implied its converse, whereas the 3 subjects who selected only E (p) expressly denied the converse. It seems that subjects need to make a conscious decision about the converse, at least when the rule uses a pair of terms not normally connected. Two of the 3 subjects who selected all 4 cards, said that the rule was an equivalence, and the other that the converse applied. This supports the hypothesised relationship between selection on the validation task and performance on the evaluation task.

Two of Kunst's subjects made the correct selection. One subject received the negative form of the rule which helped him as the rule, "vowel implies not odd" can be permissibly changed to "odd implies not vowel", unlike the conversion of "vowel implies even". The other correct subject was presented with the affirmative form of the rule. Having selected the E (p), he continues:

SUBJECT 10: "And if there is a consonant, there can also be an even number. That is not prevented. And if you should turn the even number, the 4, then there should ... can just as well be a vowel, according to this rule, as a consonant. The rule says nothing about that. And you should ... the 7, yes this you can also turn. Yes, if there should be a vowel, then this rule would not be O.K."

He is generating each possibility for the hidden symbol and testing if the resulting card would be permissible.

Kunst did not find any subjects who selected the p, q and $\bar{q}$ cards, but one of my subjects did so. He was asked to select those cards he needed to turn over to know if the rule: "*if a card has a D on one side, it has a 3 on the other*", was valid or not. He begins:

SUBJECT MM: "To test whether the rule is valid or not, one has to look at *all* cards that have a D, because the thing says 'if D then 3'. Um ... so one's not interested in the one with E on it, because that does not tell us anything about ... what you are interested in: So it is necessary to s ... look behind that one, the one with D on the front, to see what is behind. And it is necessary to look at the ones showing numbers to see whether or not in fact there are D's behind".

This "look for the p's" strategy was also used by all Kunst's subjects who selected only the p card. Here it is extended to the *back* of the cards. It is definitely not a preliminary version of the generate and test strategy used by subject 10.

A New Model

A new model of subjects processing in the evaluation, validation and inference tasks based on the protocol analysis, can account for most of the experimental findings.

It is hypothesised that after reading the rule a subject forms an internal representation of it. This takes the form of ARB triplets, in which A and B are nodes and R is link between them. The nodes A and B each stand for a class of symbols. The link represents a relationship, denoted by R, which may be → or ↔, defined by:

$A \rightarrow B ::$ the presence of A necessitates the presence of B;
$A \leftrightarrow B :: A \rightarrow B$ and $B \rightarrow A$.

The 3 common internal representations of the rule are:

$p \rightarrow q$, which is illative implication;
$p \leftrightarrow q$, which is the rule implying its converse;
$p \leftrightarrow q$, and $\tilde{p} \leftrightarrow \tilde{q}$, which is equivalence.

The truth table, as revealed by the evaluation task, can be simply deduced from the internal representation. The routine to evaluate a card, shown in Fig. 1, consists essentially of looking at the internal representation for both symbols on a card, and checking whether they necessitate the presence of a certain class for the other symbol.

The routines for the validation and inference tasks are the same. There are 4 possible strategies that a subject may use. Strategy A checks if there is any association to the visible symbol. Strategies B and C attempt to locate symbols which necessitate the presence of a certain class of other symbol, B considering only the visible symbol but C extending the search to the hidden symbol (as did subject MM). Strategy D incorporates A or B but then goes on to generate the possible classes of hidden symbol and checks if these necessitate a particular class of visible symbol (as subject 10). Strategies A and D result in the selection of a card "to see if it has ... on the back" observed in most of Kunst's protocols.

The results of applying the evaluation routine and the 4 inference strategies to the different internal representations of the rule are shown in Table I.

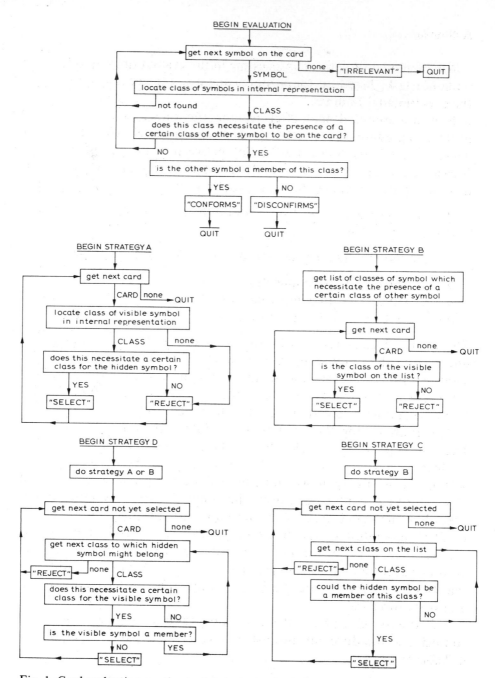

Fig. 1. Card evaluation routine and 4 strategies for inference and validation.

280

Discussion

The improvement of the new model over the old is partly that it can handle the relationship between the evaluation of $\bar{p}q$ and the selections on the inference and validation tasks, and partly that it specifies a more likely representation of the rule in the subject's memory. But it is by no means sufficient to describe all the data, and in some respects is clearly incorrect. For example, it is insufficient but can be extended to explain the very few subjects who select p and $\bar{p}$ on the validation task. They must have the internal representation: $p \to q$ and $\bar{p} \to \bar{q}$, and use strategy A or B. But in some respects the model is obviously incorrect. It cannot predict the selection of p and q by the subjects who evaluate $\bar{p}q$ as irrelevant, and often there are a few such subjects. The model cannot take account of the side of the card (left or right) on which the visible symbol is found, an important variable (Bree 'and Mcerum-Terwogt, 1971). Nor can the model differentiate between which face (front or back) of the card is seen first, and this affected the evaluations in Wason's (1968) experiments (but not in Schetagne's, 1970). These effects may be related to the spatial representation proposed by Handel et al. (1968) for relationships such as "better than" and "causes". These two effects have so far been treated as nuisance factors, but their satisfactory explanation would increase our understanding of the internal representation of the rule.

The most striking point about the new model is the simplicity of the internal representation and of each of the component parts of all the routines. The internal representation based on ARB triplets is the basis of most models of long-term memory (Frijda, 1972). The two forms of the relationship, R, are those that might also form the basis of the representation of causality. The evaluation routine and the inference strategy A, used by most people, are also extremely simple, being made up of memory location and symbol comparison routines. The complexity of behaviour comes from the way these components are assembled into a strategy, a task which might be performed by a General Problem Solver type of program (Newell and Simon, 1963). The major point that is left unexplained is the difference between the general program of a subject who develops strategy A and so only considers the visible symbol, and one who develops strategy D in which he goes on to consider the different kinds of hidden symbol. The fact that most people do not consider the hidden symbol is interesting in itself. But is the reason connected with a hardware problem such as the capacity of short-term memory, or is it a software problem that could be labelled, but not explained, by the name "set"?

There has recently been some criticism of the "Wason" task on the grounds that it is irrelevant to everyday thought (Wetherick 1970). This, of course, is not the only criterion that should be used in deciding whether or not a task should be studied. For example, the representation or strategy used by subjects might turn out to be an aspect of one of Guilford's (1967) evaluation factors. But failure to perform the *modus tollens* inference does occur every day. For example, it can be seen in the otherwise very nice Ph.D. thesis of Judith Reitman (1971), which shows that forgetting in short-term memory is not produced by time alone. She wished to demonstrate that subjects did not rehearse 3 target words, which they had just been shown, during the following period in which they performed a signal detection task. She observed that each subject's performance on the signal detection task was not altered by whether or not he had to recall the 3 words, and so she was able to conclude that "unless rehearsal can be carried out without detriment to the performance of the detection task, these subjects did not rehearse". But she failed to test the hypothesis of "if there is no difference, then there is no rehearsal" (if p then q), by simply asking the subjects to rehearse ($\tilde{q}$) and establishing that there was a difference ($\tilde{p}$). It seems that it is difficult to perform a *modus tollens* inference.

Acknowledgements

I thank Professor Frijda for suggesting that this task might be interesting to study, and M. Meerum-Terwogt and H. Kunst for collecting the data.

GEORGE W. BAYLOR*

Modelling the Mind's Eye

Summary

Two models are presented that purport to explain aspects of how people use mental imagery to solve certain problems. The task used — Guilford's Block Visualization Test (BVT) with visualization instructions — obliges subjects to construct visual mental images from memory in order to represent verbal problem statements. The experimental method chosen furnishes data in the form of a 12-minute thinking aloud protocol of one adult subject solving four of the BVT problems.

Introduction

Since the early work of Newell *et al.* (1956, 1963) in the late fifties, computer programs written in information-processing languages have come to play an increasingly important role in developing psychological theories of human thinking and problem solving. In large part this is because list-processing languages like IPL-V, LISP, SNOBAL, etc., provide precise languages for operationally defining the cognitive structures and processes responsible for intelligent behavior (Reitman, 1965; Newell and Simon, 1972).

The research sketched here makes use of the list-processing language LISP 1.5 (McCarthy *et al.*, 1963) to try to show how visual mental imagery is used in solving certain problems. The problems are Guilford's

* University of Montreal

(1967) block visualization problems, and the LISP language is used to write a program that defines what a subject means when he makes such statements as: "a 1-inch by 4-inch by 4-inch block, okay, I have that visualized". Of course, the program is also a set of processes that use these image representations to solve some of Guilford's problems.

This paper is organized as follows: first, the task and a small sample of human behavior on it are presented. Second, there follows a lengthy section showing how these data are analyzed as a preliminary step to constructing a computer program. Third, the program itself is presented and evaluated as a simulation model. Finally, some directions for future research are indicated. In an effort to illustrate this particular information processing approach to the problem of human thinking, one example is analyzed *in extenso*. It is illustrative of the full analysis that appears in Baylor (1971a), which should be consulted for clarification and elaboration of the presentation that follows.

The Task

The task is called Spatial Visualization II, a test designed by Guilford *et al.* (1952) as part of an Army—Air Forces battery; in his structure of intellect model Guilford (1967) places this test in the cell for the Cognition of Figural Transformations (CFT). The following problem is a typical item from the block visualization test (BVT):

> "Two sides of a 2 inch cube that are next to each other are painted red and the remaining faces are painted green. The block is then cut into eight 1 inch cubes.
> 8. How many cubes have *one* side painted red?
> 9. How many cubes have *no* sides painted red?
> 10. How many cubes have *three* unpainted faces?
> 11. How many cubes have only *one* color (either red or green)?"

Because words, not pictures, are used to state the problems, the subject is apparently forced to construct visual mental images that represent the words of the problem statements.

The Experiment

An adult subject solved the 15 test questions that went with the BVT problems. He followed the test instruction to "visualize the block and solve the problem by trying to imagine how the blocks look before and after they are cut into parts". He did not "make any drawings on the test pages" so that all of the problems were solved mentally, without recourse to paper and pencil (which greatly simplify the task). In addition, the subject talked out loud while solving the problems and so left behind as data a 12-minute verbal protocol of his problem-solving behavior. [1] Illustrative of this kind of data is the subject's 34 seconds of protocol on Question 8 above:

> After eventually imagining a rightside projection of a $2'' \times 2'' \times 2''$ cube with the top and leftside painted red, S says: "How many cubes have one side painted red? Have one side painted red. Well, I'm taking those two sides: the top side and the one to its left. Why that one I don't know. You take the front one, that'd apparently be easier. Uh, slicing it: there's that one red, that one red, those two both have both sides red, and the botton ones have one side red, so it's four, have *one* side painted red."

Data Analysis

Now what is to be done with this kind of data? De Groot (1965), in the tradition of Otto Selz and other Wurzburg psychologists, and more recently Newell (1968) have developed techniques for analyzing protocol data. Newell sets forth certain guidelines that will be followed here. *First,* the protocol is divided up into segments, based on pauses in the flow of speech or on what appears to constitute a single task assertion (e.g., K7–K12 below). The pauses (≥ 0.5 sec.) and speech units are timed and the latter labelled for ease of reference. Thus the above protocol fragment is rewritten as follows:

---

[1] See De Groot (1965) for a methodological assessment of the pros and cons of thinking aloud protocols.

Seconds	Protocol
2.2	$K1:''$ (8) How many cubes have one side painted red?
1.5	(Pause)
1.4	$K2$: Have *one* side painted red.
1.5	
0.2	$K3$: Well,
3.0	
1.4	$K4$: I'm taking those two sides:
1.1	
1.6	$K5$: the top side and the one to its left.
1.4	
3.6	$K6$: Why that one I don't know. You take the front one, that'd apparently be easier.
1.2	

$$
9.0 \left\{\begin{array}{l}
K7:\text{ Uh, slicing it:} \\
K8:\text{ there's that one red,} \\
K9:\text{ that one red,} \\
K10:\text{ those two both have both sides red,} \\
K11:\text{ and the bottom ones have one side red,} \\
K12:\text{ so it's four,}
\end{array}\right.
$$

2.7	
1.1	$K13$: have *one* side painted red.''
1.1	

34.0 seconds (total time)

Second, following Newell (1968), problem solving is assumed to take place in a problem space or set of problem spaces. The elements of the problem spaces are used to define *states of knowledge* through which the subject is assumed to pass in the course of solving the problems. Now inspection of the BVT protocol favored the definition of two problem spaces: an image space (I–Space) of visual mental images that the subject forms of the block, its various components, and slices; and a symbolic space (S–Space) of propositional factual (including arithmetic) information that the subject knows *about* the block, its various components, and slices. [2] In the whole 12-minute protocol the

---

[2] Recently, from their research on paired–associates learning, both Paivio (1969) and Bower (in press) argue that nonverbal imagery and verbal symbolic

subject passes through 272 states of knowledge, all 272 of which are defined in the problem spaces. Now, to effect the passage from one state to another, the subject must apply an operator; all told, nine operators are defined in the problem spaces: three I—Space operators, four S—Space operators, and two crossover links. In addition, the subject sets goals to get new states of knowledge.

Third, the sequentiality in the subject's behavior can now be described: this is done by means of a Problem Behavior Graph (PBG). The nodes of the PBG correspond to the contents of the subject's states of knowledge and the lines between nodes to the goals he sets and the operators he applies. Fig. 1 is the PBG for the subject's behavior on Question 8, presented above.

Fig. 1 is to be read from left to right and then down, following the heavy black line as though it were one long stream of behavior. The dotted lines show how goals once set are remembered ("stacked") and later "pop" to evoke operators that satisfy them.

Now it has been argued (Simons, 1969) that a PBG mirrors the processing demands of the task environment in which a problem solver finds himself. What demands, then, does the BVT environment of Fig. 1, for example, impose on the subject? First of all, he must read and understand the test question. This necessitates an operator that maps the natural language input of the test question into some parsed, internal representation of its meaning. This operator is called Encode Input in the protocol analysis and its function is to encode the test question into an S—Space schema of nested triplets (see Frijda and Meertens, 1969; Simmons, 1970) like the one at K1: {[cubes-have-((sides-color-red)-Qnt-1)]-how many?}. This is nothing more than a recoding of the test question into a more convenient format. The second task demand is to answer the test question, which means that the subject must set himself the goal of constructing mental images that fit the S—Space schema. This is his top level goal, represented in Fig. 1 as (0) get ((# cubes-have-...), where the symbol # indicates a mental image. To attain this goal, moreover, he must retrieve *some* mental image from memory: either the exact mental images that satisfy the

processes are two major components of thinking, the former relatively more attuned to the task of representing and operating on concrete information, the latter for representing abstract propositional information.

288

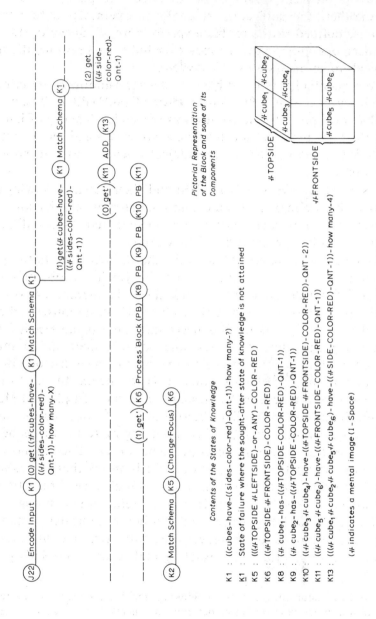

Fig. 1. Subject's Problem Behavior Graph (PBG) on BVT #3, Question 8 (K1–K13)

schema or some component part(s) that can be transformed into the sought-after image(s). Match Schema is the name of the memory retrieval operator. In Fig. 1 it eventually succeeds (at $K5$) in retrieving an image that partially matches the sought-after schema: "the top side and the one to its left", which are the faces of the block that the subject painted red when he encoded the problem statement above. An *ad hoc* pseudo-operator called Change Focus is postulated to account for the subject's decision at $K6$ to "take the front one, that'd apparently be easier". With each failure of Match Schema to attain the full image, K1, a new subgoal is generated, (1) get..., (2) get..., that drops a piece of information. Eventually Match Schema retrieves some object that matches some parts of the sought-after schema, e.g., the images of the two red faces at $K5$. While there is not much explicit evidence in the protocol for this goal structure it is a useful organizational device since "popped goals", [(1) get'], [(2) get'], can be used to control the evocation of subsequent problem solving operators.

The task requires, finally, that whatever mental image is retrieved be transformed into the desired one, as specified by the test question. This calls for certain problem-solving operators. Seven were defined throughout the protocol; two typical ones appear in Fig. 1. The first is the image operator Process Block (PB); it is evoked at $K6$ by the popped goal to (1) get' (# cubes-have-(((# TOPSIDE # LEFTSIDE)-or-ANY)-COLOR-RED)-QNT-1). PB slices the block, constructs and then points to the mental images of each of the six cubes that have red faces. The second problem-solving operator is the symbolic operator ADD; it is evoked at $K11$ in response to the popped top level goal, (0) get'.... ADD adds up the number of cubes with one red face: "so it's four, have *one* side painted red."

What this PBG primarily reflects is a straightforward problem-solving sequence in which the mental images are tailored, step by step, to the demands of the test questions. The level of the goal stack points to the difficulty the subject has in immediately translating the parsed input sentence into mental images.

Fourth, how are the subject's choice of actions at each node in the PBG to be characterized? Why does he apply one operator instead of another? Now, if it is possible to characterize his choice behavior, it is because there exists throughout the protocol a discernible *pattern* of search, that is the decisions at each of the 272 nodes in the PBG are

289

based on recurring and not unique decision criteria. Newell (1968) proposed a language of productions or condition→action rules as a means of characterizing regularities in a subject's search behavior, the action side of a production rule being evoked when its condition side holds true in the current state of knowledge. For the entire BVT protocol 14 productions were inferred from the subject's behavior. Conjoined with the goal stack, the production system shows how his choice of "what to do next" depends both on well-defined local conditions, to which the production rules are sensitive, and on a goal stack, whereupon control reverts to a previously set goal. While the production system, or some equivalent mechanism, is an essential part of protocol analysis, bearing as it does on the organization of the subject's thought processes, it cannot be adequately described except in the context of the full protocol. This is because regularities can only be detected and described when the context is sufficiently broad to expose them. Consequently, the production system will not be discussed further in this summary article, but see Baylor (1971a) as well as Newell and Simon (1972), Waterman (1970), and Klahr and Wallace (1972) for applications of production systems in a variety of tasks.

This brings the protocol analysis to a close. What has emerged is a preliminary model of the subject's behavior on this task. Hopefully, this model provides an accurate description of his behavior on the BVT problems, but it still leaves much unsaid. For instance, *how* does he make use of visual mental imagery to represent and solve the BVT problems? This requires detailed specification of the nature, content, and organization of the states of knowledge and operational demonstration of how the image operators work. The techniques of computer simulation are called upon to try to approach these questions more adequately.

The Computer Program

Now how are the subject's mental images to be represented in the computer? By making use of the list-processing capabilities of LISP 1.5 it was possible to create a vertex notation in which the image of a block is represented as a *list* of eight vertices: ($V1$ $V2$ $V3$ $V4$ $V5$ $V6$ $V7$ $V8$). The following rightside projection is one of its possible pictorial representations, with the vertices labelled as they are used consistently throughout the program:

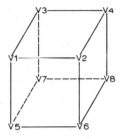

The image has a rich substructure: it is made up of six facelists (each of which is composed of four edgelists, each of which is connected to two vertices, which are interrelated). Moreover, to particularize a mental image — say to differentiate the $2'' \times 2'' \times 2''$ cube of Question 8 from the $1'' \times 4'' \times 4''$ block of Question 1 — descriptive information (about dimensions, colors, parts) is associated by means of *property lists*. So the top level structure [3] of the subject's mental image of the block at $K6$, once he has repainted the top and front red, looks like this in the program:

$(V1\ V2\ V3\ V4\ V5\ V6\ V7\ V8)$
   TOP: $(V1\ V2\ V3\ V4)$
   BOTTOM: $(V5\ V6\ V7\ V8)$
   LEFTSIDE: $(V1\ V3\ V5\ V7)$
   FRONT: $(V1\ V2\ V5\ V6)$
   RIGHTSIDE: $(V2\ V4\ V6\ V8)$
   BACK: $(V3\ V4\ V7\ V8)$
   DEPTH: 2
   WIDTH: 2
   HEIGHT: 2
   THREE-D: (2 2 2)
   HAVE: (((TOP FRONT)-COLOR-RED)-AND-((LEFTSIDE RIGHTSIDE BACK BOTTOM)-COLOR-GREEN))
    PARTS: ((CUBES THREE-D (1 1 1))-HOW MANY-8)
   NAME: BLK.

[3] The facelists, edgelists, and vertices are also described by property lists; for example, the image of the block's red top is $(V1\ V2\ V3\ V4)$, FRONTEDGE: $(V1\ V2)$, BACKEDGE: $(V3\ V4)$, LEFTEDGE: $(V1\ V3)$, RIGHTEDGE: $(V2\ V4)$, DEPTH: 2, WIDTH: 2, HEIGHT: 2, COLOR: RED, NAME: TOP.

Of course, this is "only" a representation of the subject's mental image: it is not the mental image. The issue, however, is one of functional equivalence (see Reitman, 1965; Fodor, 1968). If the above list structure leads to behavior that is indistinguishable from the human's, then it would seem reasonable to infer that such a representation adequately models his cognitive structures. Of course, this can only be tested by looking at behavior: what does the program do with this structure and how does its behavior compare with the human's in the same situation?

In the protocol analysis the subject's behavior from $K7-K11$ was identified as an instance of the image operator Process Block (PB), so this provides a basis for comparing the program's imaging activity with the human's. The input to the program's PB, at $K7$, in addition to the mental image of the $2'' \times 2'' \times 2''$ block as described above, is a set of ACTIVE-ELEMENTS, ACTIVE-ATTRIBUTES, and a FOCUS face. For Question 8 the ACTIVE-ELEMENTS, retrieved by Match Schema and modified by Change Focus at $K6$, are the images of the two red faces: the front of the block, ($V1\ V2\ V5\ V6$), and its top, ($V1\ V2\ V3\ V4$). The ACTIVE-ATTRIBUTES are what the program is looking for: the number of cubes with the attributes: (1 (COLOR RED)). This is the goal set by the test question. Finally, the block is to be viewed from the top in the mind's eye, so its focus is set to the TOP. This changes to the FRONT when the program cannot read the effects of the horizontal slice off the top.

Now at $K7$ the subject says: "Uh, slicing it." How is this process represented in the computer? Three slices must be made in the block: a horizontal slice, an in-depth vertical slice, and a lateral slice. The effect of each slice is to create two new pieces, and for the *six* new pieces formed by these three slices the program creates *partial images.* Note that the program does not yet take account of the interactions between slices, so six *independent* pieces are generated:

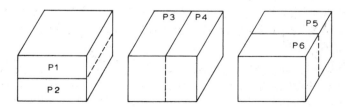

For ease of reference these pieces are labelled $P1$, $P2$, ..., $P6$, but in the program itself each is represented as a list of eight vertices. The program creates new vertices as necessary to stand for the points of intersection of the slices with the edges of the block; thus, $P1$ is the list ($V1$ $V2$ $V3$ $V4$ $G60$ $G61$ $G62$ $G63$); $P2 = (G60$ $G61$ $G62$ $G63$ $V5$ $V6$ $V7$ $V8$); etc., as in the following picture:

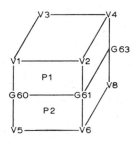

Unlike the base block these pieces are but partially defined; what this means for $P1$ and $P2$, for example, is that only their top, front, and bottom faces exist. This is a heuristic definition, which assumes that it will seldom be necessary to look at these pieces from other than these three sides (but see Baylor, 1971a, 1971b, for an interesting case of what happens when this heuristic does not hold true). Indeed, for $P1$ the front FOCUS face would probably suffice, since the front is where the effects of the horizontal slice will be read off the image. The other two facelists that are elaborated in the partial definition of a new piece are the slice itself ($P1$'s bottom) and the plane parallel to it ($P1$'s top).

Now given this preliminary set of six pieces, which ones should be sliced further into cubes? That is, which of these pieces are most probably relevant to the question: "How many cubes have *one* side painted red?" This is determined by the number of ACTIVE-ELEMENTS each piece has. Each new piece, while it is being constructed, is tagged with the number of active red faces it has. What counts as active are (1) sliced FOCUS faces plus (2) original ACTIVE-ELEMENTS on the block that serve as integral faces on a new piece. Thus, $P1$ has two ACTIVE-ELEMENTS: its top, ($V1$ $V2$ $V3$ $V4$), which is an original ACTIVE-ELEMENT on the block; and its front, ($V1$ $V2$ $G60$ $G61$), which is also red and, because it is $P1$'s FOCUS face, active. $P2$ has but one active front FOCUS face. On the other hand, $P3$ and $P4$ have active top FOCUS faces but, according to the heuristic used in the program, their cut-up red fronts are not counted as active. Finally, $P5$ has one active face, its top, while $P6$ has two: an active top plus an active front, the original uncut front of the block, ($V1$ $V2$ $V5$ $V6$).

Now the program decides that the two most salient pieces, $P1$ and $P6$, are the most relevant for further consideration. So it "chunks" them. calls them L-SHAPES, for want of a better term, and passes them on to a second image operator called Tally (TAL), which will dice them into cubes, and look for the ones that have as ACTIVE-ATTRIBUTES just *one* face painted red.

TAL *does* take account of the interactions among slices, recursively, one slice at a time. Its outputs at one level become its input arguments at the next; thus, TAL (L-SHAPES) or TAL (($P1$ $P6$)) retrieves the slices that are to be made in $P1$: a vertical in-depth slice followed by a lateral slice. TAL first creates two new pieces by slicing $P1$ vertically in depth; this can be viewed as a simple piecetree:

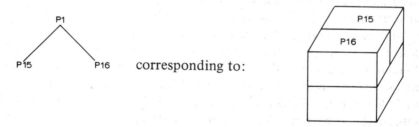

corresponding to:

Now TAL is applied to each of these two pieces by making the lateral vertical slices, yielding the following piecetree:

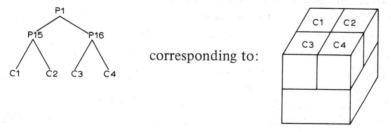

corresponding to:

The cubes, $C1$, $C2$, $C3$, $C4$, are dimensionalized (THREE—D: (1 1 1)) at the time they are created and can thus be recognized and marked as cubes because of their equi-dimensionality.

It is at this point, finally, that the program can lay claim to simulating the subject's imagerial activity:

Subject   Program
K7: "Uh, slicing it:
K8: there's that one red,   (C1)
K9: that one red..."   (C2).

TAL goes on to make the horizontal and lateral vertical slices in P6, so the following piecetree is eventually generated (with the arrows indicating the order in which pieces are created):

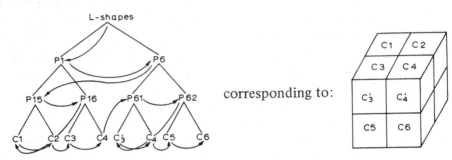

corresponding to:

TAL must be careful to identify the image of C3 (and C4) as seen from the top and the image of C_3' (and C_4') as seen from the front as being but different facets of the *same* object. It notes their identity when it tests if the facelists of the front and top of C_3' (and C_4') are the same as the facelists of the front and top of C3 (and C4). Failure to do this leads to an error of double counting — an interesting error that many people, especially children, tend to commit on these problems. Subject's behavior continues as follows:

Subject   Program
K10: "those two both have both sides red, $(C3 + C4) = (C_3' + C_4')$
K11: and the bottom ones have one side red..." $(C5 + C6)$

Finally, C1, C2, C5, and C6 are seen to be the only cubes that have just *one* side painted red since the other two, C3 and C4 have 2 active red faces. TAL counts and prints out the number of cubes with ACTIVE-ATTRIBUTES: (1(COLOR RED)).

The subject finishes the problem as follows:

Subject	Program
K12: "so it's four,	THAT MAKES 4.
K13: have *one* side painted red."	

Evaluating the Simulation

The above description of how the image operators PB and TAL make use of the program's image representation to solve this particular BVT problem deviates from the subject's behavior in at least a couple of respects. First, the subject tallies the relevant parts of the block right away, rather than applying first the operator PB followed by the operator TAL. This argues for an interwoven and more efficient operator, say PB/TAL, that, like the subject, follows a depth-first strategy in its order of generating pieces (see the piecetree below).

Second, the subject enumerates the cubes one at a time at K8–K9, but thereafter proceeds by twos, at least in his speech. If this reflects a real processing difference, and not just a more concise way he finds of talking about what he is doing, it means that from K10 onwards he no longer bothers to make the lateral vertical slice in the block. In that case his piecetree would look like this:

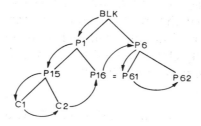

C3 through C6 are suppressed and the comparison of "those two" that "both have both sides red" is made between P16 and P61. After all, why should the subject generate C3– C6? He now "knows" (as a fact in S–Space, having learned it at K8–K9) that this is redundant information and that all he need do is to count by twos. Recall that a distinction between imagerial (I–Space) information and symbolic, factual (S–Space) information was drawn in the protocol analysis, but currently there is no provision in the program for making use of an S—Space fact to ameliorate the behavior of the subject's I—Space processes.

Both of these deviations from simulation indicate that there are small learning effects that occur throughout the subject's solution process; again, in the present program, there is no way to account for this kind of self-improvement.

These differences aside, there are a number of testable psychological hypotheses that follow from this model. For example, are the heuristic, partial definitions of the images of new pieces (and the use of the focus face) good representations of the contents of the mind's eye? Are the processes for screening the relevant parts of the block faithful to human processes? How can the distinction between S—Space and I—Space information be demonstrated to be a viable distinction? These indicate some directions for future research.

While the program is presented as a model of the subject's imagerial processes and structures on this problem, it is of course clear that a model cannot be evaluated on the basis of the behavior of one subject on one isolated test question, or even in the context of one type of problem. The case for the model on two additional BVT questions has been made elsewhere (Baylor, 1971a, 1971b), and there is some evidence for the generality of these structures and processes on other visualization tasks though these cannot be reviewed here (see Baylor, 1966; Simon, 1967; Evans, 1968; Simon and Barenfeld, 1969; Racine, 1971). Hopefully, however, this detailed analysis on one example successfully conveys the flavor of how computers, and information-processing languages in particular, can be used to try to further our understanding of human thinking.

Acknowledgements

I would like to express my gratitude to my thesis director, Dr. Herbert A. Simon, for his helpful suggestions and continued support over a number of years; and to my wife Tamara for her patience and devotion. Any mistaken views, infelicities, or errors that remain in the text are my own. This work has been financially supported by le Ministère de l'Education du Québec.

5. Experimental Studies of Human Thinking

Since an important function of the symposium was to introduce workers in the field of psychology to the potential of computer technology, it was inevitable that some of the participants should not be working primarily with computer techniques. Since, moreover, the topic is essentially the psychology of thinking, it seemed natural to invite some of these participants to present papers which illustrate the present state of research in this area. In this section, therefore, we conclude with five papers which describe interesting experimental approaches to various aspects of human thinking and problem solving. Beyond this they do not necessarily have a central theme.

In the papers by Dörner and Lüer, as in the papers by Bree and Baylor in the preceding section on Model Building and Psychological Theory, there is an emphasis on the use of protocol analysis. This is a refreshing return to techniques that have long been in disrepute, but which form a valid basis for simulation or for systematic statistical analysis. The related papers by Dörner and Lüer report analyses of protocols of subjects attempting to prove mathematical theorems. Dörner is concerned with instances of illegitimacy in thought processes in these situations, whereas Lüer is searching for the more regular sequences of problem solving strategies.

Arici compares the performance of individuals and groups of subjects in a free-recall task and Gitmez reports an experiment on children testing the role of life experience on aspects of cognitive functioning.

In the final paper Rimoldi provides a useful summary of his extensive work on developmental changes in the structure of thought processes.

GERD LÜER[*]

The Development of Strategies of
Solution in Problem Solving

Summary

One hundred and eighty-nine protocols of 25 subjects tackling 14 problems of the propositional calculus have been analysed to give a total of 10,017 separate operations or steps. These operations have been categorised into 18 types. It is shown that with increasing experience subjects develop effective sequences of operations which are used with increasing frequency. An attempt is made to describe the operators and objectives which define the operations used by the 25 subjects.

Problem

The psychology of thinking often makes use of the thinking-aloud method (Claparède, 1917) in order to get protocols from which typical sequences of steps towards the solution in a problem solving situation may be reconstructed. Analysing these protocols one can observe that the frequency of certain steps increases while that of others decreases with increasing experience. The same holds for sequences of steps. There are sequences which increase in number while others decrease. From this one may conclude that subjects are learning to build up strategies of solution by combining steps into sequences while reducing the unstructured use of single steps.

* University of Kiel

As part of a more general project (Dörner, 1971; Lüer, 1971) the present paper analyses the manner in which subjects develop strategies to systematise the evolution of their problem solving procedures.

Secondly an attempt is made to show how subjects make use of the strategies of solution once found and how they develop them. It is insufficient to take strategies as fixed and invariable systems which are governed by nothing else than principles of optimization. From the difficulties that subjects have with new problems and from the analysis of types of illegal thinking (Dörner, 1972), one can conclude that subjects rarely become optimum problem solvers even when they use relatively well-developed strategies in problem solving.

A third point of this paper will be the analysis of the conditions for further development of strategies of solution. It will be shown how "experience in problem solving" can be described more precisely by using detailed information processing units. Finally we try to demonstrate at which points of the strategies changes can be shown which result from developments of the sequences.

The changes we want to discuss take place during relatively short time intervals compared to the periods considered in developmental psychology. Starting from our specific experimental conditions, the changes begin at a time when our subjects have some but not too much experience with the problems. We stop our analysis before the subjects have developed optimum problem solving behaviour. In observing this short but very important period which is characterised by the building-up of strategies and specific modifications of modes of problem solving, we may discover principles of behaviour which might be relevant over longer periods of development.

Method

Twenty-five students were given an introduction to propositional calculus. They were taught how to prove a theorem from a given starting point by using a system of 14 rules like those used by Newell and Simon (1961). Our problems consisted of 14 theorems which had to be proved, given certain other theorems. For each problem they could choose as a starting point one of five or six given theorems, only one of which would lead to the result. This is why these problems can be classified with Reitman (1965) as "open-closed".

The given theorems as well as the theorems to be proved were partly taken from Whitehead and Russell (1963) and partly constructed by ourselves.

After introductory training the subjects were given the 14 problems in single sessions. They were asked to think aloud. Everything was recorded on tape. Our data are based on these records, as well as on the formulae written down by the subjects during theorem proving and the observations of the experimenters.

Results

Strategies of problem solving

First we looked for ways to formalize the contents of our protocols to make them comparable. We succeeded in finding a system of categories with which we could separate and note the steps of the problem solving process. There are 18 categories in total. They are listed in Table 1.

Out of the 14 problems we took 8 and coded the protocols into these categories. The 8 problems were distributed equally along the time continuum. Dropping 11 protocols that had resulted from irregular experimental conditions, our sample consisted of 189 records which on coding gave 10,017 single steps. Consequently we were able to look for systematic tendencies in the sequences by quantitative analyses.

For each problem separately we searched for systematic tendencies in the recorded sequences of thinking by a method of sequence analysis. We found that, for instance, sequences of length 5 could be discovered in all problems with a greater frequency than expected. This difference is statistically significant. These results can be interpreted as showing that our subjects preferred to combine certain steps towards solution. In these combinations we looked for strategies that stand for a frequently used way of solving problems.

Our next step was to count the frequencies of every existing sequence per problem. In advance we had defined the 1 per cent limit as a criterion for frequently observable sequences.

We define: for a problem A there are n different sequences of different lengths. All these sequences $p_1 \ldots p_n$ are used in problem A with

TABLE 1

Categories for the description of different steps during the problem-solving process

Code No.	Steps during the problem-solving process
1	Perception of the problem
2	Searching for a starting point
3	Decision between different starting points
4	Building-up a list of differences between the given situation and the goal
5	Searching for a rule to eliminate one or more of the differences in 4
6	Finding a rule to eliminate the differences
7	Experimenter intervenes and corrects a mistake or replies to a question
8	Helplessness of the subject
9	A rule and/or a theorem is schematized
10	The rule found in 6 is applied correctly
11	The rule and/or the list of differences are rejected
12	The correctness of the proof is checked
13	Illegal operations are performed
14	The subject makes a mistake (but not in connection with the application of a rule)
15	Is it convenient to apply the rule found in 6 now?
16	Subject did not find a rule for the difference in 4
17	A rule found in 6 is applied in an incorrect manner
18	Are there any more differences in 4?

a total frequency F. If each sequence were used only once then $F = n$. But as most sequences were used more than once per problem $F > n$. The 1 per cent criterion is defined as follows:

$$\frac{\text{frequency of sequence } P}{F} \cdot 100 \geqslant 1 \text{ per cent}$$

There was a total of 30 different sequences of length 5 that fulfilled the above criterion. As this was a relatively small number of rather similar sequences it was not difficult to find a typical sequence that was used frequently by every subject. We put this in the form of a flow diagram (Fig. 1).

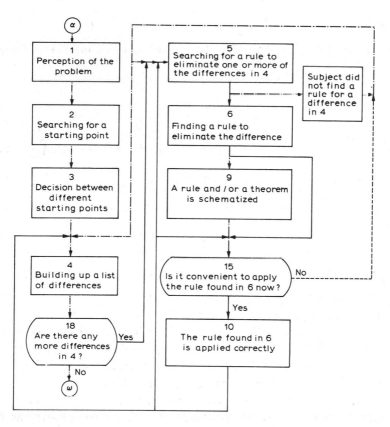

Fig. 1. A strategy in problem solving and its changes. —·—·—·— the sequence remains unchanged in frequency; —— the sequence increases in frequency; – – – – the sequence decreases in frequency.

Use of the strategies by the subjects

In order to find out changes during the problem solving process we first examined the 30 frequently used sequences of which the flow diagram is an example. We analysed whether or not these 30 sequences were used with the same frequency per problem. The frequencies of the sequences were compared to the total frequency F. In Table 2 we have put together these percentages for the 8 problems.

At first glance it seems that the 30 frequently used sequences of length 5 may be used increasingly often. Stated differently: while most

TABLE 2

Number of frequently used sequences of length 5 as percentages of total sequence

	Problem no.							
	1	*3*	*4*	*7*	*9*	*10*	*13*	*14*
No. of different sequences (*P*)	292	93	528	420	172	103	169	605
No. of sequences (*F*)	465	387	2034	1145	995	781	1100	2532
No. of 30 most frequent sequences as % of *F*	30.13	77.25	55.22	49.27	77.70	86.93	82.51	62.95

of the sequences decrease in importance, the strategy shown in the flow diagram increases in importance during the problem solving process. More precise analyses show that frequency of use of this strategy does not increase regularly with time. There are breaks in the distribution of percentages which are statistically highly significant for problems 4, 7, 13 and 14. These changes demonstrate a decrease in the frequency of usage of our strategy which contradicts our expectations.

Next we rank-ordered our problems for difficulty, difficulty being expressed in mean steps per problem. The same irregularity as found above holds for this rank order of problems. These results show clearly that our concept of experience in problem solving is not specific enough to explain the empirical facts.

Development of the strategy by storage and classification

Experiences of the subjects during the problem solving process are stored. The memorization is sustained by reinforcement and repetition. The units of experience consist of objectives which are precisely formulated and of relevant operators which are defined by the 14 rules of our system. The genesis of the objective will be discussed later. For instance, once a subject has succeeded in connecting the objective "transformation of the connective $\wedge$ into $\vee$" with the appropriate rule, this operation can be stored and held available for further problems.

We have defined storage as a matrix where every existing operation as defined by our propositional calculus system can be stored. From the status of this matrix at different times we can predict exactly the fluctuations of percentages in Table 2. When operations necessary for the solution of a problem are not available in the matrix the subjects try to solve the problem with operations that are available — in most cases without success. As a consequence they often try to use illegal operations or other inappropriate modes of solution.

A lot of new operations have to be found for problems 4, 7 and 14 while problems 3 and 10 may be solved by use of known operations. If we rank-order our problems for the number of necessary new operations we could expect our subjects to confine themselves more and more to our strategy in problem solving.

Supposing that experiences are stored as learned operations the subjects would be able to use this knowledge when trying to recognise differences. In this way stored operations could be transferred directly to new problems. As far as we know it is at this point, that is while putting up a list of differences, that subjects make up their mind how to plan their strategy. This stage may be regarded as an information process classifying the recognized differences between the starting point and the goal. For this process subjects use dimensions of the objects as well as non-specific aims which Dörner (1971) called "primary demands" (*Primärforderungen*). These non-specific aims are: extension, cutting, exchange and transformation. With this combination of the "dimensions of the objects" and the "non-specific aims" we are able to classify certain contents of the protocols, which Newell (1966) has described as "function terms". For example, if a difference in the dimension "structure" is connected with the aim of "cutting", subjects search their store specifically for an operation involving the objective "cutting the structure" and a rule of the system. Taking the differences and objectives that we found in the protocols we can show how the stored operations influence the classification of new differences. Subjects are prone to try to use their stored knowledge for new problems even where this is impossible. This leads also to the building-up of a hierarchy of planned operations which provides a fast and exact solution for a known type of problem but leads to certain detours or failure by misinterpretation of the dimensions of the object and the objective for problems with unknown requirements.

Effects of the developmental processes on the strategy

There are two points in the flow diagram (Fig. 1) where we can demonstrate the above features of problem solving. Subjects, after having applied a rule (that is after having reached a subgoal), learn to go on with a new operation at once without having to put up a new list of differences. We can explain this sequence only by supposing the subjects to have compiled a list of differences. This list represents a kind of a plan for the mode of proceeding with problem solving. These plans can only be effective when the subgoals aimed at are rank-ordered. Such organisation is only possible when experiences are available which are useful at least for reaching subgoals. This developmental process, which was found empirically, mirrors our concept of the different frequency of use of the strategy: where possible, employ existing stored operations in new situations.

A second fact fits into this concept. When subjects find an operator to eliminate a difference they check the rule to see whether it is convenient to realise it at that point. It can be shown that the rejection of an operator together with building-up a new list of differences becomes less frequent with increasing experience, while the reorganisation of the rank-order of the operations does not change in frequency. In the same way one can explain the increasing tendency to apply several rules one after the other with increasing experience. In all these developments an increasing ability to plan is evinced which is characterised by the bringing into sequence of several subgoals. Evidently there have to be reorganisations in the original planned hierarchy. We observed subjects planning up to five different steps. It is rather difficult to survey such a plan, because not only have the single operations to be considered but also the changed situation of the problem after each operation.

Discussion

From our results we can extract some principles which we can use for explaining the genesis and development of strategies of problem solving.

In problem solving subjects develop complex strategies out of single steps. These strategies consist of sequences which are partly recurrent.

After the problem has been divided into parts these sequences can be repeatedly used successfully. This is why these sequences are rather independent of the type of problem being solved. With increasing experience they are applied more and more, rejecting other unorganised modes of proceeding in problem solving.

Our results show that strategies of problem solving do not cease to develop. They are reinforced by experience and inhibited by processes of forgetting. Experiences may be thought of as stored operations made up of connections between objectives and appropriate operators. These objectives can be specified as connections between dimensions of objects and non-specific aims.

The ability to use available operations shows up in new problem solving situations. Recognized differences between the starting point and the goal are classified analogously to the stored experience. Planning becomes possible through knowledge of operations which help to transform a given state into a desired one. This experience can become a hindrance at the moment when subjects have to solve new problems where hitherto unknown operations had to be used. In such cases one can observe subjects using stored operations on problems where they are totally inappropriate. This represents so-called "conservatism" in thinking.

The development of a strategy leads to a rank-ordering of objectives and of goals. It is only when subjects succeed in building up an appropriate rank-order that they are able to plan further and more effectively. Consequently we get new sequences in the flow diagram. Stepwise planning decreases while longer chains of steps increase. Undoubtedly such planning represents changes in accordance with an optimization process. It has to be added that for the subjects the success of the optimization process is dependent on the complexity of the problem situation.

Acknowledgement

This study is supported by the Deutsche Forschungsgemeinschaft, Bad Godesberg, Germany.

DIETRICH DÖRNER*

Illegal Thinking

Summary

Subjects tackling problems in the propositional calculus showed a number of errors which could be classified into six classes of illegal thinking. The source of these errors and their relation to problem solving activities in everyday life are described and discussed.

Introduction

This paper is a product of a research project concerning processes of learning and thinking that take place in human subjects who are confronted with an unknown class of problems and have to learn how to solve problems within this class. A class of problems is defined by a set of possible objects and a set of operators which can be used to transform these objects. The problem class "chess" for instance is defined by the set of possible configurations on the chess board and by the set of possible moves. The problem class "theorem proving in propositional calculus" is defined by the set of possible formulae and by the set of deduction rules. When confronted with a new problem class, human subjects have to learn the field of application and the specific effect of the operators as well as how to organise the sequence of operator applications in order to transform a given object into the goal object.

*University of Kiel

Lüer (1971, 1972) reports the actual behaviour of subjects in such situations; Dörner (1971) discusses the necessary learning and thinking processes.

When studying the information processing of human subjects confronted with an unknown problem class we found phenomena which could not be subsumed under the categories mentioned above: subjects arbitrarily tried to modify and to amplify the set of operators. Every attempt by a subject to transform an object of a problem class by an operator which does not appear in the given set of operators we call "illegal thinking" (IT). In this investigation we have tried to find out the reason why subjects employ IT in problem solving and have analysed the forms of IT's appearance.

Experiment

Twenty-five subjects were required to learn how to prove theorems in propositional calculus and instructed to "think aloud". The subjects were given an introduction to propositional calculus and then had to solve 14 theorem-proving problems of different difficulties. For convenience the whole series was divided into two parts and analysed separately to find out whether there were any developmental tendencies. Both parts were approximately of the same duration. Altogether we considered examples of IT from 105 hours of human problem solving.

Results

The instances of IT in the protocols of the 25 subjects have been analysed in detail. A total of 361 IT cases occurred, i.e., on the average 14.5 per subject or approximately one per subject per problem. These could be classified into 6 different types:

(1) Non-consideration of the conditions for the application of an operator (NCON).

Example: Splitting of theorems into parts:

the correct way: $a \wedge b \longrightarrow a,$
an illegal way: $\ulcorner (a \wedge b) \longrightarrow \ulcorner a.$

(The condition of a non-negative main connective has not been considered for the operator.)

(2) Non-consideration of the application instructions (NEX).
Example: Transformation of "∨" into "∧":

the correct way: $a \lor b \longrightarrow \urcorner(\urcorner a \land \urcorner b)$,
an illegal way: $a \lor b \longrightarrow \urcorner\urcorner a \land \urcorner b$.

(The operator for the transformation of "∨" into "∧" has been partially applied; the brackets have been omitted.)

(3) Invention of new illegal operators by analogy transfer (AN).
Examples:

(i) $a \to (b \lor a) \longrightarrow b$
(By "division" of the formula "by a".)
(ii) $\urcorner(a \land b) \longrightarrow \urcorner a \land \urcorner b$
(By "multiplication" of the parts of the formula "by the negation sign".)

(4) Invention of new illegal operators by "semantic" considerations (SEM).
Example:

$$\urcorner a \lor b \longrightarrow b$$

("$\urcorner a$ is false, because of the negation sign, therefore I can delete it!")

(5) Invention of new illegal operators *par force* (PAR).
Example:

$$\urcorner(a \land b) \longrightarrow \urcorner a \land b$$

("The brackets are of no use; I must get rid of them!")

(6) Search for external causes for the "unsolvability" of a problem (EXT).
Examples:

"You have made mistakes in constructing the problem; the first formula cannot be right!"

"I don't like logical problems. They are not creative."

The frequencies of the six IT-forms in two parts of the series are shown in Table I. The most important IT-forms are NCON, NEX, and AN. The frequency of AN− and SEM−IT decreases significantly from the first to the second part of the series. The increasing frequency of EXT-IT from the first to the second part is due to the special effect of one problem and does not represent a general tendency.

TABLE I

Frequencies of the six IT-forms in the first and second parts of the series.

	Part 1	Part 2	Totals
NCON	104	97	201
NEX	36	35	71
AN	34	5	39
SEM	13	7	20
PAR	9	8	17
EXT	2	11	13
Total	198	163	361

Discussion

We shall concentrate on NCON–, NEX–, AN– and SEM–IT. The PAR-, and EXT-cases are of little importance.

We interpret NCON–, NEX–, AN– and SEM–IT as products of general thinking tendencies of subjects confronted with a new class of problem. These IT-forms serve to get new operators that allow an easy manipulation of the objects of a new class of problem.

The AN– and SEM–IT cases are attempts to get new operators in situations where subjects wish to attain certain objectives without knowing how. The decrease of the frequency of AN– and SEM–IT from the first to the second series is due to the fact that subjects learn what the effects of the given operators are. If one knows the effects of the given operators it is unnecessary to search for new operators since the given operators are sufficient to enable the subject to attain his objectives.

In NCON– and NEX–IT the subject ignores some of the application conditions and omits additional symbols which a correct application would produce. In the example given the brackets are omitted. NCON–IT occurs when conditions are omitted whereas NEX–IT occurs when some operator is only partially applied. With NCON– or NEX–IT the subject applies an operator without regard to the application conditions and omits additional symbols which the operation requires in the product.

TABLE II

Distribution of NCON– and NEX–IT in respect to the number of conditions and the number of effects of the operators *

(a)	Number of operators	Frequency of application	Frequency of NCON–IT	Total number of conditions	% of neglected conditions
Operators with more than one application condition	5	284	101	1052	9.60
Operators with one application condition or less	8	2101	13	1533	0.85

(b)	Number of operators	Frequency of application	Frequency of NEX–IT	Total number of effects	% of omitted effects
Operators with more than one effect	6	1238	44	3422	1.28
Operators with one effect	7	1147	16	1147	1.39

* The frequencies of NCON– and NEX– do not add to 201 and 71 respectively since IT cases of one operator have been omitted. This operator (substitution of variables) is in respect to its special nature not comparable to the other operators.

NCON– and NEX–IT minimise the application conditions as well as the products of an operator and therefore maximise the application field and simplify its effect (Table II).

Operators with a broad application field and a narrow spectrum of effects are preferable to operators which do not exhibit those attributes. By contrast one might consider an operator with a narrow application field and a broad spectrum of effects, for instance a medicament applicable only to a rare disease of the inhabitants of the Sunda Islands, which decreases fever but produces dermatitis, nausea, etc.

NCON–IT is mainly associated with operators with many application conditions. This is a trivial consequence of the fact that if there are many conditions connected with a certain operator there are many opportunities to neglect a condition. But it is non-trivial that the tendency for NCON–IT to occur is *relatively* stronger for operators with many conditions. The number of conditions of each operator was multiplied by the frequency of its application to give the total number of conditions which had to be considered by the subjects. The fourth column of Table IIa shows the total number for operators in two categories. The difference between these application categories is highly significant ($t = 10.64$). It follows that the tendency to omit conditions is not a general tendency but one which occurs mainly with operators with many application conditions.

This is not the case with NEX–IT. It can be seen from Table IIb that the tendency to omit partial operations when applying an operator seems to concern both operators with many effects (1.28% omitted) and operators which have only one effect (1.39%).

Both NCON– and NEX–IT can be reduced to an information process with the same formal structure. Both –IT forms occur when one of the tests which must precede the application of an operator in the course of a well-organised problem solving process is not carried out correctly. The tests which are of importance in respect to NCON– and NEX–IT are formally equal. This form is given in Fig. 1 as unit (2). This test determines whether a test list (L_t) is a sublist of a criterion list (L_c). That is to say whether all elements of L_t are elements of L_c. If the answer to the test question is "yes" other tests or the application of the operator will follow.

This process can be illustrated by an example of NEX–IT. Suppose that a subject at some point within a problem solving process has a "given object"

a ∨ *b*

The subject wishes to get rid of "*b*". He knows that he can slip one part of a formula when the main connective is an unnegated "∧". So he tries to change "∨" to "∧". There exists an operator – for instance op_i – which changes "∨" to "∧" and which consists of four part-operations forming the list L_t:

(1) change the connective from "∨" to "∧";

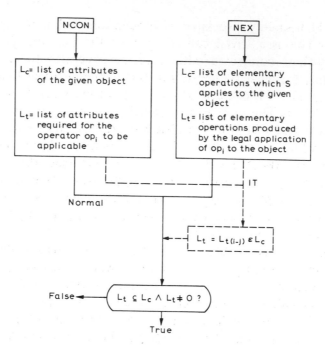

Fig. 1. Flow diagram of the information process underlying NCON— and NEX—IT

(2) add a negation sign to that part of the formula which is by the left side of the connective;

(3) add a negation sign to that part of the formula which is by the right side of the connective;

(4) add a negation sign concerning the whole formula. The correct execution of op_i would therefore produce:

$$\ulcorner(\ulcorner a \wedge \ulcorner b).\qquad\qquad(2)$$

But (2) is not exactly the formula which the subject desires since the main connective "$\wedge$" *has* an undesired negation sign produced by the fourth element of L_t.

In NEX—IT the subject therefore removes from L_t the elements whose products are undesired, those which are not in L_c (L_c being the list of operations with desired outcomes).

So in the above example the faulty application of op_i (after having removed the fourth element of op_i's list of part-operations L_t) may

316

produce:

$$\ulcorner a \wedge \ulcorner b,$$ (2')

or (when $L_{t(4)}$ has been incompletely removed)

$$\ulcorner \ulcorner a \wedge \ulcorner b.$$ (2")

NCON− or NEX−IT will occur if the test list L_t is redefined in such a way that the test is carried out only for the common elements of the list, that is, if those elements of L_t which are not elements of L_c are removed from L_t. In that case the test can only fail if L_t is empty. The test will be "over-inclusive" and will lead to the application of an operator which is not applicable or to the partial execution of the operator.

Basically NCON− and NEX−IT can be reduced to a list-matching procedure which takes account only of the common elements of two lists and disregards noncommon elements which Craig following Cameron called "over-inclusive thinking" which he believed to be characteristic of the thought processes of schizophrenics (Craig, 1971). When a schizophrenic categorises a "carrot" as "fruit" he is considering only the common attributes of the concepts and disregarding the noncommon element. Arieti (1955) and Von Domarus (1944) found in schizophrenics the tendency to regard two objects as identical when sharing a common quality. Such a tendency is also based on regarding only the common attributes and disregarding the non-common.

Now we do not believe that the over-inclusiveness of our subjects is pathological. We suppose on the contrary that over-inclusive thinking serves a useful purpose when human subjects are confronted with a new problem class. Pathological forms of over-inclusive thinking may be exacerbations of normal thinking tendencies.

The tendency to maximise the application field and confine the spectrum of effects of an operator and the tendency to search for new operators by analogy transfer and by semantic considerations are also useful techniques for dealing with a new class of problems in daily life. However, when the set of operators is sharply defined and when reality does not defend itself against the inadequate use of an operator, as in propositional calculus, these tendencies will result in "illegal thinking". A can defends itself against being opened by a screw driver, but a formula of propositional calculus does not protest against the faulty application of a deduction rule!

It is easy to predict what will happen, when there is no control of the correct use of operators. We got by chance the opportunity to observe such cases. On two occasions the instructors of the subjects did not give any feedback concerning the correct use of the operators. The problem solving behaviour of these subjects degenerated completely. The application fields of some operators became broader and broader and their effects simpler and simpler. At last the subjects showed problem solving ritual rather than problem solving behaviour, using three or four operators with a broad application field and simple effects in a constant sequence.

From these experiments it appears that human subjects faced with difficult problems adopt a variety of strategies.

Firstly, they try to find new operators by analogy transfer or by semantic considerations. Secondly, they try to broaden the application field of existing operators by disregarding some of the conditions restricting their application. Thirdly, they attempt to use existing operators without considering all the consequences.

The second and third of these tendencies can be regarded as special cases of over-inclusive thinking, that is to say a tendency to react only to the common elements of two conglomerations of elements and to disregard non-common elements.

Acknowledgement

This study is supported by the Deutsche Forschungsgemeinschaft, Bad Godesberg, Germany.

HÜSNÜ ARICI*

An Experimental Comparison of Two Models of Analysing the Problem Solving Performances of Groups and Individuals

Summary

Performance of individuals and groups of subjects on the free-recall of lists of six-letter nonsense syllables were compared. The results were analysed in terms of the conventional Model of Comparison (CM) which contrasts equal numbers of subjects in individual and group categories and in terms of Taylor's Model which contrasts the performance of "real" and "nominal" groups.

Introduction

Investigations into the relative efficiency of individuals and groups in problem solving situations have yielded conflicting results, with the implication that the differences are mainly due to the nature of the task and the type of model used to interpret the data. Most workers agree that it is necessary not to put the individual at a disadvantage in the method of comparison. Comparing equal numbers of individuals and groups clearly does so. The conventional Model of Comparison (CM) which compares results from equal numbers of subjects in group and individual conditions has limitations for multi-stage problems. Following Taylor (1955), the CM can be represented by equating 1 and 2 as follows:

*Hacettepe University, Ankara

$$\bar{X}g = \frac{Xg_1 + Xg_2 + \dots + Xg_m}{m} \quad \text{or} \quad \bar{X}g = \frac{\sum\limits_{g=1}^{m} Xg}{m} \tag{1}$$

$$\bar{X}i = \frac{Xi_1 + Xi_2 + \dots + Xi_n}{n} \quad \text{or} \quad \bar{X}i = \frac{\sum\limits_{i=1}^{n} Xi}{n} \tag{2}$$

where Xg = group performance, Xi = individual performance, m = the number of groups, n = the number of individuals.

To overcome the difficulties of this model Taylor suggests a comparison of the performance of "real" and "nominal" groups. The nature of this comparison is shown in Eqs. 3 and 4:

$$\bar{X}rg = \frac{Xrg_1 + Xrg_2 + \dots Xrg_m}{m} \quad \text{or} \quad \bar{X}rg = \frac{\sum\limits_{rg=1}^{m} Xrg}{m} \tag{3}$$

$$\bar{X}ng = \frac{Xng_1 + Xng_2 + \dots Xng_m}{m} \quad \text{or} \quad \bar{X}ng = \frac{\sum\limits_{ng=1}^{n} Xng}{m} \tag{4}$$

where $\bar{X}rg$ = the mean performance of real groups, and $\bar{X}ng$ = the mean performance of nominal groups.

Eqs. 3 and 4 give weight of $1/m$ to the performance of a highly successful subject, in both the real and nominal groups. When using the CM, however, we give weights of $1/m$ and $1/n$ respectively, to groups and individuals, thereby favouring the successful group subject with $1/k$ times more weight for his contribution than we give a subject who makes the same contribution in the individual condition.

The present experiment is based on the hypothesis that the results of a comparison between groups and individuals in a learning situation will depend on the model of comparison used. We have, therefore, used the above two models, each of which treats the data at hand differently.

Experiment

Subjects

One hundred and twenty female and 80 male second- and third-year university students of psychology and sociology, with no previous experience in experiments of this type, were randomly assigned to the group and individual condition so that there were 60 female and 40 male subjects under each condition. The 100 group subjects were again randomly divided into 20 groups of 5 members: 3 females and 2 males.

Task and procedure

Each subject was given 20 six-letter nonsense words to learn within ten minutes using the following procedure which was the same for both group and individual sessions. A short explanation of the study and instructions on the task were given. The list of nonsense words was then distributed and the subjects were given ten minutes to learn as many words as possible. The learning part of the experiment was carried out on an individual basis to avoid division of the task by the groups. After an interpolated activity the subjects were asked to write down the words they remembered. This was done individually by those in the individual condition, and in groups of 5 under the group condition. A single list of remembered words was obtained from each group, and individual lists from each individual subject. Although there was no time limit for the remembering—writing activity, the subjects were instructed to finish the task as quickly as possible and the amount of time spent was recorded. Measures were then taken for the real groups, the individuals and the nominal groups, as follows:

(1) *Number of words remembered correctly*
A score of one for each correct word and zero for each incorrect word was given to the groups and the individuals. The nominal groups were made up randomly of subjects who had worked as individuals, with 3 females and 2 males in each group. The lists for the nominal groups were made up by combining the individual lists and eliminating duplications.

(2) *Amount of time spent*

That for real groups and individuals was as recorded during the experiment. For nominal groups, the longest time taken within each group was recorded because the real groups worked at the speed of the slowest member.

(3) *Number of errors made*

For the real groups and individuals this was the number of words written incorrectly. For the nominal groups, a single list of errors was prepared for each group.

TABLE I

A comparison of real groups, nominal groups and individuals in a problem-solving situation

	Conventional Model		Taylor Model	
	Groups	Individuals	Groups	Individuals (nominal groups)
Words remembered				
$\bar{X}$	13.600	8.670	13.600	16.400
S	1.913	1.762	1.913	1.873
t		11.154*		4.560*
d.f.		118		38
Time spent				
$\bar{X}$	11.306	7.289	11.306	11.043
S	3.570	3.050	3.570	3.620
t		8.493*		0.225
d.f.		118		38
Number of errors				
$\bar{X}$	4.206	2.829	4.206	7.569
S	1.170	1.210	1.170	1.411
t		1.465		5.255*
d.f.		118		38

* Significant at 0.05 level.

Results

Table I above lists the means and standard deviations, as well as "*t*" values for the differences between the means.

Discussion

Using the CM, groups are slightly superior to individuals in the number of words remembered correctly, they spend significantly more time than the individuals and make fewer errors than the individuals, although not significantly fewer. With the Taylor Model, however, individuals are slightly superior to groups in number of words remembered (the exact reverse of results using the CM), there is no significant difference between groups and individuals in the amount of time spent and groups are significantly superior to individuals with regard to the number of errors made. Credence is, therefore, given to Taylor's argument that the CM favours groups, since when his model is used the mean measures for individuals are always higher than they are under the CM.

Conclusion

The findings of this study show that the type of results obtained from the group–individual comparison is a function of the model of comparison used. This supports the hypothesis that the results of group–individual comparisons will vary depending on the model of comparison used.

ALI S. GITMEZ*

Problem Solving as Choice Behaviour: Cost-Payoff Arrangements and Optimality of Performance

Summary

An experiment is described which relates the performance of a group of 13–14-year-old children on an intellectual task, together with their subjective evaluation of task difficulty, to three levels of reward and also to individual differences in experience as reflected in their socioeconomic background. It is concluded that an individual's cognitive skill cannot be evaluated independently of such "non-cognitive" individual differences.

Introduction

Current developments in the area of cognitive functioning indicate that problem solving abilities differ not only because of variations in individual ability, but also because strategies change under various conditions. This may indicate that the human brain converts sensory information into a model of its environment and utilizes this model to solve problems.

The Problem

Decision processes play an active role in the selection and formation

* Hacettepe University, Ankara

324

of problem solving responses. With information on the utility of each component of each outcome, it may be possible to assess the utility involved in any particular individual strategy. Hence the introduction of costs and payoffs may enable the experimenter to understand two motivational variables: incentive (the strength of the reward or punishment) and risk (the chance of the two outcomes). Extrinsic costs and payoffs may affect problem solving behaviour insofar as they affect the individual's tendency to adopt certain strategies. More liberal strategies may result from variation in the payoff for correct predictions, or anxieties may be aroused that result in the suppression of performance.

Where direct measures of anxiety levels are not available, these may be related to the socioeconomic background of the subjects. It can be argued that children with low socioeconomic backgrounds will be more anxious in competitive situations than children from homes with a high socioeconomic background.

Aims and Methods

The aims of the present inquiry were firstly to study the choice—behaviour patterns of individuals rather than their responses; secondly to inquire into how individuals deal with their uncertainties when faced with various payoffs and losses; and finally, to examine the interaction between the cost—payoff relationships and the socioeconomic background (and hence, by implication, the anxiety level) of individual subjects.

The 121 subjects

13—14-year-old school children, were divided into two groups by socioeconomic background: extended experience children (EE) and restricted experience (RE). For each group the cost—payoff arrangements were:

(A) Payoff only — payoffs were given for correct choices and no cost was involved when an incorrect choice was made (43 subjects: 26 EE and 17 RE).

(B) Linear payoff loss — subjects were penalized for making incorrect choices (39 subjects: 23 EE and 16 RE).

325

(C) Differential payoff loss — in order to create more pressure on the subjects each problem had different payoffs and costs for the various alternatives (39 subjects: 25 EE and 14 RE).

In conditions (A) and (B) the payoffs and costs were based on the confidence judgments reported by the subjects.

Each subject in each group undertook the same task which consisted of a set of 31 problems similar to intelligence test items. Eighteen were selected to form stimulus sets on the basis of standardisation data: difficult (D), where 20 per cent to 35 per cent solved the problem; moderate (M), 45 per cent to 60 per cent solved the problems; easy (E), 65 per cent to 80 per cent solved the problems.

For this task subjects' responses were evaluated by three measures: (1) confidence rating, where the subjects were asked to rate their confidence in their primary responses on a 5-point scale ("very sure" was 100 per cent and "just guessing", 20 per cent); (2) correctness, as the ratio of correct-to-total responses; (3) realism of confidence, the difference between the mean confidence score and the correctness score responses. This correlated negatively with correct responses (i.e., the higher the realism of confidence score, the worse the subject was with respect to accuracy).

Procedure

The subjects were tested in groups of 15−25. Although there was no time limit, they were instructed to turn in their responses as soon as they finished.

Monetary payoffs and losses were based on both correctness of response and confidence ratings. Subjects were told they would receive one penny for each point above, and would lose one penny for each point below the group average.

Results [1]

In analysing the relationship between payoff conditions and perform-

---

[1] Details of the results can be obtained from the author.

ance it was found that the highest mean confidence rating was for Condition (A), with (C) and (B) following in that order, the difference being highly significant; the difference between the number of correct responses in the three conditions was not significant.

With regard to the proportion of correct solutions to confidence ratings, the two loss groups [(B) and (C)] were almost identical, and the payoff only group (A) was least optimal in performance.

The mean realism of confidence was significantly higher for Condition (A) than for Conditions (B) and (C), which were both the same.

With regard to the difficulty of the task, the confidence ratings for the most difficult problems varied significantly with the payoff arrangements, whereas those of the medium difficult and easy problems did not. Judged by realism of confidence, subjects working under Condition (A) were less cautious and more casual than those working under Conditions (B) and (C). However, the difference between the three groups with regard to correct responses to the stimulus sets was not significant. Moreover an analysis of variance showed no interaction between conditions and stimulus sets.

With regard to socioeconomic factors, there was little difference between the confidence ratings of the two socioeconomic groups under the various conditions, although a one-way analysis of variance revealed that the ratings of extended experience (EE) subjects varied significantly with the variations in experimental conditions while they varied very little for the restricted experience (RE) subjects. Moreover the cumulative distributions of correct responses as a function of experimental conditions and socioeconomic background showed that the EE group varied most under Condition (A) and least under Condition (C), with very little difference between the three conditions. The RE group, however, appeared to be equally variable under all payoff arrangements, being considerably better under Condition (A) than under Conditions (B) and (C).

Although the difference between the correct responses of the two groups is negligible under Condition (A) the EE group performed at a higher level than the RE group under Condition (B) and significantly better under Condition (C).

Accuracy in confidence increased with increase in pressure in the EE group and decreased in the RE group. The accuracy of realism of confidence for the EE group varied significantly, decreasing as experimental pressure increased. For the RE group, however, there was little variance. With regard to accuracy, the EE group was slightly less accurate than the RE group under Condition (A), slightly more accurate under Condition (B) and significantly more accurate under Condition (C).

A trend analysis on confidence ratings and proportion of correct responses under each confidence category indicated that all the linear relationships are significant for both socioeconomic groups, under all conditions. They were, however, larger in the RE group than in the EE group under Condition A and smaller in Conditions (B) and (C). Linearity increased with increasing pressure in the EE group and decreased in the RE group.

With regard to the effect of the difficulty level of the stimulus sets the RE group almost always assigned higher confidence ratings than the EE group, although the latter assigned considerably higher ratings to difficult problems. While the confidence ratings of the RE group vary little with variation in treatment, those of the EE group vary significantly on difficult problems, suggesting that the difficulty of the problems was responsible for the variation. Whereas the EE group used confidence ratings indiscriminately in Conditions (B) and (C), the RE group discriminated the level of difficulty moderately significantly under all conditions.

There was no significant difference between the two groups with respect to the number of correct responses although a three-way analysis of variance of condition, socioeconomic background and stimulus sets indicated a significant interaction between condition and socioeconomic backgrounds.

Discussion

This study indicates that increasing pressure has a slightly beneficial effect on the performance of the less-anxious subjects (the extended experience group) and a considerably negative effect on the more anxious subjects (the restricted experience group), and that the less anxious subjects perform at their highest level under conditions of most pressure while anxious subjects perform best under conditions of a strong positive reward. This supplements an earlier experiment (Gitmez, 1971) and supports the findings of Atkinson and O'Connor (1966) that under conditions of strong positive motivation a tendency to avoid failure may enhance rather than hinder the efficiency of performance. The results show quite clearly that when individuals perform a task they can communicate their confidence judgments in the form of probabilities and likelihood estimates and that such subjective ratings do not interfere with the accuracy of performance. Such subjective ratings are directly related to the average accuracy of correct performance, to the experimental treatment, to the objective difficulty of the task and to individual levels of anxiety. These findings support Edwards (1961) view that costs and payoffs are of considerable importance in determining individual response tendencies in problem solving as well as in gambling, chance-related tasks. It is evident that subjective probabilities are almost linearly related to objective probabilities in problem solving situations, although the subjective always exceed the objective probabilities at all points, with the gap narrowing as the proper cost and payoff arrangement is neared.

Most important, at least for some individuals, costs and payoffs affect the ability to solve problems and the size of their confidence ratings. This contradicts findings such as those of Schum et al. (1967), who claim that costs and payoffs affect the size of confidence judgments, but not the ability to discriminate.

Conclusion

Confidence ratings may help the experimenter to evaluate qualitatively problem solving responses and to gain more information on performance patterns and on how primary responses are made. It is quite clear that performance under one condition (e.g., mental testing) may not necessarily be the best sample of an individual's performance for determining his real ability. It appears essential to collect as much information as possible on the performing individual and how he deals with his uncertainty as regards the problem and the situation, because what is called the ability of an individual cannot be measured without taking into account situational demands and his perception of the costs and rewards inherent in his action. Individual differences in overall ability cannot be discussed without first discovering under which conditions each individual performs at his highest level. In other words, one cannot study the characteristics of thinking or of cognitive function in general without considering how these are determined by external situation variables and how the performing individual feels about the task at hand.

H.J.A. RIMOLDI*

Language and Thinking Processes

Summary

This study investigates development and changes in thought processes. A large number of problems was prepared, each problem characterized by its logical structure and its mode of presentation (language). The subject solves problems by asking questions. The series of questions asked defines a tactic. A theoretical framework is developed to establish the correspondence between tactics and thinking processes. The results indicate: (1) that it is possible to differentiate experimentally the contribution of logical structure and languages in problem solving tactics; and (2) that with increasing age there is a sharp differentiation between different logical structures and different languages.

Introduction

Thinking processes will be discussed as they can be observed in a specific problem solving situation. An experimental technique was developed in which subjects are presented with a problem and a set of n cards on which possible questions that subjects may wish to ask are written. Asking a question means selecting a card and looking for the corresponding answer on the reverse side. The subject can select as many questions as he wishes in any order he desires. The task is finished when the subject gives the final answer or asks for no further questions (Rimoldi, 1955, 1960).

* University of Buenos Aires

The mode of presentation can be varied. For instance: a drawing is shown and the subject has to identify a certain area by asking questions that he himself generates. The answers to the questions can be given verbally, or by means of signs, drawings, etc. The essence of the approach is that subjects actually search for the information themselves and that E is a rather passive response mechanism that reacts to the subjects' questions following a pre-established set of instructions. The sequence of questions asked is called a tactic. By considering both tactics and final answers we partially avoid a subjective interpretation of the process that mediates between the presentation of the problem and the final solution. As far as we know there is not a one−one correspondence between processes and final answers. This technique was originally used by Rimoldi (1955, 1961) to study medical diagnostic skills. The instruments prepared proved to be highly sensitive to levels of medical training and experience.

A cognitive process is understood as the sequence of psychological events and operations directed towards the solution of a problem (goal). Different subjects reach this goal by means of various processes that serve to identify cognitive styles. Vicarious processes imply the substitution of elements and relations by other elements and relations that are functionally equivalent with regard to goal attainment.

It is assumed that the subject's tactic is the image of his process. It is further assumed that the correspondence between the domain of processes and the co-domain of tactics is of the many−one or of the one−one type. In the latter case the tactic is the exact counterpart of the process. This type of correspondence probably holds in a limited number of situations.

Studying problem solving tactics in mathematical problems we observed that elementary school children often could handle in a logical fashion the concepts involved, provided they were not presented in a language that they did not know well. These observations suggested that in every problem it might be worthwhile to differentiate two basic components: logical structures and language or manner of presentation.

By logical structure is meant the specified relational system that holds between the elements of a set. These relations may be expressed in various languages, for instance verbal, abstract symbols, pictures, etc. In our context a problem is a language function of a logical structure or the image that results from mapping a logical structure by means of a language (Rimoldi, 1971).

Problems based on the same system of logical relations presented in different languages are called isomorphic. Among these, the correspondence is of the one—one type. The tactics obtained in several isomorphic problems indicate how language (manner of presentation) affects problem solving processes. Therefore it is not enough to examine one manner of presentation and therefrom conclude on the subject's inability to operate with the logical structure involved. Another language may give a different picture.

The "difficulty of a problem" may be expressed as a function of (1) its intrinsic difficulty which relates to the logical structure; and (2) its extrinsic difficulty that depends on the mode of presentation.

Isomorphic problems will have by the definition the same intrinsic difficulty. The observed difficulty may serve to compare the contribution of language to problem solving performance. Similarly, the relative difficulty of logical structures can be indexed by comparing performance in problems presented using the same language. Therefore it is theoretically possible to define thresholds for the logical operations and for the language, and to study their interaction. In terms of these definitions and assumptions a thinking process may be tentatively characterised as an attempt to make logical structure explicit and communicable to oneself or to others.

Evaluation of Tactics

Three basic components define a tactic: number of questions, type of questions and order of the questions within a sequence. It seems desirable to develop an index that considers these three components properly weighted, though this is not a necessary condition.

Consider: (1) that logical structures can be characterised in terms of some basic laws and relations, e.g. inclusion, intersection, etc., and (2) that tactics permit us to trace how relational systems inherent to the problems are dealt with by the subjects. Based on these premises it is theoretically possible to develop a system of scoring that will give a unique index for a tactic in a given problem. The Schema Pulling out Method (SPOM) is one of our attempts at developing an evaluation procedure that would satisfy these requirements (Rimoldi, 1971).

The irrelevant questions — that provide no pertinent information —

are pulled out from the tactic. This basic tactic is analysed for order reversals and redundancy. Approximating a logical structure implies asking the more general questions first and thereafter questions of increasing specificity. An order reversal occurs when a more specific question is asked prior to a more general question. If among questions a and b with the relation $a \subset b$, a is asked first, an order reversal occurs. Questions at the same level of generality do not have order reversals. Indices to reflect the magnitude of these reversals for different types of structures have been developed. While a given question has an information value *per se*, this value is weighted by the order reversals in which the question may be involved.

Relevant questions are redundant to the extent that they appear in a tactic that already has a more general question covering the same information. When redundancies occur they are weighted negatively, and the same holds for irrelevant questions. A tactic that has no irrelevant questions, no order reversals, no redundancies and exhausts all the pertinent information is called an "ideal tactic" and obtains the maximum score.

Experimental Findings

Only studies completed after 1968 will be presented. Several authors contributed prior to that date to the development of the technique and to its application to several areas (see, for instance, Potkay, 1971). Rimoldi *et al.* (1968) examined 120 children equally distributed among 7, 9, 11 and 13 years of age. These four subsamples were homogenous with regard to scholastic achievement, intellectual endowment, etc.

Six problems were prepared involving two structures: a double dichotomy (2–2, Series 31) and a dichotomy plus a trichotomy (2–3, Series 33). These structures are shown in Fig. 1. The structures were presented in two forms. Form A had eight relevant questions and form B only six, forcing the subject to perform a detour in order to find the answer. In the concrete presentation, problems A and B consisted of coloured boxes on which were drawn circles and squares, for instance, a blue box with a circle, and so on. The subject had to find out how many beads were inside the red box with the circle. The verbal problems VA and VB were isomorphic to problems A and B. The subject's

Structure 31

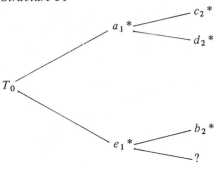

$a_1 \leqslant T_0,\ e_1 \leqslant T_0,\ c_2 \leqslant a_1,\ d_2 \leqslant a_1,$
$b_2 \leqslant e_1,\ ? \leqslant e_1$
Ideal tactic: $a_1 \to b_2$
Ideal solution: $T_0 - a_1 - b_2 = ?$

Structure 33

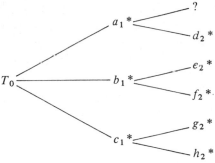

$a_1 \leqslant T_0,\ b_1 \leqslant T_0,\ c_1 \leqslant T_0$
$? \leqslant a_1,\ d_2 \leqslant a_1,\ e_2 \leqslant b_1,\ f_2 \leqslant b_1,$
$g_2 \leqslant c_1,\ h_2 \leqslant c_1$
Ideal tactic: $b_1 \leftrightarrow c_1 \to d_2$
Ideal solution: $T_0 - c_1 - b_1 - d_2 = ?$

Structure 35

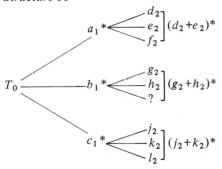

$a_1 \leqslant T_0,\ b_1 \leqslant T_0,\ c_1 \leqslant T_0,\ (d_2+e_2) \leqslant a_1,$
$f_2 \leqslant a_1,\ (g_2+h_2) \leqslant b_1,\ ? \leqslant b_1,$
$(j_2+k_2) \leqslant c_1,\ l_2 \leqslant c_1$
Ideal tactic: $a_1 \leftrightarrow c_1 \to (g_2+h_2)$
Ideal solution: $T_0 - a_1 - c_1 - (g_2+h_2) = ?$

Structure 60

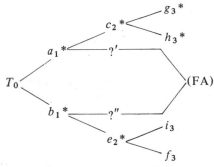

$a_1 \leqslant T_0,\ b_1 \leqslant T_0,\ c_2 \leqslant a_1,\ ?' \leqslant a_1,$
$e_2 \leqslant b_1,\ ?'' \leqslant b_1,\ g_3 \leqslant c_2,\ h_3 \leqslant c_2,$
$i_3 \leqslant e_2,\ f_3 \leqslant e_2,\ ?' \leqslant (FA),\ ?'' \leqslant (FA)$
Ideal tactic: $(a_1 \to c_2) \leftrightarrow (b_1 \to e_2)$
Ideal solution: $(T_0 - a_1 - c_2) + (T_0 - b_1 - e_2)$
$= ?' + ?'' = (FA)$

Fig.1. Problem structures

* The asterisk indicates the questions presented with the problem

tactics were scored using the SPOM and the uncertainty reduction score. This last method is equivalent to finding out the amount of information obtained after asking each question. Both approaches indicate an overall improvement as a function of age.

The analysis of variance showed that for problems A and VA only the age factor was significant at the 0.01 level. For problems B and VB, age, language and their interaction were significant at the 0.01 level. After 11 years of age the slope corresponding to the VB problem is steeper than for the B problem. No similar effect was found for the less complex problems (A and VA). This suggests that with more complex problems a differential effect in performance may be related to language. The early assumption that logical structures and language were independent has to be demonstrated in each specific case. Tentative hypotheses were made concerning the facilitating or inhibiting influence of language in problem solving and thinking in general.

To study these issues Rimoldi and Van der Woude (1969) investigated 295 subjects of both sexes at 11 age levels. These age levels were not equally spaced and covered the span between 9 and 78 years of age (mean age). The age samples were roughly matched in terms of percentiles on Raven's Progressive Matrices test. We shall analyse the results obtained by administering two isomorphic problems both based on a structure with a double dichotomy. Problem 31A is presented in ordinary verbal language and problem 31B is presented using abstract symbols. The SPOM and the agreement score were used. This last method is based on the idea that if all subjects in a group follow the same tactic then the cell values in a table that shows the frequency of occurrence of each question in each order will be zero, except for one cell in each row and each column. Disagreement among tactics can be indexed by studying the spread of frequencies within the table. Agreement and SPOM scores are independent in the sense that it is possible to obtain maximum or minimum agreement regardless of the SPOM scores.

The differences between problems 31A and 31B are always significant, except at age level 49, and approach parallelism. It seems that with increasing age, up to approximately 25 to 30 years, there is an overall improvement in tactics that goes together with higher agreement. The fact that at all ages the difference in scores for problems 31A and 31B is of about the same order of magnitude and significance can be interpreted as indicating that languages are constant factors in performance. This suggests the possibility of an experimental evaluation of languages and has a direct application in education. It raises a crucial question concerning the properties of different languages and the type of function that describes the correspondence between logical structures and languages.

This was partly answered by comparing a group of prelingual and congenitally deaf children with normal children (Van der Woude, in press). The subjects were individually matched in terms of age and performance on the Leiter International Performance Scale. The average age for both groups was approximately 8 years. The problems were built around 2–2 and 2–3 structures. They were presented using simply coloured drawings. The instructions and testing were carried through by means of signs, head movements, etc., in both normal and deaf children. The results showed no statistically significant differences between normal and deaf children.

In another study a collection of 20 problems was given to 150 subjects between 18 and 22 years of age (Rimoldi, 1971). Four structures were used: those of series 31 (2–2), those of series 33 (2–3) and those of series 35 (3–3), plus structure 60 as shown in Fig. 1. Each structure was presented in four languages (A, B, C, and K) originating 4 isomorphic problems per structure. Language A is the usual verbal language, B is abstract, C negative and K uses drawings. All the K problems were qualitative. This generated 16 problems. The remaining 4 do not represent a coherent group and were introduced for purposes that need not concern us at the present time.

The SPOM was used to score all the problems. The 4 isomorphic problems within each series were compared by means of 4 analyses of variance for repeated measures. Language was a significant factor in all cases. Problems with structures 31, 33, and 35 in the A and K languages gave no significantly different results and were the ones that gave the highest scores. The B and C languages in turn are equivalent but give lower scores. However for structure 60 the picture changes. Here the K language gives the lowest score and is significantly different from languages A, B and C which give higher scores and are not significantly different among themselves.

The factor analysis of the intercorrelations between the tactic scores identified the following: (1) one factor defined by all the K problems regardless of structure. This was tentatively identified as perceptual and

337

qualitative; (2) one factor that brings together several problems in A language regardless of structures. It seems to represent verbal language; (3) one factor defined by problems with structures 33 and 35 in B and C languages that is highly correlated with another factor defined by problems with structure 31 in B and C languages. The complexity of problems of the series 33 and 35 by comparison with those of series 31 may explain these two factors both of which include problems in B and C languages; (4) one factor that brings together problems of the 60 series in languages A, B and C.

The overall implications of these results are: (i) the possibility of showing experimentally the contribution of logical structures and languages in problem solving; (ii) the fact that some structures are better dealt with by some languages, and (iii) that some languages permit a greater variety of logical structures than others, perhaps at the risk of a decreased precision (for instance languages A and K as opposed to languages B and C).

These results, together with previous findings concerning the interaction between languages and age, indicated the opportunity of performing a longitudinal study of children between 7 and 12 years of age. A total of 705 boys were studied, of whom 349 were examined for three successive years. The 27 problems were based on structures involving series 31, series 33 and series 35. The languages used were: P (pictorial), VA (verbal), and VB (abstract). The subjects were classified in terms of the following: (1) Age, 7 to 12 years, (2) High, medium and low IQ., and (3) High, medium and low GP averages.

It would be too time-consuming to report in detail the results of this study based on well over 15,000 protocols. However we will quote some of the main conclusions. A transitional period for language was found between 9 and 11 years of age. Before this age differences were mostly due to problems expressed in P language. At later ages the VA and VB languages differentiate better than the P language. This occurs whether subjects are classified in terms of IQ levels or GPA scores. However, when problems are grouped in terms of structures, regardless of language, there is a clear differentiation whether analysed in terms of IQ, GPA or age. Problems with structure 35 obtain lower scores than those with structure 33 or 31, in this order. At the present time we are systematically studying age thresholds for logical operations and languages in relation to age.

Conclusions

In order to appraise a subject's ability it is necessary to scan his performance on problems with different structures, using languages that the subject can understand. This may avoid the risk of missing subjects with outstanding ability as well as subjects with low ability. This seems to fall in line with important questions that psychologists and educators are asking with reference to usual testing procedures. Since tactics are scored not in terms of normative samples but in terms of problem structure, it is possible to interpret a subject's score regardless of his age, cultural background, etc.

This series of studies indicates that it is experimentally possible to isolate the contribution of language and structures in problem solving tactics. Their combined influence has been studied with relation to independent variables as indicated in the previous text. Proficiency in a language is a necessary condition to establish whether or not a subject can operate with the relational system inherent to the structure of a problem. This has practical applications in determining developmental aspects of both logical operations and languages.

6. Overview

GERARD de ZEEUW*

Problems of Psychological
and Artificial Intelligence

Summary

It is argued that comparisons between psychological and artificial intelligence in terms of performance are useless, and stem from an irrelevant framework. The relevant framework is one in which psychological and artificial intelligence interact — and this interaction is described in more detail, though informally. Finally an empirical psychological approach is stressed for the development of the interaction to improve on theory construction. Prospects are optimistic.

Framework of the Discussion

Intelligence is a concept used in many areas of scientific and non-scientific inquiry. It crops up for example in history and sociology to denote the fact that a state or group of people may act adaptively, rationally and purposively; it is used in the technical area of machine construction for control of complex processes. It is also — and perhaps most properly — a central concept in psychology, which deals with different aspects of human behaviour. In all these various contexts intelligence essentially is associated with a *way* of behaving; e.g., in psychology, solving a problem efficiently, or using resources of knowledge and skill purposively with a minimum of "wrong" acts.

This rather abstract nature of intelligence has made clarification a

* University of Amsterdam

problem; indeed its interpretation is not unique, and it can be interpreted in various psychological conceptions of behaviour, such as learning — where intelligence may denote a capacity for learning to learn — or personality dynamics — where intelligence can be seen as an aspect of the evolution of a mature conception of reality.

The interpretation however which has been dominant in psychology is the one stemming from the work of Binet, who was especially interested in trying to determine which children could profit most in which type of educational program. Indeed, from 1890 onward, Binet and others insisted that the key characteristics of intelligent behaviour were its direction and organisation — and that these aspects should direct the search for indicators to measure intelligence and to recognise it at different levels of development. This led to a sustained and successful search for various tests and also to the recognition of many factors contributing to intelligent behaviour.

Thus Guilford (1966), in what seems to be a definitive model of the structure of intellect, includes a variety of components — up to 120 — for nearly all of which he developed tests. Guilford differentiates between the *kinds of thinking* in intelligent behaviour — to know, to recall, to generate, to evaluate — the *contents of thinking* — sensations, symbols, semantic information, feeling — and the *products of thinking* — problem context of units, classes, relations, transformations.

This framework may be generally characterised by the terms comparison and measurement. In other frameworks other aspects are stressed. For example in decision making one of the main difficulties lies in intelligently combining and extracting information from different sources. Here the research emphasis is less on measuring intelligence and more on studying the methods and tools which enable man to be *more* intelligent, *more* efficient and *more* rational. Indeed, in this and other examples it is necessary to know *how* people go about being intelligent, and how this can be imitated, when necessary. That is, we want to know how intelligent behaviour is produced, what mechanisms and processes make for efficiency and intelligence. Of this much less is known than of intelligence in the measurement framework.

Still, for many practical purposes there do exist rational, optimal algorithms which produce such intelligent behaviour (e.g., the calculus we teach our engineers!). Also, in many situations intelligent behaviour can be approximated adequately; for example in trying to improve on decision making in diagnosis it has been shown that the behaviour of experts can be imitated quite nicely by linear combinations and regression equations (Hoffman, 1968). However, many problems in society and in psychology have grown so difficult, or were "born" so difficult that there is no way of getting even near to intelligent behaviour in their solution. Here we need to know more about the *way* intelligent behaviour can be realised — especially as we don't know what it would or should look like in solving these problems. In this context psychologists have grabbed at new developments in computing machines.

Computing machines are designed to aid in producing intelligent behaviour by humans. Consequently they themselves show some similarities with such behaviour, and an enormously rich interaction has grown up between the problems of psychological intelligence and those of what we now call artificial intelligence (A.I.) — that is structures (formal or mechanical) which perform intelligent functions. This interaction, it should be stressed, is almost entirely in the framework of producing such functions and not of measuring them or comparing individual differences.

I make this point because in the last decade there have been many serious discussions on whether computers could be self-directed and purposive, could learn from experience, and could create novelty — that is something not easily visualised on the basis of present information — as humans can do. Neisser (1963), for example, argues that they can, but that "paradoxically" computers will not be able to be as unpurposive, as ready to change goals, as striving after as many goals, or as bent on their own growth and development as humans. This discussion is echoed even by Crosson in 1970, and in some papers of this symposium. In some definitions of what is called artificial intelligence, the same "beat the humans" idea can be detected. Such thoughts seem to me to be rooted in the measurement framework, and less in the above discussed production framework — which is the one I would advocate. Computers should not be compared with humans as such; it is their interaction in the context of solving human, social or scientific problems, i.e., where intelligent behaviour is most needed, that is important. Each changes the way the other produces intelligent behaviour and improves upon it.

For example, computers can execute the many computations that researchers are faced with when, within a given problem representation, the cues for solving a particular problem are missing. That is, they can execute a search in large problem spaces. On the other hand, one of the current main problems of artificial intelligence is how to enable machines to construct such spaces in terms of existing knowledge in the way that humans can, so that operations and computations may effectively be combined.

How humans do it we as yet know only vaguely. That is, we know that by making habits of complex sequences of acts people are able to simplify their thinking, and to combine "habitual" inductions into new ones — but this process is only partially understood (Jones, 1962; Gagné, 1965; Neisser, 1967). As Banerji in the present symposium points out, this is so to a greater extent in artificial intelligence than in psychology. Presumably this function of simplification is produced by the same mechanism which makes people prone to errors, or to sub-optimal behaviour. One of the paradoxes thus may be that to be less sub-optimal people have to make use of machines which make more mistakes.

Problems of Interaction

Having perhaps belaboured this problem of context too long, I must turn towards the task I had to perform in this symposium: namely to say something about my ideas on how the research questions and results presented in the symposium contribute to these problems. To do this I have to make some representation of the papers presented. This is difficult enough at any time, and in any case it would take too long to give each of these its proper weight. I will therefore present only a brief summary together with a few comments on some of the individual symposium papers which I hope will clarify a few of the issues. Earlier, I stressed the importance of an interaction framework — and I shall now try to make this more explicit. In both areas contributing to the symposium — psychology and artificial intelligence (I prefer to use this broad term instead of "computer techniques") — we may make a distinction between different goals and the activities expended on certain problems. Thus we usually call *applied* those research activities where in particular situations, within clear constraints of time and money, the least unsatisfying solutions have to be found and implemented. We call *theoretical* those activities where, without noticeable constraints, the best solution is sought for problems without a particular practical situation as stimulus and source. Bernard Meltzer introduced this distinction in the discussion for artificial intelligence, and I for psychology, but the distinction seems useful also in considering the interaction between aims and the methods used in reaching them in both psychology and artificial intelligence.

This division into two research activities called applied and theoretical gives four types of interaction between those two fields of research. I will consider these in turn. Giving psychology first place we may code them (a,a) applied, applied, (a,t) applied, theoretical, (t,a) theoretical, applied, and (t,t) theoretical, theoretical.

One practical psychological problem (an a,a situation) is one where too many things have to be done at the same time, or where the situation is such that people become stressed. Here computers will be of help particularly in their applied role. For example, a computer may do your arithmetic, or help in setting up an educational program, or make decisions on static issues like admissions to colleges, or clinics. Here the improvement on the psychological side stems mainly from the speed and memory size of the computer, and its data storage and retrieval facilities. Improvement on the computer side is usually technological, e.g., the development of evaluation functions borrowed from experts (heuristics), which may be built into the software or hardware for specific problems. Contributions in this area were rare in the symposium. In (a,t) activities, the situation is quite different. Here, intelligent problem solving by humans can be much improved by using formal structures developed in theoretical A.I. research. This happens for example in library organisations, or in clinical work. To take a more complex example, some theories of interacting systems where much imprecision must be allowed in the functions of the subsystems, although none in the total functioning, would be helpful in reorganising the strategy of medical therapy. As Howe's contribution to the symposium makes clear, computer aided instruction would also fall under this heading.

Thirdly, how can we characterise (t,a)? The practical aims of A.I. — to construct improved physical computing structures — may contribute much to theoretical developments in psychology. Thus, such standard models for theory construction as are exemplified by multivariate analysis, or on-line data displays are unthinkable without high-speed computers. Again, computers can help in selecting different theories for a particular situation, on the basis of sequentially incoming information (one example is given by Fogel *et al.,* 1966).

Finally, we have the (t,t) combination. The interaction in this case is quite strong — and this seems to have been one of the areas contributing most to this symposium. Again, I must add here that I do not think that artificial intelligence is some kind of theory of, or *ersatz* form of human intelligence, or even vice versa. The empirical connectivity of computers is too weak for that, as the non-specificity of human behaviour is too low. There is, however, an interactive development which should be fostered, especially in the area of inductive or inferential behaviour. Relevant here is some interesting work in the area of construction of hypotheses or formal connections between sets described by Bower (1969).

Another aspect of this interaction can be witnessed in the area of probability learning. Jones (1971) sketches how the original stimulus–sampling models of probability learning (in the S–R tradition) are gradually giving way to information processing formulations, since even in controlled laboratory situations subjects can be seen to show rather complex behaviour building up complex pattern cues, with incoming information.

I should stress that it is the empirical trial and failure of the stimulus sampling models of probability learning that has given rise to this development; not of course the theoretical structures of artificial intelligence alone. (See also Gregg and Simon, 1967). Again the interaction between theoretical developments in psychology and artificial intelligence has made people aware of the information content of reinforcement.

Having now described in more detail my representation of the research questions in which problems of intelligent behaviour in psychology and in computer science interact, it would not be difficult to classify the contributions of this symposium in this way. I will refrain from that, and instead add a few more comments. Firstly, what is the use of the representation given above? To some extent its value depends on the development of clear criteria which will define for example that some problems of psychology belong to (a,a), or to (a,t), and not to both. Such criteria I do not have; but an example may clarify the issue.

In some of the more applied forms of psychological research it would be useful to have a model of a student, detailed enough to base upon it a strategy for the presentation of learning materials. This has been tried on the basis of simple stochastic learning models. A difficulty, however, is that such models are not very parameter-sensitive, that is to say changes in parameter values don't make the fit of the models much worse. Consequently the presentation of material would not be much influenced by such changes (see, for example, Gregg and Simon, 1967). Here information processing approaches are much more useful; it is possible to be very efficient in producing changes in presentation schedules, with small changes in higher level procedures. In this sense an (a,t) approach might be less costly than an approach on the basis of simple Markov-models, or for that matter difference equations, or linear algorithms. On the other hand such models have been and are very fruitful in being precise and easily handled; in this way detailed knowledge has been acquired, about the conditions in which particular models are *best.*

Such differences in *cost* could be described by a *cost function*, or preference function, indicating how, for psychological purposes, activities in artificial intelligence with applied or theoretical aims would be more or less costly, or preferred. Such a function, if constructable, would predict when to apply "brute" computerforce, or when to think a bit more – and could thus be acceptable as a guideline. Of course, the higher the level of the procedures used, the less reliably intelligent become the results of such thinking.

Final Remarks

So far, very informally, I have tried to clarify and order some of the issues, at the "interface" of psychological and artificial intelligence. This I have done by sketching the interaction of trying to realise different aims.

One rather important aspect of the interface deserves some more attention. That is, we can distinguish between different processes – and between different optimal strategies for reaching theoretical and practical aims in psychology. The former especially interests us here, as two of the main ones were exemplified in some of the papers in the symposium. One approach is, to start with a very specific situation, e.g., behaviour in a clearly defined simple setting such as the ones used by Brée, or Mortensen, or Lüer in this symposium. Here the choice of situation is based upon some general theory of reasoning, i.e., logical or algorithmic or even game-theoretical. Such theories prescribe what subjects *should* do: when they "disobey", there is something to be explained. An explanation then is constructed out of parts of the original, formal theory, together with some processing rules. Such rules, for example, concern parameters with which to transform variables, so that the "disobedience" can be explained as rational at least in a distorted subjective world. Another example is that subjects are supposed to "stretch concepts", i.e., to interpret variables in an individual manner, due to a private experiential history, private goals, and privately identified cues which in some cases may be supplied by their interpretation — such a strategy will yield information on how subjects do *not* proceed, but also provides valid building blocks for other explanations. Thus, we may use the fact that "implication" is sometimes understood to be symmetric (one of the suggestions coming out of Brée's work) to explain the difficulties which occur in learning disjunctive concepts. Alternatively we may derive from a split-up in additive components the existence of a long-term and short-term process. This is one way in which knowledge is constructed — a type of construction which leads to what we could call inductive leaps, unexplainable in terms of classical or Baconian induction.

The other strategy may be exemplified by Wetherick's work. Here the research worker starts with a large class of intelligent behaviours — from those of fishes to those of near-angels — and tries to derive by comparison relevant similarities. An emerging fundamental pattern will thus be interpreted differently on each level of the exemplars. In this case the basic pattern is derived first, and to give it substance different families of indicators are gradually attached.

This latter strategy shows reformation and the construction of new representations from the "inside", the former from the "outside". Thus, whereas the "inside" job mainly presupposes search, the "outside" one requires construction. Both have proven their worth, and indeed may be recognised even in the general development of science itself, as Kuhn (1962) shows with many examples. Much more, however, needs to be known about ways of pursuing these processes intelligently, in order to be able to produce and improve upon them.

We can perhaps now see how much research in psychology would benefit from the development of many basically different formal A.I. structures with similar functions. These may be used in the above-mentioned strategy of construction — and thus become identified and embedded in problem solving and intelligent experience, and connected with relevant empirical psychological data. (Compare, for example, the work of Amarel, 1968; and Newell, 1965). In this way the efficiency and strategy of theories for theory construction, models for model construction, and programs for program construction can be improved. In effect, intelligent problem solving will only be achieved through the interaction of psychological and artificial intelligence.

Bibliography

Amarel, S. (1968). "On Representation of Problems of Reasoning about Actions," in Michie, D., (ed.), *Machine Intelligence 3* p. 131. Edinburgh: Edinburgh University Press.

Apostel, L. (1961). "Towards the formal study of models in the non-formal sciences," in Freudenthal, H., (ed.), *The Concept and Role of the Model in Mathematics and Natural and Social Sciences,* pp. 1–37. Dordrecht (Netherlands): D. Reidel Publishing Co.

Archibald, Y.M., Wepman, J.M. and Jones, L.V. (1967). "Performance on non-verbal cognitive tests following unilateral cortical injury to the right and left hemisphere." *J. Nerv. Ment. Dis.* 145, 25.

Arieti, S. (1955). *Interpretation of Schizophrenia.* New York: Brunner.

Atkinson, J.W. and O'Connor, P. (1966). "Neglected factors in studies of achievement oriented performance: Social approval as incentive and performance decrement." In Atkinson, J.W. and Feather, N.T. *A Theory of Achievement Motivation.* New York: John Wiley.

Atkinson, R.C. and Paulson, J.A. (1970). "An Approach to the Psychology of Instruction." *Technical Report, No. 157.* Inst. for Math. Studies in the Soc. Sciences, Stanford University.

Atkinson, R.C. and Shiffrin, R.M. (1968). "Human Memory: a Proposed System and its Control Processes." In Spence, K.W. and Spence, J.T., *The Psychology of Learning and Motivation,* Vol. II, New York: Academic Press.

Banerji, R.B. (1969). *Theory of Problem Solving; an Approach to Artificial Intelligence.* New York: Elsevier.

Banerji, R.B. (1971). "Some Linguistic and Statistical Problems in Pattern Recognition." *Pattern Recognition* 3.4.

Bar Hillel, Y. and Eifermann, Rivka R. (1970). "Who is afraid of disjunctive concepts?" *Foundation of Language* 6. 463–472.

Bartlett, F.C. (1958). *Thinking. An Experimental and Social Study.* London: Allen and Unwin.

353

Baylor, G.W. (1966). "A computer model of checkmating behavior in chess," in de Groot, A.D. and Reitman, W.R., (eds.), *Heuristic Processes in Thinking.* Moscow: "Nauka" (Science) Publishing House.

Baylor, G.W. (1971a). "A treatise on the mind's eye." Unpublished doctoral dissertation. Carnegie-Mellon University.

Baylor, G.W. (1971b). "Program and protocol analysis on a mental imagery task." *Procs. 2nd Int. Jt. Conf. on Artificial Intelligence* London: The British Computer Society. p. 218.

Beach, L.R. (1964). "Cue probabilism and inference behavior". *Psychol. Monogr.* 78.5.1.

Berry, J.W. (1966). "Temne and Eskimo perceptual skills." *Internat. J. Psychol.* I. 207–229.

Benson, A.J. and Gedye, J.L. (1963). "Logical Processes in the Resolution of Orientational Conflict." Report No. 259, Institute of Aviation Medicine, Farnborough.

Binet, A. (1894). *Psychologie des Grands Calculateurs et des Jouers d'Echecs.* Paris: Hachette.

Birnbaum, A. (1968). "Some latent trait models and their use in inferring an examiner's ability," in Lord, F.M. and Novick, M.R., (eds.), *Statistical Theories of Mental Test Scores,* Pt.5, chaps. 17–20. Reading, Mass.: Addison-Wesley.

Bitterman, M.E. (1965). "Phyletic Differences in Learning." *Amer. Psycholog.* 20.396.

Bixenstive, V.E., Potash, H.M. and Wilson, K.V. (1963). "Effects of level of cooperative choice by the other player on choice in a prisoner's dilemma game." *J. Abnorm. Soc. Psychol.* 67.139.

Black, M. (1962). *Models and Metaphors.* Ithaca, N.Y.: Cornell Univ. Press.

Bledsoe, W.W. (1971). "Splitting and reduction heuristics in automatic theorem proving." *Artificial Intelligence* 2 pp. 55–77.

Blinkov, S.M. and Glezer, I.I. (1968). *The Human Brain in Figures and Tables.* New York: Plenum Press and Basic Books Inc.

Botvinnik, M.M. (1971). "Computers, Chess and Long-Range Planning." New York: Longman/Springer Verlag.

Bovet, P. (1968). "Echelles subjectives de duree obtenues par une methode de bissection." *Annee Psychol.* 68. 23.

Bovet, P. (1969). "La methode des jugements absolus en psychophysique." *Bull. Psychol.* 22.631.

Bower, G. (1969). "Elaborative Strategies in Associative Meaning." *Proc. XVIth Int. Congr. Psych.* London.

Bower, G.H. (in press). "Mental imagery and associative learning." In Gregg, L.W. (ed.) *Cognition in learning and memory.* New York. Wiley.

Brannasky, W. (1927). *Psychologie des Schachspiels.* Berlin and Leipzig: Walter de Gruyter & Co.

Bree, D.S. and Meerum-Terwogt, M. (1971). "The relationship of evaluation and inference from an implication rule." Internal mimeo IB/71/264. Rotterdam: Interfaculteit Bedrijfskunde, Rotterdam University.

354

Bruner, J.A., Goodnow, J.J. and Austin, G. (1956) *A Study of Thinking*. New York: Wiley.

Brunswick, E. (1956). *Perception and the Representative Design of Psychological Experiments*. Berkeley: University of California Press.

Buchanan, B.G. (1966). "Logics of Scientific Discovery." *Stanford Artificial Intelligence Memo No. 47*. Department of Computer Science, Stanford University.

Buchanan, B., Sutherland, C. and Feigenbaum, E.A. (1969). "Heuristic DENDRAL: a program for generating explanatory hypotheses in organic chemistry," in Meltzer, B. and Michie, D., (eds.), *Machine Intelligence 4*, pp. 209–254. Edinburgh: Edinburgh University Press.

Butcher, H.J. (1968). *Human Intelligence: Its Nature and Assessment*. London: Methuen & Co. Ltd.

Bunderson, C.V. (1970). "The Computer and Instructional Design," in Holtzman, W.H., (ed.), *Computer-Assisted Instruction, Testing and Guidance*. New York: Harper and Row.

Carbonell, J.R. (1970). "Mixed-Initiative Man-Computer Instructional Dialogues." *Ph.D. dissertation*, M.I.T., Cambridge, Mass.

Carroll, J.D. and Chang, J.J. (1970). "Analysis of individual differences in multidimensional scaling via an N-way generalization of 'Eckart-Young' decomposition." *Psychometrika* 35.283.

Cattell, R.B. (1943). "The Measurement of Adult Intelligence." *Psychol. Bull.* 40. 153–193.

Chipman, L. (1971). "Material and illative implication." *Mind 80* pp. 179–193.

Chomsky, N. (1968). *Language and Mind*. New York: Harcourt, Brace and World.

Claparede, E. (1917). "La Psychologie de l'intelligence." *Scientia* November.

Clarke, A.D.B. (1972). "Commentary on Koluchova's 'Severe deprivation in twins: a case study'." *Journal of Child Psychology and Psychiatry*. 13. 103–106.

Clarke, M.R.B. (1973). *Some ideas for a Chess Compiler*. This volume.

Colby, K., Gilbert, J. and Watt, J. (1966). "A Computer Method of Psychotherapy: Preliminary Communication." *Jnl. of Nervous and Mental Disease*. 142.2.

Coleman, James, S. (1969). "Games as vehicles for social theory." *Amer. Behav. Sci.* 12.6. 2–5.

Cornelius, E. (1971). "Canonical correlation as a perceptual model." Unpublished master's thesis. Texas Christian University.

Craig, R.J. (1971). "Overinclusive Thinking and Schizophrenia." *J. Pers. Ass.* 35. 208.

Cronbach, L.J. (1967). "How Can Instruction be Adapted to Individual Differences?" in Gagne, R., (ed.), *Learning and Individual Differences*, p. 23, Columbia, Ohio: Merrill Books.

Crosson, F.J. (1970). Introduction to: F.J. Crosson, (ed.), *Human and Artificial Intelligence*. New York: Appleton-Century-Crofts.

Dansereau, D.F., Fenker, R.M. and Evans, S.H. (1970). "Visual pattern perception: Encoding and storage of schematic versus random patterns." *Proceedings 78th Annual Convention American Psychological Association Conference*. 49.

Darlington, J.L. (1968). "Automatic theorem-proving with equality substitutions and mathematical induction," in Michie, D., (ed.), *Machine Intelligence 3*, p. 113, Edinburgh University Press.

Darlington, J.L. (1969). "Theorem proving and information retrieval," in Meltzer, B. and Michie, D., (eds.), *Machine Intelligence 4*, Edinburgh University Press.

Davis, G.A. (1966). "The current status of research and theory in human problem solving." *Psychological Bulletin*. 66.

Davis, M. (1963). "Eliminating the irrelevant from mechanical proofs." *Proc. of Symposia in Applied Mathematics*, American Mathematical Society, 15. 15–30.

De Groot, A.D. (1946). *Het Denken van den Schaker*. Amsterdam: North-Holland.

De Groot, A.D. (1965). *Thought and choice in chess* (rev. trans.). The Hague: Mouton.

De Groot, A.D. (1966). "Perception and Memory Versus Thought: Some old ideas and recent findings." In Kleinmuntz, B., (ed.), *Problem Solving: Research, Method and Theory*. New York: Wiley.

De Soto, C.B., London, M. and Handel, S. (1965). "Social reasoning and spatial paralogic." *J. Pers. soc. Psychol*. 2. pp. 513–21.

Delamont, S. and Atkinson, P. (1971). "Preliminary Report on Attitudinal Evaluation for Computer-assisted Instruction Experiment." *Research Memorandum CAI-3*, Bionics Research Lab., Dept. of Machine Intelligence and Perception, University of Edinburgh.

Dimond, S.J. (1970). "Hemispheric refractoriness and control of reaction time." *Quart. J. Experimental Psychol*. 24. 610–617.

Domarus, E.V. (1944). "The Specific Laws of Logic in Schizophrenia." In Kasanin, J.S., (ed.), *Language and Thought in Schizophrenia*. University of California Press.

Doran, J.E. (1971). "Some recent models of the brain," in Meltzer, B. and Michie, D., (eds.), *Machine Intelligence 6*, pp. 207–220. Edinburgh University Press.

Dörner, D. (1971). "Die Fortentwicklung des Denkens beim Problemlösen." In: Reinert, G., (ed.), *Ber. 27 Kongr. DGfPs in Kiel*, Göttingen: Hogrefe.

Dörner, D. (1972). "Illegal Thinking." This Volume.

Drever, J. (1967). "The Nurture of Intelligence." *Scottish Educational Studies*. 1. pp. 3–7.

Duncker, K. 1963 (1st edition: 1935). *Zur Psychologie des produktiven Denkens*. Berlin: Springer.

Edwards, W. (1961). "Behavioural decision theory." *Ann. Rev. Psychol*. 12. 473.

Edawa, K. and Haga, J. (1966). "An inquiry into the process of human problem solving by means of an information-processing model." *Japanese Journal of Educational Psychology*. 14(2). 71–73.

Eifermann, Rivka R. (1970a). "Level of children's play as expressed in group size." *Brit. J. Ed. Psychol*. 40(2). 161–170.

Eifermann, Rivka R. (1970b). "Cooperativeness and egalitarianism in kibbutz children's games." *Human Relat*. 23(6). 579–587.

Eifermann, Rivka R. (1970c). "A cross-cultural study of children's games." Paper read at the 1st International Conference of the Founding Fellows of the Center for Human Development. The Hebrew University of Jerusalem.

Eifermann, Rivka R. (1971a). *Determinants of Children's Game Styles.* Jerusalem: The Israel Academy of Sciences and Humanities.

Eifermann, Rivka R. (1971b). "Social play in childhood." In Herron, R.E. and Sutton-Smith, B. *Child's Play.* New York: Wiley.

Eifermann, Rivka R. (1972). "It's child's play." In Bower, E. and Shears, Loyda M., (eds.), *Games in Education and Development.* Springfield, Ill.: Charles C. Thomas.

Eifermann, Rivka R. (1973). "Rules in Games." This volume.

Eifermann, Rivka R. and Steinitz, Ruth. (1971). "A comparison of conjunctive and disjunctive concept identification." *J. Gen. Psychol.* 85. 29.

Elias, Norbert and Dunning, Eric. (1970). "The Quest for Excitement in Unexciting Societies." In Luschen, G., (ed.), *The Cross-Cultural Analysis of Sport and Games.* Champaign, Ill.: Stipes Publishing Co.

Elithorn, A. and Cooper, R.L. (1973). "The Organization of Search Procedures." This volume.

Elithorn, A., Jones, D. and Kerr, M.O. (1963). "A Binary Perceptual Maze." *Am. J. Psychol.* 76 (3) 506.

Elithorn, A., Jones, D., Kerr, M.O. and Lee, D.N. (1964). "The Effects of the Variation of Two Physical Parameters on Empirical Difficulty in a Perceptual Maze Test." *Brit. J. Psychol.* 55(1). 19.

Elithorn, A. and Lawrence, C.M.D. (1955). "Central Inhibition – Some Refractory Observations." *Quart. J. Exp. Psychol.* 7. pp. 116–127.

Elithorn, A. and Telford, A. (1969). "Computer analysis of intellectual skills." *Int. J. Man-Machine Studies.* 1. 189.

Elithorn, A. and Telford, A. (1970). "Game and Problem Structure in Relation to the Study of Human and Artificial Intelligence." *Nature,* 227, No. 5264. 1205.

Elithorn, A. and Telford, A. (1973). "Design Consideration in Relation to Computer-based Problems." This volume.

Eliot, George. (1866). *Felix Holt.* London: Blackwoods.

Evans, S.H. (1970). Annotated bibliography of reports September 1967 through August 1970 from *Parameters of Human Pattern Perception,* Texas Christian University, Institute for the Study of Cognitive Systems, DAAD05-68-C-0176, U.S. Army Aberdeen Research & Development Center, Human Engineering Laboratories.

Evans, S.H. and Mueller, M.R. (1966). "VARGUS 9: Computed stimuli for schema research." *Psychon. Sci.* 6. 511.

Evans, T.G. (1968). "A program for the solution of geometric-analogy intelligence test questions." In Minsky, M., (ed.), *Semantic Information Processing.* p. 271, Cambridge, Mass: The MIT Press.

Fantz, R.L. (1957). "Form Preferences in Newly Hatched Chicks." *J. Comp. & Physiol. Psychol.* 50. 422.

Feigenbaum, E., Buchanan, B. and Lederberg, J. (1971). "Generality and Problem Solving: A Case Study Using the DENDRAL Program." In Meltzer, B. and Michie, D., (eds.), *Machine Intelligence 6.* Edinburgh: Edinburgh University Press, pp. 165–190.

Feigenbaum, E.A. and Feldman, (eds.), (1963). *Computers and Thought.* New York: McGraw-Hill.

Feldman, J. (1967). *First thoughts on grammatical inference.* Stanford Artificial Intelligence Project Memo No. 55.

Fenker, R.M. (1971). "New dimensions in psychophysics: A sure cure for methodological dyspepsia." Paper presented at Symposium "Multivariate Appraoches to Pattern Perception". Midwestern Psychological Association, Detroit.

Fikes, R. (1969). "Ref-Arf: A system for solving problems stated as procedures." SRI Artificial Intelligence Group, Note 14.

Fikes, R. and Nilsson, N. (1971). "STRIPS: A new approach to the application of Theorem-Proving to Problem-Solving." *Proceedings of the 2nd International Joint Conference on Artificial Intelligence.* Imperial College, London.

Findler, N.V. (1973). "Computer Experiments on the Formation and Optimization of Heuristic Rules." This volume.

Fisher, R.A. (1928). *Statistical Methods for Research Workers.* London: Oliver and Boyd.

Fodor, J.A. (1968). *Psychological explanation.* New York: Random House.

Fogel, L.J., Owens, A.J. and Walsh, M.J. (1966). *Artificial Intelligence Through Simulated Evaluation.* New York: John Wiley & Sons.

Frijda, N.H. and Meertens, L. (1969). "A simulation model of human information retrieval." In *The Simulation of Human Behaviour,* p. 237, Paris: Dunod.

Frijda, N.H. (1972). "The simulation of human long term memory." *Psychological Bulletin,* Vol. 77, No. 1, January, pp. 1–31.

Furneaux, W.D. (1960). "Intellectual abilities and problem-solving behaviour." In Eysenck, H.J., (ed.), *Handbook of abnormal psychology,* Chapter 5, London: Pitman.

Gagne, R.M. (1965). *The Conditions of Learning.* New York: Holt, Rinehart & Winston.

Gaines, B.R., Facey, P.V. and Gedye, J.L. (1971). *A Versatile Multi-User Interactive Language System for a Minicomputer.* Nottingham: Datafair.

Garner, W.R. and Felfoldy, G.L. (1970). "Integrality of stimulus dimensions in various types of information processing." *Cog. Psychol.* 1. 225.

Gazzaniga, M.S. and Sperry, R.W. (1966). "Simultaneous Double Discrimination Response Following Brain Bisection." *Psychon. Sci.* 4. 7. 261–262.

Gedye, J.L. (1964). "Transient Changes in the Ability to Reproduce a Sequential Operation following Rapid Decompression." Institution of Aviation Medicine, Report No. 271, Farnborough.

Gedye, J.L. (1969). "Problems in the Design of Interactive Terminals for Direct Use by Patients." In Abrams, M.E., (ed.), *Medical Computing-Progress and Problems.* London: Chatto & Windus for the British Computer Society.

Geyde, J.L. and Miller, (1969). "The Automation of Psychological Assessment." *Int. J. Man-Machine Studies,* 1. 237.

Gelernter, H. (1963). "Realisation of a geometry-theorem proving machine." In: Feigenbaum, E. and Feldman, J., (eds.), *Computers and Thought,* pp. 134–152. New York: McGraw-Hill.

George, F. (1970). "Simulating human thought." *Science Journal,* 6(1). 56.

Gilmore, P.C. (1960). "A proof method for quantification theory." *IBM Journal of Research and Development.* 4. 28.

Gitmez, A.S. (1971). "Instructions and performance: subjective reports as secondary task." *Hacettepe Bull. of Soc. Sciences & Humanities.* 3. 1.

Goffman, E. (1961). *Encounters.* Indianapolis: Bobbs-Merrill.

Goodman, Nelson (1955). *Facts, Fictions and Forecasts,* Cambridge, Mass.: Harvard University Press.

Goodwin, R.Q. and Wason, P.C. (1972). "Degrees of insight." *Br. J. Psychol.* 63. 205.

Gould, W.E. (1966). "A matching procedure for w-order logic." *Scientific Report No. 4 AFCRL 66–781,* Applied Logic Corporation, Princeton.

Gray, J.A. (1970). "Sodium Amobarbital, the Hippocampal Theta Rhythm etc." *Psychol. Rev.* 77. 465.

Green, C.C. (1969a). "Application of theorem proving solving." In Walker, D.E. and Norton, L.M. (eds.), *Proc. Int. Joint. Conf. Art. Intell.,* Washington D.C., pp. 219–239.

Green, C.C. (1969b). "Theorem-proving by resolution as a basis for question-answering systems." In Meltzer, B. and Michie, D., (eds.), *Machine Intelligence 4,* pp. 183–205, Edinburgh: Edinburgh University Press.

Greenblatt, R., Eastlake, D. and Crocker, S. (1967). "The Greenblatt Chess Program." *AFIPS Conference Proceedings, Fall Joint Computer Conference,* 31, pp. 801–810, Washington D.C.: Thompson Books.

Gregg, L.W. and Simon, H.A. (1967). "Process models and stochastic theories of simple concept formation." *J. Math. Psych.* 4. 2.

Guilford, J.P. (1966). "Intelligence: 1965 model." *Am. Psych.* 21. 20.

Guilford, J.P. (1967). *The Nature of Human Intelligence.* New York: McGraw-Hill.

Guilford, J.P., Fruchter, B. and Zimmerman, W.S. (1952). "Factor analysis of the Army-Air Forces Sheppard Field battery of experimental aptitude tests." *Psychometrika.* 17. 45.

Halmos, P. (1962). *Algebraic Logic.* New York: The Chelsea Publishing Co.

Halpin, S.M. and Pilisuk, M. (1970). "Prediction and choice in the prisoner's dilemma." *Behav. Sci.* 15. 141.

Hammond, K.R. (1971). "Computer Graphics as an Aid to Learning." *Science.* 172. 903.

Handel, S., de Soto, C.B. and London, M. (1968). "Reasoning and spatial representations." *Jnl. Verbal Learning and Verbal Behaviour.* 7. 351.

Harré, R. (1971). "Joynson's Dilemma." *Bull. Br. Psychol. Soc.* 24. 115.

Harris, R.J. (1969). A geometric classification system for 2×2 interval-symmetric games. *Behav. Sci.* 14. 138.

Hart, H.L.A. (1961). *The Concept of Law.* Oxford: Clarendon Press.

Hart, P.E., Nilsson, N. and Raphael, B. (1968). "A formal basis for the heuristic determination of minimum cost paths." *I.E.E.E. Trans. Sys. & Cyber. SSC-4*, pp. 100–7.

Hastings, D., Fenker, R.M. and Evans, S.H. (1971). "Comparison of perceived stimulus attributes across task and stimulus mapping conditions." Paper presented at the meeting of Midwestern Psychological Association, Detroit.

Hayes, P.J. (1971). "A logic of actions," in: Meltzer, B. and Michie, D., (eds.), *Machine Intelligence 6*, Edinburgh: Edinburgh University Press.

Herbrand, J. (1930). "Recherches sur la theorie de la demonstration." *Travaux de la Societe des Sciences et des lettres de Varsovie*. Nr 33. (A translation of the Key Chapter 5, is in: *From Frege to Gödel: a source book in mathematical logic*, van Heijenoort, J., (ed.), Harvard University Press, Cambridge 1967).

Heron, A. and Chown, S. (1967). *Age and Function*. London: J. and A. Churchill.

Hesse, Mary B. (1966). *Models and Analogies in Science*. Indiana: University of Notre Dame Press, p. 184.

Hodgkin, K. (1966). *Towards Earlier Diagnosis – A Family Doctor's Approach*. Second Edition, Edinburgh: Livingstone.

Hoffman, P.J. (1968). "Cue-consistency and Configurality in Human Judgement." In Kleinmuntz, B., (ed.), *Formal Representation of Human Judgement*. New York: Wiley.

Hooper, Alfred. (1949). *Makers of Mathematics*. London: Faber & Faber.

Howe, J.A.M. (1971). Edinburgh Computer-assisted Instruction Project: Progress Report 1970–1971. *Bionics Research Report No. 3*, Dept. of Machine Intelligence & Perception, University of Edinburgh.

Hintikka, J. (1967). "A Program and a Set of Concepts for Philosophical Logic." *The Monist*. 51. 69.

Hubel, D.H. and Wiesel, T.N. (1962). "Receptive Fields etc., in the Cat's Visual Cortex." *J. Physiol*. 160. 106.

Hunt, E.B., Marin, Janet and Stone, P.J. (1966). *Experiments in Induction*. New York: Academic Press, p. 247.

Johnson-Laird, P.N. and Tagart, J. (1960). "How Implication is Understood." *Am. J. Psychol* 82. 367.

Johnson-Laird, P.N. and Wason, P.C. (1970). "A Theoretical Analysis of Insight into a Reasoning Task." *Cognitive Psychol*. 1. 134.

Jones, M.B. (1962). "Practice as a Process of Simplification." *Psych. Rev*. 69. 274.

Jones, Marie Riess. (1971). "From Probability Learning to Sequential Processing: A Critical Review." *Psych. Bull*. 76(3) 153.

Kelley, M. (1971). "Edge detection in pictures by computer using planning." In Meltzer, B. and Michie, D., (eds.), *Machine Intelligence 6*. Edinburgh: Edinburgh University Press, pp. 397–409.

Kelly, G.A. (1955). *The Psychology of Personal Constructs*. New York: W.W. Norton & Co.

Kendler, H.H. and Kendler, T.A. (1962). "Vertical and Horizontal Processes in Problem Solving." *Psychol. Rev*. 69. 1.

Klahr, D. and Wallace, J.G. (1972). "Class inclusion processes," in Farnham-Diggory, Sylvia, (ed.). *Information Processing in Children*, New York: Academic Press.

Kleene, S.C. (1952). *Introduction to Metamathematics*. New York: Van Nostrand.

Kline, Morris (1962). *Mathematics, A Cultural Approach*. Reading, Mass.: Addison-Wesley Publishing.

Kling, R.E. (1971). "A paradigm for reasoning by analogy." *Artificial Intelligence*, pp. 147–178.

Klugh, H.E. (1969). "A Problem Finding Machine." *Psychological Record*. 19(2) 313.

Knuth, D. (1971). *Mathematical Analysis of Algorithms*. Stanford University Computer Science Report 206.

Koluchova, Jarmila. (1972). "Severe deprivation in twins: a case study." *J. Child Psychol. and Psychiat*. 13. 107–114.

Kowalski, R. (1969). "Search strategies for theorem proving." In Meltzer, B. and Michie, D., (eds.), *Machine Intelligence 5*, pp. 181–201. Edinburgh University Press.

Kowalski, R. (1970). "Studies in the completeness and efficiency of theorem-proving by resolution." Ph.D. Thesis, University of Edinburgh.

Kowalski, R. and Kuehner, D. (1971). "Linear resolution with selection function." *Artificial Intelligence*, pp. 227–260.

Krieger, M.H. (1964). "A control for social desirability in a semantic differential." *Brit. J. Soc. Clin. Psychol*. 3. 94.

Kripke, S. (1963). "Semantic Analysis of Modal Logic I." *Zeitschrift für math. Logik und Grundlagen der Mathematik*. 9. 67.

Kristofferson, A.B. (1965). "Attention in Time Discrimination and Reaction Time." NASA Contractor Report NASA CR-194.

Kruskal, J.B. (1964). "Nonmetric multidimensional scaling: A numerical method." *Psychometrika*. 29. 115.

Kubicka, L. (1968). "The psychological background of adolescent's behaviour in a two-person non zero sum game." *Behav. Sci*. 13. 455.

Kuhn, T.S. (1962). *The Structure of Scientific Revolutions*. Chicago: University of Chicago Press.

Kunst, H. (1971). "Een analyse van inzicht in een redeneer taak." Report FL.01.07.71.068. Amsterdam: Instituut voor Cognitie-Onderzoek, Amsterdam University.

Lee, D.N. (1965). "A Psychological and Mathematical Study of Task Complexity in Relation to Human Problem-Solving Using a Perceptual Maze Test." Ph.D. Thesis. University of London.

Lettvin, J.Y., Maturana, H., McCulloch, W.S. and Pitts, W. (1959). "What the Frog's Eye Tells the Frog's Brain." *Proceedings of the Institute of Radio Engineers*. 47.

Levine, M. (1966). "Hypothesis behaviour by humans during discrimination learning." *J. Exper. Psychol*. 71. 331.

Levy, D.N.L. (1971). "Computer Chess – A Case Study on the CDC 6600." In Meltzer, B. and Michie, D., (eds.), *Machine Intelligence 6*, pp. 151–163. Edinburgh University Press.

Levy, Jerre. (1969). "Possible Basis for the Evolution of Lateral Specialization of the Human Brain." *Nature*. 224. 5219. pp. 614–615.

Loevinger, J. (1957). "Objective Tests as Instruments of Psychological Theory." *Psych. Reports, 3.* 635.

London, R.L. (1969). "Bibliography on proving the correctness of computer programs." in Meltzer, B. and Michie, D., (eds.), *Machine Intelligence 5,* pp. 569–580, Edinburgh University Press.

Loveland, D. (1968). "A linear format for resolution." *Proceedings of IRIA Symposium on Automatic Demonstration.* Berlin: Springer Verlag. pp. 147–162.

Luckman, D. and Nilsson, N.J. (1971). "Extracting information from resolution proof trees." *Artificial Intelligence.* 2. 27.

Lüer, G. (1971). "Veränderungen im Lösungsverhalten beim Beweis aussagenlogischer Theoreme." In Reinert, G., (ed.), *Ber. 27. Kongr. DGfPs in Kiel.* Göttingen: Hogrefe.

Lüer, G. (1972). *The Development of Strategies of Solutions in Problem Solving.* This volume.

McCarthy, J. (1959). "Programs with Common Sense." *Mechanisation of Thought Processes 1.* London: HMSO. Reprinted in *Semantic Information Processing,* Minsky, M. (ed.), 1970, Cambridge, Mass.: MIT Press.

McCarthy, J. (1963a). "A Basis for a Mathematical Theory of Computation." *Computer Programming and Formal Systems.* Brafford, P. and Hirschberg, D. (eds.), Amsterdam: North-Holland.

McCarthy, J. (1963b). *Situations, Actions and Causal Laws.* Stanford Artificial Intelligence Project Memo 2.

McCarthy, J., Abrahams, P.W., Edwards, D.J., Hart, T.P. and Levin, M.I. (1963). *LISP 1.5 programmer's manual.* Cambridge, Mass.: MIT Press.

McCarthy, J. and Hayes, P.J. (1968). "Some Philosophical Problems from the Standpoint of Artificial Intelligence." In Meltzer, B. and Michie, D., (eds.), *Machine Intelligence 4,* pp. 463–502. Edinburgh University Press.

McClintock, C.G., Harrison, A.A., Strand, S. and Gallo, P. (1963). "Internationalism-isolationism, strategy of the other player, and two-person game behaviour." *J. Abnorm. Soc. Psychol.* 67. 631.

McFie, J. (1961). "Effects of hemispherectomy on intellectual functioning in cases of infantile hemiplegia." *J. Neurol. Neurosurg. & Psychiat.* 24. pp. 240–249.

Magnus, W., Karrass, A. and Solitar, D. (1966). *Combinatorial Group Theory.* New York: Interscience Publishers.

Maier, N.R. and Burke, R.J. (1966). "Test of the Concept of Availability of Functions." *Psych. Rep.* 19. 119.

Manna, Z. (1969). "The correctness of programs." *Jnl. Computer and System Sciences.* 3. 119.

Manna, Z. and Waldinger, R.J. (1970). "Towards automatic program synthesis." *Stanford Artificial Intelligence Project Memo AIM-127.* Computer Science Department, Stanford University.

Markov, A.A. (1951). *The Theory of Algorithms.* Tr. Math Inst. Steklov XLII, translated 1962 by the Office of Technical Services, U.S. Dept. of Commerce, Washington, D.C.

Mayo, B. (1951). "Rules" of language. *Philosophical Studies,* 2(1). 1−7.

Medawar, P. (1967). *The art of the soluble.* London: Metheun. pp. 147, 134.

Meltzer, B. (1969). "Power amplification for automatic theorem-provers." In Meltzer, B. and Michie, D., (eds.), *Machine Intelligence 5,* pp. 165−179, Edinburgh University Press.

Meltzer, B. (1970). "The semantics of induction and the possibility of complete systems of inductive inference." *Artificial Intelligence 1,* pp. 189−192.

Meltzer, B. (1971). "Prologomena to a theory of efficiency of proof procedures." In Findler, N.V. and Meltzer, B., (eds.), *Artificial Intelligence and Heuristic Programming,* pp. 15−33, Edinburgh University Press.

Miller, W.F. and Shaw, A.C. (1968). "Linguistic Methods in Picture Processing: A Survey." *Proc. Fall Jt. Computer Conference,* pp. 279−290.

Minsky, M. (ed.) (1968). *Semantic Information Processing.* Cambridge, Mass: MIT Press.

Morgan, C.G. (1971). "Hypothesis generation by machine." *Artificial Intelligence,* pp. 179−187.

Morris, J.B. (1969). "E-resolution: extension of resolution to include the equality relation." *Proc. Int. Joint Conf. Art. Intell.,* Washington, D.C. Walker, D.E. and Norton, L.M. (eds.), pp. 287−294.

Mott-Smith, G. (1946). *Mathematical Puzzles.* New York: Dover.

Neisser, U. (1963). "The Imitation of Man by Machine." *Science.* 139. 193. reprinted in F.J. Crosson (1970), op. cit.

Neisser, U. (1967). *Cognitive Psychology.* New York: Appleton-Century-Crofts.

Newell, A. (1965). "Limitations of the current stock of ideas about problem-solving." In Kent, A. and Taulbee, O., (eds.), *Electronic Information Handling.* New York: Spartan.

Newell, A. (1966). "On the analysis of human problem solving protocols." Paper given at the *International Symposium on Mathematical and Computational Methods in the Social Sciences.* Rome. Carnegie Institute of Technology, Pittsburgh, Pennsylvania.

Newell, A. (1967). "Studies in Problem Solving: Subject 3 on the Crypt Arithmetic Test DONALD + GERALD−ROBERT." Pittsburgh: Carnegie-Mellon University.

Newell, A. and Simon, H.A. (1956). "The logic theory machine." *IRE transactions on information theory,* IT-2, No. 3.

Newell, A. and Simon, H.A. (1963). "GPS, A Program that Simulates Human Thought." In Feigenbaum, E.A. and Feldman, J., (eds.), *Computers and Thought.* New York: McGraw-Hill.

Newell, A. and Simon, H.A. (1965). "An Example of Human Chess Play in the Light of Chess Playing Programs." In Wiener, N. and Schadé, J.P., (eds.), *Progress in Cybernetics,* Vol. 2, pp. 19−25. Amsterdam: Elsevier.

Newell, A. and Simon, H.A. (1972). *Human Problem Solving.* Englewood Cliffs, N.J.: Prentice-Hall, Inc.

Newell, A., Shaw, J. and Simon, H. (1959a). "Report on a general problem-solving program." *Proc. Int. Conf. on Information Processing,* pp. 256, Paris: UNESCO House.

Newell, A., Shaw, J.C. and Simon, H.A. (1959b). "Report on the Play of Chess-Player 1—5 of a Book Game of Morphy vs. Duke Karl of Brunswick and Count Isouard." CIP Working Paper No. 21.

Newell, A., Shaw, J.C. and Simon, H.A. (1963). "Empirical explorations with the logic theory machine," in Feigenbaum, E.A. and Feldman, J., (eds.), *Computers and Thought,* New York: McGraw-Hill, pp. 109—133.

Newman, E.A. and Scantlebury, R. (1967). "Teaching Machines as Intelligence Amplifiers." *National Physical Laboratory Report, Auto 31,* London.

Nilsson, N.J. (1969). "A mobile automaton: an application of artificial intelligence techniques." *Proc. Inf. Joint Conf. Art. Intell., Washington, D.C.,* pp. 509—520, eds., Walker, D.E. and Norton, L.M.

Nilsson, N. (1971). *Problem-Solving Methods in Artificial Intelligence.* New York: McGraw-Hill.

Opie, Iona and Opie, P. (1969). *Children's games in street and playground.* Oxford: Clarendon Press.

Ore, O. (1963). *Graphs and Their Uses.* New York: Random House.

Oskamp, S. (1970). "Effects of programmed initial strategies in a prisoner's dilemma game." *Psychon. Sci.* 19. 195.

Paivio, A. (1969). "Mental imagery in associative learning and memory." *Psychological Review,* 76. 241.

Palme, J. (1971). "Making computers understand natural language." In Findler, N.V. and Meltzer, B., (eds.), *Artificial Intelligence and Heuristic Programming,* pp. 192—244. Edinburgh University Press.

Peterson, C.R. and Beach, L.R. (1967). "Man as an intuitive statistician." *Psychol. Bull.,* 68. 29.

Phelan, J.G. and Richardson, E.D. (1969). "Cognitive complexity, strategy of the other player, and two-person game behaviour." *J. Psychol.* 71. 205.

Piaget, J. (1932). *The moral judgement of the child.* London: Routledge and Kegan Paul.

Pitrat, J. (1966). "Réalisation de programmes de démonstration de théorèmes utilisant des methodes heuristiques." Thesis. University of Paris.

Plotkin, G. (1971). "A further note on inductive generalizations." In Meltzer, B. and Michie, D., (eds.), *Machine Intelligence 6,* pp. 101—124. Edinburgh University Press.

Plotkin, G. (unpublished). "Studies of some logics for artificial intelligence." University of Edinburgh.

Pohl, I. (1969). "First results on the effect of error in heuristic search." In Meltzer, B. and Michie, D., (eds.), *Machine Intelligence 5,* pp. 219. Edinburgh University Press.

Pohl, I. (1970). "Heuristic search viewed as path finding in a graph." *Artificial Intelligence.* 1. 193.

Pollack, I., Headly, P. and Mass, E. (1966). "Modest Computer-controlled Psychoacoustical Facility." *J. Acoust. Soc. Am.* 39(1). 248.

Popper, K.R. (1959). *The Logic of Scientific Discovery.* New York: Basic Books, p. 32.

Post, E.L. (1936). "Finite combinatory processes-formulation I." *J. Symbolic Logic*, 1. 103.

Potkay, C.R. (1971). *The Rorschach Clinician. A New Research Approach and its Application.* New York: Grune and Straton.

Prawitz, D. (1960). "An improved proof procedure." *Theoria*, 26. 102.

Quinlan, J. and Hunt, E. (1958). "A formal deductive problem solving system." *JACM*. 15. 625.

Racine, B. (1971) "La transformation de l'image mentale." Unpublished M.A. thesis, Université de Montréal.

Raphael, B. (1971). "The Frame Problem in Problem-solving Systems." *Proceedings of the ASI on Artificial Intelligence and Heuristic Programming.* Edinburgh University Press.

Rapoport, A. and Chammah, A.M. (1965). *Prisoner's Dilemma. A study in conflict and cooperation.* Ann Arbor: University of Michigan Press.

Ray, W.S. (1957). "Verbal Compared with Manipulative Solution of an Apparatus Problem." *Am. J. Psychol.*, 70, 289–290.

Rayner, E.H. (1958a). "A Study of Evaluative Problem Solving: Part I, Observations on Adults." *Quart. J. Exp. Psychol.* 10(3). 155.

Rayner, E.H. (1958b). "A Study of Evaluative Problem Solving. Part II: Developmental Observations." *Quart. J. Exp. Psychol.* 10(4). 193.

Reeves, J.W. (1965). *Thinking About Thinking.* London: Secker and Warburg.

Reitman, J.S. (1971). "Mechanisms of forgetting in short-term memory." *Cognitive Psychol.*, 2. 185.

Reitman, W.R. (1965). *Cognition and Thought.* New York: Wiley.

Rescher, N. (1964). *Hypothetical Reasoning.* Amsterdam: North-Holland.

Restle, F. (1962). "The selection of strategies in cue learning." *Psychol. Rev.*, 69. 329.

Restle, F. and Greeno, J.G. (1970). *Introduction to Mathematical Psychology* Reading, Mass.

Rimoldi, H.J.A. (1955). "A Technique for the Study of Problem Solving." *Educational and Psychological Measurement*, 15(4). 450.

Rimoldi, H.J.A. (1960). "Problem Solving as a Process." *Educational and Psychological Measurement*, 20. 3.

Rimoldi, H.J.A. (1961). "The Test of Diagnostic Skills." *Journal of Medical Education.* 36. 73.

Rimoldi, H.J.A. (1971). "Logical Structure and Languages in Thinking Processes." *International Journal of Psychology.* 6(1). 65.

Rimoldi, H.J.A., Aghi, M.B. and Burger, G. (1968). "Some effects of logical structure, language and age in problem solving in children." *Journal of Genetic Psychology.* 112. 127.

Rimoldi, H.J.A. and Van der Woude, K.W. (1969). "Ageing and Problem Solving." *Archives of General Psychiatry.* 20. 215.

Robinson, J.A. (1965a). "A machine-oriented logic based on the resolution principle." *Jnl. Assoc. Comp. Mach.*, 12. 23.

Robinson, J.A. (1965b). "Automatic deduction with hyper-resolution." *Int. Jnl. Computer Mathematics,* 1. 227.

Robinson, J.A. (1967). "A review of automatic theorem-proving." *Proc. Symp. App. Math.,* 19. 1.

Robinson, J.A. (1968). "The generalised resolution principle." In Michie, D., (ed.), *Machine Intelligence 3,* pp. 77–94, Edinburgh University Press.

Robinson, J.A. (1969). "Mechanizing higher-order logic." In Meltzer, B. and Michie, D., (eds.), *Machine Intelligence 4,* pp. 151–170. Edinburgh University Press.

Robinson, John P. (1970). "Daily Participation in Sport Across Twelve Countries." In Luschen, G., (ed.), *The Cross-Cultural Analysis of Sport and Games.* Stipes Publishing Co., Champaign, Illinois.

Robinson, G.A. and Wos, L. (1969). "Paramodulation and theorem-proving in first-order theories with equality." In Meltzer, B. and Michie, D., (eds.), *Machine Intelligence 4,* pp. 135–150. Edinburgh University Press.

Runge, R.G., Uemura, M. and Viglione, S.S. (1970). "Electronic Synthesis of Aviation Retina." *IEEE Transactions on Bio-Medical Engineering, (BME),* 15(3). 138.

Samuel, A.L. (1967). "Some Studies in Machine Learning using the Game of Checkers II — Recent Progress." *IBM J. Res. Develop.,* 11(6). 601.

Sandewall, E. (1971). "Representing natural language information in predicate calculus." In, Meltzer, B. and Michie, D., (eds.), *Machine Intelligence 6,* pp. 255–277, Edinburgh: Edinburgh University Press.

Schegloff, Emanuel A. (1967). "The First Five Seconds: The Order of Conversational Openings." Unpublished PhD Dissertation, University of California, Berkeley.

Schelling, T. (1963). *The Strategy of Conflict.* New York: A Galaxy Book, Oxford University Press.

Schetagne, J.P. (1970). "L'implication logique et deux erreurs d'inferences." M.A. thesis, Montreal. University of Montreal.

Schum, D.A., Goldstein, I.L., Howell, W.C. and Southard, J.F. (1967). "Subjective propability revisions under several cost-payoff arrangements." *Organizational Behaviour and Human Performance.* 2. 84.

Sebestyen, G. (1962). *Decision Making Processes in Pattern Recognition.* New York: The Macmillan Co.

Selfridge, O.G. and Neisser, U. (1963). "Pattern Recognition by Machine." In Feigenbaum, E.A. and Feldman, J., (eds.), *Computers and Thought.* pp. 251–260. New York: McGraw-Hill.

Seltzer, R.A. (1971). "Computer Aided Instruction — What it can and what it cannot do." *Am. J. Psychol.* 373.

Sermat, V. (1967). "The effect of an initial cooperative or competitive treatment upon a subject's response to conditional cooperation." *Behav. Sci.* 12. 301.

Shannon, C.E. (1950). "Programming a Computer for Playing Chess." *Phil. Mag.,* 41. 256.

366

Shepard, R.N. and Chipman, S. (1970). "Second-order isomorphism of internal representations: Shapes of states." *Cog. Psychol.* 1. 1.

Shipstone, E.J. (1960). "Some variables affecting pattern conception." *Psychol. Monogr.*, 74 (17, Whole No. 504), 42.

Sibert, E.E. (1969). "A machine-oriented logic incorporating the equality relation." In Meltzer, B. and Michie, D., (eds.), *Machine Intelligence 4*, pp. 103–133. Edinburgh: Edinburgh University Press.

Simmons, R.F. (1970a). "Linguistic Analysis of Constructed Student Responses." In Holtzman, W.H., (ed.), *Computer-assisted Instruction, Testing and Guidance.* p. 203. New York: Harper and Row.

Simmons, R.F. (1970b). "Natural Language Question Answering Systems: 1969." In Banerji, R. and Mesarovic, M.D., (eds.), *Theoretical approaches to non-numerical problem-solving.* p. 108. New York: Springer-Verlag.

Simon, H.A. (1953). "Causal Ordering and Identifiability." In Hood, W.C. and Koopmans, T.C. (eds.), *Studies in Econometric Method,* New York: John Wiley.

Simon, H.A. (1967). "An information-processing explanation of some perceptual phenomena." *Br. J. of Psychol.* 58. 1.

Simon, H.A. and Barenfeld, M. (1969). "Information processing analysis of perceptual processes in problem solving." *Psychol. Review.* 76(5). 473.

Simon, H.A. and Rescher, N. (1966). "Cause and Counterfactual." *Philosophy of Science.* 33. Bruges, Belgium.

Simons, H.A. (1969). *The Sciences of the Artificial.* Cambridge, Mass.: MIT Press.

Slagle, J.R. and Dixon, J.K. (1969). "Experiments with some Programs that Search Game Trees." *J. Ass. Comp. Mach.,* 16(2). 189.

Slate, D. and Atkins, L. (1969). Print-out of program obtainable at University of London Computer Centre.

Smallwood, R.D. (1970). "Optimal Policy Regions for Computer-directed Teaching Systems." In Holtzman, W.H., (ed.), *Computer-assisted Instruction, Testing and Guidance.* New York: Harper and Row. p. 101.

Suppes, P.A. (1961). "A Comparison of the Meaning and Uses of Models in Mathematics and the Empirical Sciences." In Freudenthal, H., (ed.), *The Concept and the Role of the Model in Mathematics and Natural and Social Sciences.* pp. 163–177. Dordrecht (Netherlands): D. Reidel.

Suppes, P.A. (1971). "Computer-Assisted Instruction at Stanford." *Technical Report No. 174.* Institute for Mathematical Studies in the Social Sciences, Stanford University.

Suppes, P.A. and Morningstar, M. (1969). "Computer-assisted instruction." *Science,* 166. 343.

Suppes, P.A. and Morningstar, M. (1970). "Four programs in Computer-Assisted Instruction." In Holtzman, W.H., (ed.), *Computer-assisted Instruction, Testing and Guidance.* New York: Harper and Row.

Sussman, G. and Winograd, T. (1969). *Micro-Planner Reference Manual.* Internal Memorandum, Artificial Intelligence Group, M.I.T.

Sutton-Smith, B. and Roberts, J.M. (1967). "Studies of an Elementary Game of Strategy." *J. Psychol. Monographs LXXV.* pp. 3–42.

Sutton-Smith, B., Roberts, J.M. and Kozelka, R.M. (1963). "Game involvement in adults." *Journal of Social Psychology.* 60. 15.

Taylor, D.W. (1955). "Problem Solving by Groups." In *Proceedings of the Fourteenth Congress of Psychology, Amsterdam,* pp. 218–219, North-Holland Publishing Company.

Taylor, G.R. (1949). *Conditions of Happiness.* London: Bodley Head.

Taylor, M.M. and Creelman, C.D. (1967). "PEST: Efficient Estimates of Probability Function." *J. Acoust. Soc. Am.* 41, 4(1). 782.

Tedeschi, J.T., Steele, M.W., Gahagan, J.P. and Aranoff, D. (1968). "*Intensions,* predictions and patterns of strategy choices in a prisoner's dilemma game." *J. Soc. Psychol.* 75. 199.

Turing, A.M. (1950). "Computer Machinery and Intelligence." *Mind.* 59. 433.

Uhr, L. and Vossler, C. (1963). "A Pattern Recognition Program that Generates, Evaluates, and Adjusts its Own Operators." In Feigenbaum, E.A. and Feldman, J., (eds.), *Computers and Thought,* pp. 237–250. New York: McGraw-Hill.

Van der Woude, K.W. (1970). "Problem Solving and Language." *Arch. Gen. Psychiat.,* 23, 337–342.

Vergnaud, G. (1972). "Capacity and Limit of the Computer in the Study of Problem-Solving. An Example: Solving Arithmetic Problems." This Volume.

Vinacke, W.E. (1969). "Variables in experimental games: Toward a field theory." *Psychol. Bull.* 71. 293.

Von Neumann, J. (1956). "The General Logic and Theory of Automata." In Newman, J.R., (ed.), *The World of Mathematics 4,* p. 2070, New York: Simon and Schuster.

Von Neumann, John and Morgenstern, Oskar (1944). *Theory of Games and Economic Behaviour.* New York: John Wiley & Sons Inc.

Walker, G. (1840). Bell's Life in London and Sporting Chronicle.

Wang, H. (1960' "Towards mechanical mathematics." *IBM Journal of Research and Development.* 4. 2.

Winograd, T. (1970). "Procedures as a representation for data in a computer program for understanding natural language." Ph.D. Thesis. Massachusetts Institute of Technology.

Wason, P.C. (1968). "Reasoning about a rule." *Q.J. Exp. Psychol.* 20. 273.

Wason, P.C. (1969). "Regression in Reasoning?" *Br. J. Psychol.* 60. 471–480.

Waterman, D.A. (1970). "Generalization learning techniques for automating the learning of heuristics." *Artificial Intelligence.* 1. 121.

Weizenbaum, J. (1966). "ELIZA – A Computer Program for the Study of Natural Language Communication Between Man and Machine." *Communications of the ACM.,* 9. No. 1.

Wetherick, N.E. (1970a). "On the Object of Study in Psychology." *Int. J. Psychol.* 5. 149.

Wetherick, N.E. (1970b). "Concept Learning and the Short-Term Memory – Contribution to Theory." *Lang. and Speech.* 13. 271.

Wetherick, N.E. (1970c). "On the representativeness of some experiments in cognition." *Bull. Br. Psychol. Soc.* 23. 213.

Whitehead, A.N. and Russell, B. (1963). *Principia Mathematica.* Cambridge University Press.

Wilson, Andrew. (1968). *The Bomb and the Computer.* London: Barry and Rockcliffe.

Wos, L., Carson, D.F. and Robinson, G.A. (1964). "The unit preference strategy in theorem proving." *Proc. AFIPS 1964 Fall Joint Computer Conference.* 26. 616.

Wos, L., Robinson, G.A. and Carson, D.F. (1965). "Efficiency and completeness of the set of support strategy in theorem proving." *Jnl. Assoc. Com. Mach.* 12. 536.

Zusne, L. (1970). *Visual perception of form.* New York: Academic Press.

Contributors

HÜSNÜ ARICI

School of Social and Administrative Sciences,
Haceteppe University
Ankara, Turkey.

RANAN B. BANERJI

Systems Research Center,
Case Western Reserve University,
Cleveland, Ohio 44106, U.S.A.

GEORGE W. BAYLOR

Institut de Psychologie,
University of Montreal,
Montreal 3, Quebec, Canada.

PIERRE BOVET

Laboratoire de Psychologie Experimentale et
Comparée,
rue Serpente,
Paris 5, France.

DAVID S. BREE

Interfaculteit Bedrijfskunde I.O.,
Prinses Julianalaan,
Rotterdam, The Netherlands.

MICHAEL R.B. CLARK

Institute of Computer Science,
Gordon Square,
London, England.

RICHARD COOPER

Institute of Neurology,
Queen Square,
London, England.

DIETRICH DÖRNER

Institut für Psychologie,
University of Kiel,
Kiel, Germany.

RIVKA R. EIFERMANN

The Eliezer Kaplan School of Economics and
Social Sciences,
Hebrew University of Jerusalem,
Jerusalem, Israel.

ALICK ELITHORN

Medical Research Council,
Department of Psychological Medicine,
Royal Free Hospital,
London, England.

RICHARD B. FENKER

Institute for the Study of Cognitive Systems,
TCU Research Foundation,
Fort Worth, Texas 76129, U.S.A.

ROMAN FERSTL

Max-Planck Institut für Psychiatrie Klinik,
Kraepelinstrasse,
8 München 23, Germany.

NICHOLAS V. FINDLER

Department of Computer Science,
State University of New York at Buffalo,
Ridge Lea Road,
Amherst, New York 14226, U.S.A.

JOHN L. GEDYE

Electronics Centre,
University of Essex,
Colchester, England.

ALI S. GITMEZ

Department of Psychology,
Hacettepe University,
Ankara, Turkey.

WOLFGANG GRUDE

Max-Planck Institut für Psychiatrie Klinik,
Kraepelinstrasse,
8 München 23, Germany.

PATRICK J. HAYES

Metamathematics Unit,
University of Edinburgh,
Hope Park Square,
Edinburgh, Scotland.

J.A.M. HOWE

Bionics Research Laboratory,
University of Edinburgh,
Forrest Hill,
Edinburgh, Scotland.

DAVID JONES

Department of Psychology,
Birkbeck College,
Malet Street,
London, England.

DOMINIQUE LEPINE

Laboratoire de Psychologie Experimentale et
Comparée,
rue Serpente,
Paris 5, France.

GERD LÜER

Institut für Psychologie,
Christians-Albrechts Universität,
Neue Universität,
Kiel, Germany.

NORBERT MAI

Max-Planck Institut für Psychiatrie Klinik,
Kraepelinstrasse,
8 München 23, Germany.

BERNARD MELTZER

Metamathematics Unit,
University of Edinburgh,
Hope Park Square,
Edinburgh, Scotland.

UWE MORTENSEN

Fachbereich Statistik,
University of Konstanz,
Jacob Burckhardt Strasse,
775 Konstanz, Germany.

IRA POHL

Department of Computer and Information Science,
University of California,
Santa Cruz, California 95060, U.S.A.

DIRK REVENSTORFF

Max-Planck Institut für Psychiatrie Klinik
Kraepelinstrasse,
8 München 23, Germany.

JEAN-FRANCOIS RICHARD

Laboratoire de Psychologie,
Centre Universitaire de St. Maur,
Avenue Didier,
94 La Varenne St. Hilaire, France.

H.J.A. RIMOLDI

Instituto de Investigacion en Psicologia,
Matematica y Experimental,
University of Buenos Aires,
Habana 3870,
Buenos Aires, Argentina.

ROULETTE W. SMITH

Department of Psychology,
University of California,
Santa Barbara, California 93106, U.S.A.

ALEX TELFORD

Medical Research Council,
Department of Psychological Medicine,
Royal Free Hospital,
London, England.

M. FUAT TURGUT

Department of Education,
Hacettepe University,
Ankara, Turkey.

GERARD VERGNAUD

Charge de Recherche au CNRS,
Centre d'Etude des Processus Cognitifs et du
Langage,
Boulevard Raspail,
Paris 6, France.

JOHN WEINMAN

Medical Research Council,
Department of Psychological Medicine,
Royal Free Hospital,
London, England.

N.E. WETHERICK

Department of Psychology,
King's College,
University of Aberdeen,
Old Aberdeen, Scotland.

P. OWEN WHITE

Department of Psychology,
Institute of Psychiatry,
Denmark Hill,
London, England.

GERARD DE ZEEUW

University of Amsterdam,
Amsterdam, The Netherlands.

Author Index

Amarel, S., 38
Apostel, L., 227, 230
Aranoff, D., 216, 218
Archibald, Y.M., 88
Arieti, S., 317
Atkins, L., 189
Atkinson, J.W., 329
Atkinson, P., 97
Atkinson, R.C., 96, 257
Austin, G., 148

Banerji, R.B., 78
Barenfeld, M., 232, 297
Bar Hillel, Y., 148, 165
Bartlett, F.C., 11
Baylor, G.W., 284, 290, 293, 297
Beach, L.R., 133, 134
Berry, J.W., 8
Benson, A.J., 113
Binet, A., 200, 143
Birnbaum, A., 236
Bitterman, M.E., 68
Bixenstive, V.E., 215
Black, M., 148, 149
Bledsoe, W.W., 30
Blinkov, S.M., 5
Botvinnik, M.M., 192
Bovet, P., 126, 129
Bower, G., 348
Bower, G.H., 286
Brannasky, W., 144

Bree, D.S., 277, 281
Brunner, J.A., 148
Brunswick, E., 133
Buchanan, B., 30, 36
Buchanan, B.G., 31
Butcher, H.J., 9
Bunderson, C.V., 97

Carbonell, J.R., 99
Carroll, J.D., 139
Carson, D.F., 28
Cattell, R.B., 7
Chang, J.J., 139
Chipman, L., 275
Chipman, S., 135
Chomsky, N., 34
Chown, S., 88
Claparede, E., 301
Clarke, A.D.B., 148
Clarke, M.R.B., 148
Coleman, James, S., 147
Cooper, R.L., 171, 175
Cornelius, E., 133
Craig, R.J., 317
Creelman, C.D., 89
Cronbach, L.J., 97
Crosson, F.J., 345

Dansereau, D.F., 135, 137
Darlington, J.L., 29, 30
Davis, G.A., 227

Davis, M., 26
De Groot, A.D., 143, 190, 199, 200, 204, 285
De Soto, C.B., 12, 281
Delamont, S., 97
Dimond, S.J., 6
Dixon, J.K., 190
Domarus, E.V., 317
Doran, J.E., 8, 9
Dörner, D., 302, 307, 311
Drever, J., 8

Eastlake, D., 35, 189
Edwards, W., 329
Egawa, K., 234
Eifermann, Rivka, R., 147–165 *passim*
Elithorn, A., 6, 88, 148, 164, 165, 171, 175, 200, 203, 210
Eliot, George, 1
Evans, S.H., 133, 137, 139
Evans, T.G., 297

Facey, P.V., 105
Fantz, R.L., 63
Feigenbaum, E., 36
Feigenbaum, E.A., 30, 232, 233
Feldman, J., 36
Felfoldy, G.L., 132
Fenker, R.M., 132
Fikes, R., 38, 51, 54
Findler, N.V., 148
Fisher, R.A., 76
Fodor, J.A., 292
Fogel, L.J., 231, 348
Frijda, N.H., 281, 287
Fruchter, B., 284
Furneaux, W.D., 236

Gagné, R.M., 346
Gahagan, J.P., 216, 218
Gaines, B.R., 105
Garner, W.R., 132
Gazzaniga, M.S., 6
Gedye, J.L., 86, 103, 105, 113
Gelernter, H., 21

George, F., 234
Gilmore, P.C., 26
Gitmez, A.S., 328
Glezer, I.I., 5
Goffman, E., 151
Goldstein, I.L., 329
Goodman, Nelson, 71
Goodnow, J.J., 148
Goodwin, R.Q., 275
Gould, W.E., 29
Gray, J.A., 64
Green, C.C., 30, 32, 33, 46, 47, 49
Greenblatt, R., 35, 189
Greeno, J.G., 254
Gregg, L.W., 348
Guilford, J.P., 282, 283, 284, 344

Haga, J., 234
Halmos, P., 78
Halpin, S.M., 216
Hammond, K.R., 95
Handel, S., 281
Harre, R., 61
Harris, R.J., 216
Harrison, A.A., 215
Hart, H.L.A., 148
Hart, P.W., 29
Hastings, D., 139
Hayes, P.J., 29, 33, 46, 47, 50, 51, 56
Headly, P., 86
Herbrand, J., 25
Heron, A., 88
Hodgkin, K., 112
Hoffman, P.J., 345
Hooper, Alfred, 11
Howe, J.A.M., 97
Howell, W.C., 329
Hintikka, J., 47
Hubel, D.H., 62
Hunt, E., 35, 37
Hunt, E.B., 230, 233

Johnson-Laird, P.N., 274, 275
Jones, D., 88, 171, 175
Jones, L.V., 88

Jones, M.B., 346
Jones, Marie Riess, 348

Karrass, A., 78
Kellcy, M., 35
Kelly, G.A., 69
Kendler, H.H. and T.A., 69
Kerr, M.O., 171, 175
Klahr, D., 290
Kleene, S.C., 35
Kline, Morris, 226
Kling, R.E., 30
Klugh, H.E., 233
Knuth, D., 43
Koluchova, Jarmila, 8
Kowalski, R., 28, 29
Krieger, M.H., 220
Kripke, S., 47
Kristofferson, A.B., 62
Kruskal, J.B., 138
Kubicka, L., 215
Kuehner, D., 28
Kuhn, T.S., 350
Kunst, H., 277

Lawrence, C.M.D., 6
Lee, D.N., 88
Lettvin, J.Y., 72
Levine, M., 242
Levy, D.N.L., 189, 212
Levy, Jerre, 5
Loevinger, J., 85
London, M., 12
London, R.L., 33
Loveland, D., 28
Luckman, D., 32
Lüer, G., 302, 311

Maturana, H., 72
McCarthy, J., 29, 33, 38, 46, 47, 49,
    56, 283
McClintock, C.G., 215
McCulloch, W.S., 72
McFie, J., 5
Magnus, W., 78

Manna, Z., 33
Markov, A.A., 35
Mayo, B., 148
Medawar, P., 33
Meerum-Terwogt, M., 277, 281
Meltzer, B., 29, 31
Miller, W.F., 35
Minsky, M., 35
Morgan, C.G., 32
Morningstar, M., 95
Morris, J.B., 29
Mott-Smith, G., 210

Neisser, U., 231, 345, 346
Newell, A., 21, 36, 38, 41, 63, 199,
    200, 281, 283, 290, 307
Newman, E.A., 110
Nilsson, N.J., 29, 32, 35, 51, 54

O'Connor, P., 329
Opie, Iona and P., 149, 151
Ore, O., 38
Oskamp, S., 215
Owens, A.J., 231, 348

Paivio, A., 286
Palme, J., 33
Paulson, J.A., 96
Peterson, C.R., 134
Phelan, J.G., 215
Piaget, J., 148
Pilisur, M., 216
Pitrat, J., 29
Plotkin, G., 31, 36
Pohl, I., 29, 36, 41, 42
Pollack, I., 86
Popper, K.R., 30, 31
Post, E.L., 35
Potash, H.M., 215
Potkay, C.R., 334
Prawitz, D., 26, 35

Quinlan, J., 35, 37

Racine, B., 297

Raphael, B., 29, 49
Rapoport, A., 215, 218
Ray, W.S., 263
Rayner, E.H., 200, 143
Reeves, J.W., 200
Reitman, J.S., 282
Reitman, W.R., 283, 292, 302
Rescher, N., 55
Restle, F., 241, 254
Richardson, E.D., 215
Rimoldi, H.J.A., 331–337 *passim*
Roberts, J.M., 200
Robinson, G.A., 28, 29, 281
Robinson, J.A., 26, 28, 29
Robinson, John P., 145
Runge, R.G., 232
Russel, Bertrand, 303

Samuel, A.L., 190
Sandewall, E., 33, 9
Scantlebury, R., 110
Schegloff, Emanual, A., 166
Schelling, T., 116
Schetagne, J.P., 275, 281
Schum, D.A., 329
Sebestyen, G., 77
Selfridge, O.G., 232
Selzer, R.A., 84
Sermat, V., 215
Shannon, C.E., 189
Shaw, A.C., 35
Shepard, R.N., 135
Shiffrin, R.M., 257
Shipstone, E.J., 134
Sibert, E.E. 29
Simmons, R.F. 287, 98
Simon, H.A., 55, 232, 297, 348
Simons, H.A., 287
Slagle, J.R., 190
Slate, D., 189
Smallwood, R.D., 96
Sperry, R.W., 6

Strand, S., 715
Suppes, P.A., 95, 100, 227
Sussman, G., 50
Sutherland, C., 30
Sutton-Smith, B., 200

Tagart, J., 275
Taylor, D.W., 319
Taylor, G.R., 15
Taylor, M.M., 89
Tedeschi, J.T., 216, 218
Telford, A., 148, 164, 165, 200, 203, 206, 210
Turing, A.M., 230

Uemura, M., 232
Uhrm, L., 232

Van der Woude, K.W., 336
Vergnaud, G., 201
Viglione, S.S. 232
Vinacke, W.E., 223
Von Neumann, J., 144, 234
Vossler, C., 232

Waldinger, R.J., 33
Wallace, J.G., 290
Wang, H., 21
Winograd, T., 29
Wason, P.C., 12, 148, 273, 275, 277, 281
Waterman, D.A., 290
Weizenbaum, J., 116
Wepman, J.M., 88
Wetherick, N.E., 61, 67, 282
Whitehead, A.N., 303
Wiesel, T.N., 62
Wilson, Andrew, 10, 226
Wilson, K.V., 215
Wos, L., 28, 281

Zimmerman, W.S., 284
Zusne, L., 133

Subject Index

Abstraction, 20
Algebra, boolean, 25, 77−8
Algebra in concept formation, 77−9
Algebra polyadic, 77−78
ALGOL, 60, 198
ALGOL, 64, 192−198
Algorithms,
    alpha-beta, 190
    chess, 192−8
    Euclid's, 39, 43
    heuristic path (H.P.A.), 42
    ladder, 210−2
    minimax, 190
    spontaneous, 270
    unification, 28, 32
Analogical reasoning, 19, 30, 227−234, 312
Analogue computers, 234
Anxiety and performance, 325, 328−9
Artificial intelligence
    and computer aided instruction, 99
    as programmed logic, 19−34
    Chomsky's misunderstanding of, 35, 43
    comparison with human intelligence, 163−4, 343−351
    definitions of and developments in, 8−10, 14−5, 17−8, 343−351
    evaluation of simulation models, 231−4
    interaction with human intelligence, 343−351

the frame problems, 45−59
Arithmetic, 21, 37, 95, 97, 264−272
    as a binary composition, 265
    as a state transformation, 265
Attention, 18, 162, 241−250
Automated
    data collection, 130
    deduction, 19−30
    decision making, 81
    determination of win criteria for games, 30
    generation of psychological test items, 87−9
    generation of programs, 33
    grammar induction, 36, 42
    handling of mathematical symbols, 42, 228
    induction, 19−21, 30−33
    information storage, 81
    question answering, 94−101, 232
    problem solving, in complex world, 45−58
    proof procedures, 19−33, 201
    spectroscopic analysis, 30, 43
Automatic, see Automated

Bargaining
    as a dialogue, 116
Bayesian player, 186
Bluffing, 183
Belief, definition and formation of, 45

calculus of, 45–6, 56–8, 118, 122
Boolean algebra, 25

Causal connection, 50
Cerebral dominance, theories of, 5
Chess
    as complicated calculus, 13
    as favoured area of research, 160
    as model of life, 1
    changing evaluation functions in, 202–3
    comparison of machine and human play, 190
    eye movements during play, 232
    failure of early studies to develop, 143–4
    official attitude of U.S.S.R., 144
    problem behaviour graph of mate in four, 37
    programs
        and compilers (ALGOL-64), 189–198
        competence of, 35
        Greenblatt's, 35, 43
    recall of positions, 190
    skill
        as evidence military competence, 164
        as developing and strengthening intelligence, 145
    teaching by computer, 123
Chicken matrix, 214, 216
Choice behaviour, 325
"Chunking", 180, 186, 294
Cognitive abilities, 83–93
Cognitive behaviour, 34–44
Cognitive domain (see also problem areas), 36
Cognitive style, 332
Computability, theory of, 33
Computer-assisted instruction (C.A.I), 82–86, 94–114, 347
Concept development, 210
Concept formation, 70–79, 131–141, 210, 232

Concept formation, use of contingency table in, 75
Concept identification, 241–251
Concepts involved in problem solving, 269
Conflicts, curricular and social, 114–124
Conservatism, in thinking, 309
Correction procedure, 68
Counterfactual reasoning, 54–56
Creativity, 10–12
Cryptarithmetic, 122
Cue dimensions, analysed by multivariate and distance models, 133–141

Decideability, 51
Deduction or deductive thinking, 19–30, 34, 44
Dialogue, 94, 98–101, 114–124
Difficulty of problems, sources of, 333
Digit span, 85, 89
Discrimination learning, 60–69, 133, 250, 262
Disjunctive concepts, learning of, 350

Employer – employee communication, 103–104
Environment, effect of on intelligence, 8
Eye movements during chess play, 232
Evaluation factors, 281
Evaluation functions in chess, 189–190
    in halma, 204–206
    borrowed from experts, 347
Extension property obeyed by logical calculi, 46–57
Extraversion, relationship to speed accuracy preference in
    Cognitive functions, 92
Euclid's algorithm, 39, 43

Falsifiability, 31
Frame problem, 45–58

Games, 112, 123, 143–147, 200
    as models of reality, 164

as models of social interaction, 215

behaviour in, 172

board, 148, 165, 199–212

children's, as part of developmental process, 147–161

clinical decision-making, 112

environment, 178–188

inference of win criteria, 30

non-zero, 114

of strategy, 164

of strategy:
  checkers, 156, 165, 190, 232
  chess, *see* Chess
  chicken, 214–223
  five in a row, 143
  go-moko, 143,
  grasshopper, 165
  halma, 13, 160, 162–176, 199, 203–213
  kalah, 190
  peggity, 143
  pennyguessing, 145
  poker, 148, 160, 177–188
  prisoner's dilemma, 214
  ren-ju, 143
  tic-tac-toe 154, 156
  word chaining 118

rules of and their classification, 147–161

theory of, 144, 350

Generalisation, problems of, 9

induction and importance of, 20

General practitioner, job description and diagnosis, 112

Grammar, generative or phrase structure, 34–44

Group performance compared with individual, 319–323

Group theory, 30

Halma, 13, 160, 162–176, 199, 203–213

competence, 172

playing programs, 166–176

Herbrand's theorem, 25–26

Heuristics,
  hierarchy of subgoals, 19, 21, 30, 205
  in chess programs, 189–206
  in solving arithmetic problems, 264–272
  optimization of heuristic rules in poker, 177, 187
  search, 29, 42
  suggested by introspection, 19–21

Hypothesis testing 241–257, 273–282, 297, 348

in problem solving, 254

Illative implication, 275–279

Illegal thinking, 13, 273, 310–318, 345

Imagery, used to solve problems, 283–297

Image space, 286.

Implication, 273, 278–282

Implication, seen as symmetrical, 350

Individual differences, 23–40, 83–93, 94–101, 125–126, 235, 324–330

of grammars, 36

by inversion of deduction rules, 31

Induction,
  programming, 19–33
  simulation of, 60–69, 227–234

Inference task, 132–133, 227–282

Information retrieval, 19, 32

Information sampling, 62, 102

transformation, 287–293

transmission, 127

Insight, 42, 274–277

Intelligence, *see also* problem solving and thinking
  components of, 286
  crystallized (cultural), 7
  definition and key characteristics of, 2–3, 225, 283–286, 343–350
    as a set of processes, 284
    as successive states of knowledge, 286
  fluid (noncultural), 7

general 86, 326
goal-oriented, 3
non-verbal, 5
stimulation of human, 344
social 165
tests of, *see* psychological tests
Interaction
social, 172, 215
teacher−pupil, 100
Interface active, 104. 111
Introspection, 19−21 *see also* protocol
analysis
Isomorphic problems, 333

Jurisprudence, as applied to thinking,
103

Language,
computer languages, *see* programming languages
definition, 2
neurological localization, 4−5
of predicate logic, 31−33
processing program, 98
role in problem solving tactics,
331−339
three letter word (TLW), 114−124
Law of motion, 47, 52
Learning,
C.A.I. 94−101
induction and, stimulation of, 63−69
model for concept identification,
241−251
models, probability versus information processing, 348−350
nonsense syllables, alone or as a
group, 319−323
of distributional properties, 134
poker skills, 183−191
Samuels' checkers program, 190
to prove theorems, 301−318
Likelihood estimates, 236−239
List-matching, 317
List processing, 21
in human thinking, 181, 308

languages, *see* programming languages
Logic,
first order, 46
modal, 29
"normalised", 29
predicate, 21−33
resolution (Robinson's), 19
symbolic, 19
Logical structure, its relationship to
language, 331−339

Machine and machine-aided intelligence, 8−10
see also artificial intelligence
Markov models, alternatives to, 349
Material implication 275−276
MDS (multidimensional scaling analysis), 132−141
Means-end analysis, 120
Memory, 62, 86, 134, 135, 137, 306
long term, 257
short term, 85−92, 252−263
tests of, 85, 319
Mental imagery, 283
Modal categories, 55
Models, games as, 164
Models
Markov, 344
mathematical, 235−240
of comparison, 319−323
of protocols, 260−263
Modus ponens, 274
Modus tollens, 273−274, 282
Monte Carlo method, 179, 247, 250
Moral development, 148
Motivation, effects of on problem solving, 324−330

Nature versus nurture, 144
Neurophysiology, psychological events
to be consistent with, 3−6, 61, 72
Neurophyschology, contributions of,
3−6

Neurosis in relation to learning theory, 69

Observation fundamental to belief, 46
Ombudsman, 114—124
On-line, 88, 91, 122, 126, 130, 348
Operation space, 287
Operations, legal. 307
Operators,
    application fields, 314
    spectrum of effects, 314

Parameters, computer control in psychological experimentation, 83—93
Pattern encoding, 137—9
Pattern recognition, 35, 43, 77, 185—6, 232
    techniques, 185
Peasants, as good as counts, 144
Personality, related to intelligence and problem solving, 69, 91—92, 183—187, 217—218, 344
Punishment, *see* reinforcement, 160
Production system, 289
Phrase structure grammars, 35
Possible worlds, 46, 47
Predicate logic, 77
Problem behavior graph (PBG), 34—44, 287
Problem complexity, 267
Problem relationship between structure and difficulty, 267
Problem sets, 267
Problem solving, 231, 235, 252—263, 303—324
Problem solving processes,
    classification into steps, 283—309
        space, 286
        space search, 346
Problems, *see also* puzzles, psychological tests and tasks
    by name
        fifteen puzzle, 41
        missionaries and cannibals, 38
        monkeys and bananas, 38

mutilated checkerboard, 38, 41
nested bars, 266—271
pail, 38—44, 252—260
travelling salesman, 38
water-jar, *see* pail
information structure of, 267
of propositional calculus, 301- 309
"open—closed", 302
selection of, 162—176
yardstick, 38
Processing units, information processing units, 302
Production rules, 169, 200, 204, 286, 290
    unconscious nature of, 270
Production system 289
Programming languages
    ALGOL-64, a problem orientated language for chess, 191
    AMPPL-II, 186
    BASIC, 105
    BASYS, 105
    BCL, 197
    FOCAL-8, 127—130
    FORTRAN, 206, 226, 260
    IPL-V, 21, 283
    LISP, 21, 283, 290
    QUASIC, 105
    SNOBAL, 283
Programs
    EPAM, 233
    fortran deductive system (FDS), 34-44.
    general problem solver (GPS), 21, 37—38, 281
    INSCAL, 139
    MICRO-PLANNER, 50—57
    REF-ARF, 38, 42
    SPOM, 333-6
    STRIPS, 51—54
    VARGUS-9, 137
Propositional calculus, solution of problems in, 301—304, 310—318
Protocol analysis, 34, 36—8, 143—144, 260—263, 277—279, 283—318

Psycholinguistics, 34
Psychological tests,
  advanced progressive matrices
  (Raven's), 235–236, 336
  computer based, 83–93
  digit span test, 89
  limitations and potentialities of,
  83–93
  perceptual maze test (PMT), 88
  serial testing, 86–93
  spatial visualization II (Guilford),
  284
Psychologists
  difficulties of, 268
  head not in clouds, 82
  simulation of, 84
Psychology, comparative, 12–14, 18,
  20, 343–351
Psychophysics, 89, 125
Psychometric assessment, 83–93
  see also psychological tests
Punishment, see reinforcement
Puzzles, distinguished from games, 164
  see also problems

Qualification problem, 56

Recursive functions, 35
Refinement of inference system, 28
Reinforcement, 95, 215–223, 242–
  248, 306, 308, 348
Rehearsal strategies, 89
Resolution, 20, 31
Rewards, 160
  see also reinforcement
Rigidity, 309
  see also conservatism
Robots, 19, 32, 45–58
Rule, dependent experimental, 125–
  131
Rule, internal representation, 279
Rule, production, 269
Rules, as regulations and instructions,
  148

Rules, recognition, 212
Rules, classifications, 148

Search procedures, 28, 42, 199–212,
  255, 346
  diagonal, 28
  unit preference, 28
Semantics, 23, 29, 115
Sequences, in problem solving, 253–
  263
Sequences, in transformations of reality, 268
Simplicity, measure of, 73
  paradox of, 71
Simulation,
  early work, 36
  evaluation of models of, 227–234
  of eye movements in chess, 232
  of experimental subject, 268–9
  of inductive thinking, 60–69
  of natural language dialogues,
  114–124
  of opponent in game of chicken,
  214–223
  of problem solving using visual
  imagery, 283–297
  of psychologist by automated system, 84
Skolem functors, 23
Social backgrounds, comparison of,
  324
Speed-accuracy preferences, 236
Split-brain subjects, 6
Stimulus classes, 134
  schemata for, 137
Suboptimal behaviour, 346
Syllogisms, 12–13

Task analysis, 96
Tasks,
  arithmetic problems, 95
  discrimination, 132–133, 139
  evaluation, 275–282
  free recall, 299, 319–323
  inference, 273–282

judgment of duration, 126–129
judgement of similarity, 132–141, 186
mathematical problems, 332
paired associate learning, 138, 286
signal detection, 282
switching, 263
theorem proving, 301–304, 310–318
validation, 273–282
Teaching, 86, 94, 97, 105–110
drill and practice, 94
training, 75, 217
Theories of games, Borel's, 144
Thinking,
adventurous and in closed systems, 11

convergent and divergent, 11
cultural components of, 6–8, 343–351
divise, 11
overinclusive, 317
Transformation (s), 31, 36, 140, 232, 265, 306, 307, 344, 350
Turing's test, 117, 230

Universal computability, 35

Visualization, 283–297

Wolf child, 8